Aggregation

Also by Franklin M. Fisher

Industrial Organization, Economics, and the Law
Econometrics: Essays in Theory and Applications

Aggregation

Aggregate production functions and related topics

Collected Papers of
Franklin M. Fisher
Edited by
John Monz

HARVESTER
WHEATSHEAF

New York London Toronto Sydney Tokyo Singapore

First published 1992 by
Harvester Wheatsheaf
Campus 400, Maylands Avenue
Hemel Hempstead
Hertfordshire, HP2 7EZ
A division of
Simon & Schuster International Group

Typeset in 10/12 pt Times
by Keyset Composition, Colchester, Essex

Printed and bound in Great Britain by
BPCC Wheatons Ltd, Exeter

British Library Cataloguing in Publication Data

A catalogue record for this book is available from the British Library

ISBN: 0 7450 1144 6

1 2 3 4 5 96 95 94 93 92

In memory of Teddy

Contents

Introduction

The chapters in this volume all concern aggregation – chiefly the aggregation of production functions. The central question asked is whether and under what circumstances the technological relationships of a diverse economy (or even of an industry or a firm) can be summarized in a fairly simple manner. When is it appropriate to speak of such aggregates as "capital," "investment," "labor," or even "output" in the context of production theory – the context which, as the names involved suggest, is the one that would make apparent sense?

There are good reasons for believing this question to be of considerable interest to economists (and policy-makers). Strangely, there are also bad ones, and the history of the subject suggests that the bad reasons have often dominated the discussion. I begin, however, with the good reasons.

In the early 1980s I visited Harvard University for a year and taught its first-year graduate courses in microeconomic theory. Just before the first term began, there was a meeting of faculty and entering graduate students designed to inform the students of the program and reassure them as to what they were getting into. Each faculty member who taught a first-year course was supposed to give a short talk describing it.

As the teacher of the microeconomics course, I went first. Not wishing the Harvard students to think that MIT professors were colorless personalities, I began by saying: "Never mind what the guys who come after me say. Microeconomics is what economists really know about." There was some laughter, but I was soon topped by Benjamin Friedman who taught the macroeconomics course. When it was his turn to speak, he began by saying: "I agree totally with Frank Fisher. Microeconomics is what economists know about. But macroeconomics is what they *want* to know about. That's what makes it so interesting."

Friedman's remark was funny, but (although I am an exception to its rule) it is also quite true. The rigorous study of aggregation in general and of the aggregation of production functions in particular is the study of the connection between the two parts of the discipline. Starting with microeconomics, which we really do understand, is it possible to lay a foundation for macroeconomics, which many economists would like to understand and which policy-makers, the media, and the public think of when they think of economics? What justification is there for talking of "~~capital" or "labor"? Macroeconomists do these produced by capital and labor? For that matter, what justification is there for talking of "capital" or "labor?~~" Macroeconomists do these and similar things all the time, and economic policy is discussed and decided in such terms. Unless such usage and analysis can be soundly grounded in "what economists really know about," such discussions and decisions appear to be without foundation.

My position, largely based on the results reported in this book, is that the foundation is at most a very shaky one. I am fond of telling my microeconomics classes that "there is no such subject as macroeconomics," and, while that is plainly an overstatement (as well as empirically false), there is some truth in it.

Note, however, that the difficulties of aggregation affect the foundation of *macro*economics in the sense of its ability to be grounded in microeconomics. They have nothing whatever to do with the foundation of *micro*economics itself. In terms of microeconomic analysis, the existence or nonexistence of an aggregate capital stock, an aggregate labor force, or an aggregate output is at best a question of convenience. It is not a question of fundamental (if any) importance.

In particular, this is true of the question of the existence of an aggregate capital stock. Microeconomic analysis needs no such construct. It is quite comfortable with the notion that there exist n factors of production (with n as large as one likes) and that some subset, say m, of these are called "capital goods" with each one of them different and performing a different function. While aggregate capital may be a convenience, no theorem of microeconomics depends on its existence.

Note further that, in this regard, capital is no different from labor or output. Microeconomics is also comfortable (as it had better be) with the existence of a whole set of different kinds of labor and a whole collection of different kinds of output. The question of existence of aggregate labor or agggregate output just does not arise.

It is also a mistake to suppose that capital plays some special role in these matters because of the technology involved. Unless one wrongly restricts neoclassical economics to economics that requires the use of calculus, there is nothing in neoclassical microeconomics that cannot accommodate the existence of production technologies with fixed coefficients. Moreover, even if there were, more than one input, not just a particular type of capital, would typically be affected.

I mention all this because the history of the production–aggregation problem was heavily colored by the mistaken views just mentioned. Starting at least as far back as the 1950s and continuing into the 1970s, Joan Robinson pursued those views with an almost religious zealotry.[1] She was utterly convinced that the existence of an aggregate capital stock is the rock on which neoclassical microeconomics is wrecked and that fixed coefficients have a great deal to do with this. Neither proposition has any truth in it.[2]

Mrs Robinson's fervor produced what became known as the "Cambridge versus Cambridge debate" of the late 1950s and 1960s. In the view of one side, Cambridge University's economists, led by Mrs Robinson, were locked in battle against MIT's economists, led by Robert Solow and Paul Samuelson, with the entire neoclassical synthesis at stake.

The view on the other side of the Atlantic was considerably more prosaic. It was true that both Solow and Samuelson were interested in such issues, and that Solow especially engaged Mrs Robinson in a well-known exchange of articles on capital aggregation.[3] Neither they nor anyone else at MIT, however, believed that the foundations (or the *Foundations*) of economic analysis were at stake, nor was the debate, such as it was, a matter of central attention in the MIT department.

Indeed, so little did the facts match the picture of major battle, that I wandered into the subject without even realizing that I had entered the great controversy.

In about 1963, Robert Solow and James Tobin assembled a team at MIT and Yale to build an econometric model of long run economic growth in the United States. (The project was never completed.) There was considerable interest in incorporating the embodied technology model that Solow had recently put forward [26], in which the use of new technology depended on the use of new capital goods embodying it.

I became interested in the question of when, in such a model, one can write the aggregate production relation in terms of a capital "jelly" – an aggregate made up of the underlying "vintage" capitals. Among other things, I was able to prove that (in a one-output–two-factor model) this could be done under constant returns to scale if and only if all technological change was "capital augmenting," that is, if and only if embodiment of new technology simply means the shifting of a parameter multiplying the amount of capital in the production function. In such a case, capital of new vintages acts just like more capital of old vintages and an aggregate capital stock can be constructed with capital measured in efficiency units.[4] (Once one leaves constant returns to scale or introduces more types of capital in a single vintage, the matter becomes more complex.)

The resulting paper is Chapter 2 of the present volume ("Embodied technical change and the existence of an aggregate capital stock"). It was written and essentially published (in 1965) before I realized that I was contributing to the Cambridge–Cambridge debate. But of course I was. One has only to think of the vintage production functions as the production functions of different firms to realize that the analysis applies to the far more general problem of aggregation over firms with different capital and differing technologies. The paper appeared before I could make the change, and, as a result, Chapter 2 is written in terms of "vintages" rather than "firms." The thought finally did occur to me, however, and all my later writings on the subject were in the more general and more interesting context.

There quickly proved to be a number of such writings, for I came to realize that I had struck a vein of research that could be followed farther and deeper than I had first supposed. Chapter 2 dealt with the existence of an aggregate capital stock and, in its most general form, did so in the context of firm production functions with several kinds of capital and several kinds of movable factors ("labors"). The assumption that technology is embodied in capital or, equivalently, that capital is firm-specific, produces capital-aggregation difficulties for the system as a whole (the "economy") whether or not a capital aggregate exists for each firm. But no such difficulty exists for labor aggregation if there is only one type of labor to be aggregated. This is because labor is assumed to be assigned to firms efficiently.[5] Where several variable factors are present at the firm level, however, the rigidity of capital can create aggregation difficulties for the variable factors at the economy-wide level even if those factors can be aggregated within each firm (an already strong assumption).

Moreover, since one can write production functions in terms of the minimum amount of some input required to produce a set of outputs given the remaining inputs, the problem of aggregating over variable factors turns out to be isomorphic to the problem of aggregation over outputs. These twin problems were addressed in Chapter 3 ("Embodied technology and the existence of labor and output aggregates").

Furthermore, the matter does not end there. Whether a factor is fixed or movable depends on the time period and context involved.

Certain kinds of capital (typewriters or personal computers, for example) are not firm-specific save in the very short run. On the other hand, workers may have a good deal of human capital built up in a particular firm and hence be relatively immobile. There can thus be circumstances in which the ordinary definitions of "capital" and "labor" do not coincide with the distinction between fixed and variable factors. Accordingly, one may wish to aggregate some fixed factors with some movable ones. This is the subject of Chapter 4 ("Embodied technology and the aggregation of fixed and movable capital goods"), written after Chapter 3 but published with it.

These three papers, especially Chapter 3, were of considerable complexity. So, when I was invited in 1968 to deliver the Fisher–Schultz Lecture at the European meetings of the Econometric Society, I welcomed the opportunity to give an expository talk on the whole subject. The written version of that talk, "The existence of aggregate production functions," is republished as Chapter 1 of this book. The reader is referred to it for a relatively nontechnical description of what is involved and what was known of the subject at the end of the 1960s.

There now occurred my most direct (if still rather limited) entry into the Cambridge versus Cambridge debate. In the late summer of 1970, the Econometric Society held its Second World Congress at Cambridge University.[6] Dale Jorgenson organized a plenary session on aggregate production functions featuring (live, perhaps for the first time on any stage) what was planned as a direct confrontation between the protagonists, Robinson and Solow. I appeared as a discussant. Memories of such occasions can differ, but here is mine.

Mrs Robinson delivered a polemic against capital aggregation and neoclassical economics. She was followed by Solow who scolded her in an amusing way, claiming that the entire controversy existed in the head and because of the pen of one woman. He pointed out that he had stated (Solow [25, p. 312]) that "it takes something more than the usual 'willing suspension of disbelief' to talk seriously of the aggregate production function."

When it was my turn, I observed that the existence of aggregate production functions in general and of an aggregate capital stock in particular was a purely technical question. I agreed that the technical answer was that the conditions for such existence were very stringent, calling into question the use of aggregate production functions in macroeconomic applications such as Solow's famous 1957 paper [25]. But I made it quite clear that the reasons for this had nothing at all to do with those that Mrs Robinson had advanced. Indeed, Solow understood the issues, and she did not.[7]

Despite this, so powerful was Mrs Robinson's influence that it was another eleven years before I realized that the apparently special role of capital as a fixed input had relatively little to do with the problem. As discussed in Chapter 1, if a homogeneous factor is allocated across firms so as to maximize output, then maximized output depends on the total amount of that factor available; no aggregation problem arises with regard to it. The fact that capital is not so allocated (at least in the short run) appears to create the aggregation problem. This is true, but it appears as an important point only because economists are used to thinking of two-factor production functions which already assume aggregation at the level of the firm. If one works in terms of many factors and asks when it will be possible to aggregate them into groups ("capital" and "labor," for example) at the level of the entire industry or economy, it turns out that mobility of capital has relatively little to do with it. Even if such aggregation is possible on the firm level, the conditions for the existence of such aggregates at the macro level are still very stringent. It is the necessity of aggregating over firms rather than the immobility of capital that generates the real problem. These matters are discussed in Chapter 5, "Aggregate production functions revisited: The mobility of capital and the rigidity of thought," published in 1982.

The occasion that led to Chapter Five was a particularly pleasant one. My son, Abraham Fisher, was a sophomore at Carleton College, and the Carleton economics department invited me to give a lecture there. Because the seniors had to write on the microeconomic foundations of macroeconomics, I was asked to speak on that topic, so I naturally dusted off my old talk on the existence of aggregate production functions (Chapter 1).[8] In the course of preparing and delivering that talk, however, I realized that there were two problems that I had not previously thought through. The first of these was the problem of aggregation with more than two factors when all factors are mobile (Chapter 5).

The second problem was somewhat different. My first paper on aggregate production functions (Chapter 2) had explored the conditions for the existence of an aggregate capital stock and also the conditions for the existence of partial capital aggregates such as "equipment." Those conditions turned out to be very stringent, but it had not occurred to me to inquire as to the circumstances under which full and partial capital aggregates would coexist. My Carleton lecture thus also led to Chapter 6 ("On the simultaneous existence of full and partial capital aggregates").

Now, all the results so far described were obtained by the use of Leontief's "well-known theorem" on aggregation [10],[11]. Experience suggests, however, that the theorem is not so well known as its usual name suggests. It therefore seems worthwhile to explain and prove it here, in particular, since a proof is not given elsewhere in the book.[9] I begin with a lemma that states the well-known proposition that two functions generate the same marginal rates of substitution if and only if one can be derived from the other by a monotonic transformation. This is, of course, most usually applied in utility theory.

Lemma I.1: Let $F(x_1, \ldots, x_n)$ and $G(x_1, \ldots, x_n)$ be continuously differentiable, with $F_1(\mathbf{x})>0$ and $G_1(\mathbf{x})>0$ (where subscripts denote differentiation, and $\mathbf{x}$ is the vector of the x_i). Then the following two conditions are equivalent:

(a) There exists a differentiable function, $H(\cdot)$, $H'(\cdot)>0$, such that $F(\mathbf{x}) = H\{G(\mathbf{x})\}$.

(b) For every $\mathbf{x}$, $F_i(\mathbf{x})/F_1(\mathbf{x}) = G_i(\mathbf{x})/G_1(\mathbf{x})$ $(i = 2, \ldots, n)$.

Proof: First assume that (a) holds and calculate $F_i(\mathbf{x})$. This yields:

$$\frac{F_i(\mathbf{x})}{F_1(\mathbf{x})} = \frac{H'(G)G_i(\mathbf{x})}{H'(G)G_1(\mathbf{x})} = \frac{G_i(\mathbf{x})}{G_1(\mathbf{x})} \qquad (i = 2, \ldots, n), \tag{I.1}$$

which is (b).

Now suppose that (b) holds. I prove (a) by induction on n. If $n = 1$, then $\mathbf{x}$ is a scalar and $G(\mathbf{x})$ is monotonic. Hence $G(\mathbf{x})$ can be inverted, and we can write $\mathbf{x} = G^{-1}\{G(\mathbf{x})\}$. Substituting in $F(\mathbf{x})$, this yields $F(\mathbf{x}) = F[G^{-1}\{G(\mathbf{x})\}]$. This is (a) with $H(\cdot)$ defined as $F[G^{-1}\{\cdot\}]$. (The monotonicity of $H(\cdot)$ follows from the fact that $F_1(\mathbf{x})$ and $G_1(\mathbf{x})$ have the same sign.)

It remains to show that (b) implies (a) for functions of n variables on the assumption that it does so for functions of $n-1$ variables. Make that assumption. Fix x_n. then $F(x_1, \ldots, x_{n-1}, x_n)$ and $G(x_1, \ldots, x_{n-1}, x_n)$ are functions of $n-1$ variables, and inspection shows that those functions satisfy (b). Hence those functions differ by at most a monotonic transformation. Naturally, however, what that transformation is can depend on the value at which x_n is fixed. We can write this as:

$$F(\mathbf{x}) = H\{G(\mathbf{x}), x_n\}. \tag{I.2}$$

To complete the proof, we show that the separate appearance of x_n in (I.2) is unnecessary; the monotonic transformation described in the preceding paragraph does not depend on x_n at all. To see this, observe that (continuing to denote differentiation by subscripts):

$$\frac{F_n(\mathbf{x})}{F_1(\mathbf{x})} = \frac{H_G G_n(\mathbf{x}) + H_n}{H_G G_1(\mathbf{x})}. \tag{I.3}$$

But (b) then implies that $H_n \equiv 0$, and the lemma is proved.

We are now ready for Leontief's theorem. It is as follows.

Leontief's theorem: Let $\mathbf{x}$ be a vector of n variables. Let $\hat{\mathbf{x}}$ be the subvector of the first r variables and $\mathbf{x}^*$ the subvector of the remaining $n-r$ variables. Suppose that $F(\cdot)$ is a continuously differentiable function of $\mathbf{x}$ with $F_1(\cdot)>0$. Then the following two conditions are equivalent:

(a) There exist functions $G(\cdot)$ and $H(\cdot,\cdot)$ such that $F(\mathbf{x}) = H\{G(\hat{\mathbf{x}}), \mathbf{x}^*\}$.

(b) $F_i(\hat{\mathbf{x}}, \mathbf{x}^*)/F_1(\hat{\mathbf{x}}, \mathbf{x}^*)$ is independent of $\mathbf{x}^*$ for $i = 1, \ldots, r$.

Proof: First, assume that (a) holds. Direct computation of the derivatives shows

$$\frac{F_i(\hat{\mathbf{x}}, \mathbf{x}^*)}{F_1(\hat{\mathbf{x}}, \mathbf{x}^*)} = \frac{H_G G_i(\hat{\mathbf{x}})}{H_G G_1(\hat{\mathbf{x}})} = \frac{G_i(\hat{\mathbf{x}})}{G_1(\hat{\mathbf{x}})}. \tag{I.4}$$

But the ratio on the far right of (I.4) is independent of $\mathbf{x}^*$, which is the statement in (b).

Note that this could also be proved by fixing $\mathbf{x}^*$ and observing that, with $\mathbf{x}^*$ fixed, $F(\cdot,\cdot)$, considered as a function of $\hat{\mathbf{x}}$, only differs from $G(\cdot)$ by a monotonic transformation. The desired result will now follow from Lemma I.1.

This way of proceeding is the way in which I shall prove the much less obvious part of the theorem – that (b) implies (a). Assume (b) and fix $\mathbf{x}^*$ at, say, $\overline{\mathbf{x}}^*$. Define $G(\hat{\mathbf{x}}) \equiv F(\hat{\mathbf{x}}, \overline{\mathbf{x}}^*)$. Then, by (b) for *any* value of $\mathbf{x}^*$, $F(\hat{\mathbf{x}}, \mathbf{x}^*)$ has the same marginal rates of substitution between x_1 and any x_i ($i = 1, \ldots, r$) as does $G(\hat{\mathbf{x}})$. By Lemma I.1, this means that $F(\cdot, \mathbf{x}^*)$ differs from $G(\cdot)$ by at most a monotonic transformation. Plainly, the nature of that monotonic transformation can differ depending on the value of $\mathbf{x}^*$. A little thought, however, reveals that this is exactly what (a) says, and the theorem is proved.

Leontief's theorem provides the exact conditions for aggregation, with $G(\cdot)$ an aggregate of the first r variables. One question that arises is that of what happens when aggregation can be approximate rather than exact. Nobody supposes that aggregate production functions are more than approximations. Does it then matter that the conditions for exact aggregation turn out to be stringent?

One answer to this is not a helpful one. Not surprisingly, it turns out to be true that if the exact Leontief conditions (condition (b) of the theorem) are approximately satisfied, then approximate aggregates will exist. The reason that this is not helpful is that the conditions for the existence of aggregate production functions are unlikely to hold even as approximations. (In the simplest case of capital aggregation, for example, they would require that using a different kind of capital be *almost* like using a different quantity of the same kind.) So the really interesting question is whether there are any *other* cases in which an approximate aggregate exists – cases in which approximate aggregation is possible *without* the approximate satisfaction of the Leontief conditions on marginal rates of substitution.

Unfortunately, the answer is in the negative, at least so long as one requires some regularities in the derivatives of the production functions involved. Chapter 7, "Approximate aggregation and the Leontief conditions," shows that the only way for approximate aggregation to hold without approximate satisfaction of the Leontief conditions is for the derivatives of the functions involved to wiggle violently up and down, a property not generally assumed for production functions (or other functions) used in economics.

This leaves aggregation and, I think, macroeconomics with a serious problem, for the implications of the Leontief conditions are very severe indeed. If aggregate production functions (or, indeed, other aggregate relationships) are to survive, one must do more than appeal to the fact that only approximations are intended; one must find a deeper reason for believing that they work.

This is not as totally wishful as it may sound, for the history of the subject suggests that focusing attention on the technical requirements for aggregation may partly miss the point. The literature on aggregate production functions began long before Chapter 2 and long before the Cambridge versus Cambridge controversy. I have already referred (in note 8) to the contributions of May and Pu. Those papers were part of a debate on the subject that took place in the pages of *Econometrica* in the late 1940s.[10] In the course of that debate, André Nataf [15] proved what seems at first glance to be a devastating theorem.

Index firms by $v = 1, \ldots, n$, and suppose (the simplest case) that the vth firm has a two-factor production function

$$Y(v) = f^{v}\{K(v), L(v)\}, \tag{I.5}$$

where $Y(v)$ denotes output, $K(v)$ capital, and $L(v)$ labor. The appearance of the superscript in $f^{v}(\cdot,\cdot)$ reflects the fact that not all firms need have the same technology. Under what conditions will it be possible to write total output, Y, as being given by an aggregate production function:

$$Y \equiv \sum_{v} Y(v) = F(J, P), \tag{I.6}$$

where

$$J = J\{K(1), \ldots, K(n)\} \quad \text{and} \quad P = P\{L(1), \ldots, L(n)\} \tag{I.7}$$

are indices of aggregate capital and aggregate labor, respectively? Further, it is natural to assume labor homogeneous and to require

$$P = L \equiv \sum_{\nu} L(\nu). \tag{I.8}$$

Nataf's theorem: (a) A necessary and sufficient condition for (I.6) is that every firm's production function be additively separable in capital and labor, that is, that every $f^{\nu}(\cdot,\cdot)$ can be written in the form:

$$f^{\nu}\{K(\nu), L(\nu)\} = \phi^{\nu}\{K(\nu)\} + \psi^{\nu}\{L(\nu)\}. \tag{I.9}$$

(b) For (I.8) to hold as well, it is additionally necessary and sufficient that

$$\psi^{\nu}\{L(\nu)\} = cL(\nu) \quad (\nu = 1, \ldots, n), \tag{I.10}$$

where the parameter c is the same for all firms.

***Proof*:** (a) The sufficiency of (I.9) is obvious. In any case, both sufficiency and necessity follow from Leontief's theorem. The Leontief conditions for aggregation here require that the ratio of the marginal products of labor between any two firms be independent of the amounts of capital which those (or any) firms happen to have. This yields (I.9).

(b) In this case, transferring a small amount of labor from one firm to another firm does not affect aggregate output. This can only happen if labor has the same marginal product in all firms – the same regardless of how much labor each firm already has.

If this were all there were to it, then aggregate production functions would be plainly impossible and this book would never have been written. As May [13], [14] pointed out, however, this is not all. The problem with Nataf's theorem is not that it gives the wrong answer but that it asks the wrong question. A production function does not give the output that can be produced from given inputs; rather it gives the *maximum* output that can be so produced. Nataf's theorem fails to impose an efficiency condition.

Once such conditions are imposed, matters change. Observe that Nataf's theorem holds even if capital as well as labor is physically homogeneous (and even if all firms have the same production function). But if capital and labor are both physically homogeneous and are allocated to firms (by the analyst, the state, or the market) to maximize output (the efficiency conditions), then aggregate output *when maximized* is a function only of aggregate capital and aggregate labor – whether or not the firms all have the same technology.

If only labor is homogeneous and technology embodied in capital, then, in the two-factor model, we must think of labor as allocated to firms to maximize output while capital is firm-specific. In that case, the Leontief aggregation conditions are still very restrictive,[11] but not nearly so restrictive as the Nataf results. If there are several types of capital, labor, and output, the problem is more complex; hence Chapters 1–6 of this book.

The point is that there may be economic forces at work that reduce, as it were, the dimensionality of the problem with which we are dealing. In the example just given, efficient allocation of labor reduces the effective factor space from $2n$ to $n+1$ dimensions. Perhaps there are additional phenomena to be studied.

One possibility is that the size distribution of firms remains relatively constant or shifts in certain regular ways. This is the case first studied by Houthakker [9] and then generalized first by Levhari [12] and then more extensively by Sato [22], [23]. In such cases, an aggregate production function will work over the observed data and can appear quite different in form from the individual production functions of the firms composing the aggregate.

Such constancy of the size distribution seems restrictive, but the question then arises of whether there are any other circumstances under which an aggregate production function appears to do well despite a lack of foundation for it at the micro level. This is not an idle question. Aggregate production functions not only succeed in (approximately) describing the relationship between aggregate output and aggregate inputs; they also yield implications for wages as marginal products that appear roughly correct. The most famous example is that of the Cobb–Douglas production function which, when fitted to aggregate input and output data, gives an approximately correct prediction of labor's share of national output.

Chapters 8 and 9 investigate this question by means of simulation experiments. Chapter 8 ("Aggregate production functions and the explanation of wages: A simulation experiment") sets up a model in which each firm has a two-factor Cobb–Douglas production function but in which the exponents differ so that no aggregate production function exists even when labor is efficiently allocated. After such allocation, an aggregate Cobb–Douglas production function is estimated and wage predictions checked against the wages (generated as marginal products in the underlying economy). Not surprisingly, the aggregate Cobb–Douglas production function fails to perform well when labor's share of total output is not approximately constant. What is more surprising is that whenever that share *is* approximately constant, *even though that constancy is not generated by an aggregate Cobb–Douglas production function*, such a function appears to perform well.[12]

This result suggests that rather than its being the case that labor's share is approximately constant because an aggregate Cobb–Douglas production function is a good description of real economies, the reverse is true. An aggregate Cobb–Douglas production function will appear to be a good description of the real economy when labor's share happens to be approximately constant. The reasons for such constancy must then be sought elsewhere.

This result is further confirmed in Chapter 9 ("Aggregate production functions: Some CES experiments," written with Robert Solow and James Kearl). That chapter reports the results for further simulation experiments in which the underlying firms have CES rather than just Cobb–Douglas production functions. Some other results are obtained as well, but perhaps none so striking as that relating to the aggregate Cobb–Douglas.

Before leaving the subject of aggregate production functions, I must add an additional word on the literature. This discussion has not pretended to be a complete literature review in any sense, and the reader is referred to the discussions in the various chapters for a somewhat more extensive treatment. But I would be remiss were I not to mention certain pieces here.

The first of these is the important paper by W. M. Gorman [8]. Gorman, hearing that I had written a paper with the title of Chapter 2 but not yet having access to the paper itself, wrote his own paper on the same subject. While he found a number of the same results as did I, he did so by a quite different method. Where I had concentrated on conditions on the underlying production functions themselves, he worked with the dual – the restricted profits function. The two approaches are equivalent, and which one finds more congenial is likely to depend on how one was brought up in studying production theory.

In recent years, Gorman's approach has been greatly extended to other areas of production-function aggregation by Charles Blackorby and William Schworm [1], [2], and especially [3] and [4]. They have provided very general answers to aggregation questions in circumstances not restricted to the constant returns and related technologies with which economists usually operate. Their work has clarified the status of a number of issues raised in Chapters 1 through 6.

The remaining two chapters in this book do not directly concern aggregate production functions but are rather on related topics. Chapter 10 ("On perfect aggregation in the national output deflator and generalized Rybczynski theorems") uses the techniques and some of the results of the earlier chapters. It considers the question of when the production-theoretic national output deflator introduced by Karl Shell and myself [7, Essay II] can be defined over aggregate sector prices. As it happens, the problem turns out to be isomorphic to the question of the application of the famous Rybczynski theorem of international trade to models with more than two goods and more than two factors of production.

Chapter 11 ("The commodity pattern of trade and the Heckscher–Ohlin theorem in the presence of aggregate and commodity-specific factor-intensity reversals," written with Arye L. Hillman) also examines the extension of the standard $2 \times 2 \times 2$ model of international trade, this time to a two-country, two-factor world with many goods aggregated into exports and imports.

There has been some editing of the original papers before republishing in this volume. Aside from the correction of misprints, some later papers contain minor corrections of statements or proofs in earlier ones. These have been incorporated where that could be easily done. Where that would have been cumbersome, the earlier chapters refer forward to the corrections.

Once again, I am very grateful to John Monz for editorial assistance and to Theresa Benevento for skilled help and unfailing good humor even when faced with the prospect of proof reading a third volume of my collected works.

This volume is dedicated to the memory of Theodora Riva Reichman Oshiver, my Aunt Teddy. Everyone who knew her will know why.

Cambridge, Massachusetts
November, 1991 – July, 1992

Notes

1. See Robinson [17], [18], [19], [20], for example.
2. Some idea of Mrs Robinson's fervor can be gotten from the following story which I have from Jagdish Bhagwati. In conversation with him, Mrs Robinson referred to the late Leif Johansen (then still living) as a "bourgeois fascist hyena" or some similar hyperbole. "How can you say

that?" inquired Bhagwati, "He's very active in the Norwegian Communist Party." "But, but, he believes in production functions!" replied Mrs Robinson.

3. Robinson [17], [18] and Solow [24]. See also Robinson [19], Samuelson [21], Solow [27], and, generally, the Production Function Symposium in *Review of Economic Studies*, **29** (1961–62), pp. 155–266.
4. The sufficiency of this condition had already been proved by Solow [28]. See Chapters 1 and 2 for the relation to other papers, some of which proved the same theorem independently.
5. See Chapter 1 for a discussion of this.
6. The First World Congress was held in Rome in 1965. I presented a summary of Chapter 2.
7. As I say, memories differ, and, I might add, legends have a way of persisting. I have described this incident in some detail because my memory of it differs from the description in a recent book entitled *Joan Robinson and the Americans* (Turner [29]). In that book (pp. 118–20, 142), the occasion is remembered as an unpleasantly rancorous one with Paul Samuelson leaving the room because of the supposedly ill-natured tone of Solow's remarks to Robinson. Imagination does work wonders.

   Further, it is suggested that Mrs Robinson and I agreed. When Mrs Robinson [20] later took a similar view of my position, I said [6] that such an interpretation meant that "words have lost their meaning." Apparently they have. (Incidentally, the references in Turner's book, p. 266, notes 12 and 13 and p. 283, are also peculiar. One reference appears to be to a work of mine on Chow tests – [5] – which has nothing whatever to do with the subject under discussion.)
8. Lecturing on this subject at Carleton was particularly appropriate because of the earlier contributions of Kenneth O. May [13], [14] and Pu Shou-Shan [16], both of whom had been at Carleton when writing their papers. Indeed, Pu was visiting Carleton when I gave my lecture. I discuss the early history of the subject below and in Chapter 1.
9. The proof given is not Leontief's own pioneering demonstration. Indeed (so much has the world changed) that Leontief's own proof was thought too difficult to be published in *Econometrica* [10] and was given in a separate article [11].
10. See Chapter 1 for more complete references and discussion.
11. See Chapter 2.
12. Sato [23, pp. 271–2] provides reasons for this result in addition to those given in Chapter 7.

References

[1] Blackorby, C. and W. Schworm, "Aggregate investment and consistent intertemporal technologies," *Review of Economic Studies*, **49** (1982), 595–614.

[2] Blackorby, C. and W. Schworm, "Aggregating heterogeneous capital goods in adjustment-cost technologies," *Scandinavian Journal of Economics*, **85** (1983), 207–22.

[3] Blackorby, C. and W. Schworm, "The structure of economies with

aggregate measures of capital: A complete characterization," *Review of Economic Studies*, **51** (1984), 633–50.
[4] Blackorby, C. and W. Schworm, "The existence of input and output aggregates in aggregate production functions," *Econometrica*, **56** (1988), 613–43.
[5] Fisher, F. M., "Tests of equality between sets of coefficients in two linear regressions: An expository note," *Econometrica*, **38** (1970), 361–6.
[6] Fisher, F. M., "The existence of aggregate production functions: Reply," *Econometrica*, **39** (1971), 405.
[7] Fisher, F. M. and K. Shell, *The Economic Theory of Price Indices*, New York: Academic Press, 1972.
[8] Gorman, W. M., "Capital aggregation in vintage models," in J. N. Wolfe (ed.) *Value, Capital, and Growth: Papers in Honour of Sir John Hicks*, Edinburgh: University of Edinburgh Press, 1968.
[9] Houthakker, H. S., "The Pareto distribution and the Cobb–Douglas production function in activity analysis," *Review of Economic Studies*, **23** (1955–56), 27–31.
[10] Leontief, W. W., "Introduction to a theory of the internal structure of functional relationships," *Econometrica*, **15** (1947), 361–73.
[11] Leontief, W. W., "A note on the interrelation of subsets of independent variables of a continuous function with continuous first derivatives," *Bulletin of the American Mathematical Society*, **53** (1947), 343–50.
[12] Levhari, D., "A note on Houthakker's aggregate production function in a multifirm industry," *Econometrica*, **36** (1968), 151–4.
[13] May, K. O., "The aggregation problem for a one-industry model," *Econometrica*, **14** (1946), 285–8.
[14] May, K. O., "Technological change and aggregation," *Econometrica*, **15** (1947), 51–63.
[15] Nataf, A., "Sur la possibilité de construction de certains macromodèles," *Econometrica*, **16** (1948), 232–44.
[16] Pu, Shou-Shan, "A note on macroeconomics," *Econometrica*, **14** (1946), 299–302.
[17] Robinson, J., "The production function and the theory of capital," *Review of Economic Studies*, **21** (1953–54), 81–106.
[18] Robinson, J., "The production function and the theory of capital: a reply," *Review of Economic Studies*, **23** (1955–56), 247.
[19] Robinson, J., "Comment" (on Production Function Symposium), *Review of Economic Studies*, **29** (1961–62), 258–66.
[20] Robinson, J., "The existence of aggregate production functions: Comment," *Econometrica*, **39** (1971), 405.
[21] Samuelson, P. A., "Parable and realism in capital theory: The surrogate production function," *Review of Economic Studies*, **29** (1961–62), 193–206.
[22] Sato, K., "Micro and macro constant-elasticity-of-substitution production functions in a multifirm industry," *Journal of Economic Theory*, **1** (1969), 438–53.
[23] Sato, K., *Production Functions and Aggregation*, Amsterdam: North-Holland, 1975.
[24] Solow, R. M., "The production function and the theory of capital," *Review of Economic Studies*, **23** (1955–56), 101–8.

[25] Solow, R. M., "Technical change and the aggregate production function," *Review of Economics and Statistics*, **39** (1957), 312–20.
[26] Solow, R. M., "Investment and technical progress" in K. J. Arrow, S. Karlin, and P. Suppes (eds), *Mathematical Methods in the Social Sciences, 1959*, Stanford: Stanford University Press, 1960.
[27] Solow, R. M., "Substitution and fixed proportions in the theory of capital," *Review of Economic Studies*, **29** (1961–62), 207–18.
[28] Solow, R. M., "Capital, labor, and income in manufacturing," in National Bureau of Economic Research Conference in Income and Wealth, *The Behavior of Income Shares* (Studies in Income and Wealth, 26), Princeton: Princeton University Press, 1964, 101–28.
[29] Turner, M. S., *Joan Robinson and the Americans*, Armonk, New York and London: M. E. Sharpe, 1989.

1

The existence of aggregate production functions (1969)

1.1 Introduction

The estimation and use of aggregate production functions has become a widespread and important practice in economic analysis. Broadly speaking, such uses fall into two main classes. On the one hand, following Solow's seminal article [22], we have had a spurt of interest in the estimation of aggregate production functions for entire economies, for manufacturing, for durables, or for more narrowly defined industry aggregates. These papers have made empirically derived inferences about the importance of technical change, embodied or disembodied; about the rate of return to investment, social or private; about the share of wages in national product; and, generally, about the technical and economic forces making for growth.

On the other hand, different in focus but not entirely divorced in development from such empirically oriented studies, is the use of aggregate production functions by a large and growing number of authors to represent the technical possibilities of an economy in which some intertemporal welfare function is to be maximized, or as a basic constituent of a one- or two-sector descriptive growth model.

Presented as the Irving Fisher Lecture at the meeting of the Econometric Society in Amsterdam, September, 1968. I am indebted to Robert M. Solow for comments and criticism. The work was supported by National Science Foundation Grant GS-1791.

This series of lectures stands in permanent memorial to Irving Fisher and Henry Schultz on one side of the Atlantic and to Leon Walras and Arthur Bowley on the other. In view of my topic, however, it seems fitting that I should dedicate this lecture to the memory of André Nataf.

In both sorts of problems, the use of an aggregate relationship between an output aggregate on the one hand and constructs called "labor" and "capital" on the other, is an immense convenience. The question naturally arises, however, whether it is merely that. Under what circumstances can the technical relationships of a diverse economy be appropriately subsumed in such an aggregate form? What can one say about inferences drawn from such models? Is it enough for such use that we be content with approximations?

These questions are not new ones, although the particular (and, I believe, crucial) features of the model within which I shall examine them have not been employed to answer them until quite recently. Moreover, they arise at different levels of aggregation. While I shall speak generally of an aggregate production function defined over an entire economy in which production is actually carried on by individual firms, it is clear that essentially the same problems arise at the industry level. Indeed, they also arise at the firm level with production actually carried on in individual establishments or, more fundamentally, by individual workers using individual kinds of capital. The principal differences among such cases lie often merely in how closely conditions for aggregation are likely to be satisfied in practice.

Now, it is important to recognize that there is a difference between the question of the existence of an aggregate production function and such related questions as the realism of models which assume smooth substitutability between capital and labor. While the fact that different kinds of machines are different plays an important role in the discussion of both questions, the aggregation problem arises whether or not technology involves fixed coefficients, and the answers typically do not turn on this question.[1] The difference may, perhaps, be pointed out by remarking on two items. First, all the aggregation problems which I shall discuss would arise in principle even if all capital were physically homogeneous. While in many cases, such physical homogeneity would guarantee the existence of an aggregate, this is not invariably true. Second, while the different characters of different kinds of capital play a crucial role, capital aggregation is not the only problem which must be faced. Labor aggregation and output aggregation also turn out to require quite stringent conditions which are unrealistic at the economy-wide level.

Accordingly, I shall take all my production functions to be twice continuously differentiable. It turns out, so far as is known, to make no essential difference,[2] and it greatly simplifies the exposition.

1.2 Aggregation and efficiency: The simplest case

I begin by considering the simplest possible case. There are n firms. The vth firm produces a single output $Y(v)$ by utilizing a single kind of labor $L(v)$ and a single kind of capital $K(v)$. The production function for the vth firm is

$$Y(v) = f^v(K(v),L(v)). \tag{1.1}$$

To simplify matters, all the outputs are physically indistinguishable, so that it makes sense to speak of total output for the economy Y as simply the sum of individual outputs $Y(v)$. Similarly, there is only one kind of labor, so that it makes sense to speak of total labor L (more accurately, total employment) as the sum of labor employed by the individual firms. More complicated cases will be discussed later.

Capital, on the other hand, may differ from firm to firm, although it need not do so. There is hence no immediate physical sense in which total capital can be said to exist. Further, since different kinds of capital will in general have different technical properties, each firm's production function will in general be different from that of any other firm; this is represented by the superscript v on the production functions.[3]

We are interested in the conditions under which it will be possible to write total output Y as being given by an aggregate production function:

$$Y \equiv \sum_v Y(v) = F(J,P), \tag{1.2}$$

where

$$J = J(K(1), \ldots, K(n)) \quad \text{and} \quad P = P(L(1), \ldots, L(n)) \tag{1.3}$$

are indices of aggregate capital and aggregate labor, respectively. Indeed, it is natural, given the assumed physical homogeneity of labor, to require

$$P = L = \sum_v L(v).$$

Now, it has long been recognized that if nothing more than this is said, the conditions under which such aggregation can be performed are extremely restrictive.[4] It was shown by Nataf [18] that, in these circumstances, the aggregate production function (1.2) will exist if and only if every firm's production function is additively separable in capital and labor, that is, if and only if every f^v can be written in the form

$$f^v(K(v), L(v)) = \phi^v(K(v)) + \psi^v(L(v)) \qquad (v = 1, \ldots, n).^5 \quad (1.4)$$

If we further impose the condition $P = L$, then we have the even more restrictive condition that

$$\psi^v(L(v)) = cL(v) \qquad (v = 1, \ldots, n) \quad (1.5)$$

where c is a constant and is the same for all firms.

If this were all there were to it, the hope that an aggregate production function existed would be forlorn indeed. It is pretty clear, however, that this cannot be all.

Nothing in the above discussion prevented capital from being physically homogeneous, although this was not required. Further, nothing prevented each firm's production function from exhibiting constant returns to scale, although this was not assumed. The result just given holds therefore, even if all firms have the same technology, the same kind of capital, and constant returns. In this case, however, we should certainly expect an aggregate production function to exist. If "constant returns" means anything, it surely means that there is no difference between one big firm and two little ones – that total output does not depend on the way in which production is divided among the producing units. Hence something must be wrong.

Nevertheless, there is no mistake in the results presented. Mere identity of technologies and constant returns does *not* imply the existence of an aggregate production function as may be seen by trying to add up two identical Cobb–Douglas production functions without further restrictions. The catch is not in the way in which the problem has been analyzed but in the fact that the wrong problem has been posed.

At any level of aggregation, a production function is not a description of what output will be achieved for given levels of different inputs; that output is not unique. Rather a production function describes the maximum level of output that can be so achieved if the inputs are efficiently employed. The true content of the statement just made about constant returns, for example, is that there is no difference between one big firm and two little ones *if both are producing efficiently*. Accordingly, we must ask not for the conditions under which total output can be written in the form (1.2) no matter what, but rather for the conditions under which it can be so written *once production has been organized to get the maximum output achievable with the given factors*.

That such considerations can make a major difference can be seen by continuing for a moment in the case in which all capital is physically homogeneous and mobile between firms. Then efficient production requires that Y be maximized given L and $K \equiv \Sigma_v K(v)$. Calling the value of Y when so maximized Y^{**}, it is obvious that

$$Y^{**} = F(K, L) \tag{1.6}$$

since the individual allocations of labor and capital to firms will be determined in the course of the maximization problem.[6] This holds even if all firms have different production functions, f^v (because, for example, each firm has knowledge of a different secret process). Moreover, it holds whether or not there are constant returns to scale.

It has been argued, however,[7] that to allow factors to be assigned to firms so as to achieve maximum total output is to introduce institutional considerations into what ought to be a purely technological affair. In a sense this is true. If there are institutional barriers to factor mobility, then one might properly say that efficiency requires maximization within such barriers, so that the happy result of (1.6) only holds for those institutional arrangements which permit full mobility. Such arrangements are compatible with rather different social frameworks, however, since the same organization of production will be achieved in this problem by a perfectly competitive economy, a centrally planned socialist economy, and a monopolist organizing the plants under its control. Moreover, it is hard to know where to draw the line. We do not refrain from using a production function for an individual firm because it is open to that firm to behave inefficiently; yet the ability of the firm to produce efficiently also rests on institutional factors. This aspect of the problem thus seems to me to be largely one of agreeing on what we are to mean by an aggregate production function. I would prefer to speak of output produced efficiently subject only to technological constraints as given by a production function and to regard institutional barriers to efficiency as forces causing the production system in question to lie inside the efficient frontier. I recognize, however, that in dealing with actual economies, the barriers may be more important than the frontier and that it is often quite difficult to distinguish between technological and institutional constraints. (Is a slow dissemination of technical knowledge an institutional constraint in this context?)[8]

It is clear, however, that whatever one decides about the case in which all capital is homogeneous and mobile, the far more realistic case in which capital goods are different and not interchangeable provides a constraint which should be treated as technological. Accordingly, we shall again assume technology to be embodied in the capital goods and shall assume that only labor, but not capital, can be allocated to firms so as to maximize total output. This sort of distinction between fixed and movable factors (which does not always coincide precisely with conventional distinctions between labor and capital) will be maintained when we move to more complicated models.

1.3 Capital aggregation

As now constituted, the problem is the following. Given that Y is maximized with respect to the allocation of labor to firms, and denoting the resulting value of Y by Y^*, under what circumstances is it possible to write

$$Y^* = F(J, L), \quad J = J(K(1), \ldots, K(n))? \qquad (1.7)$$

It is evident that in any case Y^* can be written as

$$Y^* = G(K(1), \ldots, K(n), L), \qquad (1.8)$$

since the values of the $L(v)$ will be determined in the course of the maximizing procedure, so for this simple model there is no labor aggregation problem and the entire problem is that of the existence of a capital aggregate.[9]

By a well-known theorem of Leontief, already referred to, (1.7) and (1.8) are equivalent if and only if the marginal rate of substitution between any pair of the $K(v)$ in the production of Y^* is independent of L. The problem is to see what this implies about the original firm production functions, the f^v. If we assume strictly diminishing returns to labor, so that $f^v_{LL} < 0$ $(v = 1, \ldots, n)$, where the subscripts denote differentiation, then it can be shown[10] that a necessary and sufficient condition for capital aggregation is that every firm's production function satisfy a partial differential equation in the form

$$\frac{f^v_{KL}}{f^v_K f^v_{LL}} = g(f^v_L) \qquad (v = 1, \ldots, n), \quad (1.9)$$

where the function $g(\cdot)$ is the same for all firms. I know of no simple way to interpret this condition directly in the general case,[11] but most of its implications are clear and interpretable enough.

In the first place, one way in which (1.9) can be satisfied is for every firm's production function to be additively separable as in (1.4). This is natural, since we already know that additive separability is a sufficient condition for capital aggregation whether or not labor is optimally allocated to firms. On the other hand, since (1.9) is a necessary as well as sufficient condition for capital aggregation, it is evident that if any one firm has an additively separable production function ($f^{v}_{KL} \equiv 0$), then no capital aggregate exists unless every firm has such a production function. In other words, capital aggregation is not possible if there is both a firm which uses labor and capital in the same production process and another which has a fully automated plant. (I shall henceforth assume that there is no such separability.)

This is but the first of a number of somewhat uncomfortable results with the general characteristic that if there are one or two firms with production functions having some property, then it matters very little what reasonable properties the production functions of other firms have; aggregation will not be possible. A stronger result of this kind can easily be obtained by observing that if constant returns are not assumed, there is no reason why perfectly well-behaved production functions cannot fail to satisfy *any* partial differential equation in the form (1.9). If some firm has such a production function, then exact capital aggregation is impossible regardless of the nature of the production functions of other firms; indeed, no capital aggregate in a production function sense will exist even if all firms are exactly alike and capital physically homogeneous (but immovable).[12]

It is evident on reflection, however, that this sort of problem arises in part from the lack of constant returns, since without constant returns it *does* matter how production is organized into firms. Indeed, it is not hard to show that every *constant returns* production function does satisfy a partial differential equation such as (1.9), although naturally not all constant returns production functions satisfy the same one.

Let us therefore assume constant returns for the moment and ask what conditions are then necessary and sufficient for capital aggregation. This can be done by integrating (1.9), but at least so far as sufficiency is concerned it is more revealing to take a different route.

Suppose that the production functions of the different firms differ from each other only by a *capital-augmenting* technical difference, that is, that each f^{v} can be written

$$f^{v}(K(v), L(v)) = f^{1}(b_{v}K(v), L(v)) \qquad (v = 1, \ldots, n), \quad (1.10)$$

where the b_{v} are positive constants ($b_{1} = 1$). In this highly restrictive case, a different capital good is equivalent in all respects to more of the same capital good. It is then natural to think of measuring capital in efficiency units and natural to suppose that with constant returns aggregation of capital will be possible since firms will differ only as to amount of efficiency capital. Indeed, this is so; it will be possible in this case to allocate labor so as to make firms differ only as to scale and, moreover, it will be efficient to do so. Constant returns will then allow firms to be added together.

A formal proof along these lines is easy to give.[13] It will suffice to consider two firms. Define $J \equiv b_1 K(1) + b_2 K(2)$ (this will turn out to be the right definition) and recall that $L = L(1) + L(2)$. The sum of the outputs of the two firms is

$$Y = f^1(b_1 K(1), L(1)) + f^1(b_2 K(2), L(2)). \tag{1.11}$$

Since efficient allocation of labor requires that labor have the same marginal product in both uses, it is clear that when Y is maximized with respect to labor allocation, the ratio of the second argument to the first must be the same in each of the two firms. Thus

$$\frac{L(1)}{b_1 K(1)} = \frac{L(2)}{b_2 K(2)} = \frac{L}{J} \tag{1.12}$$

when labor is optimally allocated. Let

$$\lambda \equiv \frac{b_1 K(1)}{J} = \frac{L(1)}{L} \tag{1.13}$$

(the second equality holding when labor is optimally allocated); then

$$Y^* = f^1(\lambda J, \lambda L) + f^1((1-\lambda)J, (1-\lambda)L) = f^1(J, L) \tag{1.14}$$

because of constant returns.

So far, so good. The trouble is that the case of capital-augmenting technical differences turns out to be the *only* case under constant returns in which a capital aggregate exists.[14] Only a very limited and special kind of technical diversity can be accommodated. Just how limited that diversity is can be seen either from contemplation of the definition of capital augmentation or from the fact that if all firms differ only by a capital-augmenting parameter, then when labor is optimally allocated, *average* product per worker (as well as marginal product) and profits per worker will be the same in all firms.

As already indicated, the situation is even worse in most respects when we drop the constant returns assumption. Here there are even cases (and such cases are the rule, rather than the exception) in which no capital aggregate exists whether or not firms are technically diverse. On the other hand, for a rather limited class of cases, capital aggregation is possible under somewhat wider conditions than that of merely capital-augmenting technical differences. This is the class of cases in which each firm's production function can be made constant returns after a suitable (generally nonlinear) stretching of the capital axis. Thus (omitting henceforth the firm index on the factors, where the context is clear):

$$f^{\nu}(K, L) = F^{\nu}(H^{\nu}(K), L) \qquad (\nu = 1, \ldots, n) \quad (1.15)$$

where the $F^{\nu}(\cdot,\cdot)$ are homogeneous of degree one in their arguments and the $H^{\nu}(\cdot)$ are monotonic. I have given this class of production functions the rather noneuphonious name of "capital-generalized constant returns" or "CGCR" for short.[15]

It is easy to see that this case is really not analytically different from the constant returns case for our purposes. Since, unlike labor, capital is not allocated over firms so as to maximize output, it makes no difference whether we take the capital goods in their original units or in their transformed, stretched units as being the fundamental capital goods of the model. If we do the latter, it is evident that a necessary and sufficient condition for capital aggregation is that the production functions of the individual firms differ only in the ways in which the capital axis is stretched, in the functions $H^{\nu}(\cdot)$ but not the functions $F^{\nu}(\cdot,\cdot)$ of (1.15). This is a generalization of capital-augmenting technical differences which I have called "capital altering." Despite the fact that it is more general than capital augmentation, it allows capital aggregation only in a restricted class of cases and is itself quite restrictive. It is evident that the force of the conditions necessary for capital aggregation is not to be evaded by dropping the assumption of constant returns.[16]

One might well ask, however, whether the restrictiveness of such conditions may not be a consequence of the highly simplified nature of the model. Suppose that there are several outputs, several labor types, and several capital goods produced by or used by each firm. Unfortunately, it turns out that essentially the same results apply when there are several outputs or several labor types, although conditions such as (1.9) are replaced by rather more complicated matrix equivalents. The presence of more than one kind of capital good for each firm does make some difference, however, and this I shall now discuss.

The essentials of what is involved can be seen by examining the case of a single output, a single labor type, but two capital goods. Thus the νth firm's production function becomes $f^{\nu}(K_1, K_2, L)$, where the firm index has been omitted from the arguments. There are two questions. First, what are the conditions under which it is possible to form an aggregate of only the first capital type (for example, an equipment aggregate or a plant aggregate)? Second, when is it possible to form an aggregate of all capital together (a total capital aggregate)?

These are not the same question and the conditions for one do not imply the conditions for the other. In the formation of a K_1 aggregate only, marginal rates of substitution between K_1 for different firms must be independent of K_2; this is not required if K_2 is included in the aggregate. On the other hand, if K_2 is to be so included, then the marginal rate of substitution between K_1 and K_2 must be independent of L; this is not required if K_2 is to be left out of the aggregate.

Taking first the case in which only K_1 is to be in the aggregate, the Leontief conditions turn out to be twofold. First, the Leontief conditions with respect to labor require that every firm's production function satisfy a partial differential equation in the form

$$\frac{f^v_{K_1L}}{f^v_{K_1}f^v_{LL}} = g(f^v_L) \qquad (v = 1, \ldots, n), \quad (1.16)$$

where the function g is the same for all firms and does not depend on K_2. This is just (1.9) again, as one might expect. Unfortunately, however, whereas any two-variable, constant returns production function satisfies a partial differential equation in the form of (1.9), not every three-variable function satisfies a partial differential equation in the form of (1.16), for the presence of constant returns in K_1, K_2, and L implies the absence of constant returns in K_1 and L alone. This already means that K_1 aggregation requires conditions more stringent than we found in the one-capital case; capital augmentation or K_1 augmentation and constant returns will not do. The mere existence of a firm with a particular constant returns production function (one not satisfying any equation in the form (1.16)) will prevent K_1 aggregation.

To make matters worse, the Leontief condition with respect to K_2 is equally stringent. Assuming (1.16) to hold, that condition becomes

$$f^v_{K_1K_2} - \frac{f^v_{K_1L}f^v_{K_2L}}{f^v_{LL}} = 0 \qquad (v = 1, \ldots, n). \quad (1.17)$$

This condition can be interpreted as follows. Suppose a little K_2 is added to the vth firm. There are two effects. The first of these is a direct effect on the marginal product of K_1; it is $f^v_{K_1K_2}$. The second is an effect through the reassignment of labor. That reassignment can be thought of in two steps. First, a certain amount of labor is withdrawn from the system as a whole; second, it is assigned to the vth firm.[17] The change in labor available to the entire system has no effect on the marginal rate of substitution between K_1 in the vth firm and K_1 in any other firm, because (1.16) was assumed to hold. There is such an effect through the specific assignment of more labor to the vth firm, however; like the direct effect of the increase in K_2, such reassignment shifts the marginal product of K_1 in the vth firm but does not affect it in any other firm. It is easy to see that the amount of reassigned labor will be

$(-f^{\nu}_{K_2L}/f^{\nu}_{LL})$ as this is just what will be required to keep the marginal product of labor unaffected. Accordingly, the second term in (1.17), including the minus sign, is the indirect effect on the marginal product of K_1 in the νth firm. The condition (1.17) is that this must just cancel out the direct effect.

The condition (1.17) is obviously very strong. Just how strong it is may be grasped in part by considering one of its implications. Suppose we define two factors as complements if increasing one of them increases the marginal product of the other. In two-factor, constant returns production functions, the two factors must be complements, but not all pairs of factors need be so if there are more than two. Nevertheless, suppose that the νth firm has a production function with all three factors complements. It is easy to see that the left-hand side of (1.17) must be positive for that firm and no K_1 aggregate can exist. Thus, for example, the existence of any firm with a three-factor Cobb–Douglas production function in, say, plant, equipment, and labor, $AK_1^{\alpha}K_2^{\beta}L^{1-\alpha-\beta}$, prevents the construction of either a separate plant or a separate equipment aggregate for the economy as a whole (although, as we shall see, it does not prevent the construction of a full capital aggregate). Similar statements are true about most easy three-factor generalizations of two-factor, constant returns production functions. Even the existence of some pair of factors which are substitutes, moreover, does not guarantee either the satisfaction of (1.17) or the satisfaction of any condition in the form (1.16). So far as the present assumptions are concerned, the construction of a subaggregate of capital goods requires even less reasonable conditions than the construction of a single aggregate in the case earlier discussed.

What about the construction of a complete capital aggregate in the present case, however? Here the conditions, while not technically weaker, seem a trifle less stringent than those for the construction of subaggregates.

In the first place, it is natural to suspect that a necessary condition for such complete capital aggregation is that it be possible to construct such a capital aggregate for each firm taken separately. This indeed turns out to be the case and it already greatly restricts the admissible class of firm production functions. On the other hand, many firm production functions having reasonable appearance will allow such a construction; the three-factor Cobb–Douglas is one.

Curiously, however, whereas one might expect capital aggregation over all firms to involve the condition that the individual firm aggregates all be of the same form,[18] this is the only restriction which is *not* involved, at least in the constant returns (and the CGCR) case. As can be seen by applying the theorem for the two-factor, constant returns case to the present problem with each firm's individual capital aggregate counted as a single capital good, the necessary and sufficient condition for full capital aggregation in the constant returns case, given the existence of individual firm aggregates, is that all firms differ by at most a capital-augmenting technical difference. Interpreted in the present context, that means that firms can differ as much as we like in the way in which their individual capital aggregate is constructed; they may not differ at all in any other way. It is as though each firm used its basic capital goods to construct an intermediate capital jelly which was then combined with labor to produce output. Capital aggregation is possible (under constant returns) if and only if the only difference among firms is in the way in which the jelly is constructed, not in how it is used thereafter.

This condition leads to a rather wider class of cases than appears from the two-factor case. For example, if one firm has a three-factor Cobb–Douglas function.

$$f^1(K_1(1), K_2(1), L(1)) = AK_1(1)^{\alpha}K_2(1)^{\beta}L(1)^{\gamma} \tag{1.18}$$

(where the three exponents may or may not be restricted to sum to unity), aggregation will be possible over this firm and any other with production function

$$f^2(K_1(2), K_2(2), L(2)) = BK_1(2)^{\varepsilon}K_2(2)^{\lambda}L(2)^{\gamma} \tag{1.19}$$

or, indeed, any firm with production function in the (now completely general) form

$$f^3(K_1(3), K_2(3), L(3)) = H(K_1(3), K_2(3))\,L(3)^{\gamma}. \tag{1.20}$$

Note that the exponent of the labor term is the same in all cases; the relative importance of the $K_1(v)$ and $K_2(v)$ is allowed to vary at will. Nevertheless, the class of cases allowing aggregation is clearly still very restricted.[19]

Thus, capital aggregation turns out to require rather stringent conditions if firms are technically diverse. This will, of course, come as little surprise to some. After all, Mrs Robinson has argued this sort of position for years.[20] Indeed, one might say that the wonder is that capital aggregation can be done at all, not that it can only be done in rather restricted circumstances. Nevertheless, it is true that capital aggregation can be performed in cases in which capital goods are physically quite different and production functions allowed to differ over firms. The mere immobility and physical differentiation of capital goods does not prevent the construction of such aggregates, even though the technical diversity that can be accommodated is fairly limited. Moreover, the difficulties involved are not associated with the question of fixed coefficients versus smooth substitutability. They arise, as we have seen, in the smoothly substitutable case.

What is perhaps more surprising than the difficulty of aggregating capital itself is the fact that the immobility and physical differentiation of capital impose nearly equally stringent conditions on the aggregation of labor types and of outputs. I now turn to this question.

1.4 Labor aggregation and output aggregation[21]

To consider the problem of labor aggregation, we must, of course, drop the assumption that there is only one homogeneous type of labor and reinterpret $L(\nu)$ as an s-component vector, $(L_1(\nu), \ldots, L_s(\nu))$, where $L_j(\nu)$ denotes the amount of the jth type of labor employed by the νth firm. It does not matter whether there is one or more types of capital, so $K(\nu)$ may be interpreted either as a scalar or a vector. Clearly this provides a quite general model, save for the assumption that there is only one homogeneous output.

The case of output aggregation when there is only one labor can be handled analogously. Relabel the single homogeneous labor as $Y(\nu)$ and take $L(\nu)$ to be the vector of outputs and f^{ν} to be a labor requirements function rather than (directly) a production function. Then the same model serves to discuss output aggregation.

Moreover, it is clear that both problems can be handled simultaneously. Let $Y(\nu)$ be the amount of a particular output produced by the νth firm and consider all other outputs as negative inputs. Labor aggregation in the presence of many outputs then becomes the problem of aggregating over a subset of the variable inputs. The problem of aggregating outputs in the presence of many labor types can clearly be similarly handled. Since the results in all important cases turn out to be the same, there is no need to treat the various cases in detail here.

The principal regularity condition on the firm production functions which must be imposed is that each of them have a negative definite Hessian with respect to the variable inputs – essentially that each have strictly diminishing returns to any linear combination of movable factors. This is, of course, the natural generalization of the condition $f^{\nu}_{LL} < 0$ in the simple model.

On the other hand, another assumption appears to be required which parallels a result rather than an assumption in the capital-aggregation problem. We are here primarily interested in the cross-firm aggregation problem that arises because labors or outputs are shifted over firms, given the capital stocks and production functions, to achieve efficient production. Yet there is also a labor aggregation or output aggregation problem within each firm. Thus, a labor or output aggregate might exist for each firm separately and not for all firms together. This phenomenon is the one we are analyzing. What is strange is that apparently there can exist a labor or output aggregate for all firms together without one existing for each firm separately. (This can happen because the effect on the marginal rate of substitution between two variable factors of changing one of the capitals is different when one considers only one firm from when one considers efficient factor reallocations over all firms.) In the case of capital aggregation, this cannot happen. One can show that a necessary consequence of aggregation over all firms is that an aggregate must exist for each firm separately; in the case of the aggregation of variable factors it is possible. (An example is given in Chapter 5, p. 133.)

Nevertheless, such a case, if it exists, is only a *curiosum*. It is hard to find much interest in an aggregate so fragile that it exists over a set of firms but not over proper subsets. If the existence of an aggregate production function depended on this sort of phenomenon, then an earthquake which swallowed one or more firms would also swallow the aggregate production function. I shall thus assume, as in the capital-aggregation case, that any aggregate to be considered already exists at the firm level, even though (unlike the capital-aggregation case) such an assumption may not be technically necessary for the existence of the aggregate over the entire set of firms.

This assumption, of course, imposes an already strong condition on the production functions of the individual firms. Taking the labor-aggregation case with a single homogeneous output for simplicity and continuing to omit the firm argument in Y, K, and L, the assumption means that every firm's production function can be written in the form:

$$Y = f^{\nu}(K, L) = F^{\nu}(K, \phi^{\nu}(L)) \tag{1.21}$$

where $\phi^{\nu}(\cdot)$ is a scalar-valued function (recall that L is now a vector).

Given such restrictions, however, it turns out that the conditions for labor or output aggregation are weaker than those for capital aggregation, in the sense that the existence of a capital aggregate for the entire set of firms implies the existence of a labor or output aggregate. This is not too surprising. Recall the constructive proof (given in the preceding section) that, under constant returns, capital augmentation (which we know to be necessary for capital aggregation) implies the existence of a capital aggregate. There, essentially, we could take every $f^{\nu}(\cdot,\cdot)$ as of the same form, absorbing the differences in the efficiency parameter multiplying capital. It turned out that the aggregate production function then also had that same form. If that form is assumed to permit labor (or output) aggregation before capital aggregation, then it certainly continues to do so afterwards. Nevertheless, the content of the theorem is not restricted to constant returns nor, indeed, to the existence of a full capital aggregate, as opposed to a subaggregate. Thus, it is a bit stronger than this argument indicates.[22]

Unfortunately, the fact that labor or output aggregation turns out to require technically weaker conditions than does capital aggregation (given the restriction assumed) does not make it terribly likely that labor or output aggregates exist. Even aside from the strong requirement that the appropriate aggregate already exist at the firm level, the conditions under which a labor or output aggregate exists are quite unrealistic whether or not a capital aggregate exists. For constant returns and some related technologies,[23] those conditions can be described in several ways.

The simplest way to state such conditions (but perhaps not the most revealing one) is to say that they amount to the requirement that the individual aggregating functions, $\phi^{\nu}(\cdot)$, can be taken to be the same. The functions $F^{\nu}(\cdot,\cdot)$ can differ unrestrictedly. It is as though (for the labor case) we interpreted (1.21) as saying that each firm uses its different labors without capital to make a composite variable factor and then combines the composite with capital to produce output. A labor aggregate exists over all firms taken together if and only if the production of the composite variable factor from individual labors is the same for all firms. The way in which the composite is used with capital to produce output is not restricted.

It is interesting to note that this is just the reverse of the analogous condition for capital aggregation. In the case of aggregation over several capitals, we found that the requirement was that the use of composite capital together with labor to produce output should be the same for all firms. The construction of composite capital from individual capitals was not restricted.

Since the functions, F^{ν}, are unrestricted (save to preserve constant returns), stating the conditions for labor or output aggregation in this way makes it appear that a wide variety of technical differences among firms can be accommodated. It is evident, for example, that if one firm has a Cobb–Douglas production function, a labor aggregate can exist even if other firms have production functions in very different forms.

Unfortunately, however, even though the technical differences which can be accommodated are indeed wider than in the capital aggregation case, the realism of the cases that can be accommodated is not much greater. This can be seen by considering an alternate (but equivalent) way of stating the necessary and sufficient conditions for labor or output aggregation.

Under constant returns, it is easy to show that the individual aggregating functions, $\phi^v(\cdot)$, can be taken to be homogeneous of degree one. This means, however, that the ratio in which a particular firm hires any two labor types or produces any two outputs depends only on the relative wages of all labors or the relative prices of all outputs. If (and only if) the $\phi^v(\cdot)$ are all the same, the same set of relative wages for labor will lead to the employment of all labor types in the same relative proportions for all firms; similarly, the same set of relative prices for outputs will lead to the production of all outputs in the same relative proportions for all firms.[24] Thus the existence of a labor aggregate requires the absence of specialization in employment; faced with the same set of wages, all firms must hire the same mix of labor types, differing only as to scale of total employment. Similarly, the existence of an output aggregate requires the absence of specialization in production; faced with the same set of relative prices, all firms must produce the same market basket of outputs, differing only as to scale of production. The mix of labor types employed and the market basket of outputs produced are not constant, since they depend on relative wages and relative prices, respectively; but they are the same over all firms. Obviously, this is not a realistic condition for firms in different, rather narrowly defined industries.

What about the construction of subaggregates? Is that any easier? This question is of some importance for three reasons. First, there are natural subaggregates which one might want to discuss. The employment of skilled labor or the production of nondurables comes to mind. Even if all labors or all outputs cannot be aggregated, it would be useful if some could be.

Second, we have been pretending that the conventional distinction between capital and labor exactly corresponds to the crucial distinction in this model between fixed and movable factors. If some kinds of capital are, in fact, movable, one might want to aggregate them or aggregate the true labors without aggregating all movable factors together. I shall take up this matter in the next section.

Third (a more narrowly technical matter), if we consider the problem of labor aggregation in the presence of many outputs or the problem of output aggregation in the presence of many labors, and agree to call alternative outputs negative factors, then we are in fact considering the question of forming an aggregate from some proper subset of the variable factors. So, in a way, the existence of subaggregates is what we have been discussing all through this section.

This fact points to what the conditions for the existence of a subaggregate must be (under constant returns). There are two. First, the subaggregate in question must exist at the firm level. Second, the subaggregating functions must be the same for all firms. Equivalently, faced with the same set of relative wages for the labors to be included in the subaggregate, all firms must hire *those* labors in the same relative proportions. Faced with the same set of relative prices for the outputs to be included in the subaggregate, all firms must produce *those* outputs in the same proportions.

These are the same conditions, suitably applied, that were involved in the construction of a full aggregate. They can be more realistic in the case of subaggregates, however, for a firm producing zero of some specified list of outputs can be regarded as producing any given market basket of them at zero level. Thus, some specialization in production (or, similarly, in employment) is allowed when only a subaggregate is to be constructed. Any firm which produces any output in the subaggregate, however, must produce all of them in the same proportions as any other firm, so specialization is not permitted within the production of the outputs (hiring of the labors) in the subaggregate.

One further point before proceeding. The fact that the conditions for subaggregation turn out to be the same as those for full aggregation applied to a subset of labors or outputs makes one suspect that the existence of a full aggregate might well imply the existence of a subaggregate. This is so in the same sense that the existence of a capital aggregate implies the existence of a labor or an output aggregate. That is, under constant returns, *provided a particular subaggregate exists for every firm individually*, the existence of a full aggregate (or indeed of any larger subaggregate) for the set of firms as a whole implies the existence of the subaggregate in question for the set of firms as a whole. This is fairly easy to see from the preceding discussion; it is in sharp contrast to the case of capital aggregation already discussed where no such relationship holds.[25]

1.5 How fixed is fixed capital?[26]

So far, I have spoken as though the distinction between the elements of K and the elements of L exactly corresponded to the conventional distinction between capital and labor. Clearly, this need not be the case. The crucial distinction in the model is that between fixed and movable factors, the elements of K being firm-specific, so to speak, while the elements of L are shuffled over firms to achieve efficiency. Some kinds of human capital, however (economics professors, for example), may be capable of only one type of work in a specific place, while (rather more importantly, perhaps) some types of physical capital may be mobile over firms. Aside from such items as typewriters and other office equipment used by nearly all firms, production equipment may in some cases be thought of as mobile in the long run as efficient reallocation thereof takes place through depreciation and reinvestment. This means that such immobile labor should be counted as an element of K and such mobile capital as an element of L in our model. Since conventional definitions still make it interesting to speak of a capital aggregate or a labor aggregate rather than a fixed factor or movable factor aggregate, we must therefore ask what becomes of our results if fixed and movable factors are to be aggregated together.

Accordingly, in this section I briefly examine the case in which some, but not all, capital goods are movable (the case in which some labors are fixed can be similarly handled). Does such mobility make aggregation easier? The answer turns out to depend on whether we are considering capital aggregates including both fixed and mobile factors or whether we consider aggregates of purely fixed or purely mobile factors.

In the case of partial capital aggregates including only the mobile capital goods, the answer is clear. If one compares the conditions for subaggregation discussed above for capitals and for labors, it is obvious that the conditions for such aggregation are rather less stringent when movable factors are involved than when fixed factors are. (Whether they are any more likely to be satisfied in practice is another matter.) The primary reason for this is the fact that the construction of a subaggregate of fixed factors when there are fixed factors left out, involves conditions such as (1.17) which are very special and cannot, for example, be satisfied if all factors are complements. The construction of a subaggregate of movable factors involves no such strong conditions. Hence it seems easier to aggregate a given subset of capital goods if that subset is movable than if it is fixed.

Moreover, a similar remark applies (and for the same reason) if the subaggregate to be constructed includes all the fixed factors. Leaving mobile factors out of the aggregate just does not involve the same strong condition as does omitting fixed factors. Hence it is easier to form an aggregate from a given group of capitals if the *remaining* ones are mobile than if the remaining ones are fixed.

One would naturally expect some such result, for it is easy to see that mobility cannot hamper aggregation. The conditions for aggregation when capitals are fixed are conditions such that, when they are satisfied, aggregation becomes possible no matter what values the various capital arguments have. Hence those same conditions must imply the possibility of aggregation if some of the capital arguments just happen to have those values which occur when they are shifted over firms to achieve efficiency. Thus, if aggregation is possible with capitals fixed, it remains so when some (or all) capitals become mobile. It is therefore not too surprising that mobility helps aggregation in the cases indicated.

What is perhaps surprising is that in the rather more general (and important) case where mobile and fixed capitals are to be included in the *same* aggregate, the mobility of some capitals does not change the aggregation conditions. Yet I have shown this to be true, at least for the case of constant returns, when all fixed capitals and some mobile ones are to be aggregated. Despite the mobility of some of the capital goods, capital augmentation (or the generalization thereof discussed at the end of Section 1.3) remains necessary and sufficient for the construction of a full capital aggregate. In this, perhaps the most important case, mobility does not hurt, but it does not help either.[27]

1.6 Approximations and the real world: Do exact results matter?

So far, I have been concerned with the conditions that are sufficient and, especially, necessary for an aggregate production function to give an exact representation of a diverse set of firms with technology embodied in fixed capital goods. I have discussed those conditions assuming that the values of the variables are restricted only by the requirements of economic sense and of efficient allocation of movable factors. Obviously, the requisite conditions turn out to be terribly strong.

Yet such exact results may not be of much practical force. What we really care about is whether aggregate production functions provide an adequate approximation to reality over the values of the variables that occur in practice. This is especially so for the empirical studies of production functions, technical change, growth, and related subjects; it is less so for theoretical studies of optimal capital accumulation and growth where the variables are less likely to be restricted in range. Yet even there, one is perhaps interested less in exact results than in good approximations.

Now, there are two ways in which the values of the variables might be restricted. The first of these is simply a restriction as to range. We know that the values of the various capitals and labors observed in practice are restricted, by the finiteness of the present economy, to lie in a bounded set. It might be the case that such restriction, together with the relaxing of our requirements from exact results to good approximations, leads to a substantial relaxation of our conditions for aggregation. This is the possibility that I shall discuss in the present section.

On the other hand, whether or not the range of the variables is restricted, there may be some other conditions that, so to speak, reduce the dimensionality of the problem, just as the requirement that labor be optimally allocated reduced the problem from one in which the independent variables included each firm's employment of labor to one in which the only exogenous labor variable was the total employed by all firms. I shall return to this possibility below.

For the moment, then, I ask the following question:[28] Suppose the elements of K and L are restricted to lie in a bounded rectangular region, S. Suppose further that we no longer require that an aggregate production function exist which exactly equals the true disaggregated production function but rather require that an aggregate production function exist which comes within some specified distance, ε, of the true production function for all points in S.[29] To what extent can the rather stringent conditions already discussed be relaxed?

There is one obvious way in which such relaxation is possible. It is easy to see that if we are only interested in approximate results, we need only require that our exact conditions hold approximately. Thus, in the simplest case, it will clearly suffice for approximate capital aggregation that all technical differences among firms be approximately capital augmenting. (Naturally, how close to capital augmentation the situation must be depends on how close an approximation in the results is required.) As is usually (but not always) the case, small errors have small consequences.

Unfortunately, this is not a terribly helpful result. The reason for being unhappy with capital aggregation, for example, is not merely that one thinks technical differences are not likely all to be exactly capital augmenting but that one thinks there are some differences that are not anything like capital augmenting. It is not much comfort to know that small deviations from capital augmentation can be tolerated when one believes that such deviations may well be large.[30]

The interesting question, therefore, is whether there are any other cases – cases in which our exact conditions are *not* approximately satisfied but in which an aggregate production function gives a satisfactory approximation for all points in S. Naturally, the answer depends on what one means by a "satisfactory approximation" as well as on how badly our conditions are violated. Nevertheless, the general answer appears to be in the negative.

Without going into great detail,[31] it turns out that the only way in which such approximations could result would be if we were willing to accept production functions which were very irregular in a well-defined sense. More particularly, assuming twice differentiable production functions (and it seems vain to hope that differentiability makes any substantial difference here), such approximations could only result if either the true production function or its aggregate approximation had first or second derivatives exhibiting very large rates of change both up and down on every closed rectangular subregion of S. Put not quite precisely, those derivatives would have to fail to satisfy a Lipschitz condition in the limit as the required approximation became closer and closer to the truth. Moreover, the violation of the Lipschitz condition would have to take place both above and below. In less technical language, the derivatives would have to wiggle violently up and down all the time.[32] There is nothing wrong with functions having such properties, but we do not ordinarily expect production functions to exhibit this kind of behavior. Certainly, it is not exhibited by the aggregate production functions used in practice.

Naturally, there is a bit more to it than this. In particular, how "irregular" things have to be depends on how closely the aggregate production function is required to approximate the true state of affairs as well as on how badly our exact aggregation conditions are violated and the functional forms and range of variables involved. Nevertheless, there can be no presumption that our exact conditions do not matter simply because one is interested in reasonable approximations over a limited domain. Indeed, I think the presumption must be the other way. Such an escape from the stringency of the conditions will be available, if at all, only in rather special cases.

1.7 But it does move, all the same

Despite all this, there is, after all, considerable evidence that aggregate production functions may be appropriate approximations. I do not put much weight on the fact that estimates of aggregate production functions from output and factor data tend to yield high R^2s; the aggregates are highly correlated with the variables in the true specification, and, anyway, high correlations are fairly easy to generate. On the other hand, there is apparently nothing about the aggregation or estimation procedure involved in such studies to guarantee that the production functions so estimated will give approximately the correct picture of factor shares. Yet, clearly, this is the case. As Solow once remarked to me, we would not now be concerned with this question had Paul Douglas found labor's share of US output to be 25 per cent and capital's share 75 instead of the other way round.

How do we account for this? It is hard to be sure, but I have fairly strong suspicions.

It is clear, of course, that if something is at work behind the scenes which reduces the dimensionality of the problem in ways not accounted for in our analysis, then aggregate production functions may work well even though we conclude that they ought to work badly. The simplest example of this is the case in which, for reasons unspecified by us, firms always invested in proportion to a particular index, J. In that case, J would clearly be a suitable capital aggregate regardless of our analysis, so long as that behavior continued. If firms invested approximately in fixed ratios, then J would be an approximate aggregate. Similarly, if outputs were always produced or labors always hired in approximately fixed proportions, then an approximate output or labor aggregate would exist.

To take a different example, suppose that all capital goods were produced and rented (but not sold) under conditions of monopoly with prices administered. If all such prices were fixed over time, then firms using those goods as inputs would have to adjust to make the marginal rates of substitution between pairs of capital goods equal to the fixed price ratios. Even if each firm used a different capital good, but produced the same output as other firms, such equality would come about through the equating of marginal revenue products with factor prices. In such a case, a capital aggregate might not exist in general because the marginal rates of substitution among pairs of capitals would not generally be independent of labor. Nevertheless, a capital aggregate would appear to exist because the marginal rates of substitution in question would be fixed.[33] Naturally, the fixing of those rates could not be plausibly regarded as a purely technical matter, and the aggregate would only be appropriate so long as the capital goods industry failed to change relative prices.

Similarly, if the relative prices of outputs or of labors were administered and more or less stable, an output or a labor aggregate would appear to exist and would, indeed, be perfectly appropriate so long as such price behavior persisted.

Finally, there is the possibility that there are systematic forces at work which we simply have not thought of. Suppose in the constant-returns, one-output, one-labor case, that all technical differences were capital augmenting. As we know, a capital aggregate would then exist and an aggregate production function would give good results. An observer who had not considered the possibility that labor is efficiently allocated (by the market or by planners) would be rather puzzled, however. He or she could observe the good results, but, unless he or she thought every firm's production function were additively separable, he or she would also believe that such good results could not generally be expected. Similarly, in the present instance, it is possible that some systematic phenomenon is at work which, like the efficient allocation of labor, restricts the dimensionality of the problem and widens the class of cases in which aggregate production functions give appropriate answers.

These three possibilities are not mutually exclusive, and there may be some element of truth in all of them. For the present, anyway, I tend to favor the first over the latter two.

In a way, the third hypothesis – that there are forces at work which we have not taken into account – is not a hypothesis at all. Unless one is willing to be specific about what such forces are, it is impossible to refute the contention that they are there. I have nevertheless listed this possibility for two reasons. First, the example of the efficient allocation of labor and its effects on aggregation makes one realize that there very well may be plausible systematic effects left out of consideration and points toward the nontrivial way in which such effects might operate. Second, there is, after all, something real to be explained. To the extent that the other two possibilities (approximately constant relative proportions and approximately constant relative prices) do not succeed in accounting for the observed facts, then we must admit our ignorance in this regard. I point out, however, that if this turns out to be the case, then reliance on aggregate production functions is reliance on the continuation of badly understood phenomena. An investigation of this problem ought then to have very high priority in future research.

Turning to the hypothesis that it is administered and sticky prices that make aggregate production functions look good, I believe this should have some weight, but it is hard to say how much. The difficulty is knowing how stable relative prices have to be in order to give aggregate production functions the appearance of working. It is also not trivial to construct an index of stability for relative prices which has reasonably desirable properties (such as symmetry, freedom from scale, independence of original distribution of relative prices, and so forth). I have constructed one such index for the stability of relative output prices and of relative capital goods prices in the United States, disaggregating to fifteen outputs and six capital goods. For what it is worth, that index shows a high degree of stability relative to the rather foolish null hypothesis of independence over time, but whether that degree is high or low for the question at hand, I simply do not know, and I have thus decided not to report the details. Certainly, there are many administered prices in modern economies, but whether that alone accounts for the performance of aggregate production functions seems rather doubtful.[34] Still, sticky relative prices may be part of the explanation.

The hypothesis that seems the most promising is, as indicated, the possibility that the ratios of items in a particular aggregate do not change very much so that the aggregate is approximately correct over the observed data. In particular, if the economy does not depart too far from balanced growth, this will be the case, but it should be noted that balanced growth is only a leading, very special, case of this kind of thing. Neither exponential growth nor constant ratios among labor, output, and capital (or particular labors, particular outputs, and particular capitals) are required. All that it takes for a capital aggregate are constant ratios of capital goods; for a labor aggregate, constant ratios of labor types are involved; and for an output aggregate, we require constant ratios among outputs. This does not seem a wild departure from the facts, and, indeed, real economies may not depart too far from balanced growth, but again, how big a departure will leave aggregate production functions with good results cannot be settled easily.

I am currently in the process of conducting simulation experiments with the simple one-output, one-labor model, and the results, while very preliminary, are quite suggestive. Briefly, they indicate that an aggregate production function does quite well for small, plausible, unsystematic movements in the ratios of the capitals. A relatively large, systematic trend in such ratios of more than a few per cent a year causes things to break down rather badly. As one would expect, such sensitivity to systematic change is worse the farther the departure from exclusively capital-augmenting technical differences. A plausible extent of such departure can be tolerated, however, so long as capital ratios do not systematically move by amounts more than a very casual glance suggests are typical of real economies in the short run.

I hope to be more precise about these results in a later paper, but, if they hold up, they certainly suggest that the good performance of aggregate production functions may be due to the fact that there is not a great deal of movement in the relative variables.[35] This makes conclusions drawn from such aggregate functions valid so long as things keep on moving pretty much together; it makes such conclusions suspect if extended to movements between balanced growth paths; and it suggests that conclusions for large aggregates drawn from internationally derived estimates may be particularly shaky.

1.8 Why does it matter?

This leads directly to the final question which I wish to consider, that of the consequences of all this. Ought one to be particularly concerned over these results? Further, why should one be more concerned with aggregation difficulties in production functions than in other areas of economic analysis – consumption functions, for example?

The answers to these questions seem to me to be related, and they bear, as they must, on the uses to which production functions are put.

The first such use may be regarded as primarily descriptive. We estimate production functions to give some idea of what is happening to productivity or to use as one piece of a forecasting model, and so forth. In this kind of use, a production function plays a role not very different from that played by consumption functions, and aggregation difficulties ought perhaps not to seem more alarming in the former than in the latter case. In both cases we know that such difficulties are there in principle; in both we recognize that some degree of approximation is involved; in both we realize (if we are careful) that such approximations will get worse the more things move around.

If there is a difference here, it is perhaps in the confidence one can have as to the usefulness of the approximations. In the case of a linear consumption function (which I take merely as the simplest example), we know that an aggregate will be all right so long as either individual marginal propensities to consume are about equal or so long as the distribution of income remains relatively fixed. The former possibility does not seem outlandish, and the second has been roughly true for some time. In the production function case, however, the parallel to the equality of marginal propensities is (in the simplest example) the condition that all technical differences be approximately capital augmenting and this simply does not seem very plausible when aggregating over different industries. Similarly, rough constancy of the ratios of different capital goods, of different labor types, and of different outputs (if that is what accounts for the success of aggregate production functions), seems somehow an even less well-understood phenomenon than that of rough constancy of the income distribution and therefore a less reliable reed on which to lean. Still, I am unwilling to press this last point, and this descriptive use of aggregate production functions may well not be much worse than similar uses for other aggregates.

Production functions are not merely used in a direct descriptive way, however. For one thing, they are used together with marginal productivity theory to generate equations to help explain factor prices and employment. This indirect use has no parallel in the case of consumption functions and it means that production functions bear a relatively heavy burden in the analysis of growth. At the very least, this means that we ought to be extra careful about the analysis of a functional relationship on which we are going to put such weight.

Still, so far as empirical work and forecasting is concerned, aggregate production functions often give good results not only in the relation of outputs to inputs but also in their wage and factor share implications. Again, so long as the relevant ratios do not move too much, this is not accidental.

The real problem seems to me to come in analyses in which those ratios can be expected to move – in long run forecasting or in theoretical, descriptive, or normative growth models in which the characteristics and existence of an aggregate production function are of crucial importance. Such studies cannot afford to assume that balanced growth or constancy of ratios will continue, for they are concerned with the very forces that change such behavior. For such studies, the fact that an aggregate production function cannot be expected to exist even as an approximation is clearly very serious.

Does this vitiate the usefulness of such models? Not necessarily. Theorems derived for one- and two-sector growth models may very well have more general application. If they do, however, it will be because insights and methods developed in the analysis of such models carry over to less aggregative studies. It will not be because those models themselves directly summarize the technical relationships of highly diverse economies.

In short, it seems to me important to worry about aggregation in production functions because production functions are themselves important. They, and their implications, play central roles not only in empirical work but also in theoretical analysis. Just because it is possible to use aggregate production functions for grand statements about long run growth and technical change, it is important to be careful about the foundation for such statements. At present, that foundation seems solid only insofar as relatively small changes are concerned. The analyses which I have here summarized have convinced me that there is at least a need for great caution in this area. It may be recalled that Solow's seminal article [22, p. 312] called for "more than the usual 'willing suspension of disbelief' to talk seriously of the aggregate production function." That suspension has clearly led to very fruitful results. I am, however, finding it increasingly difficult to maintain. The conditions for the existence of aggregate production functions, at least when widely diverse industries are included, seem very, very strong.

Notes

1. For a "putty-clay" technology such as analyzed by Johansen [10], the aggregation problem essentially involves the *ex post* technology. Although, naturally, an *ex post* aggregate need not correspond to an *ex ante* one, this is not in itself a problem of aggregation since the *ex ante* and *ex post* technologies generally differ at any level of aggregation.
2. See Stigum [25] and [26].
3. Clearly, the model can also be interpreted as one of embodied technical change, with the $K(v)$ representing capital goods of different vintages. While the results apply directly to such models, and while work on this problem was greatly stimulated by Solow's introduction of the embodied model [23], the importance of the aggregation problem is best brought out by the interpretation in the text in which technical change does not enter.
4. This matter was extensively discussed in a debate in *Econometrica* in the late 1940s. See Klein [11], [12], May [16], [17], Nataf [18], and Pu [20]. A summary is given in Green [7].
5. The sufficiency of this condition is obvious. Its necessity can be easily proved among other ways by use of Leontief's well-known theorem on separable functions which states that a twice differentiable function of three variables $g(x_1, x_2, x_3)$ can be written as $G(h(x_1, x_2), x_3)$ if and only if $\partial(g_1/g_2)/\partial x_3 \equiv 0$ (where the subscripts denote differentiation). In other words, the marginal rate of substitution between x_1 and x_2 must be independent of x_3. See Leontief [14] and [15] and the Introduction. While all or nearly all of the results here discussed can be proved in other ways, I have tended to rely on the Leontief conditions.
6. This was pointed out by May [16] and [17].
7. See Klein [11] and [12], for example.
8. Whitaker [28] discusses capital aggregation in the context of immobile capitals but mobile labor with labor allocated to firms by arbitrary rules.
9. This problem has been studied in different ways by several authors. See, for example, Diamond [1], Fisher [2] (Chapter 2), Gorman [6], Hall [8], Nataf [19], Stigum [25], and Whitaker [27].
10. See [2] (Chapter 2) for the proof of this and other statements in this section.
11. If one assumes constant returns, (1.9) immediately becomes the condition that profits per worker (or, indeed, average product) be the same for all firms when labor is optimally allocated. See [2] (Chapter 2).
12. In this extreme case, however, a competitive market would lead all firms to the same equilibrium position in the long run and capital would have the same marginal product in all uses. This makes capital essentially a long run movable factor and takes us back to the case of full maximization discussed in the preceding section.
13. This proof is due to Solow [24, pp. 104–5].
14. This holds true except for the trivial case of all production functions additively separable. This result was proved independently by a number of authors. See the works cited in Note 9.
15. Examples are easy to generate, the simplest being the nonconstant returns Cobb–Douglas, $AK^{\alpha}L^{\beta}$, which is, however, the only CGCR production function which is also homogeneous of some degree other than one.

16. The class of CGCR functions differing by capital-altering differences is not the only nonconstant returns case permitting capital aggregation. There are some other very special cases. See pp. 44–5 for example.
17. This assumes that more rather than less labor will be assigned to the νth firm as a consequence of its having an increase in K_2. The opposite case is analogous.
18. A similar expectation turns out to be correct in the aggregation of labor and of output discussed below.
19. One might also add that the aggregate will look a bit odd. For the three firms just described, it is

$$J = (AK_1(1)^{\alpha}K_2(1)^{\beta})^{1/(1-\gamma)} + (BK_1(2)^{\varepsilon}K_2(2)^{\lambda})^{1/(1-\gamma)} + (H(K_1(3), K_2(3)))^{1/(1-\gamma)}.$$

The aggregate production function would be

$$Y^* = J^{1-\gamma}L^{\gamma}.$$

20. See [21], for example. Mrs Robinson was not specially concerned with aggregation over firms.
21. This section is based on Fisher [3] (Chapter 3). See also Stigum [26].
22. Details may be found in Fisher [3] (Chapter 3). The precise form of the results does appear to depend on whether there is more than one output when labor is being aggregated, or the reverse, but the sense does not.
23. Essentially, those technologies for which the individual aggregating functions, $\phi^{\nu}(\cdot)$, can all be taken to be homogeneous of degree one. There seems no point in going into great detail here. Such technologies include CGCR technologies as a special case.
24. Note, incidentally, that this form of the condition *implies* the existence of individual firm aggregates, ϕ^{ν}.
25. Similarly, in various nonconstant returns cases, the existence of a full aggregate for the system as a whole also implies the existence of system-wide subaggregates, provided the corresponding subaggregates exist at the firm level. Curiously, as opposed to the capital case where subaggregation was hindered if all factors were complements, subaggregation in the labor or output cases turns out to be aided by such pervasive complementarity. See Chapter 3 for details.
26. This section is based on Fisher [4] (Chapter 4).
27. There are some differences in the extension of the results to nonconstant returns (it matters whether a production function is CGCR because a stretching of the fixed capital axis brings it back to constant returns or whether stretching of a mobile capital axis is involved), but they do not seem worth going into in detail. See Chapter 4.
28. The following discussion is based on Fisher [5] (Chapter 7), which deals with a more general problem than the existence of aggregate production functions.
29. Similar results hold if the standard of approximation is not absolute but relative to the size of output.
30. Honesty requires me to state that I have no clear idea what technical differences actually look like. Capital augmentation seems unduly restrictive, however. If it held, all firms would produce the same market basket of outputs and hire the same relative collection of labors.

31. See Chapter 7.
32. The problem is analogous to (and indeed derived from) the problem of whether a differentiable function of one variable can be close to zero everywhere on a bounded interval and yet have its derivative not generally close to zero, that is, not be reasonably flat. The answer is clearly yes, but not if the function must also look "regular." The function $f(x) = \lambda \sin (x/\lambda)$, for $\lambda > 0$, is everywhere between $+\lambda$ and $-\lambda$. Its derivative is $f'(x) = \cos (x/\lambda)$ which is not everywhere close to zero when λ is small. The derivative fluctuates up and down, however, with the fluctuations becoming more and more frequent as we force the function closer to zero by taking smaller and smaller values of λ. As we approach the limit, the second derivative fails to exist, and, more important, the first derivative wiggles violently up and down in any small closed interval.
33. This is, of course, a special case of Hicks–Leontief aggregation. See Hicks [9, p. 33] and Leontief [13].
34. One could hope to go some way toward finding out by simulation studies, but I have not thus far done so because the simpler hypothesis about to be discussed seems more promising in this regard.
35. This seems even more plausible if we recall that recession years in which there may be such movements are frequently excluded from the estimation process or are otherwise adjusted for capacity utilization.

References

[1] Diamond, P. A., "Technical change and the measurement of capital and output," *Review of Economic Studies*, **32** (1965), 289–98.
[2] Fisher, F. M., "Embodied technical change and the existence of an aggregate capital stock," *Review of Economic Studies*, **32** (1965), 263–88 (reprinted as Chapter 2).
[3] Fisher, F. M., "Embodied technology and the existence of labour and output aggregates," *Review of Economic Studies*, **35** (1968), 391–412 (reprinted as Chapter 3).
[4] Fisher, F. M., "Embodied technology and the aggregation of fixed and movable capital goods," *Review of Economic Studies*, **35** (1968), 417–28 (reprinted as Chapter 4).
[5] Fisher, F. M., "Approximate aggregation and the Leontief conditions," *Econometrica*, **37** (1969), 457–69 (reprinted as Chapter 7).
[6] Gorman, W. M., "Capital aggregation in vintage models," in J. N. Wolfe (ed.), *Value, Capital, and Growth: Papers in Honour of Sir John Hicks*, Edinburgh: University of Edinburgh Press, 1968.
[7] Green, H. A. J., *Aggregation in Economic Analysis: An Introductory Survey*, Princeton: Princeton University Press, 1964.
[8] Hall, R. E., "Technical change and capital from the point of view of the dual," *Review of Economic Studies*, **35** (1968), 35–46.
[9] Hicks, J. R., *Value and Capital*, Oxford: Clarendon Press, 1946 (2nd edn).
[10] Johansen, L., "Substitution versus fixed production coefficients in the theory of economic growth: a synthesis," *Econometrica*, **27** (1959), 157–76.
[11] Klein, L. R., "Macroeconomics and the theory of rational behaviour," *Econometrica*, **14** (1946), 93–108.

[12] Klein, L. R., "Remarks on the theory of aggregation," *Econometrica*, **14** (1946) 303–12.
[13] Leontief, W. W., "Composite commodities and the problem of index numbers," *Econometrica*, **4** (1936), 39–59.
[14] Leontief, W. W., "A note on the interrelation of subsets of independent variables of a continuous function with continuous first derivatives," *Bulletin of the American Mathematical Society*, **53** (1947), 343–50.
[15] Leontief, W. W., "Introduction to a theory of the internal structure of functional relationships," *Econometrica*, **15** (1947), 361–73.
[16] May, K. O., "The aggregation problem for a one-industry model," *Econometrica*, **14** (1946), 285–8.
[17] May, K. O., "Technological change and aggregation," *Econometrica*, **15** (1947), 51–63.
[18] Nataf, A., "Sur la possibilité de construction de certains macromodèles," *Econometrica*, **16** (1948), 232–44.
[19] Nataf, A., "Possibilités d'agrégation de fonctions de production à variables capital et main-d'oeuvre," *Review of Economic Studies*, **34** (1967), 219–26.
[20] Pu, Shou-Shan, "A note on macroeconomics," *Econometrica*, **14** (1946), 299–302.
[21] Robinson, J., "The production function and the theory of capital," *Review of Economic Studies*, **21** (1953), 81–106.
[22] Solow, R. M., "Technical change and the aggregate production function," *Review of Economics and Statistics*, **39** (1957), 312–20.
[23] Solow, R. M., "Investment and technical progress," Ch. 7 in K. J. Arrow, S. Karlin, and P. Suppes (eds.), *Mathematical Methods in the Social Sciences, 1959*, Stanford: Stanford University Press, 1960.
[24] Solow, R. M., "Capital, labor, and income in manufacturing," in National Bureau of Economic Research Conference in Income and Wealth, *The Behavior of Income Shares* (Studies in Income and Wealth, 26), Princeton: Princeton University Press, 1964, pp. 101–28.
[25] Stigum, B. P., "On certain problems of aggregation," *International Economic Review*, **8** (1967), 349–67.
[26] Stigum, B. P., "On a property of concave functions," *Review of Economic Studies*, **35** (1968), 413–16.
[27] Whitaker, J. K., "Vintage capital models and econometric production functions," *Review of Economic Studies*, **33** (1966), 1–18.
[28] Whitaker, J. K., "Capital aggregation and optimality conditions," *Review of Economic Studies*, **35** (1968), 429–42.

2

Embodied technical change and the existence of an aggregate capital stock (1965)

2.1 Introduction

The question of when a production function which involves more than one type of capital good can be written in terms of a capital aggregate was discussed at length some time ago by various authors and settled formally by Solow in [11].[1] He observed that this can be done if and only if the production function satisfies the condition of Leontief's theorem on separable functions,[2] which in this context amounts to the requirement that the marginal rate of substitution between different types of capital be independent of the amount of labor. Unfortunately, this is a rather severe restriction on the production function.

Recently, the same problem has arisen in a somewhat different context in which the answer turns out to be of somewhat greater interest and interpretability. This is the context of the model of embodied technical change developed by Solow in a recent series of papers ([12], [13], and [14]). In that model, technical change takes effect only when new types of capital goods ("embodying" the change) are introduced. Total output is the sum of outputs obtained using each

I should like to dedicate this paper to R. M. Solow on the occasion of his return to MIT from a year's leave at Cambridge. I am grateful to A. R. Dobell, E. Kuh, D. Levhari, R. A. Pollak, P. A. Samuelson, K. Shell, R. M. Solow and J. Tobin for helpful comments at one stage or another. Despite the length and quality of this list, the responsibility for error remains my own. This paper was in part supported by a Ford Foundation grant to MIT and Yale for the construction of a model of long run economic growth in the United States.

type of capital separately. Labor is allocated over the different types of capital so as to maximize total output.

Solow has shown [14] that it is sometimes possible in such a model, *once labor has been optimally allocated*, to write the maximized value of output as a function of total labor and a homogeneous aggregate of the different types of capital goods. While the ability to do this is no more than a mild convenience in theoretical work with the embodiment model, it is of considerable practical importance in the econometric estimation of production functions and technical change. When such a construction is not available, estimation of the parameters of the production functions using the various types of capital is at best a nonlinear estimation problem of considerable magnitude, and may, in fact, be insoluble since it requires the *explicit* solution of the labor allocation problem in terms of the parameters to be estimated and the quantities of the various capital goods.

This chapter is concerned with the necessary and sufficient characteristics of embodied technical change which permit the construction of such an aggregate capital stock. We first examine the case in which each production function involves only one type of capital and in which there is only one homogeneous type of labor to be allocated. The results obtained are then generalized to the case in which there are several types of capital subject to technical change and in which there are several homogeneous factors allocated so as to maximize output. A complete solution to the existence problem posed is given for the important case in which every individual production function (whether two-factor or many-factor) exhibits constant returns to scale, and only one capital aggregate including all capital types is to be constructed. Separate sufficient conditions and necessary conditions are given for the more general case as are necessary and sufficient conditions in terms of differential equations.

While the discussion is phrased in terms of embodied technical change, the analysis is more general than this, since the defining characteristic of the problem is the optimal allocation of at least one homogeneous factor to different uses yielding the same output. Thus, it turns out that even if capital goods cannot be aggregated without taking such allocation into account, save in a rather narrow class of cases,[3] it may be possible to perform such aggregation in a rather wider class of cases when such allocation takes place. Since if *any* factors (however narrowly defined) are homogeneous, such optimal allocation is a reasonable assumption in a variety of institutional settings, the results are of considerable interest for the important problem of the use of aggregate production functions in macroeconomic analysis.[4]

2.2 The two-factor case: Preliminary results

We begin with the two-factor case. Here there is one homogeneous factor, labor, and one heterogeneous factor, capital. The amount of capital of "vintage" (type) v is denoted by $K(v)$ and the amount of labor allocated to that capital is denoted by $L(v)$. Total labor is denoted by L.

The amount of output, $Y(v)$, obtained from capital of vintage v, is given by the vintage production function:

$$Y(v) = f^v(K(v), L(v)). \tag{2.1}$$

Denoting total output by Y, we have:

$$Y = \sum_{v=1}^{n} Y(v) = \sum_{v=1}^{n} f^v(K(v), L(v)) \tag{2.2}$$

where there are n distinct vintages of capital goods.

The allocation of labor is determined by the solution of the following problem: choose $L(1), \ldots, L(n)$ so as to maximize Y, subject to

$$\sum_{v=1}^{n} L(v) = L. \tag{2.3}$$

Denote the value of Y when maximized in this way by Y^*. Our problem is the following: when is it possible (i.e., what must be true of the vintage production functions $f^v(v = 1, \ldots, n)$) to write:

$$Y^* = G(J, L) \tag{2.4}$$

where

$$J = J(K(1), \ldots, K(n)) \tag{2.5}$$

is a capital aggregate independent of L?

We shall assume that each of the vintage production functions f^v is twice continuously differentiable. It would be interesting to weaken this assumption and to examine a linear programming technology, but we have not been able to do this in the present paper.[5]

We further assume that the allocation of labor is always such that some labor (even if very little) is always employed on every vintage of capital in existence. This is not as restrictive as it looks, since it is easily seen to be guaranteed for the types of technical change which we shall show to be sufficient for the existence of the aggregate capital stock J, and since any condition which is necessary for such existence in the presence of this assumption is obviously necessary in its absence (except for the trivial case in which labor is only employed on one type of capital). Like the assumption of differentiability this assumption is required for the use of the calculus, in this case to avoid corner solutions.

By Leontief's theorem,[6] a necessary and sufficient condition for the existence of J is:

$$\partial\left(\frac{(\partial Y^*/\partial K(h))}{(\partial Y^*/\partial K(r))}\right)\Big/\partial L \equiv 0 \quad \text{for all } h, r = 1, \ldots, n. \tag{2.6}$$

We thus begin by evaluating $\partial Y^*/\partial K(h)$.

It is obvious that the solution to the labor allocation problem is to make the marginal product of labor the same in every use. Thus, in equilibrium:

$$\frac{\partial f^v}{\partial L(v)} \equiv f_L^v = \mu \quad (v = 1, \ldots, n) \tag{2.7}$$

where μ is a Lagrange multiplier and subscripts denote partial differentiation of a function with respect to its own arguments.

Now, $\partial Y^*/\partial K(h)$ apparently consists of two terms. The first of these is the direct marginal product of the hth type of capital in its own production function; the second is the sum of the effects on Y^* which come about when the optimum allocation of labor is changed as a result of a change in $K(h)$. Thus:

$$\begin{aligned}\partial Y^*/\partial K(h) &= f_K^h + \sum_{v=1}^{n} f_L^v(\partial L(v)/\partial K(h)) \\ &= f_K^h + \mu \sum_{v=1}^{n} (\partial L(v)/\partial K(h))\end{aligned} \tag{2.8}$$

in view of (2.7). However, using the labor constraint (2.3):

$$\sum_{v=1}^{n} (\partial L(v)/\partial K(h)) = \partial L/\partial K(h) = 0, \tag{2.9}$$

so that:

$$\partial Y^*/\partial K(h) = f_K^h \quad (h = 1, \ldots, n). \tag{2.10}$$

The Leontief condition (2.6) therefore becomes:

$$\frac{\partial(f_K^h/f_K^r)}{\partial L} = 0 \tag{2.11}$$

whenever $f_L^h = f_L^r$ for all $h, r = 1, \ldots, n$.

We must now evaluate $\partial f_K^h/\partial L$. Clearly:

$$\partial f_K^h/\partial L = f_{KL}^h(\partial L(h)/\partial L). \tag{2.12}$$

It therefore suffices to investigate $\partial L(h)/\partial L$, the addition to labor employed on capital of the hth vintage when a little more total labor becomes available.

Now, $L(1), \ldots, L(n)$, and μ are given by the solution of the first-order maximization conditions (2.7) and (2.3). Writing those conditions in implicit form and applying the implicit function theorem, we obtain:

$$\partial L(h)/\partial L = \frac{-\Delta^{n+1,h}}{\Delta}, \tag{2.13}$$

where

$$\Delta = \left|\begin{array}{cccccc|c} f_{LL}^1 & 0 & 0 & \cdots & & 0 & -1 \\ 0 & f_{LL}^2 & 0 & \cdots & & 0 & -1 \\ \cdot & \cdot & \cdot & \cdot & \cdot & \cdot & \cdot \\ \cdot & \cdot & \cdot & \cdot & \cdot & \cdot & \cdot \\ \cdot & \cdot & \cdot & \cdot & \cdot & \cdot & \cdot \\ 0 & \cdot & \cdot & \cdot & 0 & f_{LL}^n & -1 \\ \hline -1 & \cdot & \cdot & \cdot & \cdot & -1 & 0 \end{array}\right| \tag{2.14}$$

and $\Delta^{n+1,h}$ is the cofactor of the element in the $(n+1)$th row and hth column of Δ. Expanding Δ along the cofactors of the last row and then expanding the terms thus obtained along the cofactors of their last columns, we have:

$$\Delta = -\sum_{i=1}^{n}\prod_{\substack{v=1 \\ v\neq i}}^{n} f_{LL}^v = -\left(\prod_{v=1}^{n} f_{LL}^v\right)\left(\sum_{i=1}^{n}\frac{1}{f_{LL}^i}\right). \tag{2.15}$$

Similarly, expanding $\Delta^{n+1,h}$ along the cofactors of the hth row, we obtain:

$$\Delta^{n+1,h} = \prod_{\substack{v=1 \\ v\neq h}}^{n} f_{LL}^v = \left(\prod_{v=1}^{n} f_{LL}^v\right)\left(\frac{1}{f_{LL}^h}\right). \tag{2.16}$$

Substituting in (2.13):

$$\partial L(h)/\partial L = \frac{1}{f_{LL}^{h} \sum_{v=1}^{n} \left(1/f_{LL}^{v} \right)}. \tag{2.17}$$

Substituting this result in (2.12) and using this to write out the Leontief condition (2.11), that condition becomes:

$$\frac{\partial (f_K^h / f_K^r)}{\partial L} = (1/f_K^r)^2 \left(\frac{1}{\sum_{v=1}^{n} (1/f_{LL}^{v})} \right) \left(\frac{f_K^r f_{KL}^h}{f_{LL}^h} - \frac{f_K^h f_{KL}^r}{f_{KL}^r} \right) = 0 \tag{2.18}$$

whenever $f_L^h = f_L^r$, for all $h, r = 1, \ldots, n$.

Since we may take the marginal product of capital in any vintage production function as nonzero, and since the first two factors of the middle member of (2.18) are nonzero, this is equivalent to:

$$\frac{f_{KL}^h}{f_K^h f_{LL}^h} = \frac{f_{KL}^r}{f_K^r f_{LL}^r} \tag{2.19}$$

whenever $f_L^h = f_L^r$ for all $h, r = 1, \ldots, n$.

We may restate this result as the following basic lemma.

Lemma 2.1: In the two-factor case, a necessary and sufficient condition for the existence of an aggregate capital stock, J, is that when f_L^v is independent of v, then so is $(f_{KL}^v / f_K^v f_{LL}^v)(v = 1, \ldots, n)$.

An alternative way of stating this is as follows:

Lemma 2.1′: In the two-factor case, a necessary and sufficient condition for the existence of an aggregate capital stock, J, is that there exist a function $g(\cdot)$, independent of v, such that for all $v = 1, \ldots, n$:

$$\frac{f_{KL}^v}{f_K^v f_{LL}^v} \equiv g(f_L^v) \tag{2.20}$$

for all positive values of $K(v)$ and $L(v)$.

We observe immediately that this yields the fairly trivial result that J always exists if for all v, $f_{KL}^v \equiv 0$, so that every vintage production function can be written as the sum of a function of the amount of capital of that vintage and a function of the labor applied to that capital. Since this is not a very reasonable property for production functions to have, we shall disregard this possibility henceforth and assume that $f^v_{KL} \neq 0$ for any v.[7] We must now consider the less trivial ways in which the condition just obtained can (or cannot) be satisfied.

2.3 The two-factor case: Constant returns

In this section we examine the important leading case in which it is known that every vintage production function, $f^v(\cdot,\cdot)$, exhibits constant returns to scale. In this case, using Euler's theorem and the fact that $f^v_L(\cdot,\cdot)$ is homogeneous of degree zero when $f^v(\cdot,\cdot)$ is homogeneous of degree one, we obtain:

$$\frac{f^v_{KL}}{f^v_K f^v_{LL}} = \frac{-L(v)}{K(v) f^v_K}. \tag{2.21}$$

Since we require the left-hand (and therefore the right-hand) side of (2.21) to be independent of v when and only when f^v_L is independent of v, we may invert the ratios in (2.21) and make use of Euler's theorem again to obtain:

Theorem 2.1: In the two-factor, constant returns case, a necessary and sufficient condition for the existence of an aggregate capital stock is that when labor has been optimally allocated (so that labor's marginal product is the same for all vintages) the *average* product of labor shall be the same for all vintages.

In other words,

$$\frac{f^v}{L(v)} = \frac{K(v) f^v_K}{L(v)} + f^v_L \tag{2.22}$$

shall be the same for all $v = 1, \ldots, n$, whenever f^v_L is.

As before, this may be restated as:

Theorem 2.1′: In the two-factor, constant returns case, a necessary and sufficient condition for the existence of an aggregate capital stock is that there exist a function, $g(\cdot)$, independent of v, such that for all $v = 1, \ldots, n$:

$$\frac{f^v}{L(v)} \equiv g(f^v_L) \tag{2.23}$$

for all positive values of $K(v)$ and $L(v)$.

We now define:

DEFINITION 2.1: Technical change will be said to be *capital augmenting* if and only if there exists a function F, independent of v, and a set of positive constants, $b(1), \ldots, b(n)$, such that, for all $v = 1, \ldots, n$, and all positive values of $K(v)$ and $L(v)$:

$$f^v(K(v), L(v)) = F(b(v)K(v), L(v)). \tag{2.24}$$

If technical change is capital augmenting, one unit of new capital equipment is the same as a constant number of units of old capital equipment. This suggests immediately that an aggregate capital stock should be constructible if technical change is of this special form. Indeed, we prove that capital-augmenting technical change is necessary as well as sufficient in the present case.

Theorem 2.2: In the two-factor, constant returns case, an aggregate capital stock, J, exists if and only if all technical change is capital augmenting.[8]

Proof: It will be convenient to drop the vintage superscript or argument, as to leave it in would make the notation unduly cumbersome and the context will prevent confusion. Differentiation of the function F with respect to its ith argument will be denoted by $F_i (i = 1, 2)$. We begin with the proof of sufficiency:

(a) Sufficiency: By Theorem 2.1, it suffices to show that F/L is independent of b when L is adjusted so as to keep:

$$F_2(bK, L) = \mu. \tag{2.25}$$

It follows from (2.25) that:

$$\partial L/\partial b = \frac{-KF_{21}}{F_{22}} = \frac{L}{b}, \tag{2.26}$$

using Euler's theorem and the fact that F is homogeneous of degree one in its arguments. Using this result:

$$\begin{aligned} \frac{\partial(F/L)}{\partial b} &= (1/L)^2(LKF_1 + LF_2(\partial L/\partial b) - F(\partial L/\partial b)) \\ &= (1/bL)(bKF_1 + LF_2 - F) = 0 \end{aligned} \tag{2.27}$$

by Euler's theorem.

(b) Necessity: By Theorem 2.1′, if J exists, then there is a function $g(\cdot)$, such that for all vintages, the vintage production functions satisfy the partial differential equation:

$$f/L = g(f_L). \tag{2.28}$$

Define:

$$\lambda = \frac{L}{K};\ \Phi(\lambda) = f(1, \lambda). \tag{2.29}$$

Then, using the homogeneity of f:

$$\frac{\Phi(\lambda)}{\lambda} = g(\Phi'(\lambda)). \tag{2.30}$$

Now, we are only interested in functions, $g(\cdot)$, such that (2.28) can be satisfied for reasonable production functions. Such functions, $g(\cdot)$, must be monotonic for all positive values of f_L, since otherwise more than one marginal product of labor would correspond to the same average product. This cannot happen, since in a constant returns production function, every value of λ determines a unique value of f_L, and, using Euler's theorem:

$$\frac{d(\Phi(\lambda)/\lambda)}{d\lambda} = \frac{\lambda\Phi'(\lambda) - \Phi(\lambda)}{\lambda^2} = (1/\lambda)^2 f_1(1, \lambda) > 0.\text{[9]} \tag{2.31}$$

Thus (2.30) is an ordinary first-order differential equation whose solution $\Phi(\lambda)$ is unique up to a single arbitrary parameter.

It follows that if J exists, the vintage production functions are a one-parameter family of functions. If J existed and technical change were not capital augmenting, then it would follow from the sufficiency proof already given that we could superimpose a different arbitrary capital-augmenting change on each vintage production function and secure a two-parameter family of functions which allowed the existence of J. Since this would be a contradiction, the theorem is proved.

Two remarks on the necessity part of the theorem seem in order before proceeding. First, of course what is necessary is that technical change can be *expressed* as a capital-augmenting change. In the Cobb–Douglas production function, for example, this will be true of any change which leaves the exponents unaltered (and therefore of any true technological improvement[10]).

Second, looking at the matter of embodied technical change in a slightly different manner, our necessity result states that quality corrections to capital stock figures will only be nondistorting in two-factor constant returns production function estimates if technical change is capital augmenting.

2.4 The general two-factor case

The answer to the problem becomes rather less simple when the assumption of constant returns to scale is dropped. While I have obtained several results of some interest, I have not been able to secure a complete closed-form characterization of the class of cases in which an aggregate stock of capital exists in the same sort of terms as was possible in the constant returns case.

One's first guess in the general case might be that capital-augmenting technical change would remain a sufficient condition for the existence of J. After all, such change leads naturally to a measurement of capital in efficiency units (with the $b(v)$ as weights), and thus, apparently, to a solution of the aggregation problem. That this is false is apparent from the fact that not every reasonable looking production function will satisfy the condition of Lemma 2.1 when subjected to capital-augmenting technical change. For example, the function

$$Y(v) = AK(v)^{\alpha}\text{Log}(1 + L(v)) \qquad 0 < \alpha < 1 \tag{2.32}$$

fails to satisfy that condition when subjected to such change.[11]

The reason for this is that the argument from efficiency units is really only appropriate under constant returns. Its unstated premise is that it is always possible to aggregate capital used in two different ways if there is *no* technical change and labor is optimally allocated between the two uses. If constant returns are absent, however, there is no reason why this should be so, since the way in which the same *homogeneous* capital stock is divided is not a matter of indifference. There is no reason why in such a situation we should generally expect to be able to treat two identical plants as equivalent to one big one.

This may suggest, indeed, that J never exists without constant returns, or at least that it never exists under capital-augmenting technical change without constant returns. This too is false, however, as will be shown below. The true content of the efficiency unit argument and the intuitive feeling that capital-augmenting change ought to occupy a somehow privileged position in this problem appears to be as follows. If J exists, then it continues to exist if the vintage production functions are subjected to a generalized form of capital-augmenting technical change. To put it another way, if such generalized capital-augmenting change in a particular vintage production function does not permit construction of an aggregate capital stock, then no set of vintage production functions which includes the given one will permit such construction. Thus, no set of vintage production functions containing (2.32) as a member will permit the construction of such an aggregate. On the other hand, there do exist classes of nonconstant returns vintage production functions which do allow such a construction. To a more precise discussion of these matters we now turn.

We begin by generalizing the concept of capital-augmenting technical change.

DEFINITION 2.2: Technical change will be said to be *capital altering* if and only if there exists a function $F(\cdot,\cdot)$, independent of v, and a set of monotonic[12] functions, $H^1(\cdot), \ldots, H^n(\cdot)$, such that for all $v = 1, \ldots, n$ and all positive values of $K(v)$ and $L(v)$:

$$f^v(K(v), L(V)) = F(H^v(K(v)), L(v)). \tag{2.33}$$

If we have constant returns and capital-altering technical change, then we can always choose $F(\cdot,\cdot)$ and the $H^v(\cdot)$ $(v = 1, \ldots, n)$ so as to express that change as capital augmenting.[13] In the nonconstant returns case, capital-altering change is more general, but always includes capital-augmenting change as a special case.

Now define:

DEFINITION 2.3: A production function, $f(K, L)$, will be said to be *capital-generalized constant returns* (CGCR) if and only if there exists a function $F(\cdot,\cdot)$, homogeneous of degree one in its arguments, and a monotonic function $H(\cdot)$, such that for all positive values of K and L:

$$f(K, L) = F(H(K), L). \tag{2.34}$$

Examples of CGCR production functions can be readily generated by taking any constant returns production function and substituting for capital any monotonic function of capital. For example, a Cobb–Douglas type production function with exponents not adding to unity but with the exponent of labor less than unity is CGCR.[14] So is any function obtained from it by substituting any monotonic $H(K)$ for K. This suggests the fairly obvious:

Lemma 2.2: If technical change is capital altering and at least one vintage production function is capital-generalized constant returns, then:

(a) The function $F(\cdot,\cdot)$ in the definition of capital-altering change can be chosen to be homogeneous of degree one in its arguments.

(b) Every vintage production function is capital-generalized constant returns.

Proof: Clearly, (b) is a trivial consequence of (a) which it remains to prove. Suppose that it is $f^h(\cdot,\cdot)$ which is CGCR. Then there exists a monotonic function $P(\cdot)$ and a function $F(\cdot,\cdot)$ which is homogeneous of degree one in its arguments such that:

$$f^h(K, L) = F(P(K), L) \tag{2.35}$$

where we have omitted the index h in $K(h)$ and $L(h)$ for reasons of clarity.

Since technical change is capital altering, there exists a function $Q(\cdot,\cdot)$ independent of v and monotonic functions $R^1(\cdot), \ldots, R^n(\cdot)$, such that for all $v = 1, \ldots, n$:

$$f^v(K, L) = Q(R^v(K), L). \tag{2.36}$$

In particular, this holds for $v = h$.

Since $R^h(\cdot)$ is monotonic, it has an inverse which we shall denote by $\rho(\cdot)$. Thus:

$$K = \rho(R^h(K)). \tag{2.37}$$

Using (2.35), (2.36) with $v = h$ and (2.36), we obtain:

$$Q(R^h(K), L) = f^h(K, L) = F(P(\rho(R^h(K))), L). \tag{2.38}$$

Now define:

$$H^v(K) = P(\rho(R^v(K))) \qquad (v = 1, \ldots, n). \tag{2.39}$$

These functions are obviously monotonic in K. It follows immediately from (2.38) that:

$$f^v(K, L) = Q(R^v(K), L) = F(H^v(K), L) \qquad (v = 1, \ldots, n), \tag{2.40}$$

and the lemma is proved.

Thus the property of capital-generalized constant returns is preserved under capital-altering technical change and the function $F(\cdot,\cdot)$ may be taken to be the same in Definition 2.2 as in Definition 2.3.

We may now generalize Theorem 2.1 as follows:

Theorem 2.3: In the two-factor case, if every vintage production function is CGCR, a necessary and sufficient condition for the existence of an aggregate capital stock is that when labor has been allocated to have the same marginal product in all uses, the *average* product of labor shall be the same in all uses. In other words, f^v/L shall be independent of v when f^v_L is.

***Proof*:** We again omit the vintage argument in the expression for $K(v)$ and $L(v)$.

For every $v = 1, \ldots, n$, there exists a function $F^v(\cdot,\cdot)$, homogeneous of degree one in its arguments and a monotonic function $H^v(\cdot)$, such that:

$$f^v(K, L) = F^v(H^v(K), L). \tag{2.41}$$

Denoting differentiation of $F^v(\cdot,\cdot)$ with respect to its arguments by numerical subscripts and making use of Euler's theorem, the crucial fraction of Lemma 2.1 becomes:

$$\frac{f^v_{KL}}{f^v_K f^v_{LL}} = \frac{F^v_{12} H^{v\prime}(K)}{F^v_1 H^{v\prime}(K) F^v_{22}} = -\frac{L}{H^v(K) F^v_1}. \tag{2.42}$$

This will be independent of v whenever $f^v_L = F^v_2$ is if and only if:

$$\frac{F^v}{L} = \frac{H^v(K) F^v_1}{L} + F^v_2 \tag{2.43}$$

is so independent. QED.

Similarly, Theorem 2.2 generalizes to:

Theorem 2.4: In the two-factor case, if every vintage production function is capital-generalized constant returns, then a necessary and sufficient condition for the existence of an aggregate capital stock is that all technical change be capital altering.

***Proof*:**

(a) Sufficiency: By Lemma 2.2, the function $F(\cdot,\cdot)$ in the definition of capital-altering change can be taken as homogeneous of degree one. Choosing the $H^v(\cdot)$ as in that definition, define:

$$H(\beta_1, \ldots, \beta_n; K) = \sum_{v=1}^{n} \beta_v H^v(K). \tag{2.44}$$

Then

$$H^v(K) = H(0, \ldots 0, 1, 0 \ldots, 0; K) \quad (v = 1, \ldots, n) \tag{2.45}$$

where the unit element appears as the vth argument. The desired result now follows as in the proof of Theorem 2.2, differentiating with respect to the β_v instead of simply with respect to b.

(b) Necessity: Considering $H^v(K)$ instead of $K(v)$ as the fundamental capital variable in the vth production function the desired result follows immediately from Theorem 2.2, and the theorem is proved.

Using the sufficiency part of Theorem 2.4 and Lemma 2.2 yields immediately:

Corollary 2.1: In the two-factor case, a sufficient condition for the existence of an aggregate capital stock is that at least one vintage production function be capital-generalized constant returns and that all technical change be capital altering.

The argument used in the proof of necessity in Theorem 2.2 gives the intuitive reason why capital-generalized constant returns and capital-altering technical change play the same sort of role in the general case as constant returns and capital-augmenting change do in the constant-returns case. So long as a production function is homogeneous of degree one in labor and some function of capital, it can be split into parts, the outputs of which sum to the output from the original function. So long as the vintage production functions all have this property and are all the same function of labor and of some function of capital, the latter function need not be the same for all vintages; one might just as well think of it directly as capital. The fact that an aggregate capital stock exists in such a situation under capital-altering change yields a much wider class of cases than if only capital-augmenting change were permissible, as in the constant returns case.

The issue that now naturally arises is whether the CGCR capital-altering change cases just discussed are the only admissible ones in the general two-factor case. Despite the fact that the heuristic argument as to divisibility of production functions may indicate that this is so, it does not seem to be the case in fact. I have, on the other hand, only been able to find counter-examples which fail to exhibit at least one of the properties which one usually assumes for constant returns production functions. For example, it is a straightforward matter to verify from Lemma 2.1′ that the following set of functions, which are neither CGCR nor differ only by capital-altering change, permit the existence of J:

$$f^v(K(v), L(v)) = \phi^v(H^v(K(v)) + b(v)L(v)), \tag{2.46}$$

where $\phi^v(\cdot)$ is monotonic (as is $H^v(\cdot)$) and $b(v) > 0$.[15] For $\phi^{v\prime\prime}(\cdot) < 0$, there are diminishing returns to each factor. It is true that the cross-second partial derivative, f^v_{KL}, is negative instead of positive, but there is nothing to rule this out in a production function that does not exhibit constant returns.

It is possible that the cases which permit aggregation with changes which are not exclusively capital-altering all have negative cross-partials,[16] but this is an open question.

A further open question is the following: Suppose we require:

$$f^{v}(0, L(v)) = \psi(L(v)) \qquad (v = 1, \ldots, n) \qquad (2.47)$$

where $\psi(\cdot)$ is independent of v. This amounts to assuming that labor alone produces the same output no matter what vintage of capital is *absent*. (This is reasonable in the context of embodied technical change but perhaps not so reasonable if v denotes different firms rather than different vintages.) It is clear that the only changes then permitted in (2.46) are changes in $H^{v}(K(v))$ so that all changes are capital altering. A natural conjecture therefore is that (2.47) rules out all noncapital-altering changes which would otherwise be admissible.[17]

That this is not an easy question to settle may be seen by considering the family of functions:

$$f^{v}(K(v), L(v)) = K(v)e^{\lambda(v)L(v)} \qquad (2.48)$$

which satisfy *both* (2.47) and the condition of Lemma 2.1 but which obviously fail to be admissible as production functions because of increasing returns to labor.[18]

In any case, much of the true content of the heuristic notion that there is something privileged about capital-altering technical change in the present context appears given by:

Theorem 2.5: In the general two-factor case, consider the set of all production functions which can be formed by subjecting every vintage production function to all possible capital-altering changes. Denote that set by S. If any aggregate capital stock exists with the original vintage production functions, then one exists with those functions replaced by the elements of any subset of S.[19]

***Proof*:** By Lemma 2.1′, the existence of J implies the existence of a function $g(\cdot)$ satisfying (2.20) for every one of the original vintage production functions. It is easy to verify that the same equation will be satisfied with the same function $g(\cdot)$ for any member of S. The conclusion of the theorem now follows from the fact that the condition of Lemma 2.1′ is sufficient as well as necessary.

Put somewhat loosely, Theorem 2.5 implies that if an aggregate capital stock exists, then one also exists when capital-altering technical change is superimposed on whatever technical changes were already present. Further, it implies that if a function is to form one of any set of vintage production functions which together allow the construction of an aggregate capital stock, then any set of vintage production functions obtained by subjecting the given function to arbitrary capital-altering changes must also allow such a construction. In other words, if capital-altering change in a particular vintage production function will not allow the construction of the aggregate, then no other change (including no change at all) will either.

This latter implication can be used to state another necessary condition for the existence of an aggregate capital stock. Lemma 2.1′ shows that one such necessary condition is that for any vintage production function there exist a function $g(\cdot)$ such that (2.20) be satisfied. Indeed, it is necessary not only that $g(\cdot)$ not depend on v but also that it be the same function for all vintage production functions. Not only can it happen that $g(\cdot)$ varies with v, but also (once we leave constant returns and CGCR), it can happen that no such function exists even for a given vintage production function. This is the case, for example, with the function given in (2.32). Unfortunately, since $g(\cdot)$ can in principle be quite complicated, it may not always be easy to check this condition. It is therefore convenient to have a necessary condition which does not involve the function $g(\cdot)$.

To secure such a condition, one need only proceed as in the sufficiency proofs of Theorems 2.4 and 2.2. Since, by Theorem 2.5, for any vintage production function forming part of a set which allows the construction of an aggregate capital stock, the expression on the left-hand side of (2.20) must be unaltered by a capital-altering change, it must be unaltered by a capital-augmenting one when labor is adjusted to have the same marginal product. Obtaining $\partial L(v)/\partial b(v)$ (where $b(v)$ is the capital-augmenting parameter) from the condition that the marginal product of labor must be independent of $b(v)$, differentiate the left-hand side of (2.20) totally with respect to $b(v)$ and equate the result to zero, securing (after minor manipulations):

Corollary 2.2: In the general two-factor case, a necessary condition for the existence of an aggregate capital stock is that for every $v = 1, \ldots, n$, the vintage production function, $f^v(K(v), L(v))$ satisfy:

$$f^v_{KK}(f^v_{LL})^2 f^v_{KL} + 2f^v_K f^v_{KL} f^v_{LL} f^v_{KLL} - f^v_K (f^v_{LL})^2 f^v_{KKL} - f^v_K (f^v_{KL})^2 f^v_{LLL} - (f^v_{KL})^3 f^v_{LL} \equiv 0. \tag{2.49}$$

Despite its complicated appearance, this is not hard to check given a specific function $f^v(\cdot,\cdot)$. As stated, it has the advantage of eliminating the arbitrary function $g(\cdot)$, but the disadvantage that even if it is satisfied for every $v = 1, \ldots, n$, aggregate capital stock may not exist, since the implied function $g(\cdot)$ may vary over v. On the other hand, it is obvious that:

Corollary 2.3: In the general two-factor case, if all change is capital altering, then a necessary and sufficient condition for the existence of an aggregate capital stock is that (2.49) be satisfied for *some* $v = 1, \ldots, n$.

This completes our discussion of the two-factor case.

2.5 The multiple-factor case: Existence of individual capital aggregates

We now turn to the case in which there is more than one kind of capital and more than one kind of labor in each vintage production function. Actually, the correct distinction for our purposes is not necessarily that between capital and labor, although this is a convenient way to discuss it. The correct distinction is between factors which are not and factors which are allocated to different uses so as to maximize total output. If certain types of equipment are constantly reshuffled over plants so as to maximize output, then those types of equipment have all the characteristics of labor for our purposes. If certain types of workers are immobile, then they are a form of capital for our purposes. In general, however, one does expect our distinction to correspond to the usual one. We shall qualify this below when we observe that the results need altering if equipment is reshuffled over plants in long-run equilibrium. As a general rule, conditions which are sufficient for the construction of a capital aggregate remain so when a factor previously considered as fixed is considered allocable over uses. Necessary conditions may not survive such a transition, however.

We suppose then that there are m types of capital and s types of labor. Adopting the obvious notation, output from capitals of the vth vintage and the labors applied to them is given by the vintage production function:

$$Y(v) = f^{v}(K_1(v), \ldots, K_m(v), L_1(v), \ldots, L_s(v)). \tag{2.50}$$

As before, define:

$$Y = \sum_{v=1}^{n} Y(v). \tag{2.51}$$

We assume that the s types of labor are allocated over vintages so as to maximize output subject to the s labor constraints:

$$\sum_{v=1}^{n} L_i(v) = L_i \qquad (i = 1, \ldots, s). \tag{2.52}$$

We denote by Y^* the value of output when so maximized and seek the conditions under which it is possible to write:

$$Y^* = G(J, K_{p+1}(1), \ldots, K_{p+1}(n), \ldots, K_m(1), \ldots, K_m(n), L_1, \ldots, L_s) \quad (2.53)$$

where

$$J = J(K_1(1), \ldots, K_1(n), \ldots, K_p(1), \ldots, K_p(n)) \quad \text{for some } p,\ 1 \leq p \leq m. \quad (2.54)$$

In other words, an aggregate is to be formed from the first p types of capital. (Obviously, if we can solve this problem, the results will immediately imply the conditions for the existence of more than one capital aggregate.)

Most of our analysis in later sections will be concerned with the case in which $p = m$ so that only one aggregate containing *all* capital types is to be formed. For the present we concentrate on the problems raised when $p < m$, while providing results of general applicability.

The essence of the case of $p < m$ can be seen if we take $m = 2$ and assume that it is the first type of capital only which is to be aggregated. It will somewhat simplify the notation to do this. Further, the essence of the present problem will be preserved if we return temporarily to the case of one type of labor and drop the subscripts denoting labor type. (The results will be formally generalized below.) Proceeding as in Section 2.2, it is easy to show that the Leontief conditions in this case are:

$$\frac{\partial(f^h_{K_1}/f^r_{K_1})}{\partial L} = 0 = \frac{\partial(f^h_{K_1}/f^r_{K_1})}{\partial K_2(q)} \quad (2.55)$$

whenever labor is optimally allocated and for all $h, r, q = 1, \ldots, n$.

It is also easy to show by the implicit function theorem that:

$$\frac{\partial L(h)}{\partial K_2(q)} = \frac{f^q_{LK_2}}{f^h_{LL} f^q_{LL}\left(\sum_{v=1}^{n} \frac{1}{f^v_{LL}}\right)} \quad \text{for } h \neq q \quad (2.56)$$

$$\frac{\partial L(q)}{\partial K_2(q)} = -\frac{f^q_{LK_2}}{f^q_{LL}} + \frac{f^q_{LK_2}}{(f^q_{LL})^2\left(\sum_{v=1}^{n} \frac{1}{f^v_{LL}}\right)} \quad (q, h = 1, \ldots, n).$$

Now, since the first half of (2.55), the Leontief condition with respect to L, is a condition which holds $K_2(q)$ constant, it is evident that it is still equivalent to (2.19), *mutatis mutandis*, so that:

$$\frac{f^h_{K_1L}}{f^h_{K_1}f^h_{LL}} = \frac{f^r_{KL}}{f^r_K f^r_{LL}} \qquad h, r = 1, \ldots, n \tag{2.57}$$

whenever labor is optimally allocated.

Further, for $h \neq q \neq r$, the second half of (2.55) is equivalent (by (2.56)) to:

$$\frac{f^h_{K_1L}f^q_{K_2L}}{f^h_{K_1}f^h_{LL}f^q_{LL}\left(\sum_{v=1}^{n}\frac{1}{f^v_{LL}}\right)} = \frac{f^r_{K_1L}f^q_{K_2L}}{f^r_{K_1}f^r_{LL}f^q_{LL}\left(\sum_{v=1}^{n}\frac{1}{f^v_{LL}}\right)} \tag{2.58}$$

when labor is optimally allocated. This is guaranteed to hold if (2.57) does.

On the other hand, setting $r = q$, the second parts of (2.55) and (2.56) imply:

$$\frac{f^h_{K_1L}f^q_{K_2L}}{f^h_{K_1}f^h_{LL}f^q_{LL}\left(\sum_{v=1}^{n}\frac{1}{f^v_{LL}}\right)} = \frac{1}{f^q_{K_1}}\left(f^q_{K_1K_2} - \frac{f^q_{K_1L}f^q_{K_2L}}{f^q_{LL}}\right) + \frac{f^q_{K_1L}f^q_{K_2L}}{f^q_{K_1}(f^q_{LL})^2\left(\sum_{v=1}^{n}\frac{1}{f^v_{LL}}\right)} \tag{2.59}$$

whenever labor is optimally allocated. In view of (2.57), this implies:

$$f^q_{K_1K_2} - \frac{f^q_{K_1L}f^q_{K_2L}}{f^q_{LL}} = 0 \qquad q = 1, \ldots, n, \tag{2.60}$$

and we have:

Theorem 2.6: If $m = 2$, $p = 1$, $s = 1$, necessary and sufficient conditions for the existence of a separate aggregate of the first capital type are given by (2.57) and (2.60).

The new part of this result is (2.60). The other part, (2.57), we have already met and shall not now discuss save to observe that it must hold for *all* values of $K_2(v)$, $v = 1, \ldots, n$. Hence, even if the original vintage production functions were homogeneous of degree one in K_1, K_2, and L, the problems raised for the construction of a K_1-aggregate by (2.57) are the same as those discussed in the preceding section.

The interpretation of (2.60) is as follows. The first term of (2.56), $f^q_{LK_2}/f^q_{LL}$, can be considered as the amount of labor which must be withdrawn from general use and allocated to the qth vintage to cancel the effect on f^q_L caused by a unit increase in $K_2(q)$. So far as other vintages are concerned, (2.56) then gives the effect of changing the amount of labor by this much. (2.57) ensures that the resulting effect on $f^v_{K_1}$ is the same for all vintages. However, in vintage q, there are two additional special effects on the marginal product of K_1: a direct effect through the increase in $K_2(q)$ and an indirect effect through the allocation to vintage q of the labor withdrawn from general use. (2.60) states that these two special effects must just cancel out.

Note that (2.60) is a necessary condition for $f^v(\cdot,\cdot)$ to form part of *any* family which permits the construction of a K_1-aggregate.

It is clear that not every production function has this property. Indeed, define:

DEFINITION 2.4: Two factors of production will be called *strong complements* if an increase in one increases the marginal product of the other. They will be called *weak complements* if an increase of one does not decrease the marginal product of the other.

We have:

Corollary 2.4: If, with $m = 2$, $p = 1$, $s = 1$, there is some vintage production function for which at some factor combination all three factors are at least weak complements and either (a) K_1 and K_2 are strong complements or (b) K_1 and L as well as K_2 and L are strong complements, then that vintage production function cannot form part of any family for which a K_1-aggregate exists.

***Proof*:** For either (a) or (b), the left-hand side of (2.60) is positive.

Thus, for example, omitting the v argument, the generalized Cobb–Douglas:

$$AK_1^{\alpha}K_2^{\beta}L^{1-\alpha-\beta} \tag{2.61}$$

cannot form part of any family permitting aggregation over vintages of K_1 alone (although it can form part of a family permitting aggregation of K_1 and K_2 together, as we shall see below).

The question of what families of production functions satisfy (2.57) and (2.60) has not been answered in closed form, although Samuelson [10], following Gorman [5], has provided a way of generating such functions. Thus, it can be easily shown that:

$$f^v(K_1(v), K_2(v), L(v)) = a(v)K_2(v)\log\{H^v(K_1(v)) + b(v)L(v)\} + c(v)K_2(v)\log K_2(v) \qquad (v = 1, \ldots, n) \qquad (2.62)$$

satisfies (2.57) and (2.60). For appropriate choices of $a(v)$, $b(v)$, $c(v)$, and $H^v(\cdot)$, these can be made reasonable (and even constant returns) production functions at least over some range of values for the factors.

2.6 The multiple-factor case: General results

In this section, we generalize the preceding results to the case of m, p, and s all possibly greater than one. We obtain necessary and sufficient conditions in the form of partial differential equations for the construction of an aggregate of the first p capital stocks and use these to generalize Corollary 2.4. The results obtained in this section are then further used in the cases discussed in the remaining sections.

For convenience, we let $P \equiv \{1, \ldots, p\}$ and $\bar{P} \equiv \{p+1, \ldots, m\}$.

The first-order conditions for the optimal allocation of the s types of labor are obviously:

$$f^v_{L_i} = -\mu_i \qquad (v = 1, \ldots, n)(i = 1, \ldots, s) \qquad (2.63)$$

where the μ_i are Lagrange multipliers and

$$\sum_{v=1}^{n} L_i(v) = L_i \qquad (i = 1, \ldots, s). \qquad (2.64)$$

It will be convenient to work in matrix notation. Define:

$$\frac{\partial L(v)}{\partial L} = \left[\frac{\partial L_i(v)}{\partial L_j}\right] \qquad (i, j = 1, \ldots, s) \quad (v = 1, \ldots, n) \qquad (2.65)$$

$$\frac{\partial \mu}{\partial L} = \left[\frac{\partial \mu_i}{\partial L_j}\right] \qquad (i, j = 1, \ldots, s) \qquad (2.66)$$

$$B^v = [f^v_{L_i L_j}] \qquad (i, j = 1, \ldots, s) \quad (v = 1, \ldots, n). \qquad (2.67)$$

$$D = \left[\begin{array}{cccccc|c} B^1 & 0 & . & . & . & 0 & I \\ 0 & B^2 & 0 & . & . & 0 & I \\ . & . & . & . & . & . & . \\ . & . & . & . & . & . & . \\ . & . & . & . & . & . & . \\ 0 & . & . & . & 0 & B^n & I \\ \hline I & I & . & . & . & I & 0 \end{array}\right] \tag{2.68}$$

Differentiating (2.63) and (2.64) and writing the result in matrix form:

$$\begin{bmatrix} \partial L(1)/\partial L \\ \partial L(2)/\partial L \\ . \\ . \\ . \\ \partial L(n)/\partial L \\ \partial \mu/\partial L \end{bmatrix} = D^{-1} \begin{bmatrix} 0 \\ . \\ . \\ . \\ 0 \\ I \end{bmatrix}. \tag{2.69}$$

Inverting D by the usual rules for partitioned matrices, it is easy to show from this that:

$$\frac{\partial L(h)}{\partial L} = (B^h)^{-1} \left\{ \sum_{\nu=1}^{n} (B^\nu)^{-1} \right\}^{-1} \qquad (h = 1, \ldots, n), \tag{2.70}$$

the matrix generalization of (2.17).

Now define:

$$\frac{\partial f^\nu_{K_j}}{\partial L(\nu)} \equiv [f^\nu_{K_j L_1} \ldots f^\nu_{K_j L_s}] \quad (\nu = 1, \ldots, n) \quad (j = 1, \ldots, m). \tag{2.71}$$

$$\frac{\partial L(h)}{\partial K_j(q)} \equiv \begin{bmatrix} \dfrac{\partial L_1(h)}{\partial K_j(q)} \\ . \\ . \\ . \\ \dfrac{\partial L_s(h)}{\partial K_j(q)} \end{bmatrix} \quad (j \in \bar{P}) \; (h, q = 1, \ldots, n). \tag{2.72}$$

Similarly, differentiating (2.63) and (2.64) with respect to $K_j(q)$, it is easily seen (where primes denote transposition) that:

$$\frac{\partial L(h)}{\partial K_j(q)} = (B^h)^{-1}\left\{\sum_{\nu=1}^{n}(B^{\nu})^{-1}\right\}^{-1}(B^q)^{-1}\left(\frac{\partial f^q_{K_j}}{\partial L(q)}\right)' \text{ for } h \neq q$$

$$\frac{\partial L(q)}{\partial K_j(q)} = -(B^q)^{-1}\left(\frac{\partial f^q_{K_j}}{\partial L(q)}\right)' + (B^q)^{-1}\left\{\sum_{\nu=1}^{n}(B^{\nu})^{-1}\right\}^{-1}(B^q)^{-1}\left(\frac{\partial f^q_{K_j}}{\partial L(q)}\right)'$$

$$(j \in \bar{P})\ (h, q = 1, \ldots, n), \qquad (2.73)$$

the matrix generalization of (2.56).

Now, define:

$$\frac{\partial(f^h_{K_i}/f^r_{K_a})}{\partial L} \equiv \left[\frac{\partial(f^h_{K_i}/f^r_{K_a})}{\partial L_1} \cdots \frac{\partial(f^h_{K_i}/f^r_{K_a})}{\partial L_s}\right]$$

$$(i, a \in P)\ (h, r = 1, \ldots, n). \qquad (2.74)$$

As in Section 2.2, it is easy to show that the Leontief conditions for the construction of what we may term a P-aggregate are:

$$\frac{\partial(f^h_{K_i}/f^r_{K_a})}{\partial L} = 0 = \frac{\partial(f^h_{K_i}/f^r_{K_a})}{\partial K_j(q)}$$

$$(i, a \in P)\ (j \in \bar{P})\ (h, r, q = 1, \ldots, n), \qquad (2.75)$$

when all labors are optimally allocated. (The expression on the right is to be interpreted as a full derivative.)

Fortunately, some of these conditions are redundant given the others. The first set of redundant conditions are those for which $i \neq a$ and $h \neq r$. Since

$$f^h_{K_i}/f^r_{K_a} = (f^h_{K_i}/f^h_{K_a})(f^h_{K_a}/f^r_{K_a}), \qquad (2.76)$$

it is clear that the left-hand member has a zero derivative with respect to any magnitude such that both factors on the right have zero derivatives with respect to that magnitude. Hence we need not separately consider the case in which the Leontief conditions involve capitals of *both* different kinds and different vintages. (Further redundancies appear from the mathematics below.)

We begin therefore with the case of (2.75) in which $r = h$ but $i \neq a$. Here the Leontief conditions with respect to labor become:

$$0 = \frac{\partial(f^h_{K_i}/f^h_{K_a})}{\partial L} = \frac{\partial(f^h_{K_i}/f^h_{K_a})}{\partial L(h)} \frac{\partial L(h)}{\partial L} \qquad (i, a \in P)\ (h = 1, \ldots, n) \qquad (2.77)$$

where the first matrix on the right is defined in the obvious way. Since, by (2.70), $\partial L(h)/\partial L$ is a square nonsingular matrix, this holds if and only if:

$$\frac{\partial(f^h_{K_i}/f^h_{K_a})}{\partial L(h)} = 0 \qquad (i, a \in P)\ (h = 1, \ldots, n). \qquad (2.78)$$

Similarly, denoting by $|_{L(h)}$ the taking of a derivative with $L(h)$ held constant, the Leontief conditions with respect to capitals not in the aggregate are in this case:

$$0 = \frac{\partial(f^h_{K_i}/f^h_{K_a})}{\partial K_j(q)} = \frac{\partial(f^h_{K_i}/f^h_{K_a})}{\partial L(h)} \frac{\partial L(h)}{\partial K_j(q)} \qquad \text{for } h \neq q$$

$$0 = \frac{\partial(f^h_{K_i}/f^h_{K_a})}{\partial K_j(h)} = \left.\frac{\partial(f^h_{K_i}/f^h_{K_a})}{\partial K_j(h)}\right|_{L(h)} + \frac{\partial(f^h_{K_i}/f^h_{K_a})}{\partial L(h)} \frac{\partial L(h)}{\partial K_j(h)}$$

$$(i, a \in P)\ (j \in \bar{P})\ (h, q = 1, \ldots, n). \qquad (2.79)$$

However, using (2.78), the first part of this is redundant, while the second becomes:

$$\left.\frac{\partial(f^h_{K_i}/f^h_{K_a})}{\partial K_j(h)}\right|_{L(h)} = 0 \quad (i, a \in P)\,(j \in \bar{P})\,(h = 1, \ldots, n). \qquad (2.80)$$

Now, (2.78) and (2.80) together have a ready interpretation. They are the necessary and sufficient Leontief conditions that *considering only the* h*th vintage production function in isolation* an aggregate can be formed of the first p capitals. It is natural to encounter those conditions here, for if aggregation were not possible within vintages, we should not expect it to be possible both within and across vintages however labor is allocated.

If (2.78) and (2.80) hold, then it is possible to form what we may term "vintage aggregates." In this case, we might just as well form such aggregates and take $p = 1$ from then on. While we shall do this in the next section, we shall not do so now, in the interests of easy interpretability in the statement of the results on production functions whose factors are complements.

We now proceed to the case $i = a$ and $h \neq r$. Using (2.70), the Leontief conditions with respect to labor can easily be seen to be equivalent to:

$$(1/f^h_{K_i})\left(\frac{\partial f^h_{K_i}}{\partial L(h)}\right)(B^h)^{-1} = (1/f^r_{K_i})\left(\frac{\partial f^r_{K_i}}{\partial L(r)}\right)(B^r)^{-1}$$

$$(i \in P)\ (h, r = 1, \ldots, n) \qquad (2.81)$$

whenever all types of labor have been optimally allocated. This is clearly the generalization of Lemma 2.1 to the present case.

For $h \neq q \neq r$, using the first half of (2.73), the Leontief conditions with respect to capitals not in the aggregate are readily seen to be:

$$(1/f^h_{K_i})\left(\frac{\partial f^h_{K_i}}{\partial L(h)}\right)(B^h)^{-1}\left\{\sum_{\nu=1}^{n}(B^\nu)^{-1}\right\}^{-1}(B^q)^{-1}\left(\frac{\partial f^q_{K_j}}{\partial L(q)}\right)'$$

$$= (1/f^r_{K_i})\left(\frac{\partial f^r_{K_i}}{\partial L(r)}\right)(B^r)^{-1}\left\{\sum_{\nu=1}^{n}(B^\nu)^{-1}\right\}^{-1}(B^q)^{-1}\left(\frac{\partial f^q_{K_j}}{\partial L(q)}\right)'$$

$$(i \in P)\ (j \in \bar{P})\ (h, r = 1, \ldots, n;\ h \neq q \neq r) \qquad (2.82)$$

whenever all labors are optimally allocated. This is the generalization of (2.58), and, like that equation, is redundant in view of (2.81).

There remains only the case in which $r = q$. The second half of (2.73) and the latter part of (2.75) yield:

$$(1/f^h_{K_i})\left(\frac{\partial f^h_{K_i}}{\partial L(h)}\right)(B^h)^{-1}\left\{\sum_{\nu=1}^{n}(B^\nu)^{-1}\right\}^{-1}(B^q)^{-1}\left(\frac{\partial f^q_{K_j}}{\partial L(q)}\right)'$$

$$= (1/f^q_{K_i})\left\{f^q_{K_iK_j} - \left(\frac{\partial f^q_{K_i}}{\partial L(q)}\right)(B^q)^{-1}\left(\frac{\partial f^q_{K_j}}{\partial L(q)}\right)'\right\}$$

$$+ (1/f^q_{K_i})(B^q)^{-1}\left\{\sum_{\nu=1}^{n}(B^\nu)^{-1}\right\}^{-1}(B^q)^{-1}\left(\frac{\partial f^q_{K_j}}{\partial L(q)}\right)'$$

$$(i \in P)\ (j \in \bar{P})\ (h, q = 1, \ldots, n) \qquad (2.83)$$

whenever all labors are optimally allocated. In view of (2.81), this becomes:

$$f^q_{K_iK_j} - \left(\frac{\partial f^q_{K_i}}{\partial L(q)}\right)(B^q)^{-1}\left(\frac{\partial f^q_{K_j}}{\partial L(q)}\right)' = 0$$

$$(i \in P)\ (j \in \bar{P})\ (q = 1, \ldots, n), \qquad (2.84)$$

the generalization of (2.60).[20] The interpretation of this result is similar to that of (2.60).

We have now generalized Theorem 2.6 to:

Theorem 2.7: In the general multiple-factor case, necessary and sufficient conditions for the existence of a capital aggregate formed from the first p capitals only are given by (2.78), (2.80), (2.81), and (2.84).

Our result (Corollary 2.4) as to production functions in which all factors are complements can likewise be generalized. For the same reasons that we assume $f^v_{LL} < 0$, we assume B^v to be negative definite.[21] We prove:

Corollary 2.5: If, for some v, there is some factor combination at which:

(a) all pairs of labors are at least weak complements;

(b) for some $i \in P$, the ith capital is at least weakly complementary with every type of labor;

(c) for some $j \in \bar{P}$, the jth type of capital is at least weakly complementary with every type of labor; and

(d) for the same i and j, the ith and jth types of capital are strong complements;

then the vth vintage production function can form part of no family permitting the existence of a capital aggregate which includes the first p capital types only.

Proof: By (a), B^v has no negative off-diagonal elements. We can therefore write:

$$-B^v = \sigma I - A = \sigma\left(I - \frac{A}{\sigma}\right) \qquad (2.85)$$

where σ is a positive scalar and A is a nonnegative square matrix. Since B^v is negative definite, $-B^v$ is positive definite, whence its principal minors are all positive. It follows easily from the Hawkins–Simon condition [6] that $-(B^v)^{-1}$ is nonnegative. The remaining assumptions of the Corollary now guarantee that the left-hand side of (2.84) is positive.

This completes our discussion of the case in which aggregates are to be formed which do not include all capital types. The remainder of the chapter is concerned with the case in which only one capital aggregate is to be formed. As we have seen, a necessary condition for the existence of such a superaggregate is that, for each vintage, a vintage aggregate can be formed. Supposing that this can be done, we may as well treat the aggregate for each vintage as a single type of capital and discuss the one-capital, many-labor case, remembering to interpret the results appropriately.

There is, moreover, another reason for being interested in the one type of capital, many types of labor case. An example will make this clear. Suppose that there are two types of capital good: plant, and equipment, and that both of these are subject to embodied technical change. Every vintage production function includes just one vintage of plant and one of equipment, but all combinations are possible. It may not be unreasonable to suppose that in the long run every vintage of equipment is allocated to plants so as to maximize total output. The construction of an aggregate plant stock is then a one-capital, many-labor problem since we may treat each vintage of equipment as a type of "labor." Alternatively, we may stand the same problem on its head and think of each vintage of plant as allocated to different vintages of equipment so as to maximize output, thus allowing us to examine the question as to whether equipment can be separately aggregated as a one-capital, many-"labor" problem. We may in this way be able to avoid the force of the result obtained above that at most only aggregates of all capital exist if appropriate complementarity conditions hold for any vintage.[22]

We proceed to an examination of the one-capital, many-labor case.

2.7 The one-capital, many-labor case: Constant returns

In this section, we generalize the results found above for the two-factor, constant returns case. We assume that every vintage production function is homogeneous of degree one, whence every first partial of every such function is homogeneous of degree zero. By Euler's theorem:

$$K(v)\left(\frac{\partial f_K^v}{\partial L(v)}\right) + [L_1(v) \; . \; . \; . \; L_s(v)]\,B^v = 0 \qquad (v = 1, \ldots, s), \quad (2.86)$$

whence:

$$\left(\frac{\partial f_K^v}{\partial L(v)}\right)(B^v)^{-1} = -(1/K(v))[L_1(v) \ldots L_s(v)] \qquad (v = 1, \ldots, s). \qquad (2.87)$$

Substitute this result in (2.81). Applying Euler's theorem to the vintage production functions themselves, it is now easy to show that the following generalizations of Theorems 2.1 and 2.1′ hold.

Theorem 2.8: In the one-capital, many-labor, constant returns case, a necessary and sufficient condition for the existence of an aggregate capital stock is that when all types of labor have been optimally allocated (so that the marginal product of each type of labor is independent of vintage), then the *average* product of each type of labor shall be independent of vintage.

As before, this may be restated as:

Theorem 2.8′: In the one-capital, many-labor, constant returns case, a necessary and sufficient condition for the existence of an aggregate capital stock is that there exist functions, $g^1(\cdot, \ldots, \cdot), \ldots, g^s(\cdot, \ldots, \cdot)$, all independent of v, such that for all $v = 1, \ldots, n$:

$$\frac{f^v}{L_i(v)} \equiv g^i(f_{L_1}^v, \ldots, f_{L_s}^v) \qquad (i = 1, \ldots, s) \quad (2.88)$$

for all positive values of $K(v)$ and $L_1(v), \ldots, L_s(v)$.

Furthermore, we have:[23]

Theorem 2.9: In the one-capital, many-labor, constant returns case, a necessary and sufficient condition for the existence of an aggregate capital stock is that all technical change be capital augmenting.

***Proof*:** It will again be convenient to drop the vintage superscript and argument until further notice.

(a) Sufficiency: The proof is the obvious generalization of that of Theorem 2.2. One uses Euler's theorem to show that (where b is the capital-augmenting parameter):

$$\partial L_i/\partial b = L_i/b \qquad (i = 1, \ldots, s) \quad (2.89)$$

and then differentiates F/L_i for each i totally with respect to b substituting this result. The desired conclusion follows from another application of Euler's theorem.

(b) Necessity: The proof of necessity is not quite so straightforward a generalization of the corresponding argument in the proof of Theorem 2.2. Define:

$$\lambda_i \equiv \frac{L_i}{K} \qquad (i = 1, \ldots, s) \quad (2.90)$$

and

$$\Phi(\lambda_1, \ldots, \lambda_s) \equiv f(1, \lambda_1, \ldots, \lambda_s). \quad (2.91)$$

Then, using the homogeneity of $f(\cdot, \ldots, \cdot)$ and Theorem 2.8′, if J exists, then there exist functions $g^1(\cdot, \ldots, \cdot), \ldots, g^s(\cdot, \ldots, \cdot)$, independent of v, such that every vintage production function corresponds to a solution Φ of:

$$\frac{\Phi}{\lambda_i} = g^i(\Phi_1, \ldots, \Phi_s) \qquad (i = 1, \ldots, s) \quad (2.92)$$

where the subscripts denote differentiation with respect to the appropriate λ_i.

We first show that the system of partial differential equations (2.92) can be uniquely inverted to give the s marginal products of labor as single-valued functions of the s average products in the positive orthant. To show this, it will suffice to show that every set of average products corresponds to a unique set of factor ratios.[24] Denoting the Jacobian of the s average products $(\Phi/\lambda_1, \ldots, \Phi/\lambda_s)$ with respect to $\lambda_1, \ldots, \lambda_s$ by Q, we have:

$$Q = \begin{vmatrix} \dfrac{\lambda_1\Phi_1 - \Phi}{\lambda_1^2} & \dfrac{\Phi_2}{\lambda_1} & \cdots & \dfrac{\Phi_s}{\lambda_1} \\ \dfrac{\Phi_1}{\lambda_2} & \dfrac{\lambda_2\Phi_2 - \Phi}{\lambda_2^2} & \cdots & \dfrac{\Phi_s}{\lambda_2} \\ \vdots & \vdots & \cdots & \vdots \\ \dfrac{\Phi_1}{\lambda_s} & \dfrac{\Phi_2}{\lambda_s} & \cdots & \dfrac{\lambda_s\Phi_s - \Phi}{\lambda_s^2} \end{vmatrix} \quad (2.93)$$

$$= \left(\frac{1}{\prod_{i=1}^{s}\lambda_i}\right)\begin{vmatrix} \left(\Phi_1-\frac{\Phi}{\lambda_1}\right) & \Phi_2 & \cdots & \Phi_s \\ \Phi_1 & \left(\Phi_2-\frac{\Phi}{\lambda_2}\right) & \cdots & \Phi_s \\ \vdots & \vdots & & \vdots \\ \Phi_1 & \Phi_2 & \cdots & \left(\Phi_s-\frac{\Phi}{\lambda_s}\right) \end{vmatrix}.$$

Subtracting the second row from the first row, multiplying the resulting first column by λ_1/λ_2 and adding to the second column, we obtain:

$$Q = (-1)\left(\frac{1}{\prod_{i=1}^{s}\lambda_i}\right)\left(\frac{\Phi}{\lambda_1}\right)$$

$$\times\begin{vmatrix} \left\{\Phi_2+\Phi_1\left(\frac{\lambda_1}{\lambda_2}\right)-\frac{\Phi}{\lambda_2}\right\} & \Phi_3 & \cdots & \Phi_s \\ \left\{\Phi_2+\Phi_1\left(\frac{\lambda_1}{\lambda_2}\right)\right\} & \left(\Phi_3-\frac{\Phi}{\lambda_3}\right) & \cdots & \Phi_s \\ \vdots & \vdots & & \vdots \\ \left\{\Phi_2+\Phi_1\left(\frac{\lambda_1}{\lambda_2}\right)\right\} & \Phi_3 & \cdots & \left(\Phi_s-\frac{\Phi}{\lambda_s}\right) \end{vmatrix}. \tag{2.94}$$

Repeating the same procedure and continuing in this way, we finally secure:

$$Q = (-1)^{s-1}\left(\frac{1}{\prod_{i=1}^{s}\lambda_i}\right)(\Phi)^{s-1}\left(\frac{1}{\prod_{i=1}^{s-1}\lambda_i}\right)\times\left\{\sum_{i=1}^{s}\Phi_i\left(\frac{\lambda_i}{\lambda_s}\right)\left(-\frac{\Phi}{\lambda_s}\right)\right\}$$

$$= (-1)^{s}\left(\frac{1}{\prod_{i=1}^{s}\lambda_i}\right)^2(\Phi)^{s-1}\left(\Phi-\sum_{i=1}^{s}\lambda_i\Phi_i\right). \tag{2.95}$$

By Euler's theorem:

$$\Phi - \sum_{i=1}^{s} \lambda_i \Phi_i = f_K(1, \lambda_1, \ldots, \lambda_s) > 0 \tag{2.96}$$

so that Q has the sign of $(-1)^s$ at all positive values of the λ_i. Since every principal minor of Q is in the same general form, the principal minors alternate in sign, principal minors of odd order being negative and those of even order being positive. It follows that the Jacobian of *minus* the average products with respect to the λ_i has all principal minors strictly positive, and the desired result as to inversion of (2.92) now follows from a theorem of Gale and Nikaido.[25]

We now reintroduce the vintage superscript and argument.

Choose any set of positive values for $L_1(h), \ldots, L_s(h)$ for some $h = 1, \ldots, n$. Consider any positive value of $K(h)$. For some $r = 1, \ldots, n$ and $r \neq h$, choose K^* such that:

$$f^r(K^*, L_1(h), \ldots, L_s(h)) = f^h(K(h), L_1(h), \ldots, L_s(h)). \tag{2.97}$$

At such a point, the average product of each type of labor is the same for f^r as for f^h.[26] Therefore, if J exists, as just demonstrated, the marginal product of each type of labor is the same for r as for h. By Euler's theorem:

$$K^* f_K^r = f^r - \sum_{i=1}^{s} L_i(h) f_{L_i}^r = f^h - \sum_{i=1}^{s} L_i(h) f_{L_i}^h = K(h) f_K^h. \tag{2.98}$$

Thus:

$$K^* = K(h)\left(\frac{f_K^h}{f_K^r}\right). \tag{2.99}$$

Since the marginal product of each type of labor is the same in f^r as in f^h, however, the existence of J and the version of the Leontief conditions given in (2.75) implies that the ratio on the right-hand side of (2.99) is independent of $L_i(h), \ldots, L_s(h)$. Thus there clearly exists a monotonic function $\eta(\cdot)$, such that:

$$K^* = \eta(K(h)). \tag{2.100}$$

Substitute this result in (2.97). Note that $f^r(\cdot, \ldots, \cdot)$ is homogeneous of first degree in $\eta(K(h))$, $L_1(h), \ldots, L_s(h)$. On the other hand, $f^h(\cdot, \ldots, \cdot)$ is homogeneous of first degree in $K(h), L_1(h), \ldots, L_s(h)$. It follows immediately that $\eta(\cdot)$ is homogeneous of first degree in $K(h)$ and thus that:

$$\eta(K(h)) = bK(h) \qquad b > 0. \tag{2.101}$$

Thus, for any positive $L_1(h), \ldots, L_s(h)$:

$$f^h(K(h), L_1(h), \ldots, L_s(h)) \\ = f^r(bK(h), L_1(h), \ldots, L_s(h)), \tag{2.102}$$

so that $f^h(\cdot)$ and $f^r(\cdot)$ differ only by a capital-augmenting technical change, and the theorem is proved.

The interpretation of this result is the same as in the two-factor case if there really is only one type of capital good. We saw in an earlier section, however, that it is possible for this case to arise when that "capital good" is already an aggregate of several different types appearing in the same vintage production function. In this case, Theorem 2.9 can be read as:

Theorem 2.10: An overall aggregate capital stock exists under constant returns if and only if an aggregate exists for each vintage and the only change in the production function over vintages is change in the way in which the "vintage aggregates" are made up from their components.

Think of a two-sector world in which at each vintage the production of final output can be broken down into the production of a vintage aggregate capital from the original capital goods only and then the production of final output from vintage aggregate capital and one or more types of labor. In such a world, the sort of technical change the exclusive presence of which is necessary and sufficient for the construction of an aggregate over both types and vintages of capital goods is change in the vintage aggregate capital-producing sector.

2.8 The general one-capital, many-labor case and concluding remarks

The rest of the story is quickly told. When we drop the assumption of constant returns, the results of Section 2.4 carry over with little change in proofs to the one-capital, many-labor case. Thus, in the presence of capital-generalized constant returns, exclusive capital-altering technical change is both necessary and sufficient for the construction of an aggregate capital stock, as is average product of each type of labor constant over vintages; not every vintage production function can form part of a set which allows the construction of such an aggregate; if an aggregate can be constructed, then it can be constructed with capital-altering change superimposed on existing technical change; and so forth.

To summarize the principal results in a general way, we have shown that in the presence of constant returns, a rather interesting but still special class of cases – capital-augmenting technical change – is necessary and sufficient for the construction of a capital aggregate. (The interpretation of this class is wider than it appears in the case in which each vintage production function allows a vintage aggregate to be formed from the different types of capital goods appearing therein.) Aside from the implications for those who explicitly study the embodied technical change model, this result implies that quality corrections to capital stock figures are misleading if technical change is other than capital augmenting.

When the assumption of constant returns is dropped, the situation changes somewhat. If a capital aggregate can be formed at all, then it can be formed under a set of technical changes which is considerably wider than the set of capital-augmenting changes. On the other hand, there are some vintage production functions which if they *ever* hold forbid the construction of a capital aggregate – something which is not true in the constant returns case.

Finally, it is impossible to construct a partial capital aggregate in the many capital goods case if, for some v, all factors are at least weak complements and certain pairs are strong complements. This is the case, unless one can think of different capital goods as allocated to maximize output. In long run equilibrium such allocation may not be a bad assumption, but in the short run (which may not be so short) only a conglomerate capital aggregate can be constructed, if any can, when such complementarity is present for any vintage.

General conditions for the existence of partial or conglomerate aggregates are given in Section 2.6.

One final word may be in order. We have not discussed the question of aggregating different types of *labor*. The reason is that there is a fundamental asymmetry to the problem and our results were all obtained by heavy use of the assumption that labor is continually reassigned to different types of capital. Such reassignment may have implications for the aggregation of different types of labor so allocated, but these seem qualitatively different from the results here obtained, and I have not so far been able to derive any particularly interesting theorems about this case.[27]

Notes

1. Some of the other papers in the discussion are Robinson [9] and Champernowne [2].
2. Leontief [8, p. 364, Proposition I]. The proof is given in Leontief [7] and on pp. xv–xvi, above.

3. Those discussed in Solow [11].
4. The interpretation of our results in terms of technical change is restricted to *capital-embodied* technical change. *Disembodied* technical change which affects equally all capital and labor in existence and *labor-embodied* technical change which affects the entire labor force obviously have nothing to do with the question of the existence of a capital aggregate at a moment in time. Thus, statements such as "all technical change must be capital augmenting" should be understood to restrict the nature only of *capital-embodied* technical change.
5. As did Solow in [11]. We require the existence of third derivatives for one of the results given below. Since this paper was written, many of its results have been extended by Stigum [15] to the case of nondifferentiable production functions.
6. [7] and [8]. See also Solow [11].
7. Note that if J exists and $f^v_{KL} \equiv 0$ for *some* v, then $f^v_{KL} \equiv 0$ for *all* v. Aggregate capital therefore does not exist if only some of the vintage production functions are separable.
8. A constructive proof of sufficiency was given by Solow [14, pp. 104–5]. P. A. Diamond has independently proved necessity for the case of continuous time in another way from that used here. See [3]. Still another proof can be read out of the discussion in Arrow *et al.* [1, pp. 231–2], given our result in Theorem 2.1. Their argument also proves Theorem 2.4 as a corollary of Theorem 2.3. Finally, by reversing the names of the factors, the desired result can be obtained from Theorem 2.1′ by direct application of Uzawa's proof [16, pp. 119–20] that technical change is Harrod-neutral if and only if it is labor augmenting. Equally, the proof of Theorem 2.2 given in the text can be read as providing an alternative proof of the Harrod-neutrality labor-augmentation equivalence and, still with factors interchanged, Theorem 2.9 can be considered as generalizing that equivalence to the case of many kinds of capital and one kind of labor.
9. Here, and at the parallel point in Section 2.7, one need only assume strictly positive marginal productivity of capital in the interior of the factor space.
10. Because a shift in the exponents would not shift the production-possibility frontier outward at all points but would shift it inward at some, the production function after the frontier would not be a Cobb–Douglas. Unless old technology becomes unavailable, it is thus unreasonable to consider a shift in the exponents of a Cobb–Douglas as a technological change. I am indebted to P. A. Samuelson for pointing this out to me.
11. Probably the simplest way of showing this is to show (as in the sufficiency proof of Theorem 2.2) that after accounting for $\partial L(v)/\partial A$, the crucial fraction on the left side of (2.20) has a nonzero derivative with respect to A.
12. In this and the following definition, and their uses, monotonicity is not restrictive, since production functions may be assumed monotonic in capital.

    Apparently, a referee of the original version of Chapter 3 suggested that the definition is technically defective since such functions can always be found unless either the $H^v(\cdot)$ must have as a range the entire nonnegative half-line or the function $F(\cdot,\cdot)$ is assumed itself to be one of the $f^v(\cdot,\cdot)$. I can no longer remember (or reconstruct) the reasoning that led to this, but it really does not matter. Not only could one place such an assumption on the range of the $H^v(\cdot)$, but (more interestingly) Theorem 2.5 states that capital-altering changes do not affect the existence of a capital aggregate. Hence, in all the arguments, one could always add a phantom firm whose production function was $F(\cdot,\cdot)$ and leave all problems unchanged.

13. Using the construction given in the proof of Lemma 2.2.
14. $AK^{\alpha}L^{\beta} = A(K^{\alpha/(1-\beta)})^{1-\beta}L^{\beta}$.
15. The original version of this chapter had some special cases of (2.46). Robert Feenstra pointed the generalization out to me.
16. Such a condition does arise even in the constant returns case when there is more than one type of capital and more than one aggregate to be constructed. See Sections 2.5 and 2.6.
17. In 1991, Lawrence Lau proved a proposition related to this conjecture using a restricted profit function approach. In a recent unpublished paper ("The existence of aggregate capital when returns to scale are non-constant", 1991), he showed that, under the assumption that aggregate output is zero when capital of every vintage is zero (or, equivalently, when (2.47) reads $f^v(0, L(v)) = 0$) the capital-altering case is the only case permitting the existence of a capital aggregate for nonconstant returns production functions.
18. Since this was written, Gorman [5] has provided an alternative method of generating all families of functions permitting a capital aggregate. Unfortunately, it does not seem easy to use his results to close the present question.

    Samuelson [10] has proved that if the form of the capital aggregate is required to be independent of the number of vintages (n) in a reasonable sense, then the aggregate exists if and only if all vintage production functions are CGCR and all technical change capital altering.
19. Of course, the nature of the aggregate will generally depend on what subset is involved.
20. We have omitted the qualifying phrase: "whenever all labors are optimally allocated." If the qth vintage production function has factor positions which are not observed because of lack of appropriate concavities, then (2.84) does not apply to such positions.
21. Positions in which B^v is not negative definite are not eligible as competitive equilibria, for example. They exhibit increasing returns to some linear combination of labor inputs.
22. In his paper "Embodiment and all that: A note" (unpublished), Marc Nerlove uses this device to perform both capital *and* labor aggregation in a situation in which all capital-embodied change is capital augmenting but labor-augmenting change is "embodied" in different labor cohorts which do not work simultaneously on the same capital equipment.
23. The extension of the definition of capital-augmenting technical change to the present case is obvious and we do not bother to state it formally. A similar statement holds for the definitions of capital-altering technical change and capital-generalized constant returns.
24. Not until this paper was originally in press did it occur to me that the unique determination of factor ratios by the s average products can be given a rather less heavy-handed demonstration than that which follows in the text. Obviously, by division, f/L_1 and f/L_i uniquely determine $L_i/L_1 = \lambda_i/\lambda_1$ ($i = 2, \ldots, s$). This fact, together with the homogeneity of

$f(\cdot, \ldots, \cdot)$ and the positive marginal productivity of capital, then implies that $K/L_1 = 1/\lambda_1$ is also uniquely determined by the average products.

25. Gale and Nikaido [4]. It should be noted that a local uniqueness theorem would not suffice for our purpose.

The remainder of the proof of necessity could now proceed as in Theorem 2.2 if it were known that the s-variable functions satisfying a system of first-order partial differential equations such as (2.92) always forms a one-parameter family. While I strongly believe this to be the case, I have been unable to discover such a theorem in the literature and have thus had to use a different method of proof here.

26. The question of whether such a K^* exists is not of much moment. As the proof makes clear, all that is required is the existence of some set of $L_1(h), \ldots, L_s(h)$ and some K^* and $K(h)$ for which (2.97) holds. This is guaranteed unless for *every* positive $L_1(h), \ldots, L_s(h)$, and *every* positive value of $K(h)$ output from the rth vintage production function is strictly below (above) output from the hth vintage production function no matter how much (or how little) capital of the rth vintage is used.

27. Nerlove (see Note 22) applies the results of the present paper to labor aggregation but not where different qualities of labor enter the same vintage production function simultaneously.

References

[1] Arrow, K. J., H. B. Chenery, B. S. Minhas and R. M. Solow, "Capital–labor substitution and economic efficiency," *Review of Economics and Statistics*, **43** (1961), 225–50.

[2] Champernowne, D. G., "The production function and the theory of capital: Comment," *Review of Economic Studies*, **21** (1953–54), 112–35.

[3] Diamond, P. A., "Technical change and the measurement of capital and output," *Review of Economic Studies*, **32** (1965), 289–98.

[4] Gale, D. and H. Nikaido, "The Jacobian matrix and global univalence of mappings," *Mathematische Annalen*, **159** (1965), 81–93.

[5] Gorman, W. M., "Capital aggregation in vintage models," in J. N. Wolfe (ed.), *Value, Capital, and Growth: Papers in Honour of Sir John Hicks*, Edinburgh, University of Edinburgh Press, 1968.

[6] Hawkins, D. and H. A. Simon, "Note: Some conditions of macroeconomic stability," *Econometrica*, **17** (1949), 245–8.

[7] Leontief, W. W., "A note on the interrelation of subsets of independent variables of a continuous function with continuous first derivatives," *Bulletin of the American Mathematical Society*, **53** (1947), 343–50.

[8] Leontief, W. W., "Introduction to a theory of the internal structure of functional relationships," *Econometrica*, **15** (1947), 361–73.

[9] Robinson, J., "The production function and the theory of capital," *Review of Economic Studies*, **21** (1953–54), 81–106.

[10] Samuelson, P. A., "Simple intuitive proofs of neoclassical functions admitting of capital aggregation," unpublished.

[11] Solow, R. M., "The production function and the theory of capital," *Review of Economic Studies*, **23** (1955–56), 101–8.

[12] Solow, R. M., "Investment and technical progress," in K. J. Arrow, S.

Karlin, and P. Suppes (eds), *Mathematical Methods in the Social Sciences, 1959*, Stanford: Stanford University Press, 1960, Chapter 7.
[13] Solow, R. M., *Capital Theory and the Rate of Return* (Professor F. de Vries Lectures), Amsterdam: North-Holland, 1963.
[14] Solow, R. M., "Capital, labor, and income in manufacturing," in National Bureau of Economic Research Conference in Income and Wealth, *The Behavior of Income Shares* (Studies in Income and Wealth, 26), Princeton: Princeton University Press, 1964, pp. 101–28.
[15] Stigum, B. P., "On certain problems of aggregation," *International Economic Review*, **8** (1967), 349–67.
[16] Uzawa, H., "Natural inventions and the stability of growth equilibrium," *Review of Economic Studies*, **28** (1960–61), 117–24.

3

Embodied technology and the existence of labor and output aggregates (1968)

3.1 Introduction

This paper is concerned with certain aspects of the problem of the existence of an aggregate production function when outputs are separately produced by individual firms by means of possibly different technologies. Each firm is supposed to use different fixed factors (capitals) and certain variable factors (labors), with the latter allocated to firms to obtain efficient production. In my earlier paper [2] (Chapter 2 of this book), I considered the conditions under which the aggregate technology thus generated could be described by a production function involving an aggregate capital stock;[1] this chapter considers the parallel problems of aggregation over labor types and over different outputs.[2]

Whereas in [2], production units were referred to as "vintages," and the language of embodied technical change models used for convenience, and while the results are directly applicable to such models, the importance of the problem dictates the use of a wider terminology and the explicit consideration of aggregation over firms.

---

* This paper was in part supported by a Ford Foundation grant to MIT and Yale for the construction of a model of long run economic growth in the United States. It was revised and completed during my tenure of a Ford Foundation Faculty Research Fellowship, while visiting the London School of Economics. I am indebted to W. M. Gorman, K. Shell, E. Sheshinski, and R. M. Solow for helpful discussions, but retain responsibility for error.

3.2 The model and assumptions

We shall begin by assuming that there is only one homogeneous output produced (i.e., that output aggregation is possible) and shall concentrate on the existence of a labor aggregate. It is merely a matter of notation to shift to the case of only one homogeneous labor with alternative outputs to be aggregated by reinterpreting production functions as labor-requirements functions. Both interpretations of the results will be given, but the analysis will generally run in terms of the labor aggregation model. The general case in which either labor or output aggregation is to be performed without assuming the other is considered in a later section.

Thus, we assume that there are m fixed factors called "capitals" and s variable factors called "labors". There are n firms and the amount of the ith type of capital employed by the νth firm is denoted by $K_i(\nu)$ which we shall assume always strictly positive. The total amount of the jth type of labor is denoted by L_j, and the amount of that labor employed by the νth firm by $L_j(\nu)$. The output of the νth firm is denoted by $Y(\nu)$ and is given by the firm production function:

$$Y(\nu) = f^{\nu}(K_1(\nu), \ldots, K_m(\nu), L_1(\nu), \ldots, L_s(\nu)) \qquad (\nu = 1, \ldots, n). \quad (3.1)$$

Each firm's production function is assumed to be continuously twice differentiable[3] with nonnegative marginal products and to have negative definite Hessians in the labor arguments, so that there is diminishing marginal productivity of any linear combination of labors.[4] In general, it is only a complication in the present chapter to have more than one type of capital employed by a given firm, so, for ease of exposition, we shall for the most part take $m = 1$ and drop the subscripts in $K_i(\nu)$. (We shall, however, indicate the suitable generalization of the various results in the appropriate places.) The differences among the capital types employed by different firms are reflected in the differences among the $f^{\nu}(\cdot)$.

Total output, Y, is defined as:

$$Y \equiv \sum_{\nu=1}^{n} Y(\nu) = \sum_{\nu=1}^{n} f^{\nu}(K(\nu), L_1(\nu), \ldots, L_s(\nu)). \quad (3.2)$$

Since we are interested in representing efficient production for the economy by an aggregate production function, the allocation of labor is determined by choosing the $L_j(\nu)$ to maximize Y subject to the constraints:

$$\sum_{\nu=1}^{n} L_j(\nu) \leqq L_j > 0 \qquad (j = 1, \ldots, s). \quad (3.3)$$

We shall assume that every type of labor always has a positive marginal product in at least one use, so that (3.3) holds as an equality.

The value of Y when so maximized is denoted by Y^*. Obviously, Y^* can be written as:

$$Y^* = G(K(1), \ldots, K(n), L_1, \ldots, L_s). \tag{3.4}$$

The problem considered in [2] was the conditions under which there exists a capital aggregate, J, such that:

$$J = J(K(1), \ldots, K(n)) \tag{3.5}$$

and (3.4) can be rewritten as:

$$Y^* = F(J, L_1, \ldots, L_s). \tag{3.6}$$

The first problem to be considered in the present paper is the conditions under which there exists a labor aggregate, P, such that:

$$P = P(L_1, \ldots, L_s) \tag{3.7}$$

and (3.4) can be rewritten as:

$$Y^* = H(K(1), \ldots, K(n), P) \tag{3.8}$$

(subaggregates will also be treated). Obviously, we are also interested in the conditions under which both aggregates exist simultaneously, so that (3.4) can be rewritten as:

$$Y^* = E(J, P). \tag{3.9}$$

We shall refer to the space of $K(\nu)$ and $L_1(\nu), \ldots, L_s(\nu)$ as the νth factor space and to the space of $K(1), \ldots, K(n)$ and $L_1, \ldots, L_s$ as the overall factor space.

Throughout, differentiation will be denoted by subscripts in the obvious way, so that, for example, $f^{\nu}_{L_i} \equiv \partial f^{\nu}/\partial L_i(\nu)$, and $f^{\nu}_{KL_i} \equiv \partial^2 f^{\nu}/\partial K(\nu)\,\partial L_i(\nu)$.

For convenience, we shall begin by assuming that every firm always employs some of every kind of labor in positive amount. This restriction will be removed in Section 3.8. Making that assumption, efficiency obviously requires that the marginal product of a labor type be the same in every use, so that:

$$f^{\nu}_{L_j} = \mu_j \qquad (\nu = 1, \ldots, n;\ j = 1, \ldots, s), \tag{3.10}$$

where μ_j is a Lagrange multiplier and is independent of ν.

Now, before proceeding we must agree on one more point. The problem here analyzed is nontrivial for the following reason. Even if for each firm taken in isolation a labor aggregate can be formed, it may yet not be possible (and, in general, it will not be) to form a labor aggregate for the entire system. This is because the effect of a marginal increase in some $K(v)$ on the marginal rate of substitution between any given L_j and L_k involves not just the direct effect in the vth firm but also the effects which occur through the reallocation of all the labors. It is this that makes for an interesting problem.

Similarly, it is *possible*[5] that while an aggregate cannot be formed for some firm or subset of firms taken alone, it can be formed for the system as a whole because the effects through labor allocation just cancel out the direct effects. This is basically only a *curiosum*, if it exists, for the possibility of aggregation then depends crucially on the number as well as the nature of the individual production functions. It is an odd sort of aggregation which ceases to be possible if some firm is swallowed up by an earthquake. We shall therefore rule out this possibility and shall agree on:

DEFINITION 3.1: For any aggregation problem considered, aggregation will be said to be possible if and only if the appropriate aggregate exists both for all firms considered together *and* for any subset of firms considered in isolation.[6]

It is immediately obvious that the following is then a necessary condition for aggregation in this sense.

Assumption 3.1: A labor aggregate can be formed when each firm is considered in isolation.

As just remarked, this is not a sufficient condition for aggregation when more than one firm is present. We concentrate on the inter-firm aspect of the problem.

Now, by a well-known theorem of Leontief,[7] the necessary and sufficient conditions for labor aggregation are that the marginal rate of substitution between any pair of labors be independent of the amount of any capital. Since for a single firm this means that an increase in $K(v)$ must change all marginal products of labor in the same proportion, we may state Assumption 3.1 more formally as:

Assumption 3.1′: For every $v = 1, \ldots, n$, there exists a (not generally constant) scalar, d_v, such that:

$$f^v_{KL_i} = d_v f^v_{L_i} \qquad (i = 1, \ldots, s) \qquad (3.11)$$

everywhere in the vth factor space.

Remark 3.1: In fact, Assumption 3.1 (or 3.1′) is stronger than required for some of our results. As remarked in later sections, for those cases (including constant returns) in which we have been able to give a closed-form characterization of the necessary and sufficient conditions for labor aggregation in the presence of Assumption 3.1, technological differences turn out to be such as to make Assumption 3.1 hold for every firm's production function if it holds for any one of them. This does not make Assumption 3.1 redundant, but it does remove the need to assume it explicitly for *every* firm's production function in such cases.

3.3 Preliminary results

We are now ready to take into account the effects of capital on marginal rates of substitution when all firms are considered together. Since the marginal product of the *j*th labor is μ_j, the Leontief conditions for aggregation in the system as a whole are that changing the amount of any firm's capital alters all the μ_j in the same proportion. Thus, define μ as the column vector of the μ_j and $\partial\mu/\partial K(h)$ as the column vector whose typical element is $\partial\mu_j/\partial K(h)$ $(h = 1, \ldots, n)$. The Leontief conditions are that there exist scalars, say $c_1, \ldots, c_n$, not generally constant, such that:

$$\partial\mu/\partial K(h) = c_h\mu \qquad (h = 1, \ldots, n). \qquad (3.12)$$

We must therefore evaluate $\partial\mu/\partial K(h)$.

Define:

$$f^h_{KL} \equiv \begin{bmatrix} f^h_{KL_1} \\ \cdot \\ \cdot \\ \cdot \\ f^h_{KL_s} \end{bmatrix} \quad (h = 1, \ldots, n);\ B^v \equiv [f^v_{L_iL_j}] \quad (i, j = 1, \ldots, s) \quad (v = 1, \ldots, n) \qquad (3.13)$$

Observe that B^v is negative definite, by assumption.

Finally, define:

$$R \equiv \sum_{v=1}^{n} (B^v)^{-1}. \qquad (3.14)$$

Differentiating the first-order conditions for optimal labor allocation, (3.10) and (3.3), totally with respect to $K(h)$, and solving for $\partial\mu/\partial K(h)$, we obtain:

$$\partial\mu/\partial K(h) = R^{-1}(B^h)^{-1}f^h_{KL} \qquad (h = 1, \ldots, n). \qquad (3.15)$$

Combining this with (3.10), (3.11), and (3.12), the Leontief conditions are then that there exist scalars, $c_1, \ldots, c_n$, such that whenever all labors are optimally allocated:

$$d_h R^{-1}(B^h)^{-1}\mu = c_h \mu \qquad (h = 1, \ldots, n). \qquad (3.16)$$

Obviously, one way in which (3.16) can be satisfied is to have all d_h and therefore f^h_{KL} identically zero ($h = 1, \ldots, n$). In this case, every firm's production function is already additively separable in a function of capital and a function of the labors, and capital has no effect on the marginal product of any labor or on the way in which labors are assigned. In such a case, labor aggregation is trivial.

Moreover, if $f^h(\cdot, \ldots, \cdot)$ is constant returns, Euler's theorem shows that f^h_{KL} zero even at a point contradicts the negative definiteness of B^h.

These considerations prompt us to assume:

Assumption 3.2: There exists no open neighborhood in the overall factor space in which when all labors are optimally allocated all d_h are simultaneously identically zero ($h = 1, \ldots, n$).

This is obviously rather weak. It is required for the necessity result in the lemma to follow, but not for the proof of sufficiency.

We can now prove:

Lemma 3.1: A necessary and sufficient condition for labor aggregation is that for every v and $h = 1, \ldots, n$, there exist a nonzero scalar, t_{vh} (not generally constant) such that whenever all labors are optimally allocated,

$$(B^v)^{-1}\mu = t_{vh}(B^h)^{-1}\mu. \qquad (3.17)$$

Proof:

(a) Sufficiency: Suppose (3.17) holds. Premultiply by R^{-1} and sum over v, obtaining:

$$\mu = R^{-1}\left\{\sum_{v=1}^{n}(B^v)^{-1}\right\}\mu = t_h R^{-1}(B^h)^{-1}\mu \qquad (3.18)$$

where

$$t_h = \sum_{v=1}^{n} t_{vh}.$$

Since $\mu \neq 0$, $t_h \neq 0$, so (3.16) is satisfied with $c_h = (d_h/t_h)$. The same proof obviously holds no matter what subset of firms we consider in isolation.

(b) Necessity: We shall prove necessity for points in the overall factor space at which at least one $d_\nu \neq 0$ ($\nu = 1, \ldots, n$). The desired result for all other points then follows by continuity in view of Assumption 3.2.

Thus, assume that $d_h \neq 0$ for a particular h. It obviously suffices to show that (3.17) holds for that choice of h and for all $\nu = 1, \ldots, n$. Define

$$R(\nu) \equiv \sum_{\substack{r=1 \\ r \neq \nu}}^{n} (B^r)^{-1} = R - (B^\nu)^{-1}. \tag{3.19}$$

By (3.16),

$$(B^h)^{-1}\mu = (c_h/d_h)R\mu = (c_h/d_h)\{R(\nu) + (B^\nu)^{-1}\}\mu, \tag{3.20}$$

and $c_h \neq 0$. In view of Definition 3.1, however, aggregation must be possible considering the set of all firms except the νth. This clearly implies the existence of a scalar, $c_{\nu h}$, such that:

$$(B^h)^{-1}\mu = (c_{\nu h}/d_h)R(\nu)\mu, \tag{3.21}$$

and $c_{\nu h} \neq 0$. Thus:

$$(B^\nu)^{-1}\mu = (d_h/c_h)(B^h)^{-1}\mu - R(\nu)\mu = \left(\frac{d_h}{c_h} - \frac{d_h}{c_{\nu h}}\right)(B^h)^{-1}\mu. \tag{3.22}$$

That

$$t_{\nu h} \equiv \left(\frac{d_h}{c_h} - \frac{d_h}{c_{\nu h}}\right) \neq 0$$

follows by the negative definiteness of B^ν. QED.[8]

Remark 3.2: If *all* $d_\nu \neq 0$, $\nu = 1, \ldots, n$ (as is implied in the constant returns case by the negative definiteness of the B^ν), then (3.17) follows immediately from (3.16) without appeal to the strong definition of aggregation given in Definition 3.1. Thus, in the case of no separability in any firm's production function, the existence of an aggregate for the whole set of firms together with its existence for each individual firm implies its existence for any subset.

3.4 Simultaneous existence of capital and labor aggregates

Lemma 3.1 allows us to prove easily that, under our assumptions, if a capital aggregate exists, then a labor aggregate does also. Indeed, returning for a moment to the case where there is more than one capital type employed by each firm, we can prove that the existence of *any* capital aggregate for all firms taken together implies the existence of a labor aggregate, whether or not that capital aggregate includes all capital types.

This is not too surprising. We have assumed labor aggregation to be possible for each firm separately. If capital aggregation is possible, the macroproduction function (3.6) generally turns out to have the same form as the production functions of the individual firms, so that labor aggregation will be possible after capital aggregation if it is possible in each firm separately.

Further, it is natural to have labor aggregation across firms easier than capital aggregation. For an individual labor type, such aggregation is already performed, so to speak, without any difficulty since labor is homogeneous across firms. For a single capital type, this is not the case. It is thus natural to find that when aggregation within a single firm is assumed to be no problem, labor aggregation across firms can be performed under more general circumstances than capital aggregation. It is nevertheless useful to have a proof of this and to know that, in the presence of Assumption 3.1, labor aggregation is weaker than capital aggregation. (Assumption 3.2 is not involved in the proof.)

Theorem 3.1: If any capital aggregate exists over all firms, then a labor aggregate exists also.

Proof: It is shown in Theorem 2.7, p. 56, that a necessary condition for the existence of any such capital aggregate is (in the present notation):

$$(1/f_K^h)(B^h)^{-1} f_{KL}^h = (1/f_K^v)(B^v)^{-1} f_{KL}^v \tag{3.23}$$

for all $v, h = 1, \ldots, n$, whenever all labors are optimally allocated. (If there is more than one capital type, K in (3.23) can be taken to be any particular capital type included in the aggregate.) By (3.11), this implies:

$$(d_h/f_K^h)(B^h)^{-1}\mu = (d_v/f_K^v)(B^v)^{-1}\mu \tag{3.24}$$

under the same conditions. If any $d_v = 0$, then clearly, at such a point, all $d_{v'} = 0$ and (3.16) is trivially satisfied. At any other point, however, (3.17) is satisfied with:

$$t_{v'h} = (d_h/f_K^h)(f_K^{v'}/d_{v'}). \qquad (3.25)$$

Of course a similar result holds for output aggregates when there is only one type of labor.

While the existence of a capital aggregate is sufficient for the existence of a labor (or output) aggregate, however, it is not necessary. We therefore turn to an examination of other conditions for labor aggregation.

3.5 The constant returns case: Complete results

In this section, we assume that every firm's production function exhibits constant returns.

Define $L(v)$ as the column vector of the $L_i(v)$ $(i = 1, \ldots, s)$ $(v = 1, \ldots, n)$.

Since the first partials of $f^{v}(\cdot, \ldots, \cdot)$ are all homogeneous of degree zero, Euler's theorem states:

$$B^{v}L(v) + f_{KL}^{v}K(v) = 0 \qquad (v = 1, \ldots, n). \quad (3.26)$$

As already remarked, this, together with the negative definiteness of B^{v}, implies that f_{KL}^{v}, and therefore d_{v}, is not zero. Thus:

$$(B^{v})^{-1}\mu = \left(\frac{-1}{d_{v}K(v)}\right)L(v) \qquad (v = 1, \ldots, n). \quad (3.27)$$

Lemma 3.1 now obviously implies:

Lemma 3.2: In the constant returns case, a necessary and sufficient condition for labor aggregation is that for all $v, h = 1, \ldots, n$:

$$\frac{L_i(v)}{L_1(v)} = \frac{L_i(h)}{L_1(h)} \qquad (i = 2, \ldots, s) \quad (3.28)$$

whenever labor is optimally allocated.

It is convenient to restate this in an equivalent form as:

Lemma 3.2′: In the constant returns case, a necessary and sufficient condition for labor aggregation is that for every $i = 2, \ldots, s$, there exists a function $g^i(\cdot, \ldots, \cdot)$, the same for all firms, such that for every $v = 1, \ldots, n$:

$$\frac{L_i(v)}{L_1(v)} = g^i(f_{L_1}^v, \ldots, f_{L_s}^v). \tag{3.29}$$

In the remainder of this section, we shall explore the class of solutions to sets of partial differential equations in the form (3.29) which satisfy our assumptions and shall drop the firm argument on the $L_j(v)$ and $K_i(v)$ for ease of presentation until explictly reinstated. We write K as the vector of the K_i $(i = 1, \ldots, m)$ and L as the vector of the L_j $(j = 1, \ldots, s)$.

We begin by showing that any constant returns production function satisfying our assumptions automatically satisfies a set of partial differential equations in the form of (3.29).

Note that, by Assumption 3.1, every firm's production function can be written in the form:

$$f^v(K, L) = F^v(K, \psi^v(L)). \tag{3.30}$$

Further, in the present case of constant returns, it is obvious that $\psi^v(\cdot)$ and $F^v(\cdot,\cdot)$ can be taken to be homogeneous of degree one in their respective arguments. The negative definiteness of B^v, however, clearly implies that the ratio of any pair of labors employed by the vth firm is entirely determined, given $\psi^v(\cdot)$, by the set of marginal rates of substitution among labor pairs, that is, by the $s-1$ ratios, $r_2, \ldots, r_s$, where $r_j \equiv \mu_j/\mu_1$ $(j = 1, \ldots, s)$.

We may thus state as a lemma:

Lemma 3.3: Any constant returns firm production function satisfying our assumptions satisfies a set of partial differential equations in the form (3.29). Indeed, the $g^i(\cdot, \ldots, \cdot)$ of (3.29) are homogeneous of degree zero in their arguments, so that those equations can be rewritten as:

$$\frac{L_i}{L_1} = g^i(1, r_2, \ldots, r_s) \quad (i = 2, \ldots, s).^9 \tag{3.31}$$

With this established, we can now prove:

Theorem 3.2: In the constant returns case, each of the following three conditions is necessary and sufficient for the existence of a labor aggregate:

(a) Whenever the ratios, L_i/L_1 ($i = 2, \ldots, s$) are the same for two firms, the marginal rates of substitution between labor pairs are also the same (and vice versa, if labor is optimally allocated);

(b) The functions $\psi^\nu(\cdot)$ of (3.30) can be chosen as the same function for all firms;[10]

(c) For every $\nu = 2, \ldots, n$, there exists a function $\phi^\nu(f^1, K)$ homogeneous of degree one and monotonic in f^1, and a vector-valued function $H^\nu(K) = (H^\nu(K)_1, \ldots, H^\nu(K)_m)$, homogeneous of degree one, such that f^ν can be written in the form:

$$f^\nu(K, L) = \phi^\nu\{f^1(H^\nu(K), L), K\}. \tag{3.32}$$

Proof: By Lemma 3.3, every firm's production function satisfies a set of partial differential equations in the form (3.31). It is obvious that these can be inverted and (a) now follows from Lemma 3.2′.

To prove (b), observe that the marginal rates of substitution between labor types in the νth firm depend only on the (homothetic) isoquant map of the function $\psi^\nu(\cdot)$. By (a) it is necessary and sufficient that these maps differ at most by the numbering of the isoquants, whence the $\psi^\nu(\cdot)$ differ by at most monotonic transformations,[11] and it is a matter of notation to take them all the same.

Now, fix the first (vector) argument in $f^1(K, L)$. (a) then clearly implies that when that argument is so fixed, $f^\nu(\cdot,\cdot)$ and $f^1(\cdot,\cdot)$ can differ only by a monotonic transformation. Since the form of that transformation can depend on the value of K which is fixed, we may write it as $\phi^\nu\{f^1(K, L), K\}$ with ϕ^ν monotonic in $f^1(\cdot,\cdot)$. On the other hand, changing the value of the first argument of $f^1(\cdot,\cdot)$ does not affect marginal rates of substitution among labor types by Assumption 3.1; we are therefore free to replace K in $f^1(K, L)$ with any vector-valued function $H^\nu(K)$. This leads immediately to the form (3.34). The sufficiency of (c) is obvious, since it implies (a).

Finally, the fact that the $\phi^\nu(\cdot,\cdot)$ and $H^\nu(\cdot)$ can be taken to be homogeneous of degree one in their respective arguments can be readily shown from the homogeneity of the $f^\nu(\cdot,\cdot)$ by defining (for $K \neq 0$):

$$\lambda \equiv \sum_{i=1}^{m} K_i; \quad H^{*\nu}(K) \equiv \lambda H^\nu\left(\frac{K}{\lambda}\right);$$
$$\phi^{*\nu}(f^1, K) \equiv \lambda\phi^\nu\left(\frac{f^1}{\lambda}, \frac{K}{\lambda}\right), \tag{3.33}$$

and showing that if (3.32) holds, it also holds with $\phi^{*\nu}$ and $H^{*\nu}$ replacing ϕ^ν and H^ν, respectively. The case of $K = 0$ can be handled by continuity. QED.

An alternate form of the result is:

Corollary 3.1: In the constant returns case, a labor aggregate exists if and only if for every $\nu = 2, \ldots, n$, there exists a vector-valued function $H^\nu(K)$ defined as in Theorem 3.2 and homogeneous of degree one in K, and two functions, $\phi_1^\nu(\cdot,\cdot)$ and $\phi_2^\nu(\cdot,\cdot)$, homogeneous of degree zero in their arguments, such that:

$$f^\nu(K, L) = \phi_1^\nu\{f^1(H^\nu(K), L), K\} f^1(H^\nu(K), L) + \phi_2^\nu\{f^1(H^\nu(K), L), K\} K \tag{3.34}$$

(provided the expression on the right is monotonic in f^1).

***Proof*:** That this is sufficient follows from (c) of Theorem 3.2 and the fact that the expression on the right-hand side of (3.34) is a function (homogeneous of degree one) of f^1 and K. To prove necessity, define:

$$\phi_1^\nu(f^1, K) \equiv \frac{\partial \phi^\nu(f^1, K)}{\partial f^1}; \quad \phi_2^\nu(f^1, K) \equiv \frac{\partial \phi^\nu(f^1, K)}{\partial K}. \tag{3.35}$$

Then $\phi_1^\nu(\cdot,\cdot)$ and $\phi_2^\nu(\cdot,\cdot)$ are homogeneous of degree zero in their arguments, and the desired result follows from Euler's theorem.

Remark 3.3: If (3.11) holds for $\nu = 1$, so that labor aggregation is possible for the first firm considered alone, and if every other firm's production function can be written in the form (3.32), then (3.11) holds for every firm's production function, as can be seen by differentiation of (3.32) with respect to any labor. Thus, in this case, labor aggregation is possible for any firm or set of firms.[12]

3.6 The constant returns case: Discussion of the results

We may interpret (a) of Theorem 3.2 as follows. Under constant returns, a labor aggregate exists if *and only if* a given set of relative wages induces all firms to employ different labors in the same proportion. Similarly, an output aggregate exists if *and only if* a given set of relative output prices induces all firms to produce all outputs in the same proportion. This result is maintained when more general cases are considered below. It clearly means that aggregation of output is not possible over firms specializing in certain goods and aggregation of labor is not possible over firms offering specialized employment. If firm production functions differ enough to involve such specialization, then they also differ enough to forbid aggregation. Different labor types may be more productive in one firm than in another, but, given the proportions in which labor is hired, they must all be more productive in the same proportion. A similar statement is true of outputs and their effects on labor requirements.

Part (b) of the theorem states essentially the same condition in a different way. By Assumption 3.1, a labor (output) aggregate can be formed for each firm separately. By (b), a labor (output) aggregate exists for the system as a whole if and only if such firm aggregates are formed in the same way for all firms. The combination of the common firm aggregate with capital in the production of output is not restricted.[13]

Part (c) of the theorem is the one which it is easiest to use in generating examples and which most clearly shows the relation of the conditions for labor (output) aggregation to those for capital aggregation developed in [2]. By (c), a labor aggregate can be formed if the firms' production functions differ in at most two ways. The first of these (involved in the functions $H^{\nu}(\cdot)$) is essentially what was defined in Definition 2.2, p. 41, as a "capital-altering" technical difference. This is the generalization of capital-augmenting technical change. It essentially involves redefinition of capital units. Under constant returns, capital-altering technical differences are the only kind of technical difference permitting capital aggregation. As Theorem 3.1 also implies, we now know that they permit labor aggregation also, on our assumptions.

On the other hand, labor (or output) aggregation is permitted under some cases when capital aggregation is not. These cases (involving the $\phi^{\nu}(\cdot,\cdot)$) can be regarded as the production of output with the technology of the first firm and then the recombination of the output so produced with capital to produce further output.[14] This leads to a far wider class of cases than those permitting capital aggregation. In particular, Hicks-neutral differences are allowed, as are labor-augmenting differences provided that every kind of labor is augmented in the same proportion.

Some idea of the different classes of cases permitting labor and capital aggregation, respectively, can perhaps be gained from considering the following example. Suppose that there is only one type of capital and two types of labor employed by each firm and that the first firm's production function is given by:

$$f^1(K, L_1, L_2) = AL_1^{\alpha}L_2^{\beta}K^{(1-\alpha-\beta)}. \tag{3.36}$$

Capital aggregation will be possible if and only if all other firms have production functions differing only in A. By (c) of the theorem, however, it is easy to see that labor aggregation will remain possible even if other firms differ from the first not only in A, but also in α and β, provided that the ratio of α to β is unchanged. Indeed, labor aggregation will be possible even if some firms do not have Cobb–Doublas type production functions at all! By (c), labor aggregation remains possible, for example, if f^1 and K are combined as inputs in a constant elasticity of substitution (CES) production function, and so forth. While the conditions for labor (output) aggregation under constant returns are quite restrictive, they are not nearly so restrictive as they may at first appear and are certainly far less restrictive than the conditions for capital aggregation.

3.7 Nonconstant returns and the class of labor-homothetic production functions

As in the case of capital aggregation treated in [2], I have been unable to give a closed-form characterization of the class of cases permitting labor aggregation when constant returns is not assumed. On the other hand, the analysis of the constant returns case just completed suggests a class of more general cases to which our results can readily be extended.

As already observed, by Assumption 3.1, every firm's production function can be written in the form:

$$f^{\nu}(K, L) \equiv F^{\nu}(K, \psi^{\nu}(L)) \quad (\nu = 1, \ldots, n). \tag{3.37}$$

Now that we have left the case of constant returns, it need not be possible to take $\psi^{\nu}(\cdot)$ homogeneous of degree one, but it may be. If it is, then the marginal rates of substitution between labor types still depend only on labor ratios. As this makes the isoquant map of $f^{\nu}(\cdot,\cdot)$ in the space of the labors homothetic, a reasonable terminology is:

DEFINITION 3.2: A firm production function, satisfying (3.37), for which $\psi^{\nu}(\cdot)$ can be taken to be homogeneous of degree one, will be called *labor homothetic*.

Obviously, constant returns production functions permitting labor aggregation when considered alone are automatically labor homothetic. Some idea of the class involved may be obtained by observing that the class of labor-homothetic production functions is precisely that class which can be generated from constant returns production functions permitting labor aggregation by the sort of transformations involved in (c) of Theorem 3.2, save that the functions $\phi^\nu(\cdot,\cdot)$ and $H^\nu(\cdot)$ need no longer be restricted to be homogeneous of degree one. Thus, if and only if $f^\nu(\cdot,\cdot)$ is labor homothetic, there exist: a function $G^\nu(K, L)$, homogeneous of degree one in its arguments and permitting labor aggregation when considered alone; a function $\phi^\nu(G^\nu, K)$, monotonic in G^ν; and a vector-valued function $H^\nu(K)$, such that:

$$f^\nu(K, L) = \phi^\nu\{G^\nu(H^\nu(K), L), K\}. \tag{3.38}$$

That this is equivalent to Definition 3.2 can be seen by an argument similar to that leading to (c) of Theorem 3.2.

As in Section 3.6, (3.38) can be used to generate examples. One such is that of a Cobb–Douglas with exponents not necessarily summing to unity. It should also be observed that the class of labor-homothetic production functions includes the class of capital-generalized constant returns production functions introduced at a similar point on p. 41, given the restriction that labor aggregation is permitted when each firm is taken separately. That class was generated as in (3.38) by using the capital-altering functions, $H^\nu(\cdot)$, but with $\phi^\nu(\cdot,\cdot)$ restricted to be the identity transformation. The difference is precisely that already discussed between the conditions for labor aggregation and those for capital aggregation.

Definition 3.3: A set of labor-homothetic production functions for which the functions $\psi^\nu(\cdot)$ can be taken to be the same will be called a *family*.

An alternative definition is that the functions $G^\nu(\cdot,\cdot)$ of (3.38) can be taken to be the same.

The principal result of this section is the generalization of Theorem 3.2 to show that if every firm's production function is labor-homothetic, then a necessary and sufficient condition for labor aggregation is that they are all members of the same family. The proof of this is quite straightforward once we establish:

Lemma 3.4: If a firm's production function, $f^\nu(K, L)$, is labor homothetic, there exists for any $L \neq 0$[15] a nonzero scalar, q_ν, such that:

$$(B^\nu)^{-1} f^\nu_L = q_\nu L.\text{[16]} \tag{3.39}$$

Proof: Denoting differentiation by subscripts in the obvious way,

$$f^\nu_L = F^\nu_\psi \psi^\nu_L; \quad F^\nu_\psi \neq 0. \tag{3.40}$$

Letting D^ν be the Hessian of ψ^ν,

$$B^\nu L = F_\psi^\nu D^\nu L + F_{\psi\psi}^\nu \psi_L^\nu \psi_L^{\nu\prime} L = \left(\frac{\psi^\nu F_{\psi\psi}^\nu}{F_\psi^\nu}\right) f_L^\nu, \tag{3.41}$$

by the homogeneity of $\psi^\nu(\cdot)$ and Euler's theorem. The lemma now follows immediately from the negative definiteness of B^ν.

Theorem 3.3: If every firm's production function is labor homothetic, a necessary and sufficient condition for labor aggregation is that they all be members of the same family.

***Proof*:** By Lemmas 3.1 and 3.4, a necessary and sufficient condition for labor aggregation in this case is that every firm's production function satisfy the same set of partial differential equations in the form (3.29). However, it is obviously that Lemma 3.3 still holds, and the rest of the proof is essentially that of Theorem 3.2.

Of course, the condition that every one of a set of labor-homothetic production functions be a member of the same family is equivalent to (a), (b), or (c) of Theorem 3.2 (save that the $\phi^\nu(\cdot,\cdot)$ and $H^\nu(\cdot)$ need not be homogeneous), so that our discussion of the preceding section applies here too.

The case of every firm's production function labor homothetic is the only one for which I have been able to find a closed-form characterization of the solution in the nonconstant returns case. Indeed, an obvious open question is whether there exist any other cases in which labor aggregation is possible.[17]

The class of labor-homothetic production functions is very wide,[18] examples such as those mentioned in the preceding section no longer being restricted to preserve constant returns. It is not universal, however, and the closing of the open question just discussed is clearly a matter of some interest for further work.

3.8 Removal of the positive labor employment (output production) restriction

In this section, we remove the restriction that every firm always employs some of every labor (produces some of every output) in positive amount so that (3.10) always holds. We show among other things that all the results for constant returns and labor homotheticity are independent of that restriction. A similar development holds for the generalization of those results given below in Section 3.9, but we shall not give that discussion explicitly.

There are two possibilities to consider. First, for all points in the overall factor space differing only by sufficiently small variation in some $K(h)$,[19] there may be some firm which employs no labor of any kind. Second, there may be some firm which employs some but not all labors. It is fairly evident that the former case presents no particular difficulty. Moreover, the latter case also is no problem if the movements in $K(h)$ described do not affect the marginal products of the labors employed by the hth firm. Clearly, however, if those marginal products are affected, problems will be raised for labor aggregation, since there will be some μ_i affected by $K(h)$ in different ways than others.[20]

Thus, suppose that there is a point in the overall factor space such that for all points differing from the given one by small variations in $K(h)$ (for some $h = 1, \ldots, n$), some labor type is not employed by a particular firm. Let

$$Q_v = \{i \mid L_i(v) \neq 0 \text{ at all such points}\} \quad (v = 1, \ldots, n). \tag{3.42}$$

Then when considering movements in $K(h)$, (3.10) must be replaced by:

$$\begin{aligned} f^v_{L_i} &= \mu_i & i &\in Q_v \\ L_i(v) &= 0 & i &\notin Q_v \quad (v = 1, \ldots, n). \end{aligned} \tag{3.43}$$

Define $\tilde{B}^v$ as an $s \times s$ matrix whose elements are given as follows:

$$\tilde{B}^v_{ij} = \begin{cases} B^v_{ij} = f^v_{L_iL_j} & \text{if } i, j \in Q_v \\ 0 & \text{if } i \notin Q_v \text{ or } j \notin Q_v \text{ or both and } i \neq j \\ 1 & \text{if } i = j \text{ and } i \notin Q_v \end{cases} \tag{3.44}$$

$$(i, j = 1, \ldots, s;\ v = 1, \ldots, n).$$

Define $\tilde{I}^v$ as the $s \times s$ matrix formed as follows:

$$\tilde{I}^v_{ij} = 0 \quad \text{if } i \neq j$$

$$\tilde{I}^v_{ii} = \begin{cases} 1 & \text{if } i \in Q_v \\ 0 & \text{if } i \notin Q_v \end{cases} \quad (i, j = 1, \ldots, s;\ v = 1, \ldots, n). \tag{3.45}$$

In place of (3.17), define:

$$\tilde{R} \equiv \sum_{v=1}^{n} (\tilde{B}^v)^{-1} \tilde{I}^v. \tag{3.46}$$

Differentiating both sets of equations in (3.43) totally with respect to $K(h)$, and solving for $\partial\mu/\partial K(h)$, (3.15) is replaced by:

$$\partial\mu/\partial K(h) = \tilde{R}^{-1}(\tilde{B}^h)^{-1}\tilde{I}^h f^h_{KL}. \tag{3.47}$$

Now, it is clear that in the present case the discussion leading to Assumption 3.1 requires only that we assume that aggregation be possible within a firm considered in isolation for those labors actually employed by that firm. Hence, while it would suffice to maintain (3.11), we can weaken Assumption 3.1′ and require only the existence of scalars $\tilde{d}_v$ ($v = 1, \ldots, n$) such that:

$$\tilde{I}^v f^v_{KL} = \tilde{d}_v \tilde{I}^v f^v_L = \tilde{d}_v \tilde{I}^v \mu, \tag{3.48}$$

the last equality following from (3.43). Combining this with (3.47), the Leontief condition (3.12) with respect to $K(h)$ clearly becomes the requirement that there exist a scalar $\tilde{c}_h$ such that:

$$\tilde{d}_h \tilde{R}^{-1}(\tilde{B}^h)^{-1}\tilde{I}^h \mu = \tilde{c}_h \mu. \tag{3.49}$$

There are now two possibilities. Either $\tilde{d}_h = 0$, in which case movements in $K(h)$ do not affect the marginal products of labors employed by the hth firm, or else $\tilde{d}_h \neq 0$. It is obvious that in the former case (3.49) is trivially satisfied with $\tilde{c}_h = 0$, as it is if Q_h is empty, so we may as well take $\tilde{d}_h \neq 0$ and Q_h nonempty for the remainder of the discussion.[21] In this case, a proof identical in all essentials with that of Lemma 3.1 shows:

Lemma 3.5: A necessary and sufficient condition for the satisfying of the Leontief condition with respect to $K(h)$ is that for every $v = 1, \ldots, n$, there exists a scalar $\tilde{t}_{vh}$ such that (in the set of points in the overall factor space being considered) whenever all labors have been optimally allocated:

$$(\tilde{B}^v)^{-1}\tilde{I}^v \mu = \tilde{t}_{vh}(\tilde{B}^h)^{-1}\tilde{I}^h \mu, \tag{3.50}$$

and $\tilde{t}_{vh} \neq 0$ unless Q_v is empty.

Once more there are two cases to consider. The first of these is that in which for every v, Q_v is either empty or contains all indices from 1 to s. This is the case in which either some of every labor is employed by a given firm or else none of any labor is. If no labors whatsoever are employed by the hth firm itself, then, as already remarked, (3.49) is trivially satisfied, and again there is no problem, so we can assume for the moment that some of each labor type is employed by the hth firm. Now, if for some v, Q_v is empty, then for that v (3.45) shows that $\tilde{I}^v = 0$, so that (3.50) holds for that v with $\tilde{t}_{vh} = 0$. Since some of each labor type is employed by the hth firm, (3.50) for the νs (if any) for which Q_ν contains all indices from 1 to s simply reduces to (3.17) and our preceding analysis carries over without change.

There remains the case in which $K(h)$ does affect the marginal products of labors positively employed by the hth firm, and for some $\nu = 1, \ldots, n$, Q_ν contains some but not all of the indices from 1 to s, i.e., there exists a firm (possibly, but not necessarily, the hth) which employs some but not all labor types in positive amount. We shall refer to this as the Specialization Case.

Consider now some firm, which we may as well take to be the nth, for which Q_ν contains some but not all of the indices from 1 to s. For definiteness, we may suppose that Q_n consists of the indices from $s - s'$ to s with $0 \leqq s' < s - 1$. Consider $(\tilde{B}^n)^{-1}\tilde{I}^n\mu$. Let B^{*n} be the matrix consisting of the last s' rows and columns of $\tilde{B}^n$. Then:

$$\tilde{B}^n = \begin{bmatrix} I & 0 \\ 0 & B^{*n} \end{bmatrix}; \; (\tilde{B}^n)^{-1} = \begin{bmatrix} I & 0 \\ 0 & (B^{*n})^{-1} \end{bmatrix}; \; \tilde{I}^n = \begin{bmatrix} 0 & 0 \\ 0 & I \end{bmatrix}. \tag{3.51}$$

It is thus evident that the first $s - s'$ elements of $(\tilde{B}^n)^{-1}\tilde{I}^n\mu$ must be zero. If (3.50) is to hold, however, it is clear that the first $s - s'$ elements of $(\tilde{B}^\nu)^{-1}\tilde{I}^\nu\mu$ must be zero for *every* $\nu = 1, \ldots, n$. Formally:

Lemma 3.6: In the Specialization Case, with the firms and labors numbered as described, a necessary condition for labor aggregation is that for every $\nu = 1, \ldots, n$, there exists an s'-component column vector, λ_ν, such that when labor is optimally allocated:

$$(\tilde{B}^\nu)^{-1}\tilde{I}^\nu\mu = \begin{bmatrix} 0 \\ \lambda_\nu \end{bmatrix} \tag{3.52}$$

everywhere in the set of points in the overall factor space in question.

Premultiplying (3.52) by $\tilde{B}^\nu$, we see that an alternative statement of (3.52) is that $\tilde{I}^\nu\mu$ must be in the space spanned by the last s' columns of $\tilde{B}^\nu$.

Obviously, this condition is very special. We now consider two sets of cases in which (3.52) can be shown not to hold. The second of these will be the labor-homothetic case, but before turning to it we consider a different class of production functions (some but not all members of which are labor-homothetic). We define:

Definition 3.4: In the νth firm's production function, labor types i and j will be said to be *weakly complementary* if and only if $f^{\nu}_{L_i L_j} \geqq 0$.

Let $B^{*\nu}$ be the matrix obtained from $\tilde{B}^{\nu}$ by deleting all rows and columns not corresponding to elements of Q_{ν}. It is easy to show:[22]

Lemma 3.7: If at some point in the overall factor space, all pairs of labors employed by the νth firm in positive amount are weakly complementary, then, at that point, $(B^{*\nu})^{-1}$ is nonpositive.

By considering the case of $\nu = n$, laid out in (3.51), it is then clear that:

Lemma 3.8: Under the conditions of Lemma 3.7, $(\tilde{B}^{\nu})^{-1}\tilde{I}^{\nu}$ is nonpositive.

Lemma 3.9: Suppose the conditions of Lemma 3.7 hold and that, for that ν, $Q_{\nu} \nsubseteq Q_n$. Then $\tilde{I}^{\nu}\mu$ is not in the space spanned by the last s' columns of $\tilde{B}^{\nu}$.

***Proof*:** Suppose that the lemma were false and that (3.52) held. Since μ is positive and $(\tilde{B}^{\nu})^{-1}\tilde{I}^{\nu}$ nonpositive, λ_{ν} is nonpositive. For definiteness, suppose that $1 \in Q_{\nu}$ and $1 \notin Q_n$. Consider the first row of $\tilde{B}^{\nu}$. By weak complementarity, every element in that row and the last s' columns is nonnegative. Premultiplying (3.52) by $\tilde{B}^{\nu}$, it follows that the first element of $\tilde{I}^{\nu}\mu$ is nonpositive. This is impossible, however, for that element is $\mu_1 > 0$.

Combining this result with that of Lemma 3.6, we have:

Theorem 3.4: Suppose we are in the Specialization Case, with the firms and labors numbered as described. Suppose further that the production function of some firm which employs in positive amount a labor type not employed by the nth firm has the property that at the point in the overall factor space in question all pairs of labor types positively employed are weakly complementary. Then no labor aggregate exists.

We now return to the case of labor-homothetic production functions and prove:

Lemma 3.10: If the νth firm's production function is labor-homothetic, then $\tilde{I}^{\nu}\mu$ is not in the space spanned by the last s' columns of $\tilde{B}^{\nu}$ unless $Q_{\nu} \subseteqq Q_n$.

***Proof*:** Denote by μ^* the vector obtained by deleting from μ all elements not corresponding to components of Q_ν. Suppose that (3.52) holds and denote by λ_ν^* the vector obtained from λ_ν by the same procedure. Then (3.52) yields:

$$(B^{*\nu})^{-1}\mu^* = \begin{bmatrix} 0 \\ \lambda_\nu^* \end{bmatrix} \tag{3.53}$$

and if Q_ν is not contained in Q_n, the zero is actually present.

Now, a labor-homothetic production function in which some labors are set equal to zero is labor-homothetic in the remaining labors. By Lemma 3.4, therefore, (3.53) implies that the leading element of $L(\nu)$ must be zero, contradicting the fact that we have eliminated all elements not corresponding to elements of Q_ν.

Parallel to Theorem 3.4, we may now immediately state:

Theorem 3.5: Suppose we are in the Specialization Case with the firms and labors numbered as described. Suppose further that at the point in overall factor space in question some labor not employed in positive amount by the nth firm is employed in positive amount by a firm with a labor-homothetic production function.[23] Then no labor aggregate exists.

The main result of this section, which shows the independence of our closed-form results in previous sections from the explicit assumption that the Specialization Case is absent, may now be given. It is:

Theorem 3.6: Suppose every firm's production function is labor homothetic. Then:

(a) The absence of the Specialization Case is a necessary condition for labor aggregation;

(b) If all firm production functions are members of the same family, the Specialization Case is automatically absent.

***Proof*:**

(a) By Lemmas 3.6 and 3.10, a labor aggregate can exist in the Specialization Case only if all Q_ν are the same. This is impossible as there is then some labor type employed by no firm despite the fact that all labors were assumed to have a positive marginal product somewhere in the system.

(b) Suppose all firm production functions are labor homothetic and of the same family. It is obvious that efficient allocation requires that all firms which have any positive labor employment have all labors employed in the same proportion, since marginal rates of substitution are the same at the same labor ratios. It follows immediately that every firm either employs some of every labor in positive amount or employs no labor at all.[24]

The interpretation of the results of this section in terms of output aggregation is left to the reader. We now return to the assumption that all $L_i(v)$ are positive.

3.9 The existence of subaggregates and the separate aggregation of labor and output

Up to now, we have dealt with labor aggregation assuming output aggregation to be possible or with output aggregation assuming labor aggregation to be possible. We must now consider the more general case. This is easily done without altering the notation by considering the conditions for forming an aggregate out of the first r of the L_i only, $r < s$. We shall thus be considering at the same time the conditions for the existence of true labor subaggregates such as "skilled" or "unskilled labor."

We shall call an aggregate of the first r of the L_i an "r-aggregate." Define:

$$P \equiv [I \;\; 0]; \quad Q \equiv \begin{bmatrix} 0 \\ I \end{bmatrix}, \tag{3.54}$$

where P is $r \times s$ and Q is $s \times (s-r)$. So long as we are considering only r-aggregates, we need no longer assume that a full aggregate exists for each firm separately, but rather must assume that an r-aggregate exists for each separate firm. This implies that (3.11) should be altered to

$$Pf^v_{KL} = d_v Pf^v_L \quad (v = 1, \ldots, n). \tag{3.55}$$

However, while (3.55) is necessary for the existence of an r-aggregate for each firm, it is not itself sufficient. The conditions in (3.55) are the Leontief conditions with respect to capital. Since a less than full aggregate is involved, there are also Leontief conditions with respect to the last $(s-r)$ labors, which are left out of the aggregate.[25] Those conditions are readily seen to be:

$$PB^v Q = Pf^v_L \lambda'_v \quad (v = 1, \ldots, n) \tag{3.56}$$

where λ'_v is an $(s-r)$-component row vector.

Similarly, for the system as a whole there are Leontief conditions with respect to the last $(s-r)$ labors as well as with respect to capital. The conditions with respect to capital are:

$$PR^{-1}(B^{\nu})^{-1}f^{\nu}_{KL} = c_{\nu}P\mu \quad (\nu = 1, \ldots, n) \tag{3.57}$$

where the c_{ν} are scalars.

The Leontief conditions for the full system with respect to the last $(s-r)$ labors are readily obtained after differentiating (3.10) and (3.3) totally with respect to $L_1, \ldots, L_s$. They are:

$$PR^{-1}Q = P\mu\eta' \tag{3.58}$$

where η' is an $(s-r)$-component row vector.

We shall assume that (3.55) and (3.56) hold and summarize the results thus far as:

Lemma 3.11: Necessary and sufficient conditions for the existence of an r-aggregate are that (3.55)–(3.58) hold whenever all labors have been optimally allocated.

Now, by (3.55) and (3.56), every firm's production function can be written in the form:

$$f^{\nu}(K, L^1, L^2) = F^{\nu}\{K, \psi^{\nu}(L^1), L^2\} \quad (\nu = 1, \ldots, n) \tag{3.59}$$

where L^1 and L^2 are vectors of the first r and the last $s-r$ components of L, respectively. We generalize the class of labor-homothetic production functions by:

DEFINITION 3.5: A firm's production function satisfying (3.59) for which $\psi^{\nu}(\cdot)$ can be taken to be homogeneous of degree one is called *r-homothetic*.[26]

Labor-homothetic production functions are automatically r-homothetic if they satisfy (3.59) (i.e., if they permit r-aggregation when taken alone). The same is true for constant returns and capital-generalized constant returns production functions.[27]

DEFINITION 3.6: A set of r-homothetic production functions for which the functions $\psi^{\nu}(\cdot)$ can be taken to be the same will be called a *family*.

A family of r-homothetic production functions has the property that marginal rates of substitution among the first r labors are determined only by the ratios of those labors.

We prove:

Theorem 3.7: Let every firm's production function be r-homothetic.

(a) A sufficient condition for the existence of an r-aggregate is that they all be members of the same family.

(b) If each firm's production function is either constant returns, capital-generalized constant returns, or labor homothetic, and if $f_{KL}^{\nu} \neq 0$ for any $\nu = 1, \ldots, n$, this condition is also necessary.[28]

(The requirement that $f_{KL}^{\nu} \neq 0$ is implied by the negative-definiteness of B^{ν} for constant returns or capital-generalized constant returns, but not for labor homotheticity.)

Proof:

(a) If the $\psi^{\nu}(\cdot)$ in (3.59) can be chosen to be the same, then it is obvious that when for all firms marginal rates of substitution are the same for the first r labors, so are the ratios of the first r labors. Optimal allocation therefore requires each firm to employ the first r labors in proportion to the total amounts of such labors available in the system as a whole. Since the marginal rates of substitution between any pair of the first r labors in any firm depend only on these $r-1$ ratios, the marginal rates of substitution in the system as a whole are functions only of the total amounts of the first r labors. The desired result now follows directly from Leontief's theorem.

(b) Necessity is a rather more complicated affair. If the νth firm's production function is in any one of the classes named, then there exists a nonzero scalar, say α_{ν}, such that:

$$(B^{\nu})^{-1} f_{KL}^{\nu} = \alpha_{\nu} L.^{29} \tag{3.60}$$

For constant returns and capital-generalized constant returns, this follows from Euler's theorem; for labor-homothetic functions, it follows from Lemma 3.4.

Further, if an r-aggregate exists, then (3.57) and (3.58) are satisfied. The latter equation implies:

$$PR^{-1} = P\mu\tilde{\eta}' + XP \tag{3.61}$$

where $\tilde{\eta}' = (0 \;\; \eta')$ and X is an $r \times r$ matrix. Substituting (3.60) and (3.61) into (3.57) yields:

$$XPL = \sigma_{\nu} P\mu, \tag{3.62}$$

where

$$\sigma_\nu = \frac{c_\nu}{\alpha_\nu} - \tilde{\eta}' L. \tag{3.63}$$

Now, suppose that X were singular. Then (by (3.61)) there would exist a nonzero row vector, λ', such that:

$$\lambda' PR^{-1} = \lambda' P \mu \tilde{\eta}'. \tag{3.64}$$

Since $\lambda' P = (\lambda' \, 0)$ and $\tilde{\eta}' = (0 \, \eta')$, this would imply that the leading $r \times r$ principal submatrix of R^{-1} is singular. (Indeed, X is that submatrix.) This is impossible, however, since R is negative definite.

We may thus write:

$$PL = \sigma_\nu X^{-1} P\mu \quad (\nu = 1, \ldots, n). \tag{3.65}$$

This shows that when all labor is optimally allocated the ratios of the first r labors must be the same in each firm, since the right-hand side of (3.65) is independent of ν, save for a scalar. It is then clear that the marginal rates of substitution among the first r labors must be the same for each firm when those $r-1$ ratios are the same. This implies that the $\psi^\nu(\cdot)$ must be monotonic transformations of each other, and since the $\psi^\nu(\cdot)$ are all constant returns, the desired result follows immediately.

It seems very likely that the necessity of the condition follows without the added restrictions imposed in the statement of (b) – that is, that it follows just from r-homotheticity (and $f^\nu_{KL} \neq 0$) – but I have been unable to prove this.

Of course, the theorem allows us to carry over the discussion of the preceding sections to the more general case essentially without change. It is of some importance, however, to note that the conditions for subaggregation may be less stringent in a sense than those for full aggregation. What is required for subaggregation is that given the relative wages (relative prices) of the labors (outputs) to be included in the aggregate, every firm employs those labors (produces those outputs) in the same proportion. But zero employment of all such labors (or production of all such outputs) should be thought of as satisfying this. Thus specialization is not permitted if a firm employs any labor (produces any output) included in the subaggregate. It is permitted in the sense that there can be firms which do not employ any such labor (produce any such output) at all.

Theorem 3.7 has an obvious corollary:

Corollary 3.2: Suppose that every firm's production function is r-homothetic and, further, that they all separately permit the construction of an r'-aggregate, $r' < r$. If, in addition, they are all from the three classes mentioned in (b) of Theorem 3.7 (with all $f_{KL}^{v} \neq 0$), then the existence of an r-aggregate for the system as a whole implies the existence of an r'-aggregate for the system as a whole.

Forming subaggregates from proper subsets is thus (for the types of production functions described) easier than from a full set of labor types in the same way as labor (output) aggregation is easier than capital aggregation by Theorem 3.1. This is in very sharp contrast to the results of pp. 49–50, 56–7, where it was shown that the existence of subaggregates of capital required quite stringent conditions not required for the existence of a full aggregate.

Remark 3.4: Theorem 3.1 itself does not seem to carry over directly to the construction of subaggregates in the most general case. However, for constant returns or capital-generalized constant returns, and r-homotheticity, the existence of a full capital aggregate certainly implies the existence of an r-aggregate, since it implies that all technical differences are capital altering. Hence, in particular, for either constant returns or capital-generalized constant returns it is true that the existence of a full capital aggregate plus the existence of a labor (output) aggregate for each firm implies the existence of a labor (output) aggregate for the system as a whole.

Moreover, if we consider the case in which some types of capital are movable and are employed (perhaps in the long run) so as to produce efficiently, then such movable capitals are represented as some of the L_i. In this case, another interpretation of the result just mentioned is that, under constant returns or capital-generalized constant returns, the existence of a fixed capital aggregate for the system as a whole plus the existence of a movable capital aggregate for each separate firm implies the existence of a movable capital aggregate for the system as a whole.[30]

Even when not all firm production functions are from the three classes of (b) of Theorem 3.7 and even when they are not all r-homothetic, the existence of subaggregates (given (3.55) and (3.56)) is often weaker than the existence of a full aggregate, as we shall now show.

Lemma 3.12: Let (3.56) hold. Further, suppose a full aggregate exists and that Assumption 3.2 is valid. Then either of the following two conditions implies (3.58):

(a) $r = s - 1$, so that only one labor is left out of the r-aggregate; or
(b) for no $\nu = 1, \ldots, n$ is μ in the column space of $B^\nu Q$.

***Proof*:** From the definitions of P and Q (3.56) can be restated as:

$$B^\nu Q = \mu\lambda_\nu' + QW^\nu \quad (\nu = 1, \ldots, n) \tag{3.66}$$

where W^ν is an $(s-r) \times (s-r)$ matrix. Premultiplying by $R^{-1}(B^\nu)^{-1}$, this becomes:

$$R^{-1}Q = R^{-1}(B^\nu)^{-1}\mu\lambda_\nu' + R^{-1}(B^\nu)^{-1}QW^\nu \quad (\nu = 1, \ldots, n). \tag{3.67}$$

Now, since a full aggregate is assumed to exist, (3.55) and (3.56) hold with P deleted, or, in other words, (3.16) holds. Further, since Assumption 3.2 holds, we may assume that there exists at least one $h = 1, \ldots, n$ for which $d_h \neq 0$, the remaining case being taken care of by continuity. For that h, $R^{-1}(B^h)^{-1}\mu$ is proportional to μ. However, since a full aggregate exists, Lemma 3.1 assures us that every $(B^\nu)^{-1}\mu$ is proportional to $(B^h)^{-1}\mu$ and we may conclude that there exist scalars u_ν such that:

$$R^{-1}(B^\nu)^{-1}\mu = u_\nu\mu \quad (\nu = 1, \ldots, n). \tag{3.68}$$

Substituting this in (3.67), we obtain:

$$R^{-1}Q = \mu\beta_\nu' + R^{-1}(B^\nu)^{-1}QW^\nu \quad (\nu = 1, \ldots, n) \tag{3.69}$$

where $\beta_\nu' = u_\nu\lambda_\nu'$.

Now, either W^ν is singular or it is not. Suppose first that W^ν is singular for a particular ν. If (a) holds and $r = s - 1$, W^ν is a scalar, so if it is singular, it must be zero. In this case, the lemma follows immediately from (3.69) with $\eta' = \beta_\nu'$. If $r < s - 1$ and W^ν is singular, there exists a nonzero $(s-r)$-component column vector, say π_ν, in the null space of W^ν. Postmultiplying (3.66) by π_ν, we obtain:

$$B^\nu Q\pi_\nu = \mu\lambda_\nu'\pi_\nu. \tag{3.70}$$

Since B^ν is negative definite, it follows from the definition of Q that the left-hand side of (3.70) is not zero. Thus the right-hand side is not zero either and we may divide through by $\lambda_\nu'\pi_\nu$. This immediately shows that μ is in the column space of $B^\nu Q$ in contradiction to (b).

We may thus go on to consider the case in which for no v is W^v singular. Postmultiply (3.69) by $(W^v)^{-1}$ and sum over v to obtain:

$$R^{-1}QG = \mu\alpha' + Q; \quad G \equiv \sum_{v=1}^{n} (W^v)^{-1};$$
$$\alpha' \equiv \sum_{v=1}^{n} \beta'_v (W^v)^{-1}. \tag{3.71}$$

Suppose now that G were singular. There would then exist a nonzero $(s-r)$-component column vector, say π, in the null space of G. Postmultiplying (3.71) by π, we obtain:

$$0 = \mu\alpha'\pi + Q\pi = \mu\alpha'\pi + \begin{bmatrix} 0 \\ \pi \end{bmatrix} \tag{3.72}$$

by the definition of Q. Since $\mu > 0$, this is impossible, whence G is nonsingular.

Postmultiplying (3.71) by G^{-1} and premultiplying by P, we obtain:

$$PR^{-1}Q = P\mu(\alpha' G^{-1}) + PQG^{-1} = P\mu(\alpha' G^{-1}), \tag{3.73}$$

which is (3.58) with $\eta' = \alpha' G^{-1}$.

We further prove:

Lemma 3.13: Let a full aggregate exist and let Assumption 3.2 hold. If for some $h = 1, \ldots, n$, μ is in the column space of $B^h Q$, then μ is in the column space of $B^v Q$ for all $v = 1, \ldots, n$.

***Proof*:** Since μ is in the column space of $B^h Q$, there exists an $(s-r)$-component column vector, say π_h, such that:

$$Q\pi_h = (B^h)^{-1}\mu. \tag{3.74}$$

Since a full aggregate exists and Assumption 3.2 holds, Lemma 3.1 applies and there exist nonzero scalars t_{hv} such that:

$$Q\pi_h = t_{hv}(B^v)^{-1}\mu \tag{3.75}$$

whence

$$B^v Q\pi_v = \mu; \quad \pi_v = (1/t_{hv})\pi_h. \tag{3.76}$$

Lemma 3.13 enables us to weaken (b) of Lemma 3.12 to the requirement that there exist at least one v such that μ is not in the column space of $B^{\nu}Q$. We showed in Lemmas 3.9 and 3.10 (adapting the notation and proof to the present purpose) that if either the νth production function is labor homothetic or all labors are everywhere weakly complementary in the νth production function then μ is not in the column space of $B^{\nu}Q$. This, together with Lemmas 3.11–3.13 and the fact that (3.57) certainly holds if a full aggregate exists,[31] enables us to establish:

Theorem 3.8: Let a full aggregate exist and let Assumption 3.2 hold. Let an r-aggregate exist for each firm taken separately. Any of the following three conditions then suffice for the existence of an r-aggregate for the system as a whole.

(a) $r = s - 1$, so that only one labor is left out of the r-aggregate;
(b) For some $\nu = 1, \ldots, n$, the νth production function is labor homothetic. (Note once again that this includes constant returns as a special case.)
(c) For some $\nu = 1, \ldots, n$ all labors are everywhere weakly complementary in the νth production function.

It may be noted that (a) of the theorem is more general than it appears, since if an aggregate can be formed from the last $s - r$ labors, that will make (a) applicable. (a) can thus be weakened to the condition that an aggregate can be formed from the last $s - r$ labors.

It is just possible that (b) is implied by the existence of a full aggregate, but this is not known. (b) is a stronger result than follows immediately from Corollary 3.2 for this case, since $f^{\nu}_{KL} \neq 0$ for *all* ν is not required and since only one $f^{\nu}(\cdot,\cdot)$ is assumed labor homothetic.

Finally, it may be noted that weak complementarity of factors here aids the construction of partial labor aggregates. This is in sharp contrast to the results on pp. 50 and 56 where it was shown that such complementarity prevents the existence of any partial capital aggregate.

We conclude this section with some remarks on the role of Assumption 3.2. That assumption makes the existence of a full aggregate nontrivial in that it prevents at least one firm's production function from being additive in a function of labor and a function of capital. In the present section, this is a bit more than a matter of keeping the problem interesting, however, since the consequences of the existence of a *nontrivial* full aggregate are heavily used in establishing the existence of subaggregates in Theorem 3.8. Those results thus seem to depend on the interrelations between capital and the various labors involved in nontrivial aggregation. We have therefore included Assumption 3.2 as an explicit part of the statement of the various lemmas and of Theorem 3.8.[32]

As remarked preceding Assumption 3.2, that assumption is guaranteed to hold by the assumption of the negative definiteness of the B^v if at least one firm's production function is constant returns (or capital-generalized constant returns).

3.10 Concluding remarks

This chapter, together with Chapter 2, has shown that rather strong conditions must be satisfied for aggregation.[33] Those conditions are perhaps strongest for capital aggregation but are very strong for labor or output aggregation also where they require (*inter alia*) the absence of specialization. They are quite unlikely to be satisfied in practice for a diverse economy.

This may be discouraging, but it should not be surprising. What is surprising is the variety of cases in which firms need not have the same technology but aggregation is yet possible.

Nevertheless, these results are indeed rather discouraging. Moreover, while there at first appear to be two ways of escape, these do not turn out to be very promising. In the first place, our theorems give the exact conditions for exact aggregation with the range of the variables unrestricted except by the requirements for efficient labor allocation. Whether approximate aggregation over a limited range requires the approximate satisfaction of such conditions is by no means obvious. Unfortunately, it turns out to be the case in fact.[34]

Second, it is possible that there exist restrictions in some models on the possible values of the variables which will allow aggregation under much wider conditions than those here set forth. Thus, consider how much wider the conditions become when efficient labor allocation is assumed than when it is not. (The latter case requires additive production functions.) Similarly, if all firms always happened to invest in the same proportion, there would be no capital aggregation problem. The trouble is that while institutional organization forms part of technology, it is hard to argue that such systematic and possibly institutional restrictions on the variables are more than accidental.

On the other hand, aggregation is only a convenience (although an enormous one). It may well be that the results of models of one or two-sector economies, which assume an aggregate production function are valid for more disaggregated models. So far as the results of this chapter (and of Chapters 2, 4–7) are concerned, however, if such validity exists it is because proofs and propositions can be generalized to many-sector models, not because highly aggregate models of production are really summarizing the production processes of a diverse economy.

Notes

1. Other recent papers in this area are Diamond [1], Gorman [5], Hall [6], Nataf [14], Stigum [16], and Whitaker [18] and [19].
2. The question of the existence of aggregate production functions under various conditions is an old one in the literature. See Klein [7], [8], May [11], [12], Nataf [13], and Pu [15].
3. The differentiability assumptions can doubtless be weakened. For the capital aggregation problem, this has been done by Stigum [16]. For the present problem, cf. Stigum [17].
4. It is obviously sufficient to assume the $f^v(\cdot, \ldots, \cdot)$ strictly concave in their labor arguments, points without negative definite labor Hessians being handled by continuity.
5. An example of this sort of phenomenon is given in Chapter 5, p. 133. The parallel phenomenon in the case of capital aggregation cannot happen. See Chapter 2, p. 54. Under some circumstances, including constant returns, some manifestations of the phenomenon are ruled out in the present case as well.
6. This should be remembered when interpreting necessary conditions. Conditions which are sufficient for aggregation in the sense of Definition 3.1 obviously also suffice for aggregation in any weaker sense.
7. Leontief [10, p. 364, Proposition I]. The proof is given in Leontief [9] and in the introduction to this volume, pp. xv–xvi.
8. Incidentally, it is shown in the course of the proof of Lemma 3.12 below that Lemma 3.1 and Assumption 3.2 together imply that if an aggregate exists, $R^{-1}(B^h)^{-1}\mu = c_h^* \mu$ for some scalars c_h^* $(h = 1, \ldots, n)$, so that the d_h in (3.16) can be ignored.
9. The homogeneity of the $g^i(\cdot, \ldots, \cdot)$ can also be shown by differentiating (3.29) with respect to K and using (3.11).
10. This form of the result was pointed out to me by W. M. Gorman.
11. Indeed, since the $\psi^v(\cdot)$ are all homogeneous of degree one, they differ by at most a multiplicative constant.
12. Cf. Remark 3.1.
13. This is in interesting contrast to the case of capital aggregation with more than one type of capital good employed by each firm. There the firm aggregates can be formed in different ways, but the combinations of the firm aggregates with labor to produce output must all be the same. See Theorem 2.10, p. 62.
14. Of course, this is just a description of (3.32); the actual production processes involved need not look like this.
15. The case of $L = 0$ can be handled by continuity.
16. Taking L as a column vector.
17. The parallel question for the capital aggregation problem was settled in [2] (Chapter 2) by the construction of a class of counter-examples to the proposition that only capital-altering change and capital-generalized

constant returns production functions allow capital aggregation. (The examples are given in equation (2.46), p. 44.) The obvious extensions of that class of examples to the present case (which might otherwise settle the present question by way of Theorem 3.1) turn out either to involve labor Hessians which are not negative definite or to be labor homothetic.

18. Much wider than the parallel class of capital-generalized constant returns production functions developed in [2] (Chapter 2). Any member of the latter class which permits labor aggregation when taken separately is labor homothetic, since it differs from a constant returns function only by a capital-altering change.
19. There is no difficulty about isolated points; they can be handled by continuity. The problems under discussion only arise when some labor assignments are identically zero for small variations in some capital.
20. This is obvious if it is the *h*th firm itself which has only some labors positively employed; however, it remains true even if such semipositive employment occurs in some other firm and not in the *h*th, because the reallocation of labor consequent on movements in $K(h)$ will take place through different sets of firms for different labor types.
21. Note that, in view of Assumption 3.2, at least one $d_v \not\equiv 0$ in any open neighborhood. Hence, if for all h for which the present problem arises $d_h \equiv 0$, then there is some h for which that problem does not arise and for which $d_h \not\equiv 0$. In that case all our previous analysis goes through unchanged.
22. See pp. 56–7.
23. Indeed, it suffices for the result that the production function be labor homothetic only in the labors actually assigned to it. This will be called "*r*-homotheticity" in the next section.
24. An alternative proof can be given by first assigning to one of two firms all labors assigned to both and then transferring labor to the second firm, keeping the ratios of different labor types constant. It is easy to see that if both production functions are labor homothetic and of the same family, it either pays to asign all labor to one of the firms or to assign some of every labor to both.
25. It is this which prevents the conditions for the existence of an *r*-aggregate from being strictly weaker than the conditions for the existence of a full aggregate despite our result that for labor-homothetic cases cross-firm aggregation is no harder for partial than for full aggregates.
26. An equivalent definition can be formulated along the lines of (3.38), but this is left to the reader.
27. Note, however, that there are *r*-homothetic production functions in the latter two classes which are not labor homothetic because they do not permit full labor aggregation.
28. Note that one production function may be constant returns and another labor homothetic, and so forth. For the case of every firm's production function either constant returns or capital-generalized constant returns, these results were first obtained by W. M. Gorman using another method.
29. We are taking K to be a scalar. To take $m > 1$ would merely complicate the notation.
30. The case of movable capitals is discussed in detail in Fisher [3] (Chapter 4).

31. In other words, if the Leontief conditions with respect to capital are satisfied for all labors, they are certainly satisfied for some of them.
32. On the other hand, note that Assumption 3.2 is not required for the sufficiency proof of Theorem 3.7 but that a much stronger version of that assumption is used in the necessity proof.
33. Since the distinction is really between mobile and immobile factors rather than between labor (output) and capital, then, as already mentioned, some types of capital may be included in the L_i. This means that one ought also to consider the aggregation of some of the L_i with the elements of K to obtain complete conditions for capital aggregation. I am indebted to E. Renshaw for the suggestion which is followed up in [3] (Chapter 4).
34. This is explored in Fisher [4] (Chapter 7).

References

[1] Diamond, P. A., "Technical change and the measurement of capital and output," *Review of Economic Studies*, **32** (1965), 289–98.

[2] Fisher, F. M., "Embodied technical change and the existence of an aggregate capital stock," *Review of Economic Studies*, **32** (1965), 263–88 (reprinted as Chapter 2).

[3] Fisher, F. M., "Embodied technology and the aggregation of fixed and movable capital goods," *Review of Economic Studies*, **35** (1968), 417–28 (reprinted as Chapter 4).

[4] Fisher, F. M., "Approximate aggregation and the Leontief conditions," *Econometrica*, **37** (1969), 457–69 (reprinted as Chapter 7).

[5] Gorman, W. M., "Capital aggregation in vintage models," in J. N. Wolfe (ed.), *Value, Capital, and Growth: Essays in Honour of Sir John Hicks*, Edinburgh: University of Edinburgh Press, 1968.

[6] Hall, R. E., "Technical change and capital from the point of view of the dual," *Review of Economic Studies*, **35** (1968), 35–46.

[7] Klein, L. R., "Macroeconomics and the theory of rational behaviour," *Econometrica*, **14** (1946), 93–108.

[8] Klein, L. R., "Remarks on the theory of aggregation," *Econometrica*, **14** (1946), 303–12.

[9] Leontief, W. W., "A note on the interrelation of subsets of independent variables of a continuous function with continuous first derivatives," *Bulletin of the American Mathematical Society*, **53** (1947), 343–50.

[10] Leontief, W. W., "Introduction to a theory of the internal structure of functional relationships," *Econometrica*, **15** (1947), 361–73.

[11] May, K. O., "The aggregation problem for a one-industry model," *Econometrica*, **14** (1946), 285–8.

[12] May, K. O., "Technological change and aggregation," *Econometrica*, **15** (1947), 51–63.

[13] Nataf, A., "Sur la possibilité de construction de certains macromodèles," *Econometrica*, **16** (1948), 232–44.

[14] Nataf, A., "Possibilités d'agrégation de fonctions de production à variables capital et main-d'oeuvre," *Review of Economic Studies*, **34** (1967), 219–26.

[15] Pu, Shou-Shan, "A note on macroeconomics," *Econometrica*, **14** (1946), 299–302.
[16] Stigum, B. P., "On certain problems of aggregation," *International Economic Review*, **8** (1967), 349–67.
[17] Stigum, B. P., "On a property of concave functions," *Review of Economic Studies*, **35** (1968), 413–16.
[18] Whitaker, J. K., "Vintage capital models and econometric production functions," *Review of Economic Studies*, **33** (1966), 1–18.
[19] Whitaker, J. K., "Capital aggregation and optimality conditions," *Review of Economic Studies*, **35** (1968), 429–42.

4

Embodied technology and the aggregation of fixed and movable capital goods (1968)

4.1 Introduction

In [2] (Chapter 2 of this book), I examined the question of the existence of aggregate production functions with economy-wide capital aggregates in a model in which capitals of different types are specialized to different firms – "bolted down" – while various types of labor are shifted about so as to secure efficient production. At least for constant returns technologies and some generalizations thereof, the necessary and sufficient conditions for capital aggregation were found to be quite restrictive, being essentially that firm production functions could differ by no more than a generalized form of capital-augmenting technical change.[1] In [3] (Chapter 3 of this book), for the same model, I then considered the aggregation of labor and of output and found that for similar technologies, the conditions while still quite restrictive were rather less so than in the capital case. (The principal result for labor aggregation was that the same set of relative wages must cause the proportions in which different labor types are employed to be the same for all firms. For output aggregation, the same set of relative prices must lead each firm to produce all outputs in the same proportion as do all other firms.)

The results of these two papers, however, do not exhaust the analysis of the existence of aggregate production functions with aggregate factors for the sort of model considered. This is so because

This paper was supported by National Science Foundation grant GS-95 to the Massachusetts Institute of Technology.

in both papers the distinction between fixed and movable factors of production is taken precisely to correspond to the distinction between capitals and labors (or outputs). Yet, in the middle to long run, some types of capital may be shifted (either literally or through depreciation and investment) so as to secure efficient production. The construction of an aggregate of such movable capitals alone comes formally under the problems considered in Chapter 3, but the aggregation of such movable capitals *together with* fixed capitals remains to be considered.[2] Such consideration is the task of the present paper.

The problem is of obvious importance. One wants to know when it is appropriate to talk of an aggregate capital stock. The results of Chapter 2 settle this question when all capitals are fixed; the results of Chapters 2 and 3 together give the conditions under which a fixed capital aggregate and a movable capital aggregate can be separately formed; the conditions for the construction of a total capital aggregate when some components are fixed and some are movable must also be examined.

Further, this is not just a matter of completeness. In constant returns and related technologies, the conditions for aggregation of fixed capital are, as remarked above, rather more stringent than the conditions for the aggregation of movable factors. As will be made clear below, since one can always forget about the movability of movable capitals, the conditions for aggregating fixed and movable capitals together can be no stronger than those involved if all capitals are fixed; if they turn out to be weaker, the use of total capital aggregates will be justified in wider circumstances if just some of the capitals are not fixed. The force of the results as to fixed capitals could then be avoided in many instances.

Unfortunately, such hope turns out to be illusory. We shall show that for constant returns (and some related technologies) the aggregation of fixed and movable capitals together involves precisely the same conditions (generalized capital augmentation) as would be involved if all capitals were fixed. While movability of some capitals does make easier the construction of separate aggregates for different capital types, the construction of a total capital aggregate remains as difficult as ever.

4.2 The model and assumptions

There are n firms. The νth firm has a vector of fixed capitals, denoted $K(\nu)$, which has m components. There are r types of movable capital, and the total (positive) amounts of such capitals in the economy are denoted by $E_1, \ldots, E_r$. E denotes the r-component column vector of the E_j. The amounts of the various movable capitals assigned to the νth firm are given by the column vector $E(\nu)$ with elements $E_1(\nu), \ldots, E_r(\nu)$. Similarly, there are s types of labor; the total amounts of such labors in the economy are denoted by $L_1, \ldots, L_s$; L denotes the column vector of the L_j. The amounts of the various labors employed by the νth firm are denoted by a column vector $L(\nu)$ with elements $L_1(\nu), \ldots, L_s(\nu)$. For some purposes, it will be convenient to use a common notation for all movable factors – capitals and labors – so we let X denote the $(r+s)$-component column vector of the E_i and L_j, and $X(\nu)$ denote the $(r+s)$-component column vector of the $E_i(\nu)$ and $L_j(\nu)$.

For present purposes, we shall assume that only one homogeneous output is produced, the same for all firms; considering more than one output would merely complicate the notation. The output of the νth firm is denoted by $Y(\nu)$ and total output for all firms by Y. Thus:

$$\sum_{\nu=1}^{n} E(\nu) \leqq E; \quad \sum_{\nu=1}^{n} L(\nu) \leqq L; \quad \sum_{\nu=1}^{n} Y(\nu) \equiv Y.^3 \qquad (4.1)$$

We shall assume that all movable capitals and all labors are productive in some use, so that the weak inequalities of (4.1) can be taken to be equalities.

Technology is embodied in the fixed capitals, so the production functions of the individual firms are (in general) all different. The production function of the νth firm is given by:

$$Y(\nu) = f^{\nu}(K(\nu), E(\nu), L(\nu)) \quad (\nu = 1, \ldots, n). \qquad (4.2)$$

These production functions are assumed continuously twice differentiable[4] with nonnegative marginal products. The Hessian of $f^{\nu}(\cdot,\cdot,\cdot)$ with respect to the elements of $X(\nu)$ is denoted by B^{ν}. Thus a typical element of B^{ν} is $f^{\nu}_{X_i X_j}$ $(i, j = 1, \ldots, r+s;\ \nu = 1, \ldots, n)$, where the subscripts denote diffentiation in the obvious way. The B^{ν} are assumed negative definite, so there is diminishing marginal productivity of any linear combination of movable factors.[5]

Efficiency for the economy requires that all movable factors be allocated so as to maximize Y subject to (4.1). Denote the value of Y when so maximized by Y^*, and observe that Y^* can be written as:

$$Y^* = G(K(1), \ldots, K(n), E, L). \qquad (4.3)$$

We seek conditions under which there exists a scalar capital aggregate, J, such that:

$$J = J(K(1), \ldots, K(n), E) \qquad (4.4)$$

and (4.3) can be rewritten as:

$$Y^* = H(J, L). \tag{4.5}$$

For the case $E = 0$, these conditions were developed in Chapter 2. They are also the conditions for the existence of an aggregate including only fixed capitals but leaving out movable capitals. The condition for the existence of an aggregate including only movable capitals and leaving out fixed capitals can be read out of the results of Chapter 3.

Now, it is possible that a capital aggregate exists for each firm separately and yet fails to exist for the economy as a whole. This can occur because the effects of changing the elements of L on the marginal products of the different capital types involve rearrangement of the allocation of the movable factors. The problem considered in this paper is precisely that of the existence of aggregate capital in such circumstances.

On the other hand, if the elements of E are to be included in J, it is *possible* that an aggregate exists for the economy as a whole but fails to exist for some individual firm or subset of firms.[6] Such a possibility comes about because the direct effects on the marginal rate of substitution among capitals of an increase in a particular element of $L(v)$ are not all that is involved when some element of L is changed and movable factors reallocated. That possibility, if it exists, is basically only a *curiosum*, however, for the possibility of aggregation then depends crucially on the number of firms as well as on the nature of the production functions (4.2). It is an odd sort of aggregation which ceases to be possible if some firm is swallowed up by an earthquake. We shall therefore not be interested in this possibility and shall agree on:

Definition 4.1: For any aggregation problem considered, aggregation will be said to be possible if and only if the appropriate aggregate exists both for all firms considered together *and* for any subset of firms considered in isolation.[7]

Since we shall concentrate on the inter-firm aggregation problem, this prompts us to assume (as a necessary condition for aggregation in the above sense):

Assumption 4.1: A capital aggregate can be formed for each firm, considered in isolation. In other words, there exist scalar capital aggregates, $J(1), \ldots, J(n)$, such that:

$$J(v) = J^v(K(v), E(v)) \quad (v = 1, \ldots, n) \tag{4.6}$$

and (4.2) can be rewritten in the form:

$$f^{v}(K(v), E(v), L(v)) = F^{v}(J(v), L(v)) \quad (v = 1, \ldots, n). \quad (4.7)$$

As already remarked, this is not a sufficient condition for the existence of an economy-wide capital aggregate.

4.3 The Leontief conditions

By a well-known theorem of Leontief,[8] necessary and sufficient conditions for the existence of the capital aggregate, $J(\cdot, \ldots, \cdot, \cdot)$, of (4.4) are that the marginal rate of substitution between any two capitals in the production of Y^* be independent of the elements of L. In this section, we work out what such conditions come to in the present model and notation.

We begin with the first-order conditions for the maximization problem involved in the allocation of movable factors. Let f_X^v be the $(r+s)$-component column vector of the marginal products of the movable factors in the vth firm's production function. The first-order conditions for efficiency are:

$$f_X^v \leqq \mu \qquad (v = 1, \ldots, n); \qquad (4.8)$$

$$X(v)'(f_X^v - \mu) = 0 \qquad (v = 1, \ldots, n); \qquad (4.9)$$

$$\sum_{v=1}^{n} X(v) = X, \qquad (4.10)$$

where μ is an $(r+s)$-component column vector of Lagrange multipliers which may be taken as the shadow prices of the movable factors. For convenience, we shall assume that every movable factor is employed by every firm in positive amount, so that (4.8) holds as an equality. We shall discuss the removal of this restriction in a later section.

Now, the marginal products of the movable capitals are themselves the first r elements of μ. To determine the effect of changing the elements of L on those marginal products, it is convenient to define $\partial\mu/\partial X$ as the $(r+s)\times(r+s)$ matrix with $\partial\mu_i/\partial X_j$ the element in the ith row and jth column. Differentiating (4.8) and (4.10) totally with respect to the elements of X and solving yields:

$$\partial\mu/\partial X = R^{-1}, \qquad (4.11)$$

where

$$R \equiv \sum_{v=1}^{n} (B^v)^{-1}. \qquad (4.12)$$

Next, denote by f_K^v the m-component vector of the marginal products of the fixed capitals in the production function of the vth firm. It is not hard to show that this is also the vector of the marginal products of the elements of $K(v)$ in the production of Y^*.[9] Denote by f_{KX}^v the $m \times (r+s)$ matrix with element in ith row and jth column $\partial f_{K_i}^v / \partial X_j(v)$. Denote by $\partial f_K^v / \partial X$ the $m \times (r+s)$ matrix with element in ith row and jth column $\partial f_{K_i}^v / \partial X_j$. (Note that whereas f_{KX}^v involves only the production of $Y(v)$, $\partial f_K^v / \partial X$ involves the production of Y^*.)

To evaluate $\partial f_K^v / \partial X$ requires evaluating the derivatives of the elements of $X(v)$ with respect to the elements of X. As before, this is done by differentiating (4.8) and (4.10) totally with respect to the elements of X and solving.[10] Using the result, one obtains:

$$\partial f_K^v / \partial X = f_{KX}^v (B^v)^{-1} R^{-1} \quad (v = 1, \ldots, n). \tag{4.13}$$

For the Leontief conditions, we are interested in the last s columns of the matrices in (4.12) and (4.13), and, in the case of (4.12), we are interested in the first r rows. Define:

$$P = [I \ 0]; \quad Q = \begin{bmatrix} 0 \\ I \end{bmatrix}, \tag{4.14}$$

where P is $r \times (r+s)$ and Q is $(r+s) \times s$. Since marginal rates of substitution will be unaffected if and only if marginal products change proportionally, we may state the Leontief conditions for the present problem as:

Lemma 4.1: A necessary and sufficient condition for the existence of a total capital aggregate for all firms taken together[11] is that there exist an s-component column vector, say λ, independent of v, such that:

$$PR^{-1}Q = P\mu\lambda', \tag{4.15}$$

and

$$f_{KX}^v (B^v)^{-1} R^{-1} Q = f_K^v \lambda' \quad (v = 1, \ldots, n).^{12} \tag{4.16}$$

4.4 Constant returns

We now specialize the class of technologies considered and assume that the firm production functions $f^v(\cdot,\cdot,\cdot)$ are all homogeneous of degree one in their arguments so that constant returns prevails throughout.

Now, when no movable capitals are involved, it was proved in Theorem 2.10, p. 62 that if all firms have constant returns production functions, capital aggregation is possible if and only if all the $F^{\nu}(\cdot,\cdot)$ of (4.7) can be taken to be the same. Thus, in that case, the only differences in technology consistent with capital aggregation are what were called in Chapter 2 "capital-altering" changes, that is, changes in the way in which the individual firm capital indices $J(\nu)$ are made up from their underlying components. In the simplest case, this leads to capital-augmenting technical differences as the only kind permitted.[13]

We shall show that these same conditions are also necessary and sufficient even if there are movable capitals to be included in the aggregate, so that the formation of the total capital aggregate in constant returns technologies is no easier if some of the capitals are movable than if all are fixed.[14]

Theorem 4.1: If all production functions are constant returns, a necessary and sufficient condition for the existence of an aggregate capital stock is that all functions $F^{\nu}(\cdot,\cdot)$ of (4.7) can be taken to be the same ($\nu = 1, \ldots, n$).

Proof:

(a) Sufficiency: To begin, observe that sufficiency is obvious from the following considerations. Suppose for a moment that all elements of $E(\nu)$ were not movable but were fixed ($\nu = 1, \ldots, n$). If all $F^{\nu}(\cdot,\cdot)$ can be chosen to be the same, then we know from Chapter 2 that a total capital aggregate exists and exists no matter what the fixed values of the elements of the $E(\nu)$. In particular, such an aggregate exists if the elements of the $E(\nu)$ happen to be such as to satisfy (4.8) and (4.10).

In other words, we know that if all $F^{\nu}(\cdot,\cdot)$ are the same, then a capital aggregate exists for all points restricted only to make the marginal products of the different types of labor the same in all uses. In the present problem, we are concerned with a proper subset of such points, namely, points at which the marginal products not only of the different types of labor but also of the different types of movable capital are the same in all uses. Clearly an aggregate exists for the more heavily restricted set of points if it does for the less restricted set.

On the other hand, it is not obvious that the additional restrictions make no difference to the necessity of the stated conditions, and this we shall now prove.

(b) Necessity: Since each production function is homogeneous of degree one, each marginal product is homogeneous of degree zero.

Applying Euler's theorem to the marginal products of the movable factors thus yields:

$$K(v)' f^v_{KX} + X(v)' B^v = 0 \quad (v = 1, \ldots, n). \tag{4.17}$$

Premultiplying (4.16) by $K(v)'$ and using (4.17), we obtain:

$$-X(v)' R^{-1} Q = K(v)' f^v_K \lambda' \quad (v = 1, \ldots, n). \tag{4.18}$$

Now consider (4.15). It is a set of equations involving the first r rows and last s columns of R^{-1}. Those equations state that the first r elements of each of those columns are proportional to the corresponding elements of μ. We may state this differently, however, by stating that each such column is entirely proportional to μ, save for terms involving the last s elements. Thus, an equivalent statement to (4.15) is that there exists an $s \times s$ matrix, say S, such that:

$$R^{-1} Q = \mu \lambda' - QS. \tag{4.19}$$

Substituting in (4.18) and rearranging terms, we obtain:

$$X(v)' QS = (K(v)' f^v_K + X(v)' \mu) \lambda' = f^v \lambda' \quad (v = 1, \ldots, n), \tag{4.20}$$

where the second equality follows from (4.8) and another application of Euler's theorem.

We now show that S must be nonsingular. Suppose not. Then there would exist an s-component column vector, say q, such that $q \neq 0$ and $Sq = 0$. It would then follow from (4.20) and the fact that $f^v \neq 0$ that $\lambda' q = 0$. Postmultiplying (4.19) by q, we would then have $R^{-1} Qq = 0$, and it is easy to see that this implies $q = 0$, contrary to assumption. Hence S is nonsingular.

Postmultiply (4.20) by S^{-1} and divide through by f^v, obtaining:

$$\frac{L(v)'}{f^v} = \frac{X(v)' Q}{f^v} = \lambda' S^{-1} \quad (v = 1, \ldots, n), \tag{4.21}$$

the first equality following from the definition of Q. Since the left-hand side of each equation of (4.21) can be inverted and the right-hand side is independent of v, we have now shown:

Lemma 4.2: If all production functions are constant returns, a necesary condition for total capital aggregation is that the average product of every kind of labor be the same in every firm whenever all movable factors (labors and movable capitals) are optimally allocated.

This can be rephrased as:

Lemma 4.2′: If all production functions are constant returns, a necessary condition for total capital aggregation is that there exist functions $\phi^1(\cdot,\cdot), \ldots, \phi^s(\cdot,\cdot)$, independent of v, such that:

$$\frac{f^v}{L_j(v)} = \phi^j(f_E^v, f_L^v) \quad (j = 1, \ldots, s;\ v = 1, \ldots, n), \qquad (4.22)$$

where f_E^v and f_L^v are the vectors of marginal products of movable capitals and labors, respectively.

Now, rewrite (4.22), using (4.7), to obtain:

$$\frac{F^v}{L_j(v)} = \phi^j(F_J^v J_E^v, F_L^v) \quad (j = 1, \ldots, s;\ v = 1, \ldots, n) \quad (4.23)$$

where J_E^v is the r-component column vector of the partial derivatives of $J(v)$ with respect to the elements of $E(v)$.

Since $F^v(\cdot,\cdot)$ can clearly be taken to be constant returns, however, the left-hand side of (4.23) (the average products of the labors) is entirely determined by the s ratios:

$$L_1(v)/J(v), \ldots, L_s(v)/J(v).$$

On the other hand, by the negative definiteness of B^v, those ratios are uniquely determined by the elements of F_L^v. It follows that the first (vector) argument of the $\phi^j(\cdot,\cdot)$ is irrelevant so that we may rewrite Lemma 4.2′ as involving the existence of functions, $g^1(\cdot), \ldots, g^s(\cdot)$, independent of v, such that:

$$\frac{F^v}{L_j(v)} = g^j(F_L^v) \quad (j = 1, \ldots, s;\ v = 1, \ldots, n). \qquad (4.24)$$

Consider now each $F^v(\cdot,\cdot)$ as a function of a single capital, $J(v)$, and a vector of labors, $L(v)$. It is fairly plausible that if a total aggregate exists in the original capitals, $K(v)$ and $E(v)$, over all firms, then it is also possible to aggregate the $J(v)$ over all firms. That this is indeed the case can be seen by recognizing that by Theorem 2.8′, p. 58, (4.24) is a necessary *and* sufficient condition for such aggregation. It was shown in pp. 57–62, however, that (in the present notation) the existence of an aggregate in the $J(v)$ together with constant returns and equations (4.24) implies that the $F^v(\cdot,\cdot)$ can differ by at most a parameter entering as a $J(v)$-augmenting technical change, which difference can then be absorbed into the definition of the $J(v)$. This completes the proof of our theorem.[15]

Some remarks on the theorem and the proof now follow.

1. One way of looking at the result is along the lines indicated in the last paragraph of the proof. Once the $J(v)$ have been formed, it turns out that one might just as well consider them as the original capital goods. The fact that involved in the $J(v)$ are movable capitals which are optimally allocated does not matter once those capitals have been amalgamated with the fixed capitals which are not so allocated.

   This is of course the true state of affairs; on the other hand, one must prove that the optimal allocation of the movable capitals is indeed irrelevant to the problem. In the present constant returns case, that occurs in the above proof when it is shown that the $\phi^j(\cdot,\cdot)$ of (4.22) and (4.23) depend only on the (common) marginal products of labor and not on the marginal products of the movable capitals. In more general technologies, it does not appear to be generally true that the optimal allocation of the movable capitals is irrelevant to the problem; we shall have a bit more to say on this in the next section.[16]
2. There is an apparent exception to the theorem (which is of course ruled out by our assumptions). This is the case in which every firm's production function is already additively separable in capitals and labors, i.e., in which for all $v = 1, \ldots, n, f^v(\cdot,\cdot,\cdot)$ can be written as:

$$f^v(K(v), E(v)), L(v)) \equiv J^v(K(v), E(v)) + M^v(L(v)). \qquad (4.25)$$

   In this case, a total capital aggregate (the sum of the $J(v)$) obviously exists whether or not any factor is optimally allocated and whether or not there are constant returns.[17]

   This entirely separable case is, of course, not of much interest. It is not hard to see that it is ruled out for constant returns technologies by our assumption that the B^v are all negative definite.
3. While it is true that Theorem 4.1 states that total capital aggregation is made neither easier nor harder by the assumption that some (but not all) capitals are movable, it is important to note that this is not true of the construction of partial capital aggregates, that is, aggregates containing the fixed capitals alone or the movable capitals alone. Here the assumption that some capitals are movable makes a great deal of difference.

To see this, consider first the case in which there is exactly one type of movable capital ($r = 1$). Here it is trivial that an aggregate of movable capitals exists whatever the technologies of the individual firms. This would not be so if the type of capital involved were fixed.

To continue with rather less obvious examples, consider the problem of aggregating more than one movable capital but with no fixed capitals included in the aggregate. The conditions for doing this are different in two respects from those which would be involved were the capitals in question fixed. First, for constant returns (and certain other technologies[18]) the conditions in the movable capital case state that the same relative wages for the capitals in question must lead all firms to employ them in the same proportions, whereas in the fixed capital case what is involved is the solution to a set of partial differential equations, leading (generally) to a different set of conditions, if a solution exists.[19] Second, and more important, if a partial aggregate is to be formed when all capitals are fixed, a condition is involved which plays no role whatsoever if the capitals to be aggregated are movable; that condition has the property that if it is not satisfied by a particular firm's production function, then no such partial aggregate exists which includes that firm regardless of what other firm's production functions look like.[20] No similarly strong condition is involved if movable capitals are to be separately aggregated.

Finally, similar remarks apply if fixed capitals are to be separately aggregated or aggregated with some but not all movable capitals. If some or all of the remaining capitals are fixed, the strong condition just referred to is involved; if the remaining capitals are movable, it is not. Moreover, for constant returns (and some related technologies), if a fixed capital aggregate exists for the entire economy and a movable capital aggregate exists for each firm separately, then a movable capital aggregate also exists for the entire economy.[21] A similar property holds for the construction of any aggregate involving only some of the movable capitals.

Thus the assumption of partial movability makes a very large difference to the construction of partial aggregates. Indeed, it is wrong to interpret Theorem 4.1 as stating that for constant returns fixed capital aggregation is made no easier by the assumption that some capitals are movable. Aggregation over a given set of fixed capitals is made far easier if the *remaining* capitals are movable; Theorem 4.1 tells us that aggregation over the set of fixed capitals is not made easier if some but not all of the capitals *in that set* are assumed movable.

4.5 Capital-generalized constant returns

The question naturally arises as to the conditions for aggregation when constant returns is not assumed. Here results are much harder to obtain.

In Chapter 2, I introduced a class of production functions which I termed "capital-generalized constant returns" (CGCR). This class, in the present notation, and for present purposes, is the class for which the $F^v(\cdot,\cdot)$ of (4.7) can be taken as homogeneous of degree one, even though the original production functions, $f^v(\cdot,\cdot,\cdot)$ are not. In other words, the nonconstant returns can be concentrated, so to speak, in the $J(v)$. Apart from the assumption (expressed in (4.6) and (4.7)) that a capital aggregate exists for each firm, a production function in the CGCR class can be thought of as one which can be made constant returns by suitable redefinitions of the way in which the different capitals are measured.[22]

In the case in which all capitals are fixed, it was shown in Chapter 2 that, if all firm production functions are CGCR, it is still true that necessary and sufficient conditions for the existence of a total capital aggregate are essentially the same as in the constant returns case, namely, that all $F^v(\cdot,\cdot)$ can be chosen to be the same and that differences in technology be capable of absorption in the definition of the $J^v(\cdot,\cdot)$. It is easy to see that this must be the case, since it obviously can make no difference in the fixed capital case whether we have constant returns to begin with or whether we redefine the capital goods and then have constant returns. For purposes of this problem, the definitions and measurements of the capital goods are arbitrary anyway.

In the present case, in which some but not all capitals are movable, the situation is rather different, however. What is true of total capital aggregation in CGCR technologies is the following:

Corollary 4.1: If all firm production functions are CGCR a *sufficient* condition for total capital aggregation is that all the $F^v(\cdot,\cdot)$ of (4.7) can be chosen to be the same.

***Proof*:** This is obvious since conditions which are sufficient when only the labors are optimally allocated remain sufficient if some of the capitals are also optimally allocated.

Suppose now that there exists a (possibly vector-valued) function, $H(v) = H^v(K(v))$, such that:

$$f^v(K(v), E(v), L(v)) = F^v(J(v), L(v)) \tag{4.26}$$

and

$$J(v) = J^v(H(v), E(v)) \tag{4.27}$$

and that $J^v(\cdot,\cdot)$ and $F^v(\cdot,\cdot)$ can *both* be taken to be homogeneous of degree one in their respective arguments. In other words, suppose that the vth firm's production function can be made constant returns by redefinitions of the *fixed capital axes only*. Then $f^v(\cdot,\cdot,\cdot)$ is clearly CGCR, but a special sort of CGCR, which we may term "fixed-capital-generalized constant returns" (FCGCR).

Examples can be readily generated by taking any constant returns production function and transforming the fixed capital arguments. One such function is the three-factor, generalized Cobb–Douglas (with all arguments scalars): $AK(v)^{\alpha}E(v)^{\beta}L(v)^{\gamma}$, since, defining:

$$H(v) \equiv \{K(v)\}^{\alpha/(1-\beta-\gamma)}, \tag{4.28}$$

we have:

$$AK(v)^{\alpha}E(v)^{\beta}L(v)^{\gamma} = AH(v)^{1-\beta-\gamma}E(v)^{\beta}L(v)^{\gamma}. \tag{4.29}$$

For the special FCGCR case, it is easy to show:

Corollary 4.2: If all firm production functions are FCGCR, then a *necessary* as well as sufficient condition for total capital aggregation is that all the $F^v(\cdot,\cdot)$ of (4.7) can be chosen to be the same.

***Proof*:** It obviously makes no difference to the proof of Theorem 4.1 whether $K(v)$ or $H(v)$ is considered as the vector of fixed capitals.

Thus, for purposes of generalization of Theorem 4.1, redefinition of the *fixed* capitals makes no difference. This is apparently *not* true of redefinition of the movable capitals, and the condition of that theorem is apparently not implied by the existence of a full capital aggregate in CGCR technologies which involve such redefinitions.[23] This is a place in which the assumption of partial movability appears to make a difference.

This difference is not too surprising. Redefinition of the fixed capitals does not matter precisely because those capitals *are* fixed. The elements of the different $K(v)$ are arbitrary (nonnegative) numbers and we require aggregation to be possible whatever those numbers happen to be and whatever their relation to each other. Movable capitals, on the other hand, are a different story. They are allocated subject to (4.1) so as to make their marginal products the same in every use. If we redefine such movable capitals, however, it will not generally be true that the same conditions govern the allocation of the redefined capitals as govern the allocation of the original ones. Thus, it will not be generally true that the redefined capitals adding up to their particular totals have the same marginal product in every use. Hence such redefinition is not trivial; it changes the problem in a substantive way.

4.6 The role of the positive assignment of movable factors

In this concluding section, we remove the restriction that every firm always employs all movable factors in positive amounts. Some of our discussion will bear on the case in which all capitals are fixed as well as on the present case. It will be convenient (and also sufficient) to discuss the case in which there are just two firms, and we shall restrict our attention to constant returns technologies.

To begin, suppose that both firms employ all labors in positive amount, but that they do not both so employ all movable capitals. Clearly, movable capitals not employed by either firm make no difference to the problem, so we may concentrate on movable capitals employed by one firm and not by the other. Such movable capitals do not have the same marginal products in the two uses, and (4.8) fails to hold as an equality.[24]

It is easy to see what is involved in this case. The crucial characteristic of movable capitals which we have used in this paper is that their marginal products are equalized. If this is not so, then we may just as well consider them as fixed capitals. This means that a movable capital employed by one of the firms and not by another may just as well be treated as a fixed capital. Since our analysis of the constant returns case showed that it makes no difference for total capital aggregation whether or not some (but not all) capitals are movable, we conclude that for that case it also makes no difference whether or not all movable capitals are employed in positive amounts by all firms. In the more general case, any aid to aggregation given by the assumption that a particular capital is movable ceases when that capital is not positively employed by both firms.

We now turn to the question of the positive employment of labors. Consider first the sufficiency part of Theorem 4.1. If all the $F^{v}(\cdot,\cdot)$ can be chosen to be the same, it is easy to see that optimal allocation of labor *implies* that all labors are employed by all firms in positive amount.

Necessity is not so straightforward. Obviously, since it is necessary that an aggregate exist over any subset of firms (recall Definition 4.1), the condition of Theorem 4.1 applies to any subset such that the set of labors positively employed is the same for all firms in the subset.[25] Further, that condition is necessary over any range in which firms employ the same labors. Nevertheless, there remains the case in which the set of labors positively employed by one firm is not the same as the set positively employed by another.

The first thing to notice about this case is that the condition of Theorem 4.1 must still be involved as a limiting condition. Thus, the functions obtained from the $F^{\nu}(\cdot,\cdot)$ by setting equal to zero all labors not positively employed by both firms must be capable of being chosen the same.

Beyond this it is rather hard to obtain closed-form results. As before, the distinction between fixed and movable factors in our analysis is precisely the equalization of the marginal products of the latter. Thus labors employed by one of two firms and not by the other are no different from fixed capitals, save that they are not to be included in the capital aggregate.

The conditions for leaving a fixed capital out of the aggregate were given on pp. 47–57 for the case in which all capitals are fixed; we have referred to them above. In the present case, similarly strong conditions are involved and there seems no point in going into them in detail. It will suffice to say two things about them in the present context.

First, the amount of some labor employed by one firm and not by another may as well be considered as a parameter of that firm's production function when dealing with the Leontief conditions relative to the labors employed by both. This means that those conditions (essentially (4.15) and (4.16) with appropriate notational changes) must hold for all values of such labor employment. Even if the firm's production function was homogeneous of degree one in all employed factors it will not generally be so in the factors other than the special labor type in question, so it will not be possible to solve the Leontief conditions with respect to the labors employed in common as was done in the proof of Theorem 4.1. Indeed, those conditions can perfectly well fail to be satisfied for a given firm no matter what the other firm's technology looks like.[26]

A similar statement holds even more forcefully when dealing with the Leontief conditions relative to the labor type in question itself. Here the existence of a total capital aggregate requires that the production function of the firm which employs that labor satisfy a special condition ensuring that the direct effects of an increase in the amount of the labor in question on the marginal product of fixed capital be exactly offset by the indirect effects of the reallocation of the other movable factors.[27] Such conditions are very strong.

Thus, it is clearly most unlikely that the nonemployment of a particular labor type by a particular firm and hence the nonequalization of that labor type's marginal products makes total capital aggregation any easier. Closed-form results for this particular aspect of the problem are very hard to come by, however.

Notes

1. Other papers in this area are Diamond [1], Gorman [4], Hall [5], Nataf [9], Stigum [10], [11], and Whitaker [12] and [13].
2. I am indebted to E. Renshaw for pointing this out to me. Some forms of human capital can be immobile leading to somewhat similar problems.
3. We use the usual conventions for vector inequalities.
4. This assumption can doubtless be weakened. Cf. Stigum [10] and [11].
5. It would suffice to assume the f^v strictly concave in the elements of $X(v)$.
6. An example of this sort of phenomenon is given in Chapter 5, p. 133. A similar statement is true about aggregation involving movable factors only (see Chapter 3). In the case of aggregation involving only fixed factors, however, this sort of problem cannot arise and Assumption 4.1 emerges as a necessary condition for aggregation over all firms.
7. Note that what is involved here relates to necessary conditions for aggregation. Conditions which suffice for aggregation in the sense of Definition 4.1 also suffice for aggregation in any weaker sense.
8. Leontief [7, p. 364, Proposition I]. The proof is given in Leontief [6] and in the introduction to this volume, pp. xv–xvi.
9. The demonstration is given on p. 34. The reason that the point is not entirely trivial is that when $K(v)$ changes all movable factors are reallocated. In fact, (4.8) and (4.10) imply that the effect of such reallocation on Y^* is zero.
10. This is done in more detail on pp. 51–2.
11. Note that Definition 4.1 is not involved in this. That definition will begin to be involved when we make use of Assumption 4.1. Obviously, the conditions of the lemma can be generalized to give necessary and sufficient conditions for the existence of a total capital aggregate for any subset of firms.
12. If there are no movable capitals, (4.15) is vacuous and (4.16), as it should, becomes the condition for fixed capital aggregation, given Assumption 4.1. Cf. pp. 54–6.
13. It is interesting to note that in the case of aggregation of labor, considered in Chapter 3, the parallel theorem says just the opposite. In that case, there is no restriction on the $F^v(\cdot,\cdot)$, but the individual firm labor aggregates must be identical in form.
14. It is easier if *all* capitals are movable, but then the essence of the problem disappears.
15. See Chapter 5, pp. 136–7, Note 10.
16. Of course, as already observed, the only issue is as to necessary conditions. Conditions which suffice for aggregation whether or not movable capitals are optimally allocated certainly suffice when they are.
17. If there is no optimal allocation, this is the only case permitting capital aggregation. See Nataf [8].

18. What I have called "*r*-homothetic" technologies. See Chapter 3. The assumption that an aggregate exists for each firm separately is involved in both the fixed and the movable cases.
19. Note that a production function homogeneous of degree one in two types of capital and labor is not homogeneous of degree one in labor and one type of capital only.
20. The condition in question is discussed on pp. 47–57. It is worth noting that no production function (such as the multifactor Cobb–Douglas, for example) in which all factors are complements can ever satisfy that condition.
21. See [3] Theorem 3.7 and the ensuing discussion.
22. When there is only one capital for each firm, this involves a nonlinear stretching of the axis for that capital; when there is more than one, the redefinitions may involve combining different capitals (generally in a nonlinear way) to obtain a new set of axes on which "doses" of the new artificially constructed capitals are measured.
23. I use the word "apparently" because it is extremely difficult to find a counter-example. It is clear that the proof of necessity of Theorem 4.1 breaks down in such cases, however, the crucial place being in the use of Euler's theorem in (4.17).
24. Marginal products might just happen to be equalized even if one firm fails to employ some movable factor. In this case, our previous analysis would be unchanged. The present problem arises when marginal products are unequal; generally, this corresponds to a situation in which nonemployment of a movable factor by a firm persists over some range of the variables.
25. Labors not employed by any firm in the subset are simply irrelevant. Note that a function homogeneous of degree one in all its arguments is homogeneous of degree one in all its nonzero arguments when some arguments are identically zero.
26. It is possible to make some progress along these lines by writing all the Leontief conditions together using the notation employed in Section 3.8 for dealing with unemployed labors. This does allow one integration, but the sort of problem indicated in the text arises anyway when dealing with the set of partial differential equations parallel to (4.22). It does not seem worth going into this in any more detail.
27. See pp. 49–50. If there are no other movable factors, i.e., if the sets of labors (and movable capitals) employed by the two firms are disjoint, then capital aggregation requires each firm's production function to be additively separable into a function of capital and a function of labor.

References

[1] Diamond, P. A., "Technical change and the measurement of capital and output," *Review of Economic Studies*, **32** (1965), 289–98.
[2] Fisher, F. M., "Embodied technical change and the existence of an aggregate capital stock," *Review of Economic Studies*, **32** (1965), 263–88 (reprinted as Chapter 2).
[3] Fisher, F. M., "Embodied technology and the existence of labour and

output aggregates," *Review of Economic Studies*, **35** (1968), 391–412 (reprinted as Chapter 3).

[4] Gorman, W. M., "Capital aggregation in vintage models," in J. N. Wolfe (ed.), *Value, Capital and Growth: Essays in Honour of Sir John Hicks*, Edinburgh: University of Edinburgh Press, 1968.

[5] Hall, R. E., "Technical change and capital from the point of view of the dual," *Review of Economic Studies*, **35** (1968), 35–46.

[6] Leontief, W. W., "A note on the interrelation of subsets of independent variables of a continuous function with continuous first derivatives," *Bulletin of the American Mathematical Society*, **53** (1947), 343–50.

[7] Leontief, W. W. "Introduction to a theory of the internal structure of functional relationships," *Econometrica*, **15** (1947), 361–73.

[8] Nataf, A., "Sur la possibilité de construction de certains macromodèles", *Econometrica*, **16** (1948), 232–44.

[9] Nataf, A., "Possibilités d'agrégation de fonctions de production à variables capital et main d'oeuvre," *Review of Economic Studies*, **34** (1967), 219–26.

[10] Stigum, B. P., "On certain problems of aggregation", *International Economic Review*, **8** (1967), 349–67.

[11] Stigum, B. P., "On a property of concave functions", *Review of Economic Studies*, **35** (1968), 413–16.

[12] Whitaker, J. K., "Vintage capital models and econometric production functions," *Review of Economic Studies*, **33** (1966), 1–18.

[13] Whitaker, J. K., "Capital aggregation and optimality conditions," *Review of Economic Studies*, **35** (1968), 429–42.

5

Aggregate production functions revisited: The mobility of capital and the rigidity of thought (1982)

5.1 Introduction

In a series of papers some years ago,[1] I examined the question of the existence of aggregate production functions. I did so in the context of a model in which each firm's technology was embodied in its capital stock so that capital (of several types) was not physically homogeneous but rather specific to firms, while labor and output (each of which could be of several types) were assigned to firms so as to make the entire system produce efficiently. In such a model, the efficient production frontier is readily seen to depend on the amount of each capital type which each firm has and on the total amounts of each labor type and each output type for the system as a whole. The aggregation question was then that of the possibility of simplifying by aggregating over capital (for firms and types) or over labor types or over output types.

The necessary and sufficient conditions for such aggregation turned out to be very strong. Restricting attention to constant returns, they can be roughly summarized as follows. First, an aggregate of the desired kind must exist at the level of each firm. Second,[2] if capital is to be aggregated, firm production functions can differ by at most capital-augmenting technical changes, although the capital to be augmented can already be an otherwise unrestricted aggregate at the firm level. If labor or output is to be aggregated, on the other hand, the corresponding firm-level aggregates must all be the same, but the firm's production functions are not otherwise restricted.[3] In effect, to take output aggregation as an example, this means that every firm must produce the same market basket of outputs as every other firm, differing only as to scale, with the composition of the common basket depending on prices.

These conditions are surely very strong and unlikely to be fulfilled in practice. One question which arises, however, is the extent to which such strength really has to do with the assumption that capital is immobile and technology embodied in it. Surely many of the results depend on that assumption, but despite the impetus given to the analysis by the "Cambridge–Cambridge debate,"[4] it is not plain that all of them do. Indeed, as we shall see in this chapter, the results have at least as much to do with the fact that aggregation over individual productive units (firms) is involved as with the assumption that capital is fixed.

This chapter investigates this question and examines the aggregation issues which arise when all factors are mobile. Aside from the interest in this question which attaches to an investigation of just how much fixity of capital matters, there are some reasons for considering it on its own grounds. First, it may be considered that capital is mobile in the long run. This may be thought of (in the longest run) as the fungibility of capital funds;[5] in some shorter time period there are circumstances in which individual types of capital goods, not interchangeable among themselves, are nevertheless moved about among productive units to secure efficient production. We can think of such cases as brought about by efficient second-hand markets or by a central-planning authority. At a less grand level, we can think of a single firm managing several productive processes and efficiently allocating capital goods as well as other factors to them. The analysis below exhibits the conditions under which the resulting efficient production surface permits aggregation.

The results obtained are aesthetically rather pleasing. Aside from the obvious fact that mobility of capital goods guarantees the existence of an aggregate over firms for any *single* capital type (and thus eliminates the need for any other conditions such as capital augmentation), they are essentially as follows (for constant returns). The efficient production surface for two firms permits aggregation over some group of variables (outputs or factors) if and only if: (1) such an aggregate exists at the level of each firm separately; and (2) *either* the firm level aggregates are the same in both firms *or* the two firms' production functions differ by at most an "aggregate-augmenting" technical change.[6] Conditions for aggregation when many firms are involved can be built up from these results.

We thus see the role which fixity of capital plays (beyond preventing the aggregation over firms of a single capital type without special conditions). The mere fact that aggregation over firms is involved, whether or not capital is fixed, restricts aggregation possibilities to the two special cases just described. The effect of assuming capital is fixed is merely to go from a situation in which either special case suffices for aggregation for any group of factors or of outputs to a situation in which one special case applies to aggregation over all fixed factors and the other applies to aggregation over groups of variable factors or of outputs.[7] To put it differently, moving from a fixed to a mobile capital model does not really introduce new cases which permit aggregation; it merely makes the union of previously known cases applicable.

5.2 The model

Firms are indexed by $\nu = 1, \ldots, n$. Each firm has a production function given by:

$$Y(\nu) = f^{\nu}(X(\nu), L(\nu)). \tag{5.1}$$

This will be interpreted in more than one way. In the simplest interpretation, $Y(\nu)$ is a single output, homogeneous across firms, $X(\nu)$ is an r-vector of factors to be aggregated, and $L(\nu)$ an s-vector of other factors. $L(\nu)$ and $X(\nu)$ are allocated to firms so as to maximize $Y = \Sigma Y(\nu)$, subject to the constraints

$$\Sigma L(\nu) = L; \qquad \Sigma X(\nu) = X. \tag{5.2}$$

Calling the maximized value of output, Y^*, this makes Y^* a function of L and X, say $G(X, L)$. The question to be analyzed is that of when aggregation over the r factors in X are possible; i.e., when can we write:

$$Y^* = G(X, L) = H(\psi(X), L) \tag{5.3}$$

for some scalar-valued function, $\psi(\cdot)$?

On this interpretation, we can think of X as a vector of (mobile) capital of r different types and $\psi(X)$ as an aggregate capital index. Alternatively, we can think of X as made up of labor of all different types with $\psi(X)$ a total labor index (and L, despite the mnemonic abbreviation) as capital. Next, X can be some, but not all, types of labor with L all remaining factors and $\psi(X)$ an aggregate such as "skilled labor" and so on.

Further, it is easy to see that the analysis is not in fact restricted to only a single output. For some purposes, where firms produce different outputs, we can think of $Y(\nu)$ as dollars' worth of output at fixed prices so that total revenue is maximized. This locates points on the production possibility frontier. Where firms produce more than one output, we can interpret some elements of L as being outputs alternative to those involved in Y.

A second class of interpretations involve output aggregation. Here, $f^v(\cdot,\cdot)$ must be interpreted as a factor-requirements function, rather than as a production function, with $Y(v)$ the amount of the factor demanded given the amount of the other factors, $L(v)$, and the outputs to be produced, $X(v)$. Outputs and other factors are now assigned to firms to *minimize* total use of Y. Aggregation over X now becomes output aggregation. If some outputs are counted in L rather than in X, such aggregation is over certain categories of output and so forth.

To fix ideas, I shall discuss the proofs and give the theorems in terms of aggregation over a set of factors, with (1) a production function, remarking on the other interpretations from time to time. In addition, to simplify matters, I shall take $r = 2$ and $s = 1$ so that (5.1) becomes

$$Y(v) = f^v(X_1(v), X_2(v), L(v)) \tag{5.4}$$

and aggregation is over the two elements of X. Greater generality in this regard only makes the proofs notationally more complex without changing them in any substantive way. I discuss such generalization below.

I assume each of the $f^v(\cdot,\cdot,\cdot)$ twice continuously differentiable; subscripts denote differentiation in the obvious way. The $f^v(\cdot,\cdot,\cdot)$ are assumed nondecreasing and quasiconcave in their arguments and every factor is assumed productive in at least one use.

Now, it is possible for (5.3) to hold and aggregation over X to be possible without it being the case that aggregation is possible over X within each firm.[8] This is because changes in L, even if they altered the marginal rate of substitution between $X_1(v)$ and $X_2(v)$ within each firm with $X_1(v)$ and $X_2(v)$ fixed, might just happen to leave that marginal rate of substitution unaffected in the system as a whole through their effects on the reassignment of factors. An example is given below. However, it is uninteresting to have an aggregate which can be formed over the entire set of firms unless it can be formed over every subset, since the disappearance of one or more firms would destroy the possibility of aggregation. Hence, throughout this paper I use the following strong definition of aggregation:

DEFINITION 5.1: An aggregate over X will be said to exist if and only if an expression in the form (5.3) exists both for the entire set of firms and for every proper subset.

In other words, aggregation must be possible over every subset of firms. It follows that we must assume the equivalent of (5.3) at the firm level to get anywhere at all, and I now do so.

Assumption 5.1: Each firm's production function can be written in the form:

$$f^{\nu}(X(\nu), L(\nu)) = F^{\nu}(\phi^{\nu}(X(\nu)), L(\nu)) \tag{5.5}$$

where $\phi^{\nu}(\cdot)$ is scalar valued.

Remark 5.1: Since we have assumed constant returns, both $F^{\nu}(\cdot,\cdot)$ and $\phi^{\nu}(\cdot)$ can be taken to be homogeneous of degree one in their respective arguments.

Of course the restriction in Assumption 5.1 is already very strong.

Now there is one case in which aggregation over X is trivial. This is the case in which, for *every* $\nu = 1, \ldots, n$, $F^{\nu}(\cdot,\cdot)$ is additively separable in its two arguments. (Indeed, under constant returns, this would make all the $F^{\nu}(\cdot,\cdot)$ linear.) Note that aggregation would be possible under these conditions whether or not all factors were mobile (Nataf [9]). It is convenient to deal with this not very interesting case, which I shall call the "Nataf case," by assuming it absent, since we have now said all there is to say about it.

Assumption 5.2: At all points of interest there exists at least one $F^{\nu}(\cdot,\cdot)$ which is not additively separable ($\nu = 1, \ldots, n$).

Note that there is no reason to assume that *no* $F^{\nu}(\cdot,\cdot)$ is additively separable. In particular, such additive separability holds trivially if $L(\nu) = 0$.

Now, the additively separable case would permit aggregation even if all factors were fixed. There is another special case which would permit aggregation if the $X(\nu)$ were mobile and the $L(\nu)$ fixed. If, for some ν, $\phi^{\nu}(X(\nu)) = a_1(\nu)X_1(\nu) + a_2(\nu)X_2(\nu)$, then, in any region in which both the Xs are assigned to firm ν, the marginal rate of substitution between X_1 and X_2 in the system as a whole will be constant and independent of L. By Leontief's well-known aggregation theorem ([7] and [8]), the desired aggregate will then exist. Again it is simplest to assume this "perfect substitutes" case away for the remainder of the chapter.

Assumption 5.3: For all $\nu = 1, \ldots, n$, if efficient production makes both $X_1(\nu) > 0$ and $X_2(\nu) > 0$, then in an open neighborhood of $X(\nu)$, $\phi^{\nu}(\cdot)$ is strictly quasiconcave.

Despite the fact that the additively separable and perfect substitutes case have been assumed absent I shall refer to them below. Note that their presence would not introduce any case permitting aggregation that was not already present with only partial mobility. Hence the general result that full mobility only permits aggregation under the union of the conditions which obtained with fixed capital is unaffected by such cases.

5.3 Aggregation with two firms

The heart of the analysis will be performed for two firms ($n = 2$). As will be apparent later the results for n firms follow readily.

Now, there is one more case which permits aggregation but is totally uninteresting. It may be that efficient factor allocation sometimes requires that all of some factor be allocated to one firm with none allocated to the other. In any region in which this is true for both X_1 and X_2, with all of both X_1 and X_2 allocated to the same firm, it is plain that aggregation is trivial, given Assumption 5.1. Such an extreme case can safely be ignored, however, and I shall assume it does not occur. The less extreme cases where not all factors are allocated to both firms remain of interest, however.

One related remark before proceeding. As indicated in the introduction (Section 5.1), aggregation will turn out to be possible under either one of two conditions, the first in which the $F^v(\cdot,\cdot)$ can be taken to be the same and the second in which the $\phi^v(\cdot)$ can be taken to be the same. It is possible for one of these conditions to hold for some values of the variables and the other to hold for different values. I shall be precise about this in the proofs, but it is inconvenient to have to remember it in the discussion, so I generally speak of the $F^v(\cdot,\cdot)$ the same or the $\phi^v(\cdot)$ the same as though a given condition held everywhere.

I now proceed to the results. As already indicated, the basic theorem on aggregation to be used is the well-known theorem of Leontief ([7] and [8]) which states that aggregation is possible if and only if the marginal rates of substitution among variables in the aggregate are independent of variables left out of it. The "regions" mentioned in the analysis are in the space of total X_1, X_2, and L. "Aggregation" always means aggregation over X.

Lemma 5.1: In an open region in which all of X_1 is assigned to firm 1 and all of L is assigned to a single firm, aggregation is not possible.

***Proof*:** First consider the case in which all of X_2 is assigned to firm 2. If all of L is assigned to firm 1, then changing L affects the marginal product of X_1 but not that of X_2. Similarly, aggregation will be impossible if all of L is assigned to firm 2.

Thus we can suppose that X_2 is allocated to both firms. Begin by supposing that L is allocated entirely to firm 1 so that firm 2 operates with X_2 only. Constant returns then implies that firm 2's production function is linear in $X_2(2)$. Hence the marginal product of X_2 is constant in this region. For this to be true within firm 1, given Assumption 5.1, it must be true that $F^1_{\phi L} = 0$ where the subscripts denote differentiation in the obvious way. This means that $F^1(\cdot,\cdot)$ is additively separable and linear in its two arguments. $F^2(\cdot,\cdot)$ is trivially so separable.

The remaining case is that in which X_2 is allocated to both firms but L is allocated only to firm 2. Let M be the marginal rate of substitution between X_1 and X_2 in firm 1 (and in the system as a whole). Aggregation requires that this be independent of L, which here implies $(\partial M/\partial X_2(1))(\partial X_2(1)/\partial L) = 0$. If $(\partial X_2(1)/\partial L) = 0$, then it is easy to see that $F^2_{\phi L} = 0$ implying additive separability of $F^2(\cdot,\cdot)$. $F^1(\cdot,\cdot)$ is trivially so separable.

Suppose then that $(\partial M/\partial X_2(1)) = 0$. Plainly this implies $\phi^1_{12} = (\phi^1_1/\phi^1_2)\phi^1_{22}$ (denoting differentiation by subscripts). Euler's theorem applied to ϕ^1_2, however, shows that this is impossible unless $\phi^1_{12} = 0 = \phi^1_{22}$ so that $\phi^1(\cdot,\cdot)$ must be linear in its arguments. Since L is not assigned to firm 1 in this region, $f^1(\cdot,\cdot,0)$ must also be linear in $X_1(1)$ and $X_2(1)$. Thus the marginal product of X_2 must be constant in this region. For this to be true within firm 2, given Assumption 5.1, it must be true that $F^2_{\phi L} = 0$ and we have additive separability once more.

Lemma 5.2: Aggregation is possible in an open region in which all of either X_1 or X_2 is allocated to a single firm, if and only if the $F^\nu(\cdot,\cdot)$ can be taken to be the same, $\nu = 1, 2$.

***Proof*:** If both the $F^\nu(\cdot,\cdot)$ can be taken to be the same, then L will certainly be allocated to both firms so as to make the ratio $L(\nu)/\phi^\nu(X(\nu))$ the same in both. Further, by Lemma 5.1, if L is *not* allocated to both firms, aggregation is impossible. Hence we may as well proceed by assuming that it is so allocated.

Now suppose that all of X_1 is allocated to firm 1 everywhere in the region in question. Then, as L changes, the fact that X_1 is "really" mobile plays no role and we might as well consider it as fixed capital. If X_2 is also fixed (totally allocated to firm 2), then the desired result follows from the theorem for fixed capital aggregation (Theorem 2.2, p. 38) which states that the only differences between the $F^{\nu}(\cdot,\cdot)$ must be capital augmenting. We can take the values of the capital-augmenting parameter into the definition of the $\phi^{\nu}(\cdot)$. If X_2 is allocated to both firms, the same result follows from the similar theorem on aggregation over fixed and movable capital goods (Theorem 4.1, p. 109).

The opposite case, in which the X_i are allocated to both firms but L is not, is handled by:

Lemma 5.3: In any open region in which the X_i are assigned to both firms but L is assigned to only one firm, aggregation is possible if and only if the $\phi^{\nu}(\cdot)$ can be taken to be the same.

***Proof*:** In such a region, L might just as well be immobile. Aggregation over X is now aggregation over mobile factors in the presence of immobile ones. The desired result now follows from Theorem 3.2, p. 78.[9]

All of this cannot be very surprising. It amounts to observing that in open regions in which some factor is allocated to only one firm, then that factor might as well be treated as immobile. Aggregation conditions then reduce to those already known for the fixed capital case. Thus the cases so far considered do not really exploit the mobility of all factors. We now begin to study the case in which that mobility can be exploited – the case in which X_1, X_2, and L are assigned to both firms.

Lemma 5.4: Consider any open region in which all three factors are assigned to both firms. Suppose that, in this region, with X fixed, variations in L do not lead to reallocation of X_1 and X_2. Then the $F^{\nu}(\cdot,\cdot)$ can be taken to be the same.[10]

***Proof*:** The efficiency conditions are

$$F^1_{\phi}\phi^1_1 = F^2_{\phi}\phi^2_1; \qquad F^1_{\phi}\phi^1_2 = F^2_{\phi}\phi^2_2; \qquad F^1_L = F^2_L. \tag{5.6}$$

Consider an efficient allocation, denoting the values of the variables by bars. Choose any two scalars, ε_1 and ε_2, close to zero. Vary $\bar{X}$ by adding to it $\varepsilon_1\bar{X}(1)+\varepsilon_2\bar{X}(2)$. Vary $\bar{L}$ by adding to it $\varepsilon_1\bar{L}(1)+\varepsilon_2\bar{L}(2)$. Assign $(1+\varepsilon_1)\bar{X}(1)$ and $(1+\varepsilon_1)\bar{L}(1)$ to firm 1 and $(1+\varepsilon_2)\bar{X}(2)$ and $(1+\varepsilon_2)\bar{L}(2)$ to firm 2. By constant returns all marginal products remain the same, so this allocation is efficient, but $\phi^1(\bar{X}(1))$ and

$\phi^2(\bar{X}(2))$ have been multiplied by $(1 + \varepsilon_1)$ and $(1 + \varepsilon_2)$, respectively. Since ε_1 and ε_2 can be chosen arbitrarily, if close enough to zero, every pair of values of the $\phi^v(\cdot)$ in an open neighborhood of their original values can be reached in this way.

Now, from (5.6),

$$F^1_\phi / F^2_\phi = \phi^2_1 / \phi^1_1. \tag{5.7}$$

The right-hand side of (5.7), however, depends only on $X(1)$ and $X(2)$ and is independent of L in the region in question. Thus (5.7) shows that, considering $\phi^1(X(1))$ and $\phi^2(X(2))$ themselves as factors, so to speak, their marginal rate of substitution is independent of L. Hence it must be possible to aggregate the $\phi^v(\cdot)$. Since this must be true for all values of the $\phi^v(\cdot)$ in an open neighborhood of any original point, no efficiency condition applies to the $\phi^v(\cdot)$ themselves. Hence aggregation of the $\phi^v(\cdot)$ is isomorphic to the fixed capital aggregation problem with the $\phi^v(\cdot)$ the fixed capital, and the result now follows from Theorem 2.2.

Lemma 5.5: In any open region in which all three factors are assigned to each firm, aggregation is possible only if either (a) the $F^v(\cdot,\cdot)$ can be taken to be the same or (b) the $\phi^v(\cdot)$ can be taken to be the same.

***Proof*:** Consider changing L with X_1 and X_2 (the system totals) constant. If the $F^v(\cdot,\cdot)$ cannot be taken to be the same, this will require reallocation of at least one of the X_i. If the $\phi^v(\cdot)$ cannot be taken to be the same, there must be some point at which the equality of the marginal rate of substitution between X_1 and X_2 in both firms requires that the ratios $X_1(1)/X_2(1)$ and $X_1(2)/X_2(2)$ not be identical. Then reallocation of at least one of the X_i must alter at least one of these ratios. By strict quasiconcavity of the $\phi^v(\cdot)$, such alteration will change the marginal rate of substitution between X_1 and X_2 for the system as a whole (as well as within each firm). Thus that marginal rate of substitution is not invariant to changes in total L, and, by Leontief's theorem, no aggregate exists, completing the proof.

The fact that the conditions of Lemma 5.5 are sufficient as well as necessary is developed as part of the principal result of this section for which we are now ready.

Theorem 5.1: Apart from the Nataf case and the perfect substitutes case an aggregate over two firms exists if and only if, for any open region in the space of the $X_1(v)$, $X_2(v)$, and $L(v)$,[11] at least one of (a) and (b) below holds:

(a) The $F^v(\cdot,\cdot)$ can be taken to be the same.
(b) The $\phi^v(\cdot)$ can be taken to be the same.

Proof:

(a) Necessity. This follows directly from Lemmas 5.1, 5.2, 5.3, and 5.5.

(b) Sufficiency. That (a) is sufficient follows from the fact that it would be sufficient even if the values of the $X(v)$ were unrestricted by efficiency considerations (Chapter 2). Similarly, that (b) is sufficient follows from the fact that it would be sufficient even if the values of the $L(v)$ were unrestricted (Chapter 3). Nevertheless, a more self-contained proof is more instructive and desirable for later purposes.

First suppose that the $F^v(\cdot,\cdot)$ can be taken to be the same.[12] Then optimal allocation of L requires that the quasifactor ratio, $\phi^v/L(v)$, be the same for both firms. Define

$$J \equiv \phi^1(X(1)) + \phi^2(X(2)). \tag{5.8}$$

Then whenever L is optimally allocated

$$\phi^1/L(1) = \phi^2/L(2) = J/L. \tag{5.9}$$

Let $\lambda \equiv L(1)/L = \phi^1/J$. Total output, when optimized, will be given by (omitting the superscripts on the $F^v(\cdot,\cdot)$ since they are both the same):

$$\begin{aligned} Y^* &= F(\phi^1, L(1)) + F(\phi^2, L(2)) \\ &= F(\lambda J, \lambda L) + F((1-\lambda)J, (1-\lambda)L) \\ &= F(J, L) \end{aligned} \tag{5.10}$$

by constant returns. It now follows that X_1 and X_2 must be allocated to the two firms to maximize J as defined in (5.8), whence the value of J depends only on X_1 and X_2 and not on L, and $F(J, L)$ is seen from (5.10) to be the required aggregate production function.

Now suppose instead that the $\phi^v(\cdot)$ can be taken to be the same.[13] Optimal allocation of X_1 and X_2 then requires that they be assigned in the same ratio to each firm. In that case, however, the ratios $X_1(v)/X_2(v)$ must be the same as the overall ratio X_1/X_2 for $v = 1, 2$. Since the marginal rate of substitution between X_1 and X_2 is the same within each firm and depends only on the ratio $X_1(v)/X_2(v)$, that marginal rate of substitution in the system as a whole depends only on X_1/X_2 and not on L. The fact that X_1 and X_2 can be aggregated now follows from Leontief's theorem, and the proof is complete.

In the latter case, let $\phi^v(\cdot) = \phi(\cdot)$ for all v. Then $X(v) = \mu_v X$ for some set of positive scalars μ_v which sum to unity. Since $\phi(\cdot)$ is homogeneous of degree one, it is easy to see that the aggregate production function is:

$$Y^* = \max \sum_v F^v(\mu_v \phi(X), L(v))$$
$$\text{subject to: } \sum_v \mu_v = 1; \qquad \sum_v L(v) = L. \tag{5.11}$$

It is interesting to note that in this case the form of the aggregate for X is defined in closed-form and that of the aggregate production function is not, whereas in the case of the $F^v(\cdot,\cdot)$ all the same, the opposite is true.

Note that if either the $F^v(\cdot,\cdot)$ or the $\phi^v(\cdot)$ can be taken to be the same, certain of the cases treated in Lemmas 5.1–5.3 cannot arise.

5.4 More than two firms

Suppose now that there are many firms ($n \geqq 2$). We shall derive most of our results from the fact that, given Definition 5.1, aggregation over the entire set of firms requires aggregation over every pair. Before doing so, however, there are two matters which need attention.

The first of these concerns the trivial case ruled out for two firms in which all of X_1 and X_2 is assigned to one firm and none to the other. Where there are more than two firms, the equivalent statement of the triviality of this case is that the existence of firms to which neither X_1 nor X_2 is assigned presents no difficulties for aggregation of X. We may as well assume there are no such firms.

The second matter is the case considered in Lemma 5.1 which requires explicit extension to the case of $n > 2$ since with more than two firms there is no reason to rule out additive separability for any given pair of firms. Hence the case considered in Lemma 5.1 must be ruled out in some other way. We accomplish this with:

Lemma 5.6: In any open region in the space of X_1, X_2, and L, suppose that for firms 1 and 2, $X_2(2) = 0$ and either $L(1) = 0$ or $L(2) = 0$. Then aggregation is not possible unless *all* the $F^v(\cdot,\cdot)$ are additively separable.

Proof: It is sufficient to prove this result for $n = 3$. If aggregation is possible, then (Definition 5.1) it is possible over every pair of firms. Lemma 5.1 then implies additive separability for firms 1 and 2.

Consider firm 3. If $L(3) = 0$, then $F^3(\cdot,\cdot)$ is trivially additively separable. So assume $L(3) \neq 0$. Suppose first that $X_1(3) \neq 0$. If $L(2) = 0$, then aggregation over firms 2 and 3 is another case of Lemma 5.1. If $L(2) \neq 0$, then such aggregation is covered by Lemma 5.2. In this latter case $F^3(\cdot,\cdot)$ can be taken to be the same as $F^2(\cdot,\cdot)$ which we know to be (nontrivially) additively separable.

Now suppose that $X_1(3) = 0$. If $L(1) = 0$, then aggregation over firms 1 and 3 is another case of Lemma 5.1. If $L(1) \neq 0$, then Lemma 5.2 shows that such aggregation implies that $F^3(\cdot,\cdot)$ can be taken to be the same as $F^1(\cdot,\cdot)$ which we know to be (nontrivially) additively separable. This completes the proof.

Since additive separability for all firms has been ruled out in Assumption 5.2, aggregation in the case of Lemma 5.1 cannot arise. This makes Theorem 5.1 applicable to aggregation over every pair of firms and we can now generalize it. The interesting fact about the generalization is that aggregation requires *either* that the $F^v(\cdot,\cdot)$ can be taken to be the same over *all* firms *or* that the $\phi^v(\cdot)$ have this property. Combinations of the two cases for different pairs of firms are not allowed.

Theorem 5.2: Apart from additive separability of *all* the $F^v(\cdot,\cdot)$ $(v = 1, \ldots, n)$ or the perfect substitutes case, an aggregate over n firms exists if and only if, for any open region in the space of $X_1(v)$, $X_2(v)$, and $L(v)$ at least one of (a) and (b) below holds:

(a) All the $F^v(\cdot,\cdot)$ can be taken to be the same.
(b) All the $\phi^v(\cdot)$ can be taken to be the same.

***Proof*:**

(a) Sufficiency. The proofs given for sufficiency in Theorem 5.1 do not require $n = 2$.

(b) Necessity. By the strong definition of aggregation (Definition 5.1, above), aggregation requires the existence of an aggregate over every *pair* of firms. Theorem 5.1, therefore, shows that every pair of firms must have either the same $F^v(\cdot,\cdot)$ or the same $\phi^v(\cdot)$ if an aggregate exists. Now suppose that an aggregate exists but that not all firms have $F^v(\cdot,\cdot)$ which can be taken to be the same. Let A be the set of all firms whose $F^v(\cdot,\cdot)$ can be taken to be the same as $F^1(\cdot,\cdot)$. Let B be the set of all remaining firms. Then neither A nor B are empty. However, the existence of an aggregate requires that every firm in A

and every firm in B have $\phi^v(\cdot)$ which can be taken to be the same. Evidently, then, *all* the $\phi^v(\cdot)$ can be taken to be the same.

Note that appeal to the strong definition of aggregation is required here. Otherwise we could have the following situation. Suppose $n = 3$ and $F^1(\cdot,\cdot)$ and $F^2(\cdot,\cdot)$ can be taken to be the same but $F^3(\cdot,\cdot)$ is essentially different. Using the construction in the sufficiency proof of Theorem 5.1 which led to (5.10), aggregate over firms 1 and 2 to form the aggregate production function $F^1(\tilde{J}, \tilde{L})$ where $\tilde{L} \equiv L(1) + L(2)$ and

$$\tilde{J} = \max\{\phi^1(X(1)) + \phi^2(X(2))\} \tag{5.12}$$

subject to $X(1) + X(2)$ fixed. If it now turns out that $\tilde{J}(\cdot)$ and $\phi^3(\cdot)$ can be taken to be the same, then the third firm can be combined with the aggregate of the first two.

The trouble with this is that unless $\phi^1(\cdot)$ and $\phi^2(\cdot)$ can be taken to be the same, it will *not* in general be true that they can be taken to be the same as $\tilde{J}(\cdot)$ or $\phi^3(\cdot)$. So if the first firm were not present no aggregate would exist.

Thus, were we to drop the strong definition of aggregation (but retain Assumption 5.1 as to aggregation within each firm), we would permit a somewhat wider class of cases along the lines just described. This widening seems of no practical importance, however.

5.5 Generalizations

I now briefly consider two generalizations, the first to more than three factors and the second to nonconstant returns technologies.

The case in which there are more than three factors, with one exception, presents no substantive changes. The single exception involves the generalization of the cases treated in Lemmas 5.1–5.3 above. Suppose that L has more than one element and that some but not all factors in L are assigned to both firms. Suppose further that at least one X_i is not assigned to both firms. Aggregation of X then becomes isomorphic to capital aggregation when not all capital types are to be included in the aggregate. Closed-form results are not known for this case, although necessary and sufficient conditions are.[14] These conditions are extremely restrictive. Similarly, suppose that X has more than two elements and that some but not all factors in X are assigned to both firms. Aggregation of X then becomes isomorphic to aggregation of fixed and mobile capitals when not all fixed capitals are included in the aggregate. This case seems likely to reduce to the previous one (Chapter 4) if aggregation is possible at all. The flavour of Theorem 5.2 is preserved even with such exceptions by observing that at best the assumption that all factors are mobile permits aggregation under various conditions which would hold without such an assumption but does not do more than to permit the union of such conditions.

Further, for the exceptions just noted to apply, it must be the case that full mobility fails to come into play. I shall ignore this minor complication in the remainder of the discussion.

The case of nonconstant returns technologies has the property that, in general, no aggregate will exist whether or not the $F^v(\cdot,\cdot)$ or the $\phi^v(\cdot)$ can be taken to be the same.[15] It is easy to see, however, that (with the exception of a few special cases in which full mobility does not come into play – Lemma 5.1) the necessity as well as the sufficiency results obtained above apply if the $F^v(\cdot,\cdot)$ can be taken to be constant returns in ϕ^v, and $L(v)$ and the $\phi^v(\cdot)$ are merely homothetic. They do not require that *both* the $F^v(\cdot,\cdot)$ *and* the $\phi^v(\cdot)$ can be taken to be constant returns at the same time.[16] A complete closed-form characterization of the nonconstant returns cases permitting aggregation is not easy to come by.

5.6 Interpretations

As indicated in Section 5.1, these results can be interpreted in various ways in terms of factor or output aggregation. I shall give some remarks along these lines for the simplest cases.

In terms of factor aggregation, the existence of aggregates at the firm level (Assumption 5.1) can be thought of as stating that each firm can be regarded as if it had a two-stage production process (although such a description is only a parable and not necessarily a literal one). In the first stage, the factors to be aggregated (the $X_i(v)$) are combined together to produce an intermediate output (the $\phi^v(X(v))$). That intermediate output is then combined with the remaining factors (the $L(v)$) to produce final output. Aggregation of X in the system as a whole can be done if and only if firms are *either* all alike as regards the first stage of production *or* all alike as regards the second stage. If they are all alike as regards the first stage (the $\phi^v(\cdot)$ all the same), then the fact that L is mobile plays no role; this is the condition for aggregation of mobile factors when the remainder are fixed.[17] If they are all alike as regards the second stage (the $F^v(\cdot,\cdot)$ all the same), then the fact that the X_i are mobile plays no role; this is the condition for aggregation of fixed factors when the remainder are mobile.[18]

This is not to say that mobility does not help.[19] Apart from the fact that it permits instant aggregation over firms of any single factor, it aids in other ways. If the X_i were fixed, taking the $\phi^\nu(\cdot)$ as the same would not permit aggregation; if L were fixed, taking the $F^\nu(\cdot,\cdot)$ as the same would not help.

A different insight into the results can be obtained by considering the case of output aggregation. Here, Assumption 5.1 is the assumption that outputs can be aggregated within each firm with the firm thought of as producing a composite good (the $\phi^\nu(\cdot)$) which is then split up into individual outputs. The condition that the $\phi^\nu(\cdot)$ all be the same is the condition that each firm, faced with the same relative output prices, produce the same market basket with individual outputs in the same ratio as every other firm. (What the ratios are can depend on prices.) Firms can then differ in the scale of their composite market basket and in the way in which it is produced, but not in its composition.

The other condition – that the $F^\nu(\cdot,\cdot)$ can all be taken to be the same – can be thought of as requiring that the production functions with which the composite goods (the $\phi^\nu(\cdot)$) are produced differ only by Hicks-neutral differences.[20] In this case, however, the make-up of the composite good is unrestricted.

Output aggregation requires, however, either that all composite goods be the same *or* that the technologies for producing them be essentially the same. One implication of this concerns the case of complete specialization. Suppose that every firm produces a single good, different from that produced by any other firm. Then the $\phi^\nu(\cdot)$ cannot all be the same and aggregation requires only Hicks-neutral differences in technology. With only such differences, however, the production possibility frontier for the entire system will consist only of flats; relative output prices will be fixed (for all outputs actually produced) and it is hardly surprising that output aggregation is possible.

It is interesting to note, however, that even this restrictive case becomes admissible only because all factors are assumed mobile. With fixed capital, output aggregation is possible only with all firms producing the same composite market basket.[21]

When we leave complete specialization in outputs we obtain a somewhat similar, but perhaps less intuitive, result. Aggregation of outputs will be possible even if each firm does not produce the same composite bundle as every other, but only if the composite bundles produced are produced with the same technology. In effect, the relative prices of the composite bundles must be fixed.

In general, then, the assumption that all factors are mobile does aid aggregation somewhat. First (a point not the focus of this paper), it permits instantly the aggregation of any *single* factor across firms.

Were it reasonable to assume that each firm (or production process) only used one capital type, this would end the matter, but of course that is not the case. So far as aggregation involving more than one factor is concerned, the conditions are seen still to be very restrictive. Aggregation is possible only under circumstances which, in some sense, would have allowed it anyway. The only gain is that now either the conditions which would have permitted aggregation of fixed factors (the $F^v(\cdot,\cdot)$ the same or additive separability) or the conditions which would have permitted aggregation of movable factors or outputs (the $\phi^v(\cdot)$ the same or the perfect substitutes case) will do. Aggregation can thus take place in somewhat wider circumstances; however, in a sense, no new cases are introduced. It thus turns out that aggregation across firms plays quite as big a role in the difficulties of aggregate production functions as does the fixity of capital. Aggregate production functions practically never exist – but this is true whether or not capital is mobile. The implications for the intellectual history of the "Cambridge versus Cambridge" debate are left to the reader.

Notes

1. For present purposes, the important papers in the series are Fisher [2], [3], and [4] (Chapters 2, 3, 4). [5] (Chapter 1) presents a nontechnical survey. (I am not, of course, the only one to work in this area. See [5] for other references.)
2. Some of the specific statements which follow in this introduction strictly apply to strictly quasiconcave production functions. They ignore the additively separable case (Nataf [9]) and the perfect substitutes case treated below. As shown below, the general nature of the results is not affected by the inclusion of these cases, although the exact aggregation conditions are different from those in the more general case.
3. There are similar conditions – and one additional very strong one in the case of capital – for the construction of partial rather than full aggregates but these will not directly concern us here. See Fisher [2], [3], [4], [5], and [6] (Chapters 1–4, 6).
4. See, in particular, Robinson [10] and Solow [11].
5. See Brown and Chang [1] for an analysis which can be so interpreted.
6. This means, in effect, that they will not differ at all, since such changes can be absorbed into the definition of the aggregate.
7. As already observed, the assumption of fixed capital also produces stringent conditions if only *some* capital types are to be aggregated.
8. In the case in which X is capital and capital is fixed this cannot happen; where L is capital and fixed it may. See Fisher [2] and [3].
9. That theorem is proved for the case in which each firm has a nonzero amount of capital (here L). However, careful reading of the proof of Lemma 3.1, pp. 74–5, shows that this is immaterial.
10. I am greatly indebted to W. M. Gorman for pointing out a lacuna in an

earlier proof of Lemma 5.4. Indeed, that lacuna also occurs in the proof of the main necessity result of Chapter 4 where (p. 111), the argument from (4.23) fails to establish that the functions $g^i(\cdot)$ in (4.24) must be independent of v. This is because the functions which map the marginal product of labor into the (quasi) factor ratios can differ for different v. Nevertheless, that necessity result is true as can be seen from the fact that Lemma 5.4 applies even if one of the $X_i(v)$ is immobile. In that case, even if the $\phi^v(\cdot)$ were the same, an increase in total L would change the ratios of the $X_i(v)$ within each firm altering the marginal rate of substitution between the Xs.

11. Note that this is not the same as the open regions used in the lemmas which were in the space of the factor *totals*. Of course, it turns out to make no difference. Strictly speaking, the theorem only applies to regions in which factors can ever be assigned.
12. The following proof is based on Solow's proof of the sufficiency of capital augmentation for the aggregation of fixed capital [12, pp. 104–5]. See also pp. 7–8.
13. The following sufficiency proof follows that given on p. 92.
14. See pp. 10–11, 17–19, 47–57, 112–13 and Chapter 6. Incidentally, the existence of this case shows that the results given on pp. 84–90, that under constant returns absence of specialization is necessary for aggregation of mobile factors in the presence of fixed capital is limited to the case in which *all* mobile factors are to be included in the aggregate. (The remarks on p. 93, following Theorem 3.7, overlook this possibility.) This is not unimportant since, along lines observed in the introduction, output aggregation when capital is fixed *and* there is more than one mobile factor can be cast into this form. Other cases also arise. The cases permitting aggregation in such circumstances are extremely special, however.
15. Cf. p. 40.
16. Cf. pp. 40–4, 82–4, and 91–4.
17. See Chapter 3.
18. See Chapter 2. Cf. Chapter 4.
19. Cf. pp. 17–19 and 112–13.
20. Scalar multiplication of ϕ^v in (5.5) is a Hicks-neutral shift if the $f^v(\cdot,\cdot)$ are interpreted as factor-requirements functions.
21. See Chapter 3.

References

[1] Brown, M., and W. W. Chang, "Capital aggregation in a general equilibrium model of production," *Econometrica*, **44** (1976), 1179–200.

[2] Fisher, F. M., "Embodied technical change and the existence of an aggregate capital stock," *Review of Economic Studies*, **32** (1965), 263–88 (reprinted as Chapter 2).

[3] Fisher, F. M., "Embodied technology and the existence of labour and output aggregates," *Review of Economic Studies*, **35** (1968), 391–412 (reprinted as Chapter 3).

[4] Fisher, F. M., "Embodied technology and the aggregation of fixed and movable capital goods," *Review of Economic Studies*, **35** (1968), 417–28 (reprinted as Chapter 4).
[5] Fisher, F. M., "The existence of aggregate production functions," *Econometrica*, **37** (1969), 553–77 (reprinted as Chapter 1).
[6] Fisher, F. M., "On the simultaneous existence of full and partial capital aggregates," *Review of Economic Studies*, **50** (1983), 197–208 (reprinted as Chapter 6).
[7] Leontief, W. W., "A note on the interrelation of subsets of independent variables of a continuous function with continuous first derivatives," *Bulletin of the American Mathematical Society*, **53** (1947), 343–50.
[8] Leontief, W. W., "Introduction to a theory of the internal structure of functional relationships," *Econometrica*, **15** (1947), 361–73.
[9] Nataf, A., "Sur la possibilité de construction de certains macromodèles," *Econometrica*, **16** (1948), 232–44.
[10] Robinson, J., "The production function and the theory of capital," *Review of Economic Studies*, **21** (1953–54), 81–106.
[11] Solow, R. M., "The production function and the theory of capital," *Review of Economic Studies*, **23** (1955–56), 101–8.
[12] Solow, R. M., "Capital, labor, and income in manufacturing," in *National Bureau of Economic Research Conference in Income and Wealth, The Behavior of Income Shares* (Studies in Income and Wealth, 26), Princeton: Princeton University Press, 1964, pp. 101–28.

6

On the simultaneous existence of full and partial capital aggregates (1983)

6.1 Introduction

Some years ago Fisher [1] (Chapter 2) examined the question of the existence of an aggregate capital stock in the context of a model in which technology was embodied in capital and capital was fixed (i.e., firm-specific) but labor was assigned to firms so as to maximize output. This was the beginning of a more general examination into the existence of aggregate production functions.[1] Not surprisingly, the conditions for such existence turned out to be quite restrictive. For example, the best known theorem in this area[2] states that under constant returns with one kind of capital per firm, a necessary and sufficient condition for the existence of an aggregate capital stock is that all technical differences be capital augmenting, with one unit of a different kind of capital being equivalent to a fixed number of units of a given type. Similar results hold for more general models.

Such conditions are not even approximately likely to be satisfied and, one would think, are dispositive of the use of aggregate production functions at least as a theoretical tool. Despite this, the use of aggregate production functions has remained at least a flourishing empirical industry (and perhaps properly so since, where small movements are concerned and approximations acceptable, aggregate production functions may be the best tools we have). Moreover, the common use of such macroeconomic concepts as "investment," "capital," "plant," "equipment," "labor (skilled or unskilled)," or even "output," to refer to the productive sector implicitly assumes that these are approximately thought of in terms of production relationships. It is well then to understand precisely what is involved in such an assumption.

This chapter returns to the subject and cleans up an important loose end. As indicated, it is common in applied macroeconomic work to think in terms not only of a full capital aggregate but also of subaggregates such as "plant" or "equipment." Yet the conditions under which such aggregates can rigorously be constructed are severe. In particular, as we shall see, the conditions under which full *and* partial aggregates exist are interesting, but wildly restrictive.

More specifically, the use of a full capital aggregate together with any partial aggregate such as "equipment" implies that such a partial aggregate and its complementary partial aggregate (e.g., "plant") are perfect substitutes. Since this is very far from what is usually assumed about "plant" and "equipment," models or discussions that use them should not *also* speak in terms of "capital" as a whole, but should proceed with even greater caution than is called for by the strict conditions for the existence of a single partial aggregate alone.

How one feels about this chapter will probably be determined by how one feels about aggregate production functions before reading it. To those convinced that aggregate production functions are dangerous to the health, this chapter can only be of interest for the sake of intellectual completeness. It closes certain questions in a satisfying way. To those who employ aggregate production functions, this chapter may be of more substantive interest, pointing out the nature of the assumptions underlying the use of full and partial capital aggregates.

Turning to the problem itself, when each firm employs more than one type of capital good (surely the general case), the simple capital-augmentation theorem referred to above generalizes, but there are two related but certainly not identical questions which arise. The first of these is that of the existence of a full capital aggregate; the second is that of the existence of an aggregate including some but not all of the capital types. (As indicated, to fix ideas, one may think of these as the question of the existence of a meaningful aggregate called "capital" on the one hand and of the existence of "equipment" or "plant" aggregates or both on the other.) It is not the case that the conditions for one kind of aggregation are stronger than those for the other.[3]

Thus, to consider two particular examples, let the νth firm produce output $Y(\nu)$ according to the three-factor production function

$$Y(\nu) = f^{\nu}(K_1(\nu), K_2(\nu), L(\nu)) \tag{6.1}$$

where $K_1(\nu)$ and $K_2(\nu)$ denote the amounts of two different types of capital (plant and equipment) which the νth firm has, and $L(\nu)$ denotes the amount of labor assigned to the firm. Labor – assumed homogeneous – is allocated to firms to maximize the sum of outputs – also assumed homogeneous – but the v superscript on the production function indicates the fact that technology is embodied in the capital stocks so that $K_j(v)$ and $K_j(v')$ can generally be physically quite different for $v \neq v'$, $j = 1, 2$ (physically different equipment used by different firms, for example). $f^v(\cdot,\cdot,\cdot)$ is assumed continuously twice differentiable with positive first derivatives and $f^v_{LL} < 0$, where subscripts indicate differentiation. The strong assumption that labor and output are homogeneous (i.e., that they can themselves be aggregated) makes no difference to the results but permits substantial notational simplification.[4]

Now suppose that one of the firms, say the hth, has a production function of the form:

$$f^h(K_1(h), K_2(h), L(h)) = AK_1(h)^{\alpha}K_2(h)^{\beta}L(h)^{\gamma}. \tag{6.2}$$

Then no partial aggregate exists, no matter what other firms look like. A full capital aggregate will exist, however, so long as every other firm has a production function in the form:

$$f^v(K_1(v), K_2(v), L(v)) = \{J^v(K_1(v), K_2(v))\}\, L(v)^{\gamma}\text{[5]} \tag{6.3}$$

where $J^v(\cdot,\cdot)$ is monotonic in its arguments.

On the other hand, suppose instead that all firms (including the hth) have production functions of the form:

$$f^v(K_1(v), K_2(v), L(v)) = H_1^v(K_1(v))\{H_2^v(K_2(v)) + c_v L(v)\}^{\gamma_v} \tag{6.4}$$

where $H_1^v(\cdot)$ and $H_2^v(\cdot)$ are monotonic functions and c_v and γ_v parameters. Then a partial aggregate exists for K_2. If, further, γ_v is the same for all firms, a partial aggregate exists for K_1 as well. Yet even in this case there exists no full aggregate of K_1 and K_2 together.[6]

In general, therefore, the cases permitting full and partial capital aggregation are different ones – both restrictive but not identical. A natural question, however, is that of what class of cases simultaneously permits the construction of *both* full and partial aggregates, fulfilling a macroeconomist's production fantasies. That question was not examined in Chapter 2 and is the subject of this chapter.

Briefly, the results turn out as follows. First, such cases do exist. Further, simultaneous existence of a total aggregate and one partial aggregate implies the existence of another partial aggregate consisting of all the kinds of capital left out of the first partial aggregate.[7] Similarly, the simultaneous existence of one partial aggregate and a subaggregate of that partial aggregate implies the existence of the complementary subpartial aggregate. These tidings of apparent good news should not be overrated, however. They come about because the conditions for the existence of a total and even one partial aggregate are already extremely restrictive. Thus, for example, in the three-factor case under constant returns, a total aggregate and a K_1-aggregate will both exist if and only if[8] all firms have production functions of the form:

$$f^{v}(K_1(v), K_2(v), L(v)) = F(b_v K_1(v) + c_v K_2(v), L(v)) \qquad (6.5)$$

where $F(\cdot,\cdot)$ is the same for all v, and b_v and c_v are parameters which are allowed to vary. In this case, it is plain that $K_1(v)$ and $K_2(v)$ are perfect substitutes within firm v; a unit of one can be treated as equivalent to a fixed number of units of the other. Since $F(\cdot,\cdot)$ does not vary, $K_j(v)$ and $K_j(v')$ are also related in this way ($j = 1, 2$; $v \neq v'$), and we are looking at a generalization of the capital-augmenting theorem. In this context, it is hardly surprising that a K_2-aggregate exists as well.

Note that all this is true even if all firms have the *same* production function. The requirement that total and all partial aggregates exist imposes a very stringent burden on the form that production functions can have.

This is the most restrictive case, however. I derive it below as a consequence of more general considerations, some of which lead to conditions at least somewhat less onerous.

6.2 The general case: Preliminary results

While the case of two kinds of capital within the firm is an interesting one, it is best to begin with the more general case of several kinds. The assumption of a single homogeneous labor and a single homogeneous output will be maintained for simplicity; this does not affect the results. Also for simplicity, I assume that all factors have positive marginal products in every firm and that it is always efficient to assign a positive amount of labor to every firm.[9]

Each firm, then, has m types of capital as well as labor. There are n firms. The vth firm's production function (twice continuously differentiable with strictly diminishing returns to labor) is given by:

$$Y(v) = f^{v}(K_1(v), \ldots, K_m(v), L(v)). \qquad (6.6)$$

Labor is assigned to firms to maximize total output. This makes maximized output for the system as a whole a function of total labor and of the nm amounts of each of the m capital stocks possessed by each of the n firms. The questions being examined have to do with the simplification of that function by aggregation over capital types and over firms.

It is convenient to begin by stating the necessary and sufficient conditions for the existence of an aggregate consisting of the first p capital types.[10] They are:

Lemma 6.1: Necessary and sufficient conditions for the existence of an aggregate consisting of the first p capital types, $1 \leqq p \leqq m$, are given by (a), (b), and (c) below.

(a) Such an aggregate exists within each of the n firms taken separately. That is, for all $v = 1, \ldots, n$,

$$f^v(K_1(v), \ldots, K_m(v), L(v)) = F^v(J(v), K_{p+1}(v), \ldots, K_m(v), L(v)) \quad (6.7)$$

where

$$J(v) = J^v(K_1(v), \ldots, K_p(v)). \quad (6.8)$$

(b) For all $v = 1, \ldots, n$, all $i = 1, \ldots, p$, and all $j = p+1, \ldots, m$,

$$f^v_{K_iK_j} - \frac{f^v_{K_iL} f^v_{K_jL}}{f^v_{LL}} \equiv 0 \quad (6.9)$$

(where the subscripts denote differentiation in the obvious way).

(c) There exists a function $g(\cdot)$, independent of v and of i, such that, for all $v = 1, \ldots, n$, $i = 1, \ldots, p$,

$$\frac{f^v_{K_iL}}{f^v_{K_i} f^v_{LL}} = g(f^v_L). \quad (6.10)$$

***Proof*:** Immediate from Theorem 2.7, p. 56. The fact that $g(\cdot)$ is independent of i as well as of v follows from (a).

Lemma 6.2: In the presence of (a) of Lemma 6.1, (b) and (c) of Lemma 6.1 can be respectively replaced by (b′) and (c′) below.

(b′) For all $v = 1, \ldots, n$ and all $j = p+1, \ldots, m$,

$$F^v_{JK_j} - \frac{F^v_{JL} F^v_{K_jL}}{F^v_{LL}} \equiv 0. \quad (6.9')$$

(c′) There exists a function $g(\cdot)$, independent of v, such that, for all $v = 1, \ldots, m$,

$$\frac{F_{JL}^{v}}{F_{J}^{v} F_{LL}^{v}} = g(F_{L}^{v}). \tag{6.10′}$$

***Proof*:** Obvious.

Lemmas 6.1 and 6.2 show that aggregation over the first p capitals for the system as a whole can be thought of in two stages. First there is aggregation at the level of the individual firm. Second, the individual firm aggregates, $J(v)$, are themselves aggregated over firms. This fact permits some notational simplification, since it means that – so far as the second stage of such aggregation (conditions (b) and (c) of Lemma 6.1) is concerned – we might as well take $p = 1$. I shall occasionally do so and later reinterpret the results.

It is also convenient to state:

Lemma 6.3: In the presence of (a) of Lemma 6.1, if there exists a $g(\cdot)$ such that (6.10′) holds, then (6.10) holds with that same $g(\cdot)$ for all $i = 1, \ldots, p$. Further, if there exists a $g(\cdot)$ such that (6.10) holds for any $i = 1, \ldots, p$, then (6.10′) holds with that same $g(\cdot)$ and hence (6.10) also holds with that same $g(\cdot)$ for all $i = 1, \ldots, p$.

***Proof*:** Direct computation.

In view of the discussion following Lemma 6.2, this result applies even if the K_i in (6.10) are themselves subaggregates.

6.3 Complementary subaggregates in the general case

We can now state immediately:

Theorem 6.1: Suppose an aggregate consisting of the first two capital types exists. Suppose further that an aggregate consisting only of the second capital type exists. Then an aggregate consisting only of the first capital type also exists.

***Proof*:** (a) of Lemma 6.1 is trivially satisfied here. Considering (b), it is evident that (6.9) holds for $i = 1$, $j = 3, \ldots, m$ by the existence of an aggregate containing the first two capital types. (6.9) is satisfied for $i = 1$, $j = 2$ because it is symmetric in i and j and an aggregate consisting of the second capital type only exists. So (b) is also satisfied. Finally, (6.10) is satisfied for $i = 1$, since an aggregate of the first two capital types exists, implying that (6.10) is satisfied for $i = 1, 2$.

Corollary 6.1: Suppose that an aggregate consisting of the first q capital types exists for some q, $1 < q \leqq m$. Suppose further that an aggregate consisting of types $(p + 1, \ldots, q)$ also exists for some p, $1 \leqq p < q$. Finally, suppose that an aggregate consisting of the first p capital types exists for each firm taken separately. Then an aggregate consisting of the first p capital types exists for the system as a whole.

***Proof*:** Follows from Lemmas 6.1–6.2 and Theorem 6.1.

Corollary 6.2: Suppose that an aggregate consisting of the first q capital types exists for some q, $1 < q \leqq m$. Suppose further that an aggregate consisting of capital types $(2, \ldots, q)$ also exists. Then an aggregate consisting of capital of type 1 exists as well.

***Proof*:** Obvious.

Thus, in particular, if a full capital aggregate and also a partial capital aggregate exist for the system as a whole, then the complementary partial capital aggregate will also exist for the system as a whole provided that it exists at the level of each firm. This latter condition is guaranteed if only one capital type is left out of the first partial aggregate. Roughly speaking, provided that they all exist at the level of the individual firm, the existence of a full capital aggregate plus the existence of a plant aggregate implies the existence of an equipment aggregate (where all capital types are either plant or equipment). Similarly, the existence of a full aggregate and of an equipment aggregate implies the existence of a plant aggregate.

This seems like relatively good news, in contrast to the usual results as to the restrictive conditions required for aggregation, and in a way that is true. Indeed, the news will appear to get better, for it will turn out that the condition in Corollary 6.1 that an aggregate of the first p capital types exist at the firm level is redundant. Alas, reconsideration of what is going on reveals that this occurs only because the simultaneous existence of two aggregates, one of which involves a subset of the capital types involved in the other, is already extremely restrictive.

As might be expected in view of Lemma 6.3, such further results involve (a) and (b) of Lemma 6.1 which restrict the form of individual production functions, in contrast to (c) which, while also so restrictive, involves a condition across production functions. As a result, it is convenient to drop the v superscript and argument in what follows. We prove:

Lemma 6.4: Let $f(\cdot)$ be one of the production functions. Suppose that for some q, $1 < q \leqq m$, $f(\cdot)$ can be written as:

$$f(K_1, \ldots, K_m, L) = F(J(K_1, \ldots, K_q), K_{q+1}, \ldots, K_m, L) \qquad (6.11)$$

and also, for every $i = 1, \ldots, q-1$,

$$f_{K_q K_i} - \frac{f_{K_q L} f_{K_i L}}{f_{LL}} \equiv 0. \qquad (6.12)$$

Then $J(K_1, \ldots, K_q)$ can be written as

$$J(K_1, \ldots, K_q) = R(K_q) + S(K_1, \ldots, K_{q-1}). \qquad (6.13)$$

Proof: Using (6.11), (6.12) becomes

$$0 = F_{JJ} J_{K_q} J_{K_i} + F_J J_{K_q K_i} - \frac{F_{JL}^2 J_{K_q} J_{K_i}}{F_{LL}} \qquad (6.14)$$

whence

$$\frac{J_{K_q K_i}}{J_{K_q} J_{K_i}} = \frac{F_{JL}^2}{F_J F_{LL}} - \frac{F_{JJ}}{F_J} \qquad (6.15)$$

and this holds for all $i = 1, \ldots, q-1$. However, the right-hand side of (6.15) depends only on J, $K_{q+1}, \ldots, K_m$, and L and not (given the value of J) on $K_1, \ldots, K_q$. Hence (6.15) can only hold if both sides are the same function of J, say $M(J)$. This implies that the left-hand side must equal $M(J)$ for all $i = 1, \ldots, q-1$. There are two cases to consider.

(a) $M(J) \equiv 0$. Then $J_{K_q K_i} \equiv 0$ for all $i = 1, \ldots, q-1$, and the desired result is immediate.

(b) $M(J) \not\equiv 0$. Then

$$\frac{\partial \log J_{K_q}}{\partial K_i} = M(J) \frac{\partial J}{\partial K_i} \qquad (6.16)$$

for $i = 1, \ldots, q-1$. Integrating with respect to K_i,

$$\log J_{K_q} = N(J) + \log G^i(K^i) \qquad (6.17)$$

where $K^i \equiv (K_1, \ldots, K_{i-1}, K_{i+1}, \ldots, K_q)$, $N(J)$ is an integral of $M(J)$, and $G^i(\cdot)$ is some function. However, the fact that $M(J)$ is the same for all $i = 1, \ldots, q-1$ implies with (6.17) that $G^i(K^i)$ is the same for all such i. Hence we can write

$$G^i(K^i) = r(K_q) \tag{6.18}$$

for all $i = 1, \ldots, q-1$. Substituting in (6.17), we obtain:

$$J_{K_q} = r(K_q)\mathrm{e}^{N(J)} \tag{6.19}$$

$$\mathrm{e}^{-N(J)}\frac{\partial J}{\partial K_q} = r(K_q). \tag{6.20}$$

Integrating with respect to K_q, this implies

$$C(J) = R(K_q) + S(K^q) \tag{6.21}$$

where $C(J)$ is an integral of $\mathrm{e}^{-N(J)}$, $R(K_q)$ is an integral of $r(K_q)$, and $S(K^q)$ is some function of $K_1, \ldots, K_{q-1}$. Since $C(\cdot)$ is obviously invertible,

$$J = C^{-1}(R(K_q) + S(K_q)). \tag{6.22}$$

However, the transformation in (6.22) can be absorbed into the definition of J by suitable redefinition of $F(\cdot, \ldots, \cdot)$ so this is equivalent to the statement of the lemma, completing the proof.

Remark 6.1: Lemma 6.4 itself shows that the function $M(J)$ involved in the proof can always be taken as zero by writing J as in (6.13) and redefining F appropriately. Note that, if $q = m$ and F exhibits constant returns in its arguments, then that function is *already* zero and $J(\cdot, \ldots, \cdot)$ additive in that further redefinition. This follows from (6.15) and Euler's theorem applied to $F_J(\cdot,\cdot,\cdot)$ and $F_L(\cdot,\cdot,\cdot)$ which are both homogeneous of degree zero.

This result enables us to state the most general result of this section.

Theorem 6.2: Suppose that an aggregate consisting of the first q capital types exists for some q, $1 < q \leqq m$. Suppose further that an aggregate consisting of capital types $(p+1, \ldots, q)$ also exists for some p, $1 \leqq p < q$. Then an aggregate consisting of the first p capital types also exists.

***Proof*:** Lemmas 6.1 and 6.2 and the discussion following them show that an aggregate of capital types $(p+1, \ldots, q)$ exists at the level of each firm. Further, we might as well start with such an aggregate and take $p = q - 1$. Now the existence of an aggregate over the first q capital types together with Lemma 6.1 implies that (6.11) is applicable to $f^v(\cdot)$ for all $v = 1, \ldots, n$. Further, the existence of an aggregate consisting of capital of type q implies that (6.12) also holds. This makes Lemma 6.4 applicable whence an aggregate consisting of the first p capital types exists for each firm taken separately. The desired result now follows from Corollary 6.1.

We can also state a partial converse.

Theorem 6.3: Suppose that an aggregate consisting of the first p capital types exists for the system as a whole, for some p, $1 \leqq p < m$. Suppose further that an aggregate consisting of capital types $(p+1, \ldots, q)$ exists for the system as a whole for some q, $p < q \leqq m$. Finally, suppose an aggregate consisting of the first q capital types exists for each firm separately. Then an aggregate consisting of the first q capital types exists for the system as a whole.

***Proof*:** Condition (a) of Lemma 6.1 holds by assumption. So does condition (b). Condition (c) follows from Lemma 6.3.

In the case of $q = m$ where a full aggregate is involved, Theorem 6.2 can be strengthened to:

Theorem 6.4: Suppose that a full capital aggregate exists *for each firm taken separately*. Suppose further that an aggregate consisting of capital types $(p+1, \ldots, m)$ exists *for the system as a whole* for some p, $1 \leqq p < m$. Then a full capital aggregate and an aggregate consisting of the first p capital types also exist for the system as a whole.[11]

***Proof*:** Consider first the existence of a full capital aggregate. By assumption, (a) of Lemma 6.1 is satisfied (with $p = m$). Further, (b) is vacuous since all capital types are to be included in the aggregate. Finally, (c) holds by Lemma 6.3 and the existence of an aggregate consisting of capital types $(p+1, \ldots, m)$. Hence a full capital aggregate exists. The simultaneous existence of an aggregate consisting of the first p capital types now follows from Theorem 6.2.

The fly in the ointment occurs because Lemma 6.4, on which these results depend, does not merely ensure the existence of an aggregate of the first $q-1$ capital types for each firm separately given that an aggregate of K_q exists. This would involve only

$$J(K_1, \ldots, K_q) = H(R(K_q), S(K_1, \ldots, K_{q-1})) \qquad (6.23)$$

whereas (6.13) shows that J is actually *additively* separable. As we shall see most clearly when we come to closed-form results, this is so restrictive as to take any surprise out of Theorem 6.4. We state the restrictive consequence as:

Theorem 6.5: Suppose that an aggregate consisting of the first q capital types exists. Suppose further that an aggregate consisting of capital types $(p+1, \ldots, q)$ exists for some p, $1 < p \leqq q$. Then every firm's production function can be written in the form:

$$f^v(K_1(v), \ldots, K_m(v), L(v)) = F^v(\{S^v(K_1(v), \ldots, K_p(v)) + R^v(K_{p+1}(v), \ldots, K_q(v))\}, K_{q+1}(v), \ldots, K_m(v), L(v)). \tag{6.24}$$

Proof: Follows from Lemmas 6.1, 6.2, and 6.4.

Corollary 6.3: Suppose that a full capital aggregate exists (either for the system as a whole or for each firm separately) and that an aggregate consisting of capital types $(p+1, \ldots, m)$ also exists for the system as a whole for some p, $1 \leqq p < m$. Then each firm's production function can be written in the form:

$$f^v(K_1(v), \ldots, K_m(v), L(v)) = F^v(\{S^v(K_1(v), \ldots, K_p(v)) + R^v(K_{p+1}(v), \ldots, K_m(v))\}, L(v))$$

Proof: Follows from Theorems 6.3 and 6.4.

The simplest interpretation of these conditions occurs when we consider technologies for which necessary and sufficient conditions for aggregation are known in closed form. For the most part, these are constant returns and related technologies,[12] but there is one very special case which we must dispose of first. If *every* firm's production function is additively separable in a function of the first q capitals and a function of the remaining factors, so that:

$$f^v(K_1(v), \ldots, K_m(v), L(v)) = J^v(K_1(v), \ldots, K_q(v)) + \psi^v(K_{q+1}(v), \ldots, K_m(v), L(v)) \quad (v = 1, \ldots, n) \tag{6.25}$$

then it is evident that an aggregate of the first p capital types, $p < q$ exists if and only if

$$J^v(K_1(v), \ldots, K_q(v)) = S^v(K_1(v), \ldots, K_p(v)) + R^v(K_{p+1}(v), \ldots, K_q(v)) \quad (v = 1, \ldots, n) \tag{6.26}$$

and that an aggregate of type $p+1, \ldots, q$ also exists. Here necessity follows from Theorem 6.5 and sufficiency from inspection (or both directly from Lemma 6.1), the case being essentially that of Nataf [5] in which efficient allocation of labor plays no role.

The Nataf case of *every* firm having an additively separable production function in the form (6.25) is not very interesting, however, and we shall henceforth assume that it does not occur. With that assumption, we can now turn to the more interesting closed-form cases which arise under constant returns and related technologies.

6.4 Constant returns and related technologies

DEFINITION 6.1: Suppose that the νth firm's production function can be written in the form

$$f^\nu(K_1(\nu), \ldots, K_m(\nu), L(\nu)) = G^\nu(H^1(K_1(\nu)), \ldots, H^m(K_m(\nu)), L(\nu)) \qquad (6.27)$$

where the $H^i(\cdot)$ are monotonic and $G^\nu(\cdot, \ldots, \cdot, \cdot)$ is homogeneous of degree one in its arguments. Then $f^\nu(\cdot, \ldots, \cdot, \cdot)$ will be called capital-generalized, constant returns (CGCR). See p. 41.

A CGCR function is one which can be made constant returns by (possibly nonlinear) stretching of the capital axes. Equations (6.2) and (6.3) above provide examples.[13] We prove:

Theorem 6.6: Let every firm have a CGCR production function.

(a) A necessary and sufficient condition for the simultaneous existence of a full capital aggregate and an aggregate consisting of capital types $(p+1, \ldots, m)$ for some p, $1 \leqq p < m$ is that, for all $\nu = 1, \ldots, n$,

$$f^\nu(K_1(\nu), \ldots, K_m(\nu), L(\nu)) = F(\{S^\nu(K_1(\nu), \ldots, K_p(\nu)) + R^\nu(K_{p+1}(\nu), \ldots, K_m(\nu))\}, L(\nu)) \qquad (6.28)$$

where $F(\cdot,\cdot)$ is homogeneous of degree one and is independent of ν.

(b) Further, in this case, an aggregate consisting of the first p capital types also exists.

(c) When the aggregates exist, the aggregate production function can be written as

$$Y^* = F\left(\left\{\sum_{\nu=1}^{n} S^\nu(K_1(\nu), \ldots, K_p(\nu)) + \sum_{\nu=1}^{n} R^\nu(K_{p+1}(\nu), \ldots, K_m(\nu))\right\}, L\right) \qquad (6.29)$$

where Y^* is maximized output and L is total labor.[14]

Proof:

(a) 1. Necessity. From Lemma 6.1 the existence of a full aggregate implies that for every $\nu = 1, \ldots, n$,

$$f^\nu(K_1(\nu), \ldots, K_m(\nu), L(\nu)) = F^\nu(J^\nu(K_1(\nu), \ldots, K_m(\nu)), L(\nu)). \qquad (6.30)$$

Since $f^\nu(\cdot, \ldots, \cdot, \cdot)$ is CGCR, $F^\nu(\cdot,\cdot)$ can be taken to be homogeneous of degree one in its arguments by suitable redefinition of $J^\nu(\cdot, \ldots, \cdot)$. The fact that the $F^\nu(\cdot,\cdot)$ must then all be the same is the standard capital-augmenting result for the existence of a full capital aggregate given in Theorem 2.2, p. 38 and Theorem 2.4, p. 43.[15] That $J^\nu(K_1(\nu), \ldots, K_m(\nu))$ can be written in the additive form given in (6.28) follows from Corollary 6.3 above. This does not quite complete the proof of necessity, however, since one must show that the two arguments just given hold simultaneously – that is, that $F^\nu(\cdot,\cdot)$ can be taken as homogeneous of degree one when $J^\nu(\cdot, \ldots, \cdot)$ is written in its additive form. This follows from Remark 6.1.

2. Sufficiency. This can be proved in (at least) two ways. One such way is by construction as in the proof of (c), below. The other way is as follows. From (6.28) and the fact that $F(\cdot,\cdot)$ is homogeneous of degree one, Chapter 2, Theorem 2.4 implies that a full aggregate exists. Further, (6.28) itself shows the existence at the firm level of two aggregates consisting respectively of capital types $(p+1, \ldots, q)$ and the first p capital types, so that (a) of Lemma 6.1 is satisfied for such partial aggregates. Lemma 6.3 then shows that (c) of Lemma 6.1 is also so satisfied. Since $F(\cdot,\cdot)$ is constant returns, F_J and F_L are homogeneous of degree zero (where $J(\nu)$ is the first argument of $F(\cdot,\cdot)$). As in Remark 6.1, Euler's theorem applied to F_J and F_L shows that the right-hand side of (6.15) above is zero, and since the left-hand side is also zero when K_q and K_i are replaced by S^ν and R^ν, respectively, (6.15) and thus (6.14) and (6.12) hold so that (b) of

Lemmas 6.1 and 6.2 are also satisfied. Lemma 6.1 now shows the existence of the partial aggregates.

(b) The proof of sufficiency just given proves the simultaneous existence of both partial aggregates. This would also follow from Theorem 6.2 or Theorem 6.3.

(c) The nature of the aggregate follows from an alternative proof of sufficiency along lines following Solow [6, pp. 104–5] (see also p. 8). Begin with (6.28). Optimal allocation of labor requires the same marginal product of labor in every use. Since $F(\cdot,\cdot)$ is constant returns and $F_{LL} < 0$, this means the ratio of the two arguments of $F(\cdot,\cdot)$ must be the same for every v. Letting $J(v)$ denote the first argument, there then exist scalars, λ_v, $v = 1, \ldots, n$, such that $\lambda_v > 0$, $\Sigma_{v=1}^{n} \lambda_v = 1$, and

$$L(v) = \lambda_v L; \qquad J(v) = \lambda_v J \tag{6.31}$$

where

$$J = \sum_{v=1}^{n} J(v) \equiv \sum_{v=1}^{n} S^v(K_1(v), \ldots, K_p(v)) + \sum_{v=1}^{n} R^v(K_{p+1}(v), \ldots, K_m(v)) \tag{6.32}$$

when labor is optimally allocated. Then, at such points,

$$Y^* = \sum_{v=1}^{n} F(J(v), L(v)) = \sum_{v=1}^{n} F(\lambda_v J, \lambda_v L) = \sum_{v=1}^{n} \lambda_v F(J, L) = F(J, L) \tag{6.33}$$

using the fact that $F(\cdot,\cdot)$ is homogeneous of degree one. This simultaneously shows the existence of a full capital aggregate, J, and of partial capital aggregates,

$$S \equiv \sum_{v=1}^{n} S^v(K_1(v), \ldots, K_p(v))$$

and (6.34)

$$R \equiv \sum_{v=1}^{n} R^v(K_{p+1}(v), \ldots, K_n(v))$$

as well as proving (c).

Theorem 6.6 shows fairly plainly what is going on. In the CGCR case, the requisite full and partial aggregates will exist in the system as a whole if and only if: (1) the corresponding partial aggregates exist at the firm level *and* are perfect substitutes for each other within the firm; and (2) firms differ *only* in the way in which the partial aggregates are constructed but not in the way in which their capital aggregates are combined with labor to produce final output. This leads to a situation in which, once aggregation has been performed at the firm level, the firm's two partial capital aggregates are perfect substitutes for those of any other firm as well as for each other.

This set of conditions is even plainer in its implication when we consider constant returns and partial capital aggregates consisting of a single capital type.

Corollary 6.4: Suppose all firms have constant returns production functions. Then the results of Theorem 6.6 apply. Further, $R^{\nu}(\cdot, \ldots, \cdot)$ and $S^{\nu}(\cdot, \ldots, \cdot)$ can be taken as homogeneous of degree one in their arguments.

***Proof*:** Constant returns is a special case of CGCR, so only the final statement requires a separate proof which is left to the reader.[16]

Corollary 6.5: Suppose all firms have constant returns production functions. A necessary and sufficient condition for the simultaneous existence of a full capital aggregate and an aggregate consisting of capital type m *only* is as in Theorem 6.6 with $R^{\nu}(K_m(\nu)) = b_m(\nu) K_m(\nu)$ for some scalar $b_m(\nu)$, so that aggregate capital for the system as a whole is given by

$$J \equiv \sum_{\nu=1}^{n} b_m(\nu) K_m(\nu) + \sum_{\nu=1}^{n} S^{\nu}(K_1(\nu), \ldots, K_{m-1}(\nu)). \quad (6.35)$$

The other results of Theorem 6.6 continue to apply.

***Proof*:** Obvious from Corollary 6.4.

Corollary 6.6: Suppose all firms have constant returns production functions. A necessary and sufficient condition for the simultaneous existence of a full capital aggregate and of $m-1$ partial capital aggregates each consisting of a single capital type is that, for every $\nu = 1, \ldots, n$, there exist scalars, $b_1(\nu), \ldots, b_m(\nu)$, such that:

$$f^{\nu}(K_1(\nu), \ldots, K_m(\nu), L(\nu)) = F\left(\sum_{i=1}^{m} b_i(\nu) K_i(\nu), L(\nu)\right) \quad (6.36)$$

where $F(\cdot,\cdot)$ is the same for all firms. In this case, aggregate capital stock is given by

$$J \equiv \sum_{v=1}^{n} \sum_{i=1}^{m} b_i(v) K_i(v) \tag{6.37}$$

and the aggregate production function by

$$Y^* = F(J, L). \tag{6.38}$$

In this case, the mth possible partial aggregate consisting of a single capital aggregate and, indeed, every possible partial capital aggregate also exists.

***Proof*:** Let the $m-1$ partial aggregates whose existence is assumed be types $2, \ldots, m$. Let the full aggregate for firm v be $J^v(K_1(v), \ldots, K_m(v))$ which can be taken to be homogeneous of degree one. As in the proof of Theorem 6.6, consideration of Remark 6.1 and (6.15), (6.14), and (6.12) shows that

$$J^v_{K_iK_j} \equiv 0 \qquad (i, j = 1, \ldots, m, \quad i \neq j) \tag{6.39}$$

whence, by homogeneity, there exist $b_1(v), \ldots, b_m(v)$ such that

$$J^v(K_1(v), \ldots, K_m(v)) = \sum_{i=1}^{m} b_i(v) K_i(v). \tag{6.40}$$

The corollary now follows from Theorem 6.6.

Corollary 6.6 exhibits the case in which all capital aggregates exist. In it, any capital of any type within any firm is equivalent to a fixed amount of capital of any other type in or out of the same firm, where the equivalences depend both on type and firm. All capital assets are perfect substitutes both within and across firms and there is a natural capital aggregate consisting of capital measured in efficiency units. Such an aggregate only exists, however, because firms differ only as regards the size of their capital stock measured in efficiency units. This is the capital-augmentation theorem applied both across and within firms, as it were.

This is, of course, the most restrictive case. Theorem 6.6 or Corollaries 6.4 and 6.5 exhibit cases where perfect substitution only occurs between groups of capital types without requiring it among individual capital types. Still the restrictive implications are clear. Suppose for simplicity that all capital is considered either plant or equipment. Then the simultaneous existence of a full capital aggregate and of either a plant or an equipment aggregate (the existence of either of which implies the existence of the other given a full aggregate) implies that plant and equipment – as aggregates – are perfect substitutes. Under constant returns or CGCR (essentially the only important cases where aggregates are likely to exist at all), firms can differ only in how the plant and equipment aggregates are constructed. They cannot differ as to how they are used or as to the fact that they are perfect substitutes. Indeed, the fact that plant and equipment must be perfect substitutes would still be true even if all firms were identical. The simultaneous existence of full *and* partial capital aggregates imposes a stringent burden on the form of production functions.

Notes

1. See [4] (Chapter 1) for a relatively nontechnical summary and for a more general bibliography.
2. See p. 38. A number of authors have provided alternate proofs. See the works cited at p. 27, Note 9 and p. 64, Note 8.
3. See the discussion on pp. 9–10.
4. See [1] (Chapter 2). The mutually isomorphic questions of labor and output aggregation were analyzed in [2] (Chapter 3). See also [3] (Chapter 4).
5. See pp. 11–12, 50, and 62.
6. The existence of the partial aggregates can be verified by direct – although tedious – computation from Theorem 2.6, p. 49. See also Lemmas 2.1 and 2.1′, p. 36. The nonexistence of the full aggregate follows from the fact that the marginal rate of substitution between $K_1(\nu)$ and $K_2(\nu)$, even within the νth firm, is not independent of $L(\nu)$. See p. 54.
7. Somewhat similar results hold for labor or output aggregation. See Chapters 3 and 4. The results are not the same, however. In the case of labor aggregation, there is a natural partial aggregate consisting of any single labor so the existence of such a partial aggregate is not restrictive, as it is in the capital case (see especially Lemma 6.4). On the other hand, for the result in question on complementary subaggregates to apply, it is necessary to assume the existence of the complementary subaggregate at the firm level which is not additionally necessary for capital.
8. This ignores the trivial Nataf case treated at the end of Section 6.3.
9. For discussion of these matters see Chapters 1–4.
10. Throughout this chapter I use unmodified the phrase "existence of an aggregate" to mean the existence of an aggregate for the system as a whole rather than the existence of an aggregate within particular firms' production functions. When the latter is meant, I shall say so. Of course, the two are closely related; indeed, existence within each firm's production function is necessary but not sufficient for existence for the system as a whole.
11. Note that the result is not symmetric as regards the assumptions made on full and partial aggregates. The existence of a full aggregate for the

system as a whole plus the existence of a partial aggregate for each firm separately does *not* suffice for the existence of any partial aggregate for the system as a whole. Otherwise a full aggregate for the whole system would immediately imply an aggregate for the whole system of each separate capital type and this is false. (Equations (6.2) and (6.3) provide a counter-example.) This is because of the crucial role of (b) of Lemma 6.1 which is vacuous for a full aggregate.

12. These are not the only such cases, however. (See p. 44.) A full aggregate exists if all production functions are in the form

$$f^v(K_1(v), \ldots, K_m(v), L(v)) = F^v(J^v(K_1(v), \ldots, K_m(v)) + c_v L(v)).$$

The full set of nonconstant returns-related cases permitting capital aggregation is not known. It is plain, however, that such cases are very special in that, for most nonconstant returns-related cases, capital aggregates will not exist for the system as a whole even if they exist for each firm separately and all firms are exactly alike.

13. A more general class of technologies would be ones which are homogeneous of degree one in labor and monotonic functions of the first q capital types but not necessarily in monotonic functions of the remaining capital types. The necessity results of this section concerning the nature of the aggregate apply to such cases with the existence of a full aggregate replaced by the existence of an aggregate consisting of the first q capital types and partial aggregates being understood to involve capital types lower-numbered than q. Explicit discussion of this case does not seem useful because closed-form necessary and sufficient conditions for the existence of such aggregates are not known for $q < m$.
14. Generalization to more than two partial aggregates is left to the reader.
15. See also Note 7, Chapter 2.
16. Cf. p. 80.

References

[1] Fisher, F. M., "Embodied technical change and the existence of an aggregate capital stock," *Review of Economic Studies*, **32** (1965), 263–88 (reprinted as Chapter 2).

[2] Fisher, F. M., "Embodied technology and the existence of labour and output aggregates," *Review of Economic Studies*, **35** (1968), 391–412 (reprinted as Chapter 3).

[3] Fisher, F. M., "Embodied technology and the aggregation of fixed and movable capital goods," *Review of Economic Studies*, **35** (1968), 417–28 (reprinted as Chapter 4).

[4] Fisher, F. M., "The existence of aggregate production functions," *Econometrica*, **37** (1969), 553–77 (reprinted as Chapter 1).

[5] Nataf, A., "Sur la possibilité de construction de certains macromodèles," *Econometrica*, **16** (1948), 232–44.

[6] Solow, R. M., "Capital, labor, and income in manufacturing," in *National Bureau of Economic Research Conference in Income and Wealth, The Behavior of Income Shares* (Studies in Income and Wealth, 26), Princeton: Princeton University Press, 1964, pp. 101–28.

7

Approximate aggregation and the Leontief conditions (1969)

7.1 The nature and importance of the problem

Some twenty years ago, W. W. Leontief proved what is now a well-known and classic result on the conditions under which a continuously twice differentiable function can be written with two or more of its arguments grouped in an aggregate.[1] He showed that if $F(x_1, x_2, x_3)$ is continuously twice differentiable, then there exists a function $\phi(x_1, x_2)$ and a function $G(\phi, x_3)$ such that

$$F(x_1, x_2, x_3) \equiv G(\phi(x_1, x_2), x_3) \tag{7.1}$$

if and only if F has the property

$$\frac{\partial(F_1/F_2)}{\partial x_3} \equiv 0, \tag{7.2}$$

where the subscripts denote differentiation.[2]

The problem of the presence or absence of such a separability property and of the satisfaction of the Leontief conditions naturally arises in several important connections in economic analysis. It has occurred in utility theory where it involves the possibility of grouping commodities into budget aggregates as well as a number of other behavioral implications;[3] it has occurred in the theory of the firm

This research was supported by National Science Foundation Grant GS-95. I am indebted to Karl Shell for helpful discussions but retain the usual responsibility.

where it involves the aggregation of factors.[4] Most recently, the problem has received wide attention in a closely related connection, that of the existence of macro production functions aggregated over firms and with economy- or industry-wide factor aggregates as arguments.[5] For the sake of definiteness, I shall concentrate discussion on the latter problem, although the results of the present chapter are by no means restricted thereto.

The leading theorem in the problem of aggregation over firms is the following. Suppose that technical differences among firms are embodied in the capital goods used by them, so that capital goods are not homogeneous or shiftable among firms. Suppose further that labor or other factors are assigned to firms so as to achieve efficient production for the set of firms taken as a whole. If there are constant returns, then efficient production for the set of firms can be expressed as a production function involving an overall capital aggregate if *and only if* all technical differences among firms are capital augmenting.[6] Similarly strong results are available on the aggregation of labor and of outputs in the same model,[7] but for ease of presentation, I shall concentrate on the capital-aggregation theorem as an example here.

Now, the force of the capital-aggregation theorem is not the sufficiency of capital-augmenting technical differences for the existence of a capital aggregate; it is the fact that *only* such differences can be accommodated.[8] If, in the circumstances described, macro production functions with a single capital argument are to give an exact description of production possibilities, if exact quality-corrected index numbers for capital exist, if the results of the analysis of one- or two-sector growth models apply directly to the analysis of more realistically diverse economies,[9] then the extent of technical diversity among firms must be greatly and unrealistically circumscribed. Similar strong statements arise from practically any application of the necessity of the Leontief conditions.

Yet it might still be the case that this is irrelevant for practical purposes. All models are approximations, and what really matters are the conditions under which aggregate models give satisfactory approximations to reality.[10] Naturally, if it turns out that the existence of such a satisfactory approximation implies that the exact Leontief conditions must be approximately satisfied, the acceptance of such approximations does not lead very far, but is this true? Suppose, for example, that in the capital-aggregation problem we merely require that a macro production function with capital aggregate be approximately accurate over some bounded range of the variables. It is obvious that this will happen if technical differences are approximately capital augmenting, but it is not at all clear that this is the *only* way in which such an approximation can occur. If there are other ways, then the force of the exact theorem is considerably evaded in practice.

This chapter goes some distance toward answering this question. Formally, we seek the conditions on a function $F(\cdot,\cdot,\cdot)$ under which there exists a function $\phi(\cdot,\cdot)$ and a function $G(\cdot,\cdot)$ such that, for all x_1, x_2, x_3 in a closed, bounded rectangular region, S[11]

$$H(x_1, x_2, x_3) \equiv F(x_1, x_2, x_3) - G(\phi(x_1, x_2), x_3) \tag{7.3}$$

satisfies

$$|H(x_1, x_2, x_3)| < \varepsilon \tag{7.4}$$

for some small $\varepsilon > 0$.[12] Clearly, this will occur if the Leontief condition (7.2) is approximately satisfied; we ask whether it can occur in any other way.

Our principal result is that if $F(\cdot,\cdot,\cdot)$ and $G(\cdot,\cdot)$ must satisfy fairly strong but fairly reasonable regularity conditions, then *only* the approximate satisfaction of the Leontief condition can lead to (7.4) in a sense to be made precise below. This strongly suggests that the hope of evading the force of theorems such as the capital-aggregation theorem is forlorn. It does not settle that question, since how closely the Leontief condition must be satisfied naturally depends on how close an approximation is required in (7.3) and (7.4), and we can give little or no guidance on this point. We shall return to this below after establishing our results.

7.2 Definitions and lemmas

Throughout what follows, a and b are both finite,[13] $b > a$, and $f(x)$ is a function defined on $[a, b]$.

DEFINITION 7.1: $f(\cdot)$ will be said to satisfy an *upper half Lipschitz condition* on $[a, b]$ if and only if there exists a finite $M > 0$, such that for all x_0, x_1 in $[a, b]$, $x_1 > x_0$,

$$\frac{f(x_1) - f(x_0)}{x_1 - x_0} < M. \tag{7.5}$$

DEFINITION 7.2: $f(\cdot)$ will be said to satisfy a *lower half Lipschitz condition* on $[a, b]$ if and only if there exists a finite $M > 0$, such that for all x_0, x_1 in $[a, b]$, $x_1 > x_0$,

$$\frac{f(x_1) - f(x_0)}{x_1 - x_0} > -M. \tag{7.6}$$

Obviously, if $f(\cdot)$ satisfies both a lower and an upper half Lipschitz condition on $[a, b]$, then it satisfies a Lipschitz condition on $[a, b]$; that is, there exists a finite $M > 0$, such that for all x_1, x_0 in $[a, b]$, $x_1 \neq x_0$,

$$\frac{|f(x_1) - f(x_0)|}{|x_1 - x_0|} < M. \tag{7.7}$$

Now, consider a set of functions, $\mathscr{F}$, each defined on $[a, b]$.

DEFINITION 7.3: A set of functions, $\mathscr{F}$, will be said to satisfy a *uniform* upper half Lipschitz condition on $[a, b]$ if and only if there exists an $M > 0$, such that for any $f(\cdot)$ in $\mathscr{F}$, and any x_0, x_1 in $[a, b]$, $x_1 > x_0$, (7.1) is satisfied. Similar statements define $\mathscr{F}$ as satisfying a uniform lower half Lipschitz condition and a uniform full Lipschitz condition.

Clearly, requiring $\mathscr{F}$ to satisfy a uniform (half or full) Lipschitz condition is stronger than requiring each of its elements to satisfy a (half or full) Lipschitz condition because the same M must serve for each element. This means there exists no sequence of functions in $\mathscr{F}$ for which the corresponding sequence of Ms goes to infinity. The plausibility of such a condition will be discussed later.[14]

We prove the following lemma.

Lemma 7.1: Let $\mathscr{F}$ be a set of continuous functions defined on $[a, b]$. Let $f(\cdot)$ be any function with first derivative $f'(\cdot)$ a member of $\mathscr{F}$ and satisfying

$$|f(x)| < \varepsilon \qquad \text{for all } x \text{ in } [a, b], \tag{7.8}$$

where $\varepsilon > 0$. For any $\eta > 0$, let $P(\eta)$ be the set of points in $[a, b]$ for which $|f'(x)| > \eta$.

(a) If $\mathscr{F}$ satisfies either a uniform lower or a uniform upper half Lipschitz condition on $[a, b]$, then for any $\eta > 0$ there exists an $\varepsilon^* > 0$, such that for all $\varepsilon < \varepsilon^*$, $P(\eta)$ is empty on any given closed interior subinterval of $[a, b]$.

(b) If $\mathscr{F}$ satisfies a uniform full Lipschitz condition on $[a, b]$, then for any $\eta > 0$, there exists an $\varepsilon^* > 0$, such that for all $\varepsilon < \varepsilon^*$, $P(\eta)$ is empty.

In other words, provided a function has a sufficiently regular derivative, the function can only approach zero if its derivative does.[15]

Proof: The first part of the proof uses the fact that $f'(x)$ cannot stay large and on one side of zero for too long without having (7.8) violated together with the fact that the uniform Lipschitz assumptions keep $f'(x)$ from changing very quickly.

Thus, suppose that $\mathscr{F}$ satisfies a uniform upper half Lipschitz condition on $[a, b]$. We begin by showing that for any $\eta > 0$ and $\lambda > 0$, there exists an $\varepsilon^* > 0$, such that for all $\varepsilon < \varepsilon^*$, $f'(x) < -\eta$ can occur on $[a, b]$ only for $x > b - \lambda$.

Suppose not. Then there exists an $x_0 < b - \lambda$, such that $f'(x_0) = -\rho$, for some $\rho > \eta$. There are two possibilities. Either for some x, $x_0 < x \leqslant b$, $f'(x) = -\eta$, or else for all x, $x_0 < x \leqslant b$, $f'(x) < -\eta$. In the latter case, take $x_1 = b$; in the former case, choose x_1 as the smallest $x > x_0$ for which $f'(x) = -\eta$. Then

$$x_1 - x_0 > \frac{\rho - \eta}{M}. \tag{7.9}$$

Clearly, by the mean value theorem,

$$f(x_0) - f(x_1) > \eta(x_1 - x_0) \geqslant \eta \min \left\{ \begin{matrix} \lambda \\ \dfrac{\rho - \eta}{M} \end{matrix} \right\} > 0. \tag{7.10}$$

By (7.8), however, $2\varepsilon > f(x_0) - f(x_1)$, and for sufficiently small ε, this contradicts (7.10).

Similarly, if satisfies a uniform lower half Lipschitz condition, then for any $\eta > 0$ and $\lambda > 0$, and sufficiently small ε, the only x in $[a, b]$ for which $f'(x) > \eta$ are those for which $x < a + \lambda$.

With this result, (b) can now be proved. Choose $\eta > 0$ and $\lambda > 0$ such that $(b - a) > \lambda$. For sufficiently small ε, $f'(x) < -\eta$ is impossible for $x \leqslant b - \lambda$. Now suppose that $f'(x_0) = -\rho$, $\rho > \eta$, for some x_0, with $(b - \lambda) < x_0 \leqslant b$. Consider $f'(b - \lambda)$. If $\mathscr{F}$ satisfies a uniform full Lipschitz condition on $[a, b]$, then

$$|f'(b - \lambda) - (-\rho)| < M\{x_0 - (b - \lambda)\} \leqslant M\lambda, \tag{7.11}$$

so

$$f'(b - \lambda) < -\rho + M\lambda. \tag{7.12}$$

Since λ can be made as small as desired, for small enough ε, this implies $f'(b - \lambda) < -\eta$ which is a contradiction. This establishes (b).

Thus, return to the case in which $\mathscr{F}$ satisfies only a uniform upper half Lipschitz condition (the case in which a uniform lower half Lipschitz condition is involved differing only trivially). Choose a small

$\lambda > 0$. Consider the interval $[a, b-\lambda]$. For small enough ε^*, $f'(x) < -\eta$ cannot occur for $x > b-\lambda$. By choosing λ close enough to $(b-a)$, we can place any subregion of $[a, b]$ not including point a into the region where $f'(x) \geqslant -\eta$. Similarly, consider the interval $[a+\lambda, b]$. $f'(x) > \eta$ cannot occur for $x < a+\lambda$. By choosing λ close enough to $(b-a)$, we can place any subregion of $[a, b]$ not including point b into the region where $f'(x) \leqslant \eta$. This establishes Lemma 7.1(a).

We consider one more point before proceeding. We shall speak of a function $f(\cdot,\cdot, \ldots, \cdot)$ as satisfying a (half or full) Lipschitz condition in x_1 on a closed bounded rectangular region S if and only if, for all fixed values of $x_2, \ldots, x_n$, say $\bar{x}_2, \ldots, \bar{x}_n$, for which there exists a point $(x_1, \bar{x}_2, \ldots, \bar{x}_n)$ in S, the function $g(\cdot) \equiv f(\cdot, \bar{x}_2, \ldots, \bar{x}_n)$ satisfies such a condition.

Similarly, a set of functions $\mathscr{F}$ with typical member $f(\cdot,\cdot, \ldots, \cdot)$ will be said to satisfy a uniform (upper half, lower half, or full) Lipschitz condition in x_1 on S if and only if all the functions generated by taking a member of $\mathscr{F}$ and fixing the values of $x_2, \ldots, x_n$ arbitrarily satisfy such a condition at all points of S *with the same value of M*.

7.3 The principal theorem

We are now ready to proceed with the question of approximate separability and the approximate satisfaction of the Leontief conditions. We suppose that a given twice continuously differentiable function, $F(x_1, x_2, x_3)$, is to be approximated by another twice continuously differentiable function, $G(\phi(x_1, x_2), x_3)$, drawn from a set of functions, $\mathscr{F}$, satisfying certain regularity conditions. A similar analysis would apply if we were to ask what functions, $F(\cdot,\cdot,\cdot)$, satisfying certain regularity conditions could be approximated by a given function, $G(\cdot,\cdot,\cdot)$. Throughout, we define $H(x_1, x_2, x_3) \equiv F - G$ and our standard of approximation is

$$|H(x_1, x_2, x_3)| < \varepsilon \tag{7.13}$$

for some $\varepsilon > 0$ and all points in the interior of a closed, bounded, rectangular region, S.

Theorem 7.1: Consider the following conditions:

(1) For all x in S, $F_2 \neq 0$.[16]

(2) F_1, F_2, F_{13}, and F_{23} satisfy Lipschitz conditions on S in x_1, x_2, x_3, and x_3, respectively.

(3) Each of the following sets of functions, $(\partial G/\partial x_1)$, $(\partial G/\partial x_2)$, $(\partial^2 G/\partial x_1\,\partial x_3)$, and $(\partial^2 G/\partial x_2\,\partial x_3)$ for all G in $\mathscr{F}$ satisfies either a uniform upper or a uniform lower half Lipschitz condition on S in x_1, x_2, x_3, and x_3, respectively.

(3′) The sets of functions described in (3) all satisfy uniform full Lipschitz conditions on S in the variables listed.

For any $\gamma > 0$, let $Q(\gamma)$ be the set of points in S at which

$$\left|\frac{\partial(F_1/F_2)}{\partial x_3}\right| > \gamma. \tag{7.14}$$

(a) If (1)–(3) hold, then for any $\gamma > 0$ and $\mu > 0$, there exists an $\varepsilon^* > 0$, such that for all $\varepsilon < \varepsilon^*$, (7.13) implies $Q(\gamma)$ is empty.

(b) If (1), (2), and (3′) hold, then for any $\gamma > 0$, there exists an $\varepsilon^* > 0$ such that for all $\varepsilon < \varepsilon^*$, (7.13) implies that $Q(\gamma)$ is empty.

***Proof*:** We shall prove the theorem assuming (1), (2), and (3′). The proof using (3) in place of (3′) is similar and is sketched in Note 17.

Differentiating the definition of H and rearranging:

$$\frac{F_1}{F_2} = \frac{\phi_1}{\phi_2} + \frac{H_1 - H_2(\phi_1/\phi_2)}{F_2} = \frac{\phi_1}{\phi_2}\left(1 - \frac{H_2}{F_2}\right) + \frac{H_1}{F_2}. \tag{7.15}$$

First, observe that if (2) and (3′) hold, then the set of H_1 generated by taking the set of all G in $\mathscr{F}$ satisfies a uniform Lipschitz condition in x_1, whence, for any $\eta_1 > 0$, we can choose ε sufficiently small to make $|H_1| < \eta_1$. Similarly, we can make $|H_2| < \eta_1$.

Next, we shall show that there exists a finite $P_1 > 0$ such that $|\phi_1/\phi_2| < P_1$. Since $F_2 \neq 0$ anywhere in S and S is closed and bounded, there exists a $P_2 > 0$ such that $|F_2| > P_2$. Further, since F is continuously differentiable, there exists a $P_3 > 0$ such that $|F_1/F_2| < P_3$. Hence, choose $\eta_1 < P_2$. Then by (7.15):

$$P_3 > \left|\frac{F_1}{F_2}\right| \geqslant \left|\frac{\phi_1}{\phi_2}\right|\left|1 - \frac{H_2}{F_2}\right| - \left|\frac{H_1}{F_2}\right| \geqslant \left|\frac{\phi_1}{\phi_2}\right|\left(1 - \left|\frac{H_2}{F_2}\right|\right)$$

$$- \left|\frac{H_1}{F_2}\right| > \left|\frac{\phi_1}{\phi_2}\right|\left(1 - \frac{\eta_1}{P_2}\right) - \frac{\eta_1}{P_2} \tag{7.16}$$

whence

$$P \equiv \frac{P_3 + \dfrac{\eta_1}{P_2}}{1 - \dfrac{\eta_1}{P_2}} > \left| \frac{\phi_1}{\phi_2} \right|. \tag{7.17}$$

It follows that

$$|H_1 - H_2(\phi_1/\phi_2)| \leqslant |H_1| + |H_2||\phi_1/\phi_2| < \eta_1(1 + P_1). \tag{7.18}$$

Moreover, by (2) and (3), the sets of H_{13} and H_{23} generated by taking the set of all G in $\mathscr{F}$ satisfy uniform Lipschitz conditions in x_3. Since η_1 can be made as small as desired by taking ε sufficiently small, a second application of Lemma 7.1 shows that we can make both $|H_{13}| < \eta_2$ and $|H_{23}| < \eta_2$ for any $\eta_2 > 0$. Hence,

$$|H_{13} - H_{23}(\phi_1/\phi_2)| < \eta_2(1 + P_1). \tag{7.19}$$

Now, since F_{23} is continuous and S is closed and bounded, there exists a $P_4 > 0$, such that $|F_{23}| < P_4$. Using this together with (7.18) and (7.19), we have

$$\begin{aligned} \left| \frac{\partial(F_1/F_2)}{\partial x_3} \right| &= \left| \frac{H_{13} - H_{23}(\phi_1/\phi_2)}{F_2} - \frac{F_{23}(H_1 - H_2(\phi_1/\phi_2))}{(F_2)^2} \right| \\ &\leqslant \left| \frac{H_{13} - H_{23}(\phi_1/\phi_2)}{F_2} \right| + \left| \frac{F_{23}(H_1 - H_2(\phi_1/\phi_2))}{(F_2)^2} \right| \\ &< \frac{\eta_2(1 + P_1)}{P_2} + \frac{\eta_1 P_4(1 + P_1)}{(P_2)^2}. \end{aligned} \tag{7.20}$$

Since, by making ε sufficiently small, both η_1 and η_2 can be made as small as desired, the final expression can be made less than γ. QED.[17]

7.4 Discussion of the theorem: Leontief and Lipschitz

Theorem 7.1 essentially states that if a twice differentiable separable function approximates a given reasonable-looking twice differentiable function, then either the given function approximately satisfies the Leontief conditions or else the approximating function exhibits some kind of peculiar behavior. In this section, we shall discuss the reasonableness and applicability of the assumptions of the theorem as well as the sense in which such behavior is indeed peculiar.

In the first place, assumption (1) of the theorem is essentially a matter of housekeeping, required to ensure the existence of the appropriate derivatives in the very statement of the Leontief conditions. Aside from the fact that F_1 could be used instead of F_2, this condition can be weakened in the following way. Suppose that there exist points at which $F_2 = 0$. Construct closed rectangular subregions of S excluding such points; the theorem then holds on every such subregion.

On the other hand, the requirement that certain derivatives of $F(\cdot,\cdot,\cdot)$ satisfy a Lipschitz condition on S may appear too strong. The derivatives of the Cobb–Douglas production function, for example, do not satisfy a Lipschitz condition on any rectangular region which includes points on an axis. Unfortunately, this objection does not really affect the practical force of the theorem. In the Cobb–Douglas case, for example, the function and all its derivatives satisfy Lipschitz conditions everywhere in the interior of the positive quadrant. The theorem then applies to any closed rectangular region S entirely contained in that quadrant. It is true that the theorem cannot be extended to include the axes, but this is not a matter of much direct practical interest. (It is a matter of indirect interest, however, because it bears on how closely the Leontief conditions must be approximated. We shall return to this below.) Similarly, in other cases, the theorem applies to any closed bounded region so constructed as to rule out points where Lipschitz conditions are not satisfied. Only if such points are the rule rather than the exception, as it were, does their existence destroy the applicability of the theorem. Needless to say, cases in which such points are of general importance are cases in which the function $F(\cdot,\cdot,\cdot)$ exhibits behavior very different from that usually assumed in economic analysis.[18]

Similar remarks apply to the possibility that the derivatives of a particular function $G(\cdot,\cdot)$ of F fail to satisfy the appropriate half or full Lipschitz condition at a particular set of points or that the uniformity requirement fails at such a set.

That requirement, the assumption of the satisfaction of *uniform* (half or full) Lipschitz conditions, is perhaps the strongest assumption of the theorem. We have already observed that those Lipschitz conditions could be satisfied by the appropriate derivatives of every $G(\cdot,\cdot)$ in $\mathscr{F}$ without being uniformly satisfied. Nevertheless, the uniformity assumption does not seem unrealistic. This is so for a number of reasons.

First, it is clearly not unreasonable to require that any function

$G(\cdot,\cdot)$ which is to be a reasonable-looking approximation to a function $F(\cdot,\cdot,\cdot)$ satisfy the same sort of regularity conditions which $F(\cdot,\cdot,\cdot)$ does. If the real world is thought to be regular, it is natural to require that what we say about the world also be regular. Functions exhibiting too grossly irregular behavior will not be deemed acceptable. Clearly, an example of such a function is one which fails to have derivatives satisfying Lipschitz conditions. Yet it also seems reasonable to suppose that functions whose derivatives only satisfy Lipschitz conditions with extremely large M will also be ruled out. If the reason for requiring a derivative to satisfy a Lipschitz condition is that functions whose derivatives move too fast seem unrealistic, then that reason seems also to require (at least in a closed bounded region) that the rate at which such derivatives move must not exceed some fixed large finite bound, beyond which unrealism seems evident. The force of this sort of argument depends, of course, on the particular purposes to which such functions are to be put; in no sense can the argument establish a general proposition.

The argument for uniform Lipschitz conditions is, however, very much strengthened by a further consideration. For practical purposes, it is enough if (3) rather than (3′) of the theorem holds. In other words, it is not necessary for the application of the results that the appropriate derivatives of functions in $\mathscr{F}$ satisfy uniform *full* Lipschitz conditions; it is enough that they satisfy either uniform upper or uniform lower half Lipschitz conditions. This means that the results of our theorem do not become inapplicable simply because there exists no fixed upper bound such that the absolute rates of change of derivatives of acceptable functions do not exceed that bound. To escape the applicability of our theorem, the rate of change of such derivatives must be unbounded *both above and below* as we consider a sequence of acceptable functions.

The force of this may be illuminated if we look at the matter in a different way. Choose a standard of approximation to the Leontief conditions (γ in (7.14)). Consider any finite $M>0$. The theorem tells us that if we wish to approximate $F(\cdot,\cdot,\cdot)$ sufficiently closely by a separable function, $G(\cdot,\cdot)$, there are only two ways in which this can be done. Either $F(\cdot,\cdot,\cdot)$ must meet the chosen standard of approximation to the Leontief conditions or else at least one of the derivatives of $G(\cdot,\cdot)$ described in the theorem has the property that there exist points in S such that the rate of change of that derivative between those points is positive and greater than M, and also points for which that rate of change is negative and less than $-M$. Any function not approximately satisfying the Leontief conditions and with rates of change of derivatives bounded either above by M or below by $-M$ will not serve.

In other words, if we insist that $F(\cdot,\cdot,\cdot)$ be approximated closely enough and that $F(\cdot,\cdot,\cdot)$ not approximately satisfy the Leontief conditions, we are also insisting that the rates of change of the appropriate derivatives of the approximating function be very large, both positively and negatively.

That such behavior is peculiar is pointed up even more strongly if we recall our earlier point that it is not enough that such behavior exists at isolated points. If S is divided into small rectangular closed subregions, then the Leontief conditions will have to be approximately satisfied on each such subregion unless the rates of change of the appropriate derivatives exceed a fixed reasonable bound *both above and below on each such subregion*. This can happen, of course. The function $\lambda \sin(x/\lambda)$ has a first derivative whose rate of change both above and below exceeds any given bound on any given interval for small enough λ; for small λ, however, it is not a function whose behavior resembles that of functions generally used in economic analysis.

Thus, if we restrict our attention to functions with reasonable-looking first and second derivatives and insist on approximating $F(\cdot,\cdot,\cdot)$ sufficiently closely, we are also assuming that $F(\cdot,\cdot,\cdot)$ approximately satisfies the Leontief conditions. Applying this to the capital-aggregation theorem earlier discussed, this result becomes the following. A macro production function with an aggregate capital stock will approximate the true state of affairs only if either technical differences among firms are almost entirely capital augmenting or if the firm production functions or the macro production function itself fails to exhibit the kind of regular behavior which production functions used in practice are generally assumed to possess. Something has to give if we require such reasonable behavior together with general types of technical differences and closeness of approximation.

Naturally, the importance of this type of result in practice depends on the standards of approximation and of regularity applied in particular cases and also on the particular region S in which it is desired to work. To take the latter point first, consider again an example in which Lipschitz conditions are violated on the axes. If one takes a closed region S with boundaries very close to the axes, then a given standard of approximation to $F(\cdot,\cdot,\cdot)$ can be satisfied and the Leontief conditions not approximated everywhere in S more easily than if attention is restricted to a region with boundaries farther from the axes. This is not much help if we require approximations to be good everywhere; it is only important if we are especially interested in what happens on or near the axes.

Similarly, the theorem will not matter much if standards of regularity or of approximation are loose ones. What those standards are or ought to be depends on the particular problem to be analyzed, as do the relations among them enforced by the theorem. It does not seem possible, therefore, to give any detailed guidance in this regard. The conclusion seems warranted, nevertheless, that the hope of approximating given functions with separable ones unless the given functions also approximately satisfy the Leontief conditions is not generally justifiable. In the capital-aggregation problem, for example, use of quality-corrected capital aggregates as approximately correct seems likely to rest on the unrealistic assumption that technical differences are almost all capital augmenting. The use of such aggregates in theory and practice is thus a matter for considerable caution.[19]

Notes

1. See Leontief [15]. The proof is given in Leontief [14] and in the introduction to this volume pp. xv–xvi.
2. The necessity of (7.2) is, of course, obvious. Leontief's contribution was the proof of sufficiency.
3. See, for example, Barton [1], Fisher and Shell [7], Frisch [8], Goldman and Uzawa [9], Gorman [10], Houthakker [12], Pollak [18], and Strotz [23] and [24].
4. See, for example, Champernowne [2], Robinson [19], and Solow [20].
5. See Chapters 1–6, Diamond [3], Gorman [11], Nataf [17], Stigum [21], [22], and Whitaker [25] and [26].
6. There can be more than one type of labor and more than one type of output. This theorem was independently proved by (at least) Diamond, Gorman, Whitaker, and myself, although my proof was the only one to use the Leontief conditions directly. For a full discussion of the theorem, see Chapters 1 and 2.
7. See Chapter 3.
8. If each firm has more than one kind of capital, the interpretation of this result is somewhat weaker, although additional conditions on each firm's production function taken alone must then be satisfied. See Chapter 2.
9. Such analyses can apply directly if aggregation conditions are satisfied. They can also apply indirectly and lead to important insights if the results and methods of proof can be generalized. The latter possibility in no way rests on the existence of aggregate production functions.
10. In the capital-aggregation problem, one way in which this might happen is if the distribution of capital or other magnitudes over firms were known to be constant. See Houthakker [13] and Levhari [16]. This possibility is not explored in this chapter.

11. Boundedness, and especially closure, of S are largely matters of convenience in the present context.
12. If $G \neq 0$ everywhere in S, the same analysis applies to the case in which the standard of approximation is the size of the ratio of H to G.
13. This is merely a matter of convenience.
14. If $\mathscr{F}$ is closed (with an appropriate norm), then it satisfies a uniform (half or full) Lipschitz condition if each of its members satisfies such a condition.

    An example of a set of functions each of whose members satisfies a full Lipschitz condition but which fails to satisfy a uniform upper half Lipschitz condition is the set of all functions in the form $f(x) = x/\lambda$ for some $\lambda > 0$. Another example in which all the functions in the set are uniformly bounded and satisfy a full Lipschitz condition but in which the set satisfies neither a uniform lower nor a uniform upper half Lipschitz condition is the set of all functions in the form $f(x) = \sin(x/\lambda)$ for some $\lambda > 0$. Note that in both examples as λ approaches zero, the functions exhibit increasingly "irregular" behavior in some sense.
15. This lemma is fairly obvious and its proof fairly easy. I am sure it must be known, but I have been unable to find this precise result in the literature.
16. Obviously, one can work with F_1 equally well.
17. Since all that is required in the proof is that various derivatives of H satisfy uniform half or full Lipschitz conditions, (a) will still follow if condition (2) is weakened to require the appropriate derivatives of F to satisfy only upper (or lower) half Lipschitz conditions, provided that condition (3) is strengthened to specify that the corresponding derivatives of G satisfy those uniform half Lipschitz conditions which will lead to the appropriate conditions on the derivatives of H. This can be done by observing that if $f(\cdot)$ satisfies an upper half Lipschitz condition and $g(\cdot)$ satisfies a lower half Lipschitz condition, then $h(\cdot) \equiv f(\cdot) - g(\cdot)$ satisfies an upper half Lipschitz condition. Similarly, if $f(\cdot)$ satisfies a lower half Lipschitz condition and $g(\cdot)$ satisfies an upper half Lipschitz condition, then $h(\cdot)$ satisfies a lower half Lipschitz condition.
18. Assumption (2) is guaranted to hold if $F(\cdot,\cdot,\cdot)$ is assumed thrice continuously differentiable. Of course, the two times continuous differentiability of $F(\cdot,\cdot,\cdot)$ makes the Lipschitz conditions on $F_1(\cdot,\cdot,\cdot)$ and $F_2(\cdot,\cdot,\cdot)$ redundant.

    The assumption that the stated derivatives of $F(\cdot,\cdot,\cdot)$ satisfy full Lipschitz conditions can also be weakened to the imposition of half Lipschitz conditions. See Note 17.

    In the following discussion, (1) and (2) are assumed to hold.
19. There remains open the possibility that the assumptions of differentiability used in the present analysis are crucial and that the present results can be avoided if differentiability is dropped. While I am unable to prove that this is false – extensions of the analysis not seeming particularly easy – I have little doubt that it is. Differentiability is a great convenience in this sort of analysis, but it seems wishful thinking to suppose that it is anything more. See Stigum [21] and [22], and Chapters 2 and 3.

References

[1] Barten, A. P., "Consumer demand functions under conditions of almost additive preferences," *Econometrica*, **32** (1964), 1–38.

[2] Champernowne, D. G., "The production function and the theory of capital: A Comment," *Review of Economic Studies*, **21** (1953–54), 112–35.

[3] Diamond, P. A., "Technical change and the measurement of capital and output," *Review of Economic Studies*, **32** (1965), 289–98.

[4] Fisher, F. M., "Embodied technical change and the existence of an aggregate capital stock," *Review of Economic Studies*, **32** (1965), 263–88 (reprinted as Chapter 2).

[5] Fisher, F. M., "Embodied technology and the existence of labour and output aggregates," *Review of Economic Studies*, **35** (1968), 391–412 (reprinted as Chapter 3).

[6] Fisher, F. M., "Embodied technology and the aggregation of fixed and movable capital goods," *Review of Economic Studies*, **35** (1968), 417–28 (reprinted as Chapter 4).

[7] Fisher, F. M., and K. Shell, "Taste and quality change in the pure theory of the true cost-of-living index" in J. N. Wolfe (ed.), *Value, Capital, and Growth: Essays in Honour of Sir John Hicks*, Edinburgh: University of Edinburgh Press, 1968.

[8] Frisch, R., "A complete scheme for computing all direct and cross demand elasticities in a model with many sectors," *Econometrica*, **27** (1959), 177–96.

[9] Goldman, S. M., and H. Uzawa, "A note on separability in demand analysis," *Econometrica*, **32** (1964), 387–98.

[10] Gorman, W. M., "Separable utility and aggregation," *Econometrica*, **27** (1959), 469–81.

[11] Gorman, W. M., "Capital aggregation in vintage models" in J. N. Wolfe (ed.), *Value, Capital, and Growth: Essays in Honour of Sir John Hicks*, Edinburgh: University of Edinburgh Press, 1968.

[12] Houthakker, H. S., "Additive preferences," *Econometrica*, **28** (1960), 244–57.

[13] Houthakker, H. S., "The Pareto distribution and the Cobb–Douglas production function in activity analysis," *Review of Economic Studies*, **23** (1955–56), 27–31.

[14] Leontief, W. W., "A note on the interrelation of subsets of independent variables of a continuous function with continuous first derivatives," *Bulletin of the American Mathematical Society*, **53** (1947), 343–50.

[15] Leontief, W. W., "Introduction to a theory of the internal structure of functional relationships," *Econometrica*, **15** (1947), 361–73.

[16] Levhari, D., "A note on Houthakker's aggregate production function in a multifirm industry," *Econometrica*, **36** (1968), 151–4.

[17] Nataf, A., "Possibilités d'agrégation de fonctions de production à variables capital et main d'oeuvre," *Review of Economic Studies*, **34** (1967), 219–26.

[18] Pollak, R. A., "Conditional demand functions and the implications of separable utility," *Southern Economic Journal*, **37** (1971), 423–33.

[19] Robinson, J., "The production function and the theory of capital," *Review of Economic Studies*, **21** (1953–54), 81–106.

[20] Solow, R. M., "The production function and the theory of capital," *Review of Economic Studies*, **23** (1955–56), 101–8.

[21] Stigum, B. P., "On certain problems of aggregation," *International Economic Review*, **8** (1967), 349–67.
[22] Stigum, B. P., "On a property of concave functions," *Review of Economic Studies*, **35** (1968), 413–16.
[23] Strotz, R. H., "The empirical implications of a utility tree," *Econometrica*, **25** (1957), 269–80.
[24] Strotz, R. H., "The utility tree – A correction and further appraisal," *Econometrica*, **27** (1959), 482–8.
[25] Whitaker, J. K., "Vintage capital models and econometric production functions," *Review of Economic Studies*, **33** (1966), 1–18.
[26] Whitaker, J. K., "Capital aggregation and optimality conditions," *Review of Economic Studies*, **35** (1968), 429–42.

8

Aggregate production functions and the explanation of wages: A simulation experiment (1971)

8.1 Introduction

Recent work[1] has shown pretty clearly that the conditions under which the production possibilities of a technologically diverse economy can be represented by an aggregate production function are far too stringent to be believable. This is true not only of the conditions for the existence of an aggregate capital stock, where what is required is that the production functions of individual firms differ at most by capital-augmenting technical differences, but also of the existence of labor and output aggregates, where every firm must hire the same proportions of each type of labor and produce the same market basket of outputs. Moreover, the view that aggregate production functions are only approximations anyway cannot be sustained merely because such approximations are required only to hold over a limited range of the variables.[2]

Yet aggregate production functions apparently work nevertheless and do so in a way which is *prima facie* not easy to explain. It is easy enough to understand why, in economies in which things move more or less together, a relationship giving an aggregate measure of output as dependent on aggregate measures of capital and labor should give a good fit when applied to the data. What is not so easy to explain is the fact that the marginal product of labor in such an estimated relationship appears to give a reasonably good explanation of wages as well. In its simplest form, this puzzle is set by a remark which Solow

This research was supported by NSF Grant #GS-1791. I am indebted to Nancy Greene and, especially, Hossein Askari for programming and computational assistance.

once made to me that, had Douglas found labor's share to be 25 per cent and capital's 75 per cent instead of the other way around, we would not now be discussing aggregate production functions.

If the fact that estimated aggregate production functions explain wages fairly well is a statistical artifact, then it is certainly not an obvious one. There seems little reason why a function fitted to time series of output and input data on an aggregate basis should have this property; yet coincidence seems hard to swallow.[3]

This chapter reports on a simulation experiment which may cast some light on this issue. Aggregate Cobb–Douglas production functions were estimated for data produced by numerous fictitious and very simple economies in which there was only one homogeneous output and one homogeneous kind of labor but in which the conditions for the existence of an aggregate capital stock were definitely violated. Various measures of the performance of such an aggregate function were computed, among them measures of how well the aggregate production function did in explaining the history of wages. The histories of the economies were varied in a number of ways and the performance measures compared to see under what circumstances the aggregate production function did well.

The general object of the study was thus to determine whether economies in which we know with certainty that an aggregate production function is a poor description of the actual technology *and* in which forces which may make for approximate aggregation possibilities in the real world have been suppressed can nevertheless generate wages which can fairly accurately be predicted by a fictitious aggregate production function. If this can happen, then the fact that aggregate production functions do indeed give good wage predictions in practice cannot be taken as evidence that for some deep reason they really summarize the true technology. On the other hand, if such good wage predictions (and good fits to input and output data) are produced in our experiments under systematic circumstances of some sort, then reliance on aggregate production functions as a descriptive device in empirical work can be taken to be reliance on the persistence of such systematic circumstances in the real world.

The principal result of this investigation, while necessarily only suggestive, is very suggestive indeed. It is obvious that, since a Cobb–Douglas production function implies the constancy of labor's share, such a function cannot be expected to explain wages well in an economy in which that share is not constant. What is not obvious is that in economies in which labor's share *happens* to be roughly constant, even though the true relationships are far from yielding an aggregate Cobb–Douglas, such an aggregate production function *will* yield a good explanation of wages. Yet this is generally what we find for our fictitious economies, and the relationship between the variance in labor's share and the goodness-of-fit of the wage predictions is close, although certainly not perfect.

If such a result holds for other than our simplified and fictitious economies, it has important implications. It suggests that the view that the constancy of labor's share is due to the presence of an aggregate Cobb–Douglas production function is mistaken. Causation runs the other way, and the apparent success of aggregate Cobb–Douglas production functions is due to the relative constancy of labor's share. The explanation of such constancy remains to be found.[4] Our results suggest that should the forces making for it suddenly change, then aggregate Cobb–Douglas production functions would cease to give reasonable wage explanations.

Briefly then, the answer suggested by the present results to Solow's question is that an aggregate Cobb–Douglas production function estimated from input and output data does well in wage prediction not because wages are truly generated by it but because the behavior of labor's share just happens to approximate the central stylized fact generated by such a function, even though the mechanism actually generating wages and output is rather different. Such a view obviously has extensions to the performance of aggregate production functions other than Cobb–Douglas.

Should one be disturbed by these results? That depends on one's prior position regarding the nature of an estimated aggregate production function. There are several possible positions:

1. An aggregate production function works well in relating outputs to inputs and in predicting wages because it really summarizes the underlying technological relationships at the micro level. This view is demonstrably false as a matter of theory unless one also believes that there are unknown underlying forces which in some sense restrict the dimensionality of the aggregation problem.[5] This makes the use of such functions for wide-ranging theoretical purposes rather suspect.
2. An aggregate production function appears to be a useful empirical approximation only because the underlying variables move more or less together. So long and only so long as such common movement continues can we rely on such functions to give good predictions. This view is only partly correct. It is true that an aggregate production function works well so long as there is little relative movement (this is borne out in the results below). These are by no means the only cases in which our results show an

aggregate production function working well. Even when there is a great deal of relative movement in the underlying variables, an aggregate Cobb–Douglas does well in our experiments so long as labor's share just happens to be roughly constant. The low relative movement experiments are just special cases of this general result.

3. An aggregate Cobb–Douglas *only* works well so long as labor's share is relatively constant. Were labor's share to change, predictions made with an aggregate Cobb–Douglas would cease to be good ones. This view is obviously correct, since an aggregate Cobb–Douglas predicts a constant share for labor. The point of our results, however, is not that an aggregate Cobb–Douglas fails to work well when labor's share ceases to be roughly constant, but that an aggregate Cobb–Douglas will continue to work well so long as labor's share continues to be roughly constant, even though that rough constancy is not itself a consequence of the economy having a technology that is truly summarized by an aggregate Cobb–Douglas.

Our results, then, may be said to support the use of aggregate production functions as interesting descriptive and empirical devices (in the eyes of those who already regarded such use as appropriate) only so long as certain underlying regularities continue. At the same time, our results damage the view that the apparent success of aggregate production functions in wage predictions shows that the true technological relationships of a diverse economy can really be summarized for theoretical purposes in an aggregate production function.

8.2 The model

Our economies each consist of *n* units which hire the same kind of labor and produce the same kind of output. We shall refer to these units as "firms," although they might equally well or better be thought of as industries, each of which consists of a number of identical firms. In our experiments, *n* was taken to be 2, 4, or 8. Much higher numbers would have led to greatly increased computing time and the results do not suggest that it would have made much difference.

Each firm has a different kind of capital stock and its technology is embodied in that stock. Thus, different firms have different production functions and capital is not transferable among firms (although labor is). The *i*th firm's production function is given by:

$$y_i(t) = A_i(t)\, L_i(t)^{\alpha_i}\, K_i(t)^{1-\alpha_i} \quad (i = 1, \ldots, n). \tag{8.1}$$

Here, K_i is the amount of the ith firm's capital; L_i the amount of labor employed by the firm; and y_i the amount of output it produces. Calendar time is denoted by t (running from 1 to 20 in each economy); $A_i(t)$ is a function of time representing disembodied Hicks-neutral technical change (which, given the fact that the production functions are Cobb–Douglas, is indistinguishable from disembodied factor-augmenting change);[6] α_i is a parameter.

At any moment of time, the aggregate labor force employed is, of course,

$$L(t) \equiv \sum_{i=1}^{n} L_i(t). \tag{8.2}$$

Total output produced is

$$Y(t) \equiv \sum_{i=1}^{n} y_i(t). \tag{8.3}$$

However, whereas $L(t)$ is one of the givens of the economy, $Y(t)$ is not, since it obviously depends on the way in which employment is allocated to firms.

Such allocation is performed so as to make total production efficient. As would a perfect labor market or a socialist planning board, the $L_i(t)$ are chosen each period so as to maximize $Y(t)$, given $L(t)$, $K_1(t)$, . . ., $K_n(t)$, $A_1(t)$, . . ., $A_n(t)$, and (8.1) and (8.2). We denote output so maximized as $Y^*(t)$.

Now, it is not hard to show that if all the α_i were the same, then Y^* would be given by an aggregate Cobb–Douglas production function:

$$Y^*(t) = A(t)\,L(t)^{\alpha}J(t)^{1-\alpha} \tag{8.4}$$

where $J(t)$ depends only on the $K_i(t)$ and the $A_i(t)$ and not on $L(t)$. (This would *not* be true, incidentally, of $Y(t)$.) The results on the existence of aggregate production functions, already referred to, imply that this will certainly not be the case if the α_i are different for different firms. Indeed, they show that there exists *no* aggregate production function:

$$Y^*(t) = F(J(t), L(t), t) \tag{8.5}$$

in which $J(t)$ is merely a capital index independent of labor.[7] For each economy, however, we ignore this and estimate an aggregate Cobb–Douglas production function in the form (8.4) with $J(t)$ chosen as about to be described. As already stated, the relative performance of such estimated functions is compared across economies.

A single experiment, then, consists of choosing values for the parameters and of generating twenty-year time series for $L(t)$, $K_1(t)$, . . ., $K_n(t)$, and $A_1(t)$, . . ., $A_n(t)$. For each year, the $L_i(t)$ are chosen so as to maximize $Y(t)$ subject to (8.2).[8] Given the labor assignments, wages and capital rentals for the n different capital types are computed by taking marginal products in the individual production functions. We denote by $w(t)$ the resulting wage at time t and by $r_i(t)$ the marginal product of the ith capital type at that time.

It will be noted that the individual capital stocks are given exogenously rather than having the marginal value of the last dollar invested the same in all firms. It might be suspected that aggregate production functions are relatively more likely to do well when such an investment process is going on at the micro level. Such a conjecture is very far from being a proof, however, and is in any case irrelevant for present purposes. Our results show that an aggregate production function can do well in predicting wages *even when all such forces which one might expect to aid aggregation have been suppressed*. This makes the inferences that can be drawn from the success of aggregate production functions in practice as to their accuracy as theoretical summaries of the underlying technological relationships rather weak.[9]

Now, it is obvious from Euler's theorem that:

$$Y^*(t) = w(t)L(t) + \sum_{i=1}^{n} r_i(t)K_i(t) \quad (t = 1, \ldots, 20). \qquad (8.6)$$

This means that, at any moment of time, the sum of the right-hand side of (8.6) makes an excellent capital index. The problem, of course, occurs because the relative magnitudes of the $r_i(t)$ not only do not remain constant over time but also are not independent of the magnitude of $L(t)$; this is the essence of the capital-aggregation problem.

Nevertheless, it seems clear that an aggregate production function will do best if its capital index comes as close as possible to weighting different capital goods by their rentals.[10] Accordingly, we constructed $J(t)$ for use in (8.4) by

$$J(t) \equiv \sum_{i=1}^{n} \bar{r}_i K_i(t) \quad (t = 1, \ldots, 20), \qquad (8.7)$$

where

$$\bar{r}_i \equiv \frac{\sum_{t=1}^{20} r_i(t)K_i(t)}{\sum_{t=1}^{20} K_i(t)} \quad (i = 1, \ldots, n). \qquad (8.8)$$

8.3 The experiments: Detailed description

Obviously, the choice of the parameters and time series which define an experiment and the choice of measures of performance of the aggregate production function are crucial. In the present section we discuss the former choice, taking up the latter in the next section.

We begin with the crucial parameters of the production functions, α_i. As aggregate estimates for the United States tend to show a Cobb–Douglas exponent for labor of about 0.75, we chose the α_i around this value. In one set of experiments, the α_i were chosen in the range 0.7–0.8; in a second, they were chosen in the range 0.6–0.9. In both cases, the n individual α_i were chosen so that α_1 was at the lower and α_n at the upper end of the range, with the remainder (if any) of the exponents uniformly spread over the range. Thus, for example, in the 0.6–0.9 case, with $n = 4$, the exponents were 0.6, 0.7, 0.8, 0.9. Note that in all cases the unweighted average of the α_i was kept constant at 0.75.

As already indicated, n was chosen at 2, 4, or 8. A little reflection, however, shows that changing the number of firms represented in this model is not merely a matter of changing n, despite the terminology. One has two choices in increasing the number of firms. The first of these is to add firms without altering the set of α_i to be examined. Given constant returns and efficient labor allocation, however, adding a firm with a labor exponent identical to that of an existing firm is equivalent to increasing the size of the existing one by giving it more capital stock. Since one of the other choices described below involves doing just this, changes in n are not the only way in which the experiments reflect changes in the number of firms.

Aside from this, however, a change in n which is not merely equivalent to an increase in firm size must involve a change in the set of α_i. One cannot merely change n alone. The way in which increases in n were in fact reflected in the set of α_i has already been indicated. Note that whereas the average α_i is always the same, an increase in n involves a reduction in the variance of the α_i around their mean, other things equal. (Weighting by firm size, of course, that variance can increase when we increase the number of firms by changing firm size at given α_i; so can the weighted mean.) An increase in n involves a greater number of different firms, but also involves less polarization among firms.

The three sets of exogenously specified time profiles were all chosen to be approximately exponential trends. Thus:

$$\log L(t) = \lambda_0 + \lambda_1 t + \lambda_2 \varepsilon_t; \tag{8.9}$$

$$\log K_i(t) = \beta_{i0} + \beta_{i1} t + \beta_{i2} \eta_{it} \quad (i = 1, \ldots, n); \tag{8.10}$$

$$\log A_i(t) = \gamma_{i0} + \gamma_{i1} t + \gamma_{i2} \nu_{it} \quad (i = 1, \ldots, n), \tag{8.11}$$

where the λ_j, β_{ij}, and γ_{ij} are parameters, and ε_t, the η_{it}, and the ν_{it} are independently distributed standard normal deviates. The random elements (which were kept small) were introduced partly for minor reasons of realism, partly to see what difference they made, and partly to avoid multicollinearity in the estimation of the aggregate production function. This is particularly important in the cases in which allowance for exponential disembodied technical change is made in estimating (8.4), since the variables in that regression will be $\log(J(t)/L(t))$ and t. Moreover, as reported below, some regressions were made without imposing constant returns, so that the variables in such cases would be $\log J(t)$, $\log L(t)$, and t.

After considerable gross experimentation to discover what parameter choices made much difference, the random terms were standardized for the main experiments reported here by always taking $\lambda_2 = 0.02$, $\beta_{i2} = 0.0001$, and $\gamma_{i2} = 0$ $(i = 1, \ldots, n)$.

Further, λ_1 was chosen as 0.03 and λ_0 as zero. Thus, labor always grows at an average 3 per cent trend with deviations normally distributed with mean zero and standard deviation 0.02. The initial experimentation referred to showed the measures of performance of the aggregate production function not to be terribly sensitive to choices of λ_0 and λ_1, so these were standardized to reduce the gigantic number of different cases examined. For similar reasons, all the γ_{i0} were chosen as 0. (This is merely a choice of units.)

The performance measures *are* sensitive, as one might expect, to the choices made as to the capital and technical change parameters, the principal sensitivity being to the trend terms. If all firms are growing at the same rate, then an aggregate capital index can be expected to perform rather well; if firms grow at rather different rates, this is less likely to be the case.

The initial conditions for the K_i were chosen as follows. The n firms were divided into two halves, one with relatively low values of α_i and one with relatively high values. We shall refer to these as "low-α" and "high-α" firms, respectively. The β_{i0} were chosen in three sets. In the first of these, all $\beta_{i0} = 0$ $(i = 1, \ldots, n)$. In the second set, all β_{i0} for the low-α firms were set at 0 and the β_{i0} for the high-α firms were set at 2. In the third set, these values were reversed. As already remarked, these choices can also be thought of as changing the number of firms. Since all logarithms were natural, changing a β_{i0} from 0 to 2 amounts to multiplying the initial capital stock by something over 7.

The selection of the trend parameters was done rather more finely. In one set of experiments, which I shall refer to as "two-group capital" experiments, β_{i1} was set at 0 for firms in the high-α group, while all β_{i1} for firms in the low-α group were set equal to each other and, in successive runs, allowed to vary from -0.05 to $+0.05$ in steps of 0.01.[11]

Similarly, in a second set of experiments, which I shall call "two-group Hicks" experiments, the γ_{i1} for the high-α firms were set at 0. To secure comparability with the two-group capital experiments, however, the γ_{i1} for the remaining firms were chosen so that the equivalent trends in their capital stocks would all be equal and move in steps of 0.01 from -0.05 to $+0.05$. Such equivalent trends, of course, are such that a choice of a particular value for β_{i1} corresponds to a choice of $\gamma_{i1} = \beta_{i1}(1-\alpha_i)$. We also report results for preliminary runs of the two-group Hicks experiments, in which the γ_{i1} for the low-α firms were chosen all equal and moving from -0.05 to $+0.05$ in steps of 0.01.

Now, since in these two-group experiments, all firms in a given group grow or shrink together, there is a real sense in which they are roughly all one firm for our purposes, so that, were these the only experiments performed, we would not be giving too much scope to the effects of increases in n. This is particularly so, since the way in which the α_i were chosen, as already described, means that the average α_i for each of the two groups in such an experiment is getting closer to the other one when n increases.

Accordingly, we performed two more sets of experiments, which I shall refer to as "fanning capital" and "fanning Hicks" experiments, respectively.

In the fanning capital experiments, β_{i1} was set equal to zero for the firm with the highest α_i. Call this firm 1 and number the firms so that α_i decreases.[12] The remaining β_{i1} were chosen as:

$$\beta_{i1} = (i-1)\mu \qquad (i = 1, \ldots, n) \tag{8.12}$$

where μ was allowed to go from -0.05 to $+0.05$ in steps of 0.01. Thus the rates of growth of the firms "fanned out" from that of the first firm. Note that much bigger relative rates of growth are involved here (for $n > 2$) than in the case of the two-group experiments.

The fanning Hicks experiments were chosen analogously. In these,

$$\gamma_{i1} = (1-\alpha_i)(i-1)\mu \qquad (i = 1, \ldots, n) \tag{8.13}$$

with μ chosen as before.

Since the number of separate experiments to be run would be gigantic if all possible combinations were tried, all γ_{i1} were set at zero in performing capital experiments and all β_{i1} were set at zero when performing Hicks experiments.

The number of different experiments was still high. Each of the two-group sets (including the preliminary two-group Hicks set) and each of the fanning sets involves eleven experiments for each choice of the other parameters. Since there are three choices of n, two choices of the range of the α_i, and three choices of initial conditions for the capital stocks, each five sets of experiments involves 198 separate runs. In addition, to ensure that the random variation involved had little effect on the conclusions, we performed five runs instead of one each time all the β_{i1} were set at zero in the capital experiments or all the γ_{i1} were set at zero in the Hicks experiments. This brought the total number of runs to 202 for each of the five sets or a grand total of 1010 exclusive of the preliminary experimentation referred to earlier.[13] However, since for $n = 2$ a fanning experiment is identical to a two-group experiment, the actual total of runs, exclusive of the extensive preliminary experimentation, was 830.

The various choices of parameters are summarized in Table 8.1.

8.4 Aggregate regressions and measures of performance

In each of the experiments, four regressions were performed on the aggregate data. In two of these constant returns was imposed and in two no such imposition was made; further, given the imposition or nonimposition of constant returns, regressions were run both with and without a trend term allowing for Hicks-neutral disembodied technical change. This was done both for Hicks experiments in which there was such change at the firm level and for capital experiments in which there was not.

Thus the four equations estimated, all versions of (8.4), were (omitting the time argument):

$$\log Y^* = a + b \log J + c \log L; \tag{8.14}$$

$$\log Y^* = a + b \log J + c \log L + \mathrm{d}t; \tag{8.15}$$

$$\log (Y^*/L) = a + b \log (J/L); \tag{8.16}$$

and

$$\log (Y^*/L) = a + b \log (J/L) + \mathrm{d}t. \tag{8.17}$$

We now turn to the question of how the performance of such estimated aggregate production functions ought to be measured.

The first such measure is an obvious one; it is the R^2 of the regressions. While we should not expect such correlations to be low so long as aggregate capital, J, is correlated with its components, it

Table 8.1 Different choices of parameters for experiments.

Parameters	Choice of values
n	2; 4; 8
α_i	evenly distributed over range 0.7–0.8 or 0.6–0.9
λ_0	0
λ_1	0.03
λ_2	0.02
β_{i0}	0 all firms; 0 low-α firms and 2 high-α firms; 0 high-α firms and 2 low-α firms
β_{i1}	0 all firms in Hicks experiments; in two-group capital experiments, 0 for high-α firms and μ for low-α firms; in fanning capital experiments, $(i-1)\,\mu$
β_{i2}	0.0001 all firms
γ_{i0}	0 all firms
γ_{i1}	0 all firms in capital experiments; in final two-group Hicks experiments, 0 for high-α firms and $(1-\alpha_i)\,\mu$ for low-α firms; in preliminary two-group Hicks experiments, 0 for high-α firms and μ for low-α firms; in fanning Hicks experiments, $(1-\alpha_i)\,(i-1)\,\mu$
γ_{i2}	0 all firms
μ	−0.05, −0.04, . . ., 0, . . ., 0.04, 0.05

remains a necessary feature of the good performance of an aggregate production function that when fitted to aggregate output and input data it yield a close fit in explaining the dependent variable.[14]

A second natural measure is relevant to the equations in which constant returns is not imposed. The underlying structure certainly is constant returns. It is therefore of some interest to know whether or not an aggregate production function when estimated from data generated by that structure reveals that fact.

Somewhat similarly, in the Hicks experiments, there is underlying Hicks-neutral technical change and in the capital experiments there is not. It is of some interest to see whether this will be detected in the aggregate estimates.

Further, the underlying firm production functions are all in fact Cobb–Douglas with or without Hicks-neutral technical change. In general, we would expect a well-performing aggregate Cobb–Douglas production function to give parameter estimates which are averages of the individual firm production function parameters.

All of this, however, while interesting, is subsidiary to our main focus, that of the explanation of wages. Our principal performance measure, therefore, will measure the degree of success of the aggregate production functions in explaining the generated wage data, to which they are not directly fitted. What measure should be used?

The measure which first naturally suggests itself is the squared coefficient of determination:

$$I^2 = 1 - \frac{\sum_t (w(t) - \hat{w}(t))^2}{\sum_t (w(t) - \bar{w})^2}, \tag{8.18}$$

where $w(t)$ is the actual wage, $\hat{w}(t)$ the predicted wage,[15] and $\bar{w}$ the average actual wage over the twenty years. This has the usual property of having an upper bound of unity, although it is not bounded below by zero (or anything else).

A little thought (and some hindsight), however, suggests that this is not a terribly appropriate measure for our purposes. There is no reason why our experiments cannot generate economies in which the variance of wages is very small. This would make I^2 also very small, even if predicted wages came very close to actual ones. This possibility occurs in practice in a way that is convincing as to the inappropriateness of I^2. There are numerous cases in which, when performing a given series of experiments which differ only in relative growth rates (μ) but have identical initial conditions and other parameters, I^2 suddenly becomes very negative at a particular value of μ while being satisfactorily positive on both sides of that value. Examination of the histories of the corresponding economies reveals that for smaller values of μ, say, wages are going up and, for larger values, they are going down, while, for the critical value of μ, they are nearly constant. Predicted wages pretty much duplicate that behavior, and the numerator of the fraction in (8.18) stays small, so that the erratic behavior of I^2 is entirely due to the behavior of the denominator and the accident that wages happen to have a small variance in a particular experiment.

This naturally suggests the use of the numerator in (8.18) as itself the measure of performance as to wage explanation, and the natural form in which to use this is as the root-mean-square prediction error. Since this is not scale-free, we used instead the relative root-mean-square error, calculated as:

$$S = \frac{\sqrt{[(1/20)\Sigma_t(w(t) - \hat{w}(t))^2]}}{\bar{w}} \tag{8.19}$$

as our primary measure of performance.[16]

8.5 Subsidiary results

As more or less suspected, R^2 turns out not to be a particularly sensitive measure of performance. Essentially without exception, it is very high, generally around 0.99. This holds for all four of the regressions (8.14)–(8.17) and all sets of experiments. It reflects the fact that, with everything moving in trends of one sort or another, an excellent fit is obtained regardless of misspecification of different sorts.

The estimated coefficients, however, do reflect misspecification in different ways. Without going into great detail, the following comments convey the general impression given.

Consider first cases in which the correct specification as to the presence or absence of Hicks-neutral technical change is made. In such cases, it often makes a great difference whether or not constant returns is imposed, particularly in experiments where things are moving about. Not only do the nonconstant returns regressions (8.14) and (8.15) often yield estimates of the degree of homogeneity $(b + c)$ which are widely different from unity, but also there are numerous (but less frequent) cases in which the individual coefficients are ridiculous, including many cases in which marginal products are estimated as negative. On the other hand, there are many cases in which the individual coefficients are plausible and some in which they add up to something around unity.

If constant returns is imposed, however, such wild behavior essentially completely disappears and the exponents of labor and capital in the aggregate regressions almost always lie in the range covered by the corresponding firm coefficients.

One obvious explanation for such behavior is that of multicollinearity. $J(t)$ is composed of several variables trending at different rates with small random fluctuations; $L(t)$ is such a trend variable with larger fluctuations. It is not then too surprising that when both $\log J(t)$ and $\log L(t)$ appear in the regressions, particularly when t itself does, results as to individual coefficients look peculiar. When only $\log(J(t)/L(t))$ appears, one would expect to do better in this respect. Still, there is in many cases nothing like exact collinearity so this may only be part of the explanation.

Multicollinearity may also play some part in the explanation of a second phenomenon, this one relating to the correct or incorrect specification of the presence of Hicks-neutral technical change. Concentrating on the constant returns results, we find, as one might expect, that when dealing with Hicks experiments it makes a considerable difference whether or not we allow for technical change at the aggregate level. If we do, then results look plausible and, for low levels of movement, the relative root-mean-square error in the prediction of wages (S) is low. If no allowance for technical change is made in such cases, results are far worse.

What is somewhat more surprising than this, however, is the fact that in the capital experiments when there is no underlying technical change, results are nevertheless somewhat better when technical change at the aggregate level is assumed to be absent than when allowance is made for its possible presence. Despite the fact that, in all such cases, the estimated coefficient of time in the aggregate regression turns out to be very small in absolute value, there is a definite deterioration in relative root-mean-square error, S, as compared with the same cases with that coefficient set equal to zero in the estimation of the aggregate production function. Conceivably, this is due to the fact that there are only twenty observations to begin with, so that the use of one degree of freedom to estimate a zero coefficient is not a trivial loss of efficiency. This may particularly be so when the estimation of that coefficient involves the introduction of time, a variable which makes the regressions pretty collinear, even with constant returns.

Similar considerations may also explain why the Hicks experiments tend to have higher root-mean-square errors than the corresponding capital experiments in the results below.

Given all this, our analysis of the results as to wage prediction proceeded by taking, in each experiment, the wage prediction generated by the best of the aggregate production functions estimated, as indicated by the above considerations. These were the predictions generated by the estimates imposing constant returns and making the correct specification as to the presence or absence of Hicks-neutral technical change. In general, these were also the best wage predictions in terms of relative root-mean-square error. Thus the results in the next section are based on (8.16) for the capital experiments and on (8.17) for the Hicks experiments.

8.6 The principal results: Variance of labor's share and the prediction of wages

We now come to the principal focus of the experiments, the prediction of wages as measured by S. It is perfectly clear that there are some cases in which we would naturally expect S to be small and some in which we would expect it to be large.

Certainly, for the cases in which μ is zero or almost zero, we would expect an aggregate production function to do reasonably well. For such cases, the individual capital stocks are roughly proportional to each other and any average of them will provide a good capital index. It is true that the correct form of the aggregate production function in such cases will not be Cobb–Douglas,[17] but one would expect an aggregate Cobb–Douglas to do pretty well, nevertheless. We shall refer to such cases as "low-movement" cases.

One would also expect such good performance in quite an opposite case. Suppose that one of the firms starts out very large relative to the others; suppose also that the large firm is growing relative to the others. Then the entire economy is largely dominated by that firm and output and wages are largely determined by its production function. In such a case, treating the economy as though it were just one big firm is obviously not going to be far off the mark. Note that this will be true whether the large and growing firm has a growing capital stock or a growing technical efficiency parameter.

This sort of case is most obvious when there are only two firms and one of them is much bigger than the other; there are similar cases, however, for $n = 4$ or $n = 8$. In the two-group capital or two-group Hicks experiments (but *not* in the fanning experiments), the high-α firms are treated as a group, as are the low-α firms. The firms in each group start out large or small together; they also grow proportionally (a slight exception being the two-group Hicks experiments where identical growth rates are adjusted by slightly different capital exponents for different firms). Considering just one of the groups of firms, then, it forms a low-movement case and we should expect to be able to treat it more or less as a single unit. If one of those units is big and growing relative to the other, however, this closely parallels the case of two firms with one dominating the other. Again in such cases we should expect that treating the entire economy as a single firm gives fairly good results.

We shall refer to such cases as "specialization cases," observing that, for $n > 2$, they have some aspects of low-movement cases as well. There are not too many such cases even for the two-group experiments. For the fanning experiments in which $n > 2$,[18] there can be no cases which are exactly specialization cases as just defined. On the other hand, when one group of firms starts out very big and grows relative to the other, then, even in the fanning cases, it is misleading to take the relevant rate of growth as that of the big firms relative to the small ones. The big firms dominate throughout and what matters are the rates of growth of those firms relative to each other. For $n = 4$, this is μ; for $n = 8$, this is 3μ (taking the maximum of such relative growth rates). In the results below, we have accounted for this by indexing such cases under growth rates μ and 3μ instead of 3μ and 7μ, respectively, as would be done were all *n* firms treated symmetrically. This means, for example, that a fanning case in which there are four firms with two of them big and growing, with the growth rates of the four firms being 0, 0.01, 0.02, and 0.03, is treated as a case of 0.01 relative growth rather than a case of 0.03 relative growth in the tables below and is thus counted with the low-movement cases.

There is also a large class of cases in which it is obvious that the wage predictions of the estimated aggregate production functions will be poor. Since those predictions are from Cobb–Douglas functions, they involve the prediction that labor's share of total output will be constant. If, in fact, labor's share has a high variance in a given experiment, one would hardly expect such wage predictions to be accurate.

While it is thus obvious that a low variance of labor's share is a necessary condition for a good set of wage predictions, it is by no means obvious that this is also a sufficient condition. Yet, by and large, we find this to be the case. Even excluding the a priori obvious low-movement and specialization cases, we find that a low variance of labor's share is associated with a low relative root-mean-square error in wage prediction. This phenomenon thus occurs even in cases in which there is high relative movement and no domination by a set of proportionally growing firms, so that the underlying technical relationships do not look anything like an aggregate Cobb–Douglas (or indeed, *any* aggregate production function) in any sense. Cases which seem a priori similar to these generate a relatively high variance of labor's share and do badly on the relative root-mean-square error criterion.

We now present the results, postponing heuristic argument as to the plausibility of this finding to the next section.

Each of Tables 8.2–8.11 gives the joint distribution of the relative root-mean-square error of the wage predictions (S) and the standard deviation of labor's share. The latter, for comparability, is divided into intervals which are 0.003 75 in absolute value, this being 0.5 per cent of 0.75 which is the overall mean of labor's share in all the experiments. Columns are thus labelled "Relative standard deviation of labor's share." Table 8.2 summarizes all capital experiments; and Table 8.3, all Hicks experiments. Tables 8.4 and 8.5 provide the same summary deleting specialization cases and all cases in which the relevant growth rates are zero or 1 per cent. Tables 8.6–8.8 and 8.9–8.11 give the results broken down by growth rates (for rates higher than 1 per cent),[19] but still excluding pure specialization cases.

In all cases, growth rates are taken as μ, so that Hicks cases are grouped with capital cases with equivalent growth rates. In the fanning cases, the relevant growth rate is taken to be that of the fastest-growing firm, except in cases in which one group of firms is large and growing, in which case, as noted above, it is taken to be the growth rate of the fastest-growing large firm relative to the slowest-growing large firm.

Each box in each of the capital tables has three entries, corresponding to two-group, fanning, and all experiments, respectively; each box in each of the Hicks tables has four entries, corresponding to preliminary two-group, final two-group, fanning, and all experiments, respectively. The total of the entries for the individual experiment types is not always that given in the last line of the box because final two-group and fanning experiments are identical for $n = 2$ and are counted in each category separately but included in the total only once.

The sparseness of entries in the upper right-hand corners of the tables corresponds to the obvious fact that an aggregate Cobb–Douglas cannot give a good explanation of wages when the variance of labor's share is high. The point of interest is the sparseness of entries in the lower left-hand corners and the density of entries in the upper left-hand corners showing the cases in which the variance of labor's share is low and (for the upper corners) the relative root-mean-square error of wage prediction low. This phenomenon is particularly marked if one observes that the left-hand axis is rather finely subdivided at the upper end, so that the first four boxes only get up to 2 per cent relative root-mean-square error and the first seven boxes only up to 5 per cent, but it generally appears even within the first few boxes.[20]

Obviously, the results of the capital experiments fit the described pattern extremely tightly, there being few cases much off the principal diagonals. The results of the Hicks cases also fit it, particularly looking at the number of cases in each box and not merely at whether or not the box is empty, but not so strikingly well as the capital experiment results. This is probably due to the greater problems of multicollinearity encountered in the aggregate regressions in the Hicks experiments, as we shall discuss in the next section.

8.7 Heuristics

Why should an aggregate Cobb–Douglas do well in explaining wages when labor's share has a small variance? With the benefit of hindsight it is possible to give a fairly convincing heuristic explanation as to the reasonableness of our principal result for these experiments, showing that it is, in part, a consequence of the subsidiary results discussed

Table 8.2 Summary of all capital experiments.

Relative standard deviation of labor's share (per cent)		0.0–0.5	0.5–1.0	1.0–1.5	1.5–2.0	2.0–2.5	2.5–3.0	Above 3.0
Relative root-mean-square error in predicting wages (per cent)								
0.0–0.5								
	Two-group	87						
	Fanning	52						
	Total	108						
0.5–1.0								
	Two-group	27	30	1				
	Fanning	8	28	1				
	Total	34	47	1				
1.0–1.5								
	Two-group		4	17	2			
	Fanning		6	17	1			
	Total		10	29	2			
1.5–2.0								
	Two-group		0	0	10	2		
	Fanning		1	8	6	3		
	Total		1	8	13	3		
2.0–3.0								
	Two-group		0	0	1	5	5	1
	Fanning		1	3	5	5	7	4
	Total		1	3	5	7	10	4

3.0–4.0						
	Two-group	0	0	1		3
	Fanning	1	2	0		11
	Total	1	2	1		13
4.0–5.0						
	Two-group		0	0		1
	Fanning		1	1		8
	Total		1	1		8
5.0–10.0						
	Two-group				0	1
	Fanning				2	14
	Total				2	14
10.0–20.0						
	Two-group					0
	Fanning					1
	Total					1
Above 20						
	Two-group					
	Fanning					
	Total					

Items sometimes do not add to totals because each two-firm experiment was counted in both categories but added into total only once.

Table 8.3 Summary of all Hicks experiments.

Relative standard deviation of labor's share (per cent)	0.0–0.5	0.5–1.0	1.0–1.5	1.5–2.0	2.0–2.5	2.5–3.0	Above 3.0
Relative root-mean-square error in predicting wages (per cent)							
0.0–0.5							
Prelim. two-group	63	1	1				
Two-group	61	0	0				
Fanning	33	0	0				
Total	138	1	1				
0.5–1.0							
Prelim. two-group	30	15					
Two-group	21	12					
Fanning	12	12					
Total	55	33					
1.0–1.5							
Prelim. two-group	10	5	3				
Two-group	11	8	3				
Fanning	5	8	1				
Total	24	18	6				
1.5–2.0							
Prelim. two-group	3	4	5	3			
Two-group	9	2	6	0			
Fanning	1	0	7	1			
Total	12	6	15	4			

2.0–3.0							
Prelim. two-group	5	5	7	2	3	1	
Two-group	5	4	2	5	3	0	
Fanning	3	1	0	5	3	1	
Total	13	10	9	8	7	2	
3.0–4.0							
Prelim. two-group	0	3	0	3	1	1	1
Two-group	4	4	2	1	2	0	0
Fanning	2	4	1	0	1	1	1
Total	4	11	3	4	3	2	2
4.0–5.0							
Prelim. two-group	0	2	1	1	1		1
Two-group	1	0	3	1	0		2
Fanning	2	0	2	0	0		1
Total	3	2	5	2	1		3
5.0–10.0							
Prelim. two-group	3	1	1	2	2	1	1
Two-group	0	5	2	5	2	3	2
Fanning	2	8	3	2	3	2	5
Total	5	11	5	8	5	4	7
10.0–20.0							
Prelim. two-group		0	0	1		1	4
Two-group		1	0	0		2	2
Fanning		4	6	4		1	6
Total		5	6	5		4	11
Above 20							
Prelim. two-group	0	0	0	0	0	0	0
Two-group	0	1	0	0	0	0	1
Fanning	1	0	8	5	2	3	25
Total	1	1	8	5	2	3	25

Items sometimes do not add to totals because each two-firm experiment was counted in both categories but added into total only once.

Table 8.4 Summary of nontrivial capital experiments.

Relative standard deviation of labor's share (per cent)	0.0–0.5	0.5–1.0	1.0–1.5	1.5–2.0	2.0–2.5	2.5–3.0	Above 3.0
Relative root-mean-square error in predicting wages (per cent)							
0.0–0.5							
Two-group	24						
Fanning	21						
Total	36						
0.5–1.0							
Two-group	17	22					
Fanning	6	23					
Total	22	37					
1.0–1.5							
Two-group		3	9				
Fanning		6	13				
Total		9	19				
1.5–2.0							
Two-group		0	0	3	0		
Fanning		1	8	3	1		
Total		1	8	5	1		
2.0–3.0							
Two-group		0	0	1	4	5	1
Fanning		1	3	5	4	7	4
Total		1	3	5	6	10	4

3.0–4.0					
Two-group	0	0	1		3
Fanning	1	2	0		11
Total	1	2	1		13
4.0–5.0					
Two-group		0	0		1
Fanning		1	1		8
Total		1	1		8
5.0–10.0					
Two-group				0	1
Fanning				2	14
Total				2	14
10.0–20.0					
Two-group					0
Fanning					1
Total					1
Above 20					
Two-group					
Fanning					
Total					

Does not include growth rates of −1 to +1 per cent or pure (two-group) specialization cases. Items sometimes do not add to totals because each two-firm experiment was counted in both categories but added into total only once.

Table 8.5 Summary of nontrivial Hicks experiments.

Relative standard deviation of labor's share (per cent)	0.0–0.5	0.5–1.0	1.0–1.5	1.5–2.0	2.0–2.5	2.5–3.0	Above 3.0
Relative root-mean-square error in predicting wages (per cent)							
0.0–0.5							
Prelim. two-group	23	1	1				
Two-group	11	0	0				
Fanning	10	0	0				
Total	40	1	1				
0.5–1.0							
Prelim. two-group	19	11					
Two-group	9	3					
Fanning	6	7					
Total	30	18					
1.0–1.5							
Prelim. two-group	7	4	2				
Two-group	8	7	1				
Fanning	4	7	0				
Total	18	15	3				
1.5–2.0							
Prelim. two-group	3	4	1	0			
Two-group	7	2	3	0			
Fanning	1	0	5	1			
Total	10	6	7	1			

2.0–3.0							
Prelim. two-group	3	5	4	2	2	1	
Two-group	4	4	2	1	1	0	
Fanning	2	1	0	2	1	1	
Total	9	10	6	4	4	2	
3.0–4.0							
Prelim. two-group	0	3	0	2	1	1	1
Two-group	1	4	0	0	2	0	0
Fanning	0	4	1	0	1	1	1
Total	1	11	1	2	3	2	2
4.0–5.0							
Prelim. two-group	0	2	0	1	1		1
Two-group	1	0	1	1	0		2
Fanning	2	2	1	0	0		1
Total	3	2	2	2	1		3
5.0–10.0							
Prelim. two-group	3	1	0	2	1	1	1
Two-group	0	5	1	2	1	3	2
Fanning	2	8	3	1	2	2	5
Total	5	11	3	4	3	4	7
10.0–20.0							
Prelim. two-group		0	0	0		1	4
Two-group		1	0	0		2	2
Fanning		4	6	4		1	6
Total		5	6	4		4	11
Above 20							
Prelim. two-group	0	0	0	0	0	0	0
Two-group	0	1	0	0	0	0	1
Fanning	1	0	8	5	2	3	25
Total	1	1	8	5	2	3	25

Does not include growth rates of −1 to +1 per cent or pure (two-group) specialization cases. Items sometimes do not add to totals because each two-firm experiment was counted in both categories but added into total only once.

Table 8.6 Capital experiments, 2–5 per cent growth.

Relative standard deviation of labor's share (per cent)	0.0–0.5	0.5–1.0	1.0–1.5	1.5–2.0	2.0–2.5	2.5–3.0	Above 3.0
Relative root-mean-square error in predicting wages (per cent)							
0.0–0.5							
Two-group	24						
Fanning	19						
Total	34						
0.5–1.0							
Two-group	17	22					
Fanning	3	14					
Total	19	28					
1.0–1.5							
Two-group		3	9				
Fanning		2	5				
Total		5	11				
1.5–2.0							
Two-group				3	0		
Fanning				1	1		
Total				3	1		
2.0–3.0							
Two-group				1	4	5	1
Fanning				1	3	4	2
Total				1	5	7	2

3.0–4.0		
Two-group	1	3
Fanning	0	2
Total	1	4
4.0–5.0		
Two-group		1
Fanning		1
Total		1
5.0–10.0		
Two-group		1
Fanning		1
Total		1
10.0–20.0		
Two-group		
Fanning		
Total		
Above 20		
Two-group		
Fanning		
Total		

Does not include pure (two-group) specialization cases.

Table 8.7 Capital experiments, 6–10 per cent growth.

Relative standard deviation of labor's share (per cent)	0.0–0.5	0.5–1.0	1.0–1.5	1.5–2.0	2.0–2.5	2.5–3.0	Above 3.0
Relative root-mean-square error in predicting wages (per cent)							
0.0–0.5							
Two-group	0						
Fanning	2						
Total	2						
0.5–1.0							
Two-group	0	0					
Fanning	2	8					
Total	2	8					
1.0–1.5							
Two-group		0	0				
Fanning		4	4				
Total		4	4				
1.5–2.0							
Two-group			0	0			
Fanning			1	1			
Total			1	1			
2.0–3.0							
Two-group				0		0	
Fanning				2		2	
Total				2		2	

3.0–4.0	
Two-group	0
Fanning	5
Total	5
4.0–5.0	
Two-group	0
Fanning	1
Total	1
5.0–10.0	
Two-group	
Fanning	
Total	
10.0–20.0	
Two-group	
Fanning	
Total	
Above 20	
Two-group	
Fanning	
Total	

Does not include pure (two-group) specialization cases.

Table 8.8 Capital experiments, 11–35 per cent growth.

Relative standard deviation of labor's share (per cent)	0.0–0.5	0.5–1.0	1.0–1.5	1.5–2.0	2.0–2.5	2.5–3.0	Above 3.0
Relative root-mean-square error in predicting wages (per cent)							
0.0–0.5							
Two-group							
Fanning							
Total							
0.5–1.0							
Two-group	0	0					
Fanning	1	1					
Total	1	1					
1.0–1.5							
Two-group			0				
Fanning			4				
Total			4				
1.5–2.0							
Two-group		0	0	0			
Fanning		1	7	1			
Total		1	7	1			
2.0–3.0							
Two-group		0	0	0	0	0	0
Fanning		1	3	2	1	1	2
Total		1	3	2	1	1	2

3.0–4.0					
Two-group	0	0			0
Fanning	1	2			4
Total	1	2			4
4.0–5.0					
Two-group		0	0		0
Fanning		1	1		6
Total		1	1		6
5.0–10.0					
Two-group				0	0
Fanning				2	13
Total				2	13
10.0–20.0					
Two-group					0
Fanning					1
Total					1
Above 20					
Two-group					
Fanning					
Total					

Does not include pure (two-group) specialization cases.

Table 8.9 Hicks experiments, 2–5 per cent growth.

Relative standard deviation of labor's share (per cent)	0.0–0.5	0.5–1.0	1.0–1.5	1.5–2.0	2.0–2.5	2.5–3.0	Above 3.0
Relative root-mean-square error in predicting wages (per cent)							
0.0–0.5							
Prelim. two-group	10						
Two-group	11						
Fanning	10						
Total	27						
0.5–1.0							
Prelim. two-group	5	3					
Two-group	9	3					
Fanning	5	5					
Total	15	8					
1.0–1.5							
Prelim. two-group	1	1	0				
Two-group	8	7	1				
Fanning	3	4	0				
Total	11	9	1				
1.5–2.0							
Prelim. two-group	0	0	0				
Two-group	7	2	3				
Fanning	1	0	2				
Total	7	2	3				

2.0–3.0							
Prelim. two-group	0	0	1	1	0	0	
Two-group	4	4	2	1	1	0	
Fanning	2	0	0	1	1	1	
Total	6	4	3	2	2	1	
3.0–4.0							
Prelim. two-group	0	0	0	1	0		
Two-group	1	4	0	0	2		
Fanning	0	1	1	0	1		
Total	1	5	1	1	2		
4.0–5.0							
Prelim. two-group	0		0	0			0
Two-group	1		1	1			2
Fanning	1		0	0			1
Total	2		1	1			2
5.0–10.0							
Prelim. two-group		0	0	1	0	0	0
Two-group		5	1	2	1	3	2
Fanning		7	1	1	2	2	1
Total		9	1	3	2	3	2
10.0–20.0							
Prelim. two-group		0	0			0	0
Two-group		1	0			2	2
Fanning		0	1			1	2
Total		1	1			3	3
Above 20							
Prelim. two-group		0					0
Two-group		1					1
Fanning		0					2
Total		1					2

Does not include pure (two-group) specialization cases. Items sometimes do not add to totals because each two-firm experiment was counted in both categories but added into total only once.

Table 8.10 Hicks experiments, 6–10 per cent growth.

Relative standard deviation of labor's share (per cent)	0.0–0.5	0.5–1.0	1.0–1.5	1.5–2.0	2.0–2.5	2.5–3.0	Above 3.0
Relative root-mean-square error in predicting wages (per cent)							
0.0–0.5							
Prelim. two-group	10						
Two-group	0						
Fanning	0						
Total	10						
0.5–1.0							
Prelim. two-group	5	1					
Two-group	0	0					
Fanning	1	2					
Total	6	3					
1.0–1.5							
Prelim. two-group	1	1					
Two-group	0	0					
Fanning	1	3					
Total	2	4					
1.5–2.0							
Prelim. two-group	1		0	0			
Two-group	0		0	0			
Fanning	0		2	1			
Total	1		2	1			

2.0–3.0							
Prelim. two-group		1		0	1		
Two-group		0		0	0		
Fanning		1		1	0		
Total		2		1	1		
3.0–4.0							
Prelim. two-group		0			1	0	0
Two-group		0			0	0	0
Fanning		3			0	1	1
Total		3			1	1	1
4.0–5.0							
Prelim. two-group	0			1			
Two-group	0			0			
Fanning	1			0			
Total	1			1			
5.0–10.0							
Prelim. two-group	0		0		1		0
Two-group	0		0		0		0
Fanning	2		1		0		3
Total	2		1		1		3
10.0–20.0							
Prelim. two-group		0	0				0
Two-group		0	0				0
Fanning		2	1				2
Total		2	1				2
Above 20							
Prelim. two-group			0	0			0
Two-group			0	0			0
Fanning			1	1			1
Total			1	1			1

Does not include pure (two-group) specialization cases.

Table 8.11 Hicks experiments, 11–35 per cent growth.

Relative standard deviation of labor's share (per cent)	0.0–0.5	0.5–1.0	1.0–1.5	1.5–2.0	2.0–2.5	2.5–3.0	Above 3.0
Relative root-mean-square error in predicting wages (per cent)							
0.0–0.5							
Prelim. two-group	3	1	1				
Two-group	0	0	0				
Fanning	0	0	0				
Total	3	1	1				
0.5–1.0							
Prelim. two-group	9	7					
Two-group	0	0					
Fanning	0	0					
Total	9	7					
1.0–1.5							
Prelim. two-group	5	2	2				
Two-group	0	0	0				
Fanning	0	0	0				
Total	5	2	2				
1.5–2.0							
Prelim. two-group	2	4	1				
Two-group	0	0	0				
Fanning	0	0	1				
Total	2	4	2				

2.0–3.0						
Prelim. two-group	3	4	3	1	1	1	
Two-group	0	0	0	0	0	0	
Fanning	0	0	0	0	0	0	
Total	3	4	3	1	1	1	
3.0–4.0							
Prelim. two-group		3		1		1	1
Two-group		0		0		0	0
Fanning		0		0		0	0
Total		3		1		1	1
4.0–5.0							
Prelim. two-group		2	0		1		1
Two-group		0	0		0		0
Fanning		2	1		0		0
Total		2	1		1		1
5.0–10.0							
Prelim. two-group	3	1	0	1		1	1
Two-group	0	0	0	0		0	0
Fanning	0	1	1	0		0	1
Total	3	2	1	1		1	2
10.0–20.0							
Prelim. two-group		0	0	0		1	4
Two-group		0	0	0		0	0
Fanning		2	4	4		0	2
Total		2	4	4		1	6
Above 20							
Prelim. two-group	0		0	0	0	0	0
Two-group	0		0	0	0	0	0
Fanning	1		7	4	2	3	22
Total	1		7	4	2	3	22

Does not include pure (two-group) specialization cases.

earlier. Indeed, that heuristic explanation strikes me as so convincing that I hesitate to give it lest the reader mistake it for a proof and believe that all the experiments were unnecessary. In experiments such as this in which the data are all internally generated with little stochastic element, any organizing principle for the results which can be made to seem very reasonable will also misleadingly appear afterwards to have been deducible without the experiments.

Consider the polar case in which labor's share just happens to be constant. Call that share $\bar{\alpha}$. Then wages and output per man are certainly related by:

$$w(t) = \bar{\alpha}(Y^*(t)/L(t)). \tag{8.20}$$

We have already noted, however, that our regressions invariably give an extremely close fit to $\log(Y^*(t)/L(t))$, so that we would expect to do well in explaining wages in such a case with labor's share constant, provided that we obtained a decent estimate of $\bar{\alpha}$.

It is clear, however, that since the marginal product of labor is equal to $w(t)$ in every firm:

$$\bar{\alpha} = \frac{w(t)L(t)}{Y^*(t)} = \frac{\sum_{i=1}^{n} w(t)L_i(t)}{\sum_{i=1}^{n} Y_i^*(t)} = \frac{\sum_{i=1}^{n} \alpha_i \left(\frac{Y_i^*(t)}{L_i(t)}\right) L_i(t)}{\sum_{i=1}^{n} Y_i^*(t)} = \frac{\sum_{i=1}^{n} \alpha_i Y_i^*(t)}{\sum_{i=1}^{n} Y_i^*(t)}, \tag{8.21}$$

where $Y_i^*(t)$ is the output produced by the ith firm when labor has been efficiently allocated. Thus $\bar{\alpha}$ is a weighted average of the individual α_i, the weights being proportional to the individual firm outputs.[21] We have already seen, however, that the estimate of labor's share given by the aggregate Cobb–Douglas α, like the other parameters, is usually within the range of the corresponding microparameters, in this case the α_i, so that it is plausible that when labor's share is constant, the estimate of α will come close to $\bar{\alpha}$ (although the estimated α need not be a weighted average of the α_i and does not have the same weights as does $\overline{\alpha}$).

It thus follows from the success of the aggregate regressions in explaining output per man and the plausible appearance of α as within the range of the α_i that wages will tend to be well predicted when labor's share is roughly constant. Indeed, the exceptions to this general rule observed in the tables reporting the Hicks experiments are typically cases in which the estimated α fails to lie in the indicated range, an occurrence which is probably due to the multicollinearity which affects the Hicks regressions considerably more than the capital regressions.[22]

This argument makes it very plausible that in these experiments rough constancy of labor's share should lead to a situation in which an aggregate Cobb–Douglas gives generally good results including good wage predictions, even though the underlying technical relationships are not consistent with the existence of any aggregate production function and even though there is considerable relative movement in the underlying firm variables. Whether such an argument or such results have much bearing on a real world in which underlying relationships are more complicated and aggregation takes place over labor and output as well as capital is necessarily a somewhat open question. The suggestion is clear, however, that labor's share is not roughly constant because the diverse technical relationships of modern economies are truly representable by an aggregate Cobb–Douglas but rather that such relationships appear to be representable by an aggregate Cobb–Douglas *because* labor's share happens to be roughly constant. If this is so, then the reason for such rough constancy becomes an important subject for further research.[23]

It hardly needs remarking that I have throughout dealt with constancy of labor's share and the Cobb–Douglas because that is the simplest case and not because it is the best-fitting aggregate production function in practice. If one rejects the Cobb–Douglas form in favor of an alternative aggregate production function, the suggestion (though less direct this time) remains that the apparent success of such a function in explaining wages occurs not because such functions really represent the true state of technology but rather because their implications as to the stylized facts of wage behavior agree with what happens to be going on anyway. The development of the CES, for example, began with the observation that wages are an increasing function of output per man and that the function involved can be approximated by one linear in the logarithms.[24] The present results suggest (but only suggest) that the explanation of that wage–output-per-man relationship may not be in the existence of an aggregate CES but rather that the apparent existence of an aggregate CES may be explained by that relationship.

Notes

1. Summarized in Fisher [7] (Chapter 1). Relevant pieces include Diamond [2], Fisher [3], [4], [5], [6] (Chapters 2–4, 7), Gorman [8], Solow [10], [13], and Whitaker [14] and [15], among others.
2. See Chapter 7.
3. Phelps Brown [9] simply dismisses the time series results as poor or implausible, largely because of their failure to allow for technical change. In the light of Solow's seminal paper [11] and its successors, this can no longer be done. Phelps Brown's arguments as to cross-section estimates explain nothing about the time series results, nor do they show why a cross-sectionally estimated production function should give reasonable wage predictions for years far from that of the original cross-section.
4. For purposes of this discussion, I assume that such constancy is really there and that an aggregate Cobb–Douglas fits the facts pretty well. Obvious extensions to the case of other more complex aggregate production functions suggest themselves and are commented on briefly below, but the central tenor of the text is unaffected.
5. See Chapter 1.
6. Embodied technical change, of course, is, in a sense, what the whole model is about. Cobb–Douglas production functions for individual firms were used because they allow great simplifications in the labor-allocation algorithm described below and because they ought to provide the best chance for an aggregate Cobb–Douglas to work well. It is planned to extend the study to different functional forms in later work.
7. See Chapter 2.
8. This was done as follows, making use of the property that, with Cobb–Douglas production functions, every $L_i(t) > 0$. It is easy to write an algorithm which equalizes (by iteration) the marginal product of labor in any given pair of firms, given the total amount of labor employed by those firms. When $n = 2$, this is all there is to it, since equality of marginal product is obviously the condition for efficient allocation. For $n > 2$, we first divided labor equally among all n firms; then we took the total labor assigned to firms 1 and 2 and reallocated it between the firms to equalize marginal product. The next step took the labor then allocated to firms 2 and 3 and reassigned it to them efficiently; then we went on to firms 3 and 4, and so forth up to firms $n - 1$ and n. The process was then repeated starting at firms 1 and 2 and continued until all marginal products were equalized (approximately). It is easy to prove convergence of this algorithm and, although it is not particularly efficient, it did not take a prohibitive amount of computer time for $n = 8$.
9. Although it has other implications for their usefulness in empirical work, as already discussed.
10. The fact that other ways of constructing the index might have led to worse results hardly seems relevant. In any case, early experimentation with a capital index constructed using base-year rentals did not reveal any striking differences in the results.

11. Note that, in view of constant returns, there is no essential difference between allowing one group of firms to shrink and allowing the other to grow.
12. Thus the high-α firms are firms 1, . . ., $n/2$ and the low-α ones are firms $n/2+1, \ldots, n$.
13. Since, as it turned out, there was only negligible difference in the results of the experiments with zero growth which differ only by random variation, we used only one of the five sets each time in analyzing the results as reported below.
14. R^2 is a sensible measure of goodness-of-fit here. t-statistics are not, since the problem is nonstochastic.
15. There is an apparent issue as to how $\hat{w}(t)$ should be computed. From (8.4):

$$\hat{w}(t) = \alpha(Y^*(t)/L(t)),$$

where α, of course, is estimated from the aggregate regressions (8.14)–(8.17). Should $Y^*(t)$ be taken as the actual value of $Y^*(t)$ or the predicted value? Fortunately, R^2 for all the regressions is so very high that it turns out to make no practical difference which one is used. In the results reported, we used the actual value of $Y^*(t)$.
16. There are other associated measures which might be used. One might, for example, regress $w(t)$ on $\hat{w}(t)$ and observe whether the constant term was close to zero and the slope close to unity as well as computing the correlation coefficient. While we did in fact do this, the results did not seem to provide much information not already contained in the relative root-mean-square error and they are not reported here. In any case, the relative root-mean-square error seems the most natural single measure.
17. The correct form is the sum of the individual firms' production functions, with each $K_i(t)$ set equal to $k_i J(t)$ and the $L_i(t)$ determined by the efficiency conditions. This last makes the writing of the aggregate production function in closed form unhelpful, at best.
18. For $n = 2$, fanning experiments are identical to two-group experiments.
19. The 1 per cent growth rate cases also exhibit the same phenomenon as do finer breakdowns of the other results.
20. It does not seem worthwhile to compute a formal test of association. The most obvious chi-square test would involve the guaranteed emptiness of the upper right-hand corner, a point of little interest. Moreover, the appearance of very many cases in the upper left-hand corner would be important regardless of the rest of the table. In any case, the pattern in the results is strong enough to be obvious at a glance.
21. This shows that labor's share will be roughly constant if relative outputs are roughly constant, which will occur, for example, if the 3 per cent labor trend, given the coefficients, just happens to offset the other trends because increasing amounts of labor are assigned to relatively slow-growing firms. If $n = 2$, such rough constancy of relative outputs is the only way in which labor's share can be roughly constant; for $n > 2$, there are other ways.
22. Recall that the results presented in the tables are those from regressions including t for the Hicks experiments and excluding t for the capital experiments.
23. It is hard to believe that it is explained along the lines of (8.21) by the existence of underlying Cobb–Douglas functions at the micro level

together with rough constancy of relative outputs. Relative outputs do not seem very constant and, if they were, one would still want to know why. For a discussion of the reasons for apparent constancy, see Solow [12].

24. See Arrow *et al.* [1].

References

[1] Arrow, K. J., H. B. Chenery, B. S. Minhas, and R. M. Solow, "Capital–labor substitution and economic efficiency," *Review of Economics and Statistics*, **43** (1961), 225–50.

[2] Diamond, P. A., "Technical change and the measurement of capital and output," *Review of Economic Studies*, **32** (1965), 289–98.

[3] Fisher, F. M., "Embodied technical change and the existence of an aggregate capital stock," *Review of Economic Studies*, **32** (1965), 263–88 (reprinted as Chapter 2).

[4] Fisher, F. M., "Embodied technology and the existence of labour and output aggregates," *Review of Economic Studies*, **35** (1968), 391–412 (reprinted as Chapter 3).

[5] Fisher, F. M., "Embodied technology and the aggregation of fixed and movable capital goods," *Review of Economic Studies*, **35** (1968), 417–28 (reprinted as Chapter 4).

[6] Fisher, F. M., "Approximate aggregation and the Leontief conditions," *Econometrica*, **37** (1969), 457–69 (reprinted as Chapter 7).

[7] Fisher, F. M., "The existence of aggregate production functions," *Econometrica*, **37** (1969), 553–77 (reprinted as Chapter 1).

[8] Gorman, W. M., "Measuring the quantities of fixed factors," in J. N. Wolfe (ed.), *Value, Capital, and Growth: Papers in Honour of Sir John Hicks*, Edinburgh: University of Edinburgh Press, 1968, 141–72.

[9] Phelps Brown, E., "The meaning of the fitted Cobb–Douglas function," *Quarterly Journal of Economics*, **71** (1957), 546–60.

[10] Solow, R. M., "The production function and the theory of capital," *Review of Economic Studies*, **23** (1955–56), 101–8.

[11] Solow, R. M., "Technical change and the aggregate production function," *Review of Economics and Statistics*, **39** (1957), 312–20.

[12] Solow, R. M., "A skeptical note on the constancy of relative shares," *American Economic Review*, **48** (1958), 618–31.

[13] Solow, R. M., "Capital, labor, and income in manufacturing," in National Bureau of Economic Research Conference in Income and Wealth, *The Behavior of Income Shares* (Studies in Income and Wealth, 26), Princeton: Princeton University Press, 1964, 101–28.

[14] Whitaker, J. K., "Vintage capital models and econometric production functions," *Review of Economic Studies*, **33** (1966), 1–18.

[15] Whitaker, J. K., "Capital aggregation and optimality conditions," *Review of Economic Studies*, **35** (1968), 429–42.

9

Aggregate production functions: Some CES experiments (1977)

Written jointly with Robert M. Solow and James M. Kearl

9.1 Introduction

As a purely theoretical matter, aggregate production functions exist only under conditions too stringent to be believed satisfied by the diverse technological relationships of actual economies. There is a summary discussion and bibliography in Fisher [2] (Chapter 1). Yet aggregate production functions estimated from real data do appear to give good results, at least sometimes, and to do so in an apparently nontrivial way. Not only do such estimated relationships give good fits to input and output data, but also the calculated marginal products appear to be related to observed factor payments. Alternatively, production functions with parameters estimated from factor payments turn out to fit input and output data pretty well sometimes.

It is not a simple matter to decide why this should be so as a matter of theory. Indeed, the problem is sufficiently complicated that perhaps the most promising mode of attack on it is through the construction and analysis of simulation experiments. By constructing simplified economies in which the conditions for aggregation are known not to be satisfied, we can hope to find out inductively the circumstances under which aggregate production functions appear to give good results in the double sense just discussed. Moreover, such experiments can cast

---

This research was supported by National Science Foundation Grant #GS-43185 to the National Bureau of Economic Research. We are indebted to Nancy Greene Burstein for programming assistance and to Martin Osborne for research assistance.

light on other aspects of the estimation of aggregate production functions from underlying nonaggregatable data.

The related papers of Houthakker [4], Levhari [6], and Sato [8] do not bear directly on the problems here addressed. Those papers show what aggregate production functions can be expected when the distribution of capital over firms with related technologies is fixed (or changes in very restricted ways). Such fixity of distribution, however, can hardly be expected in the real world and is certainly not true in the world of simulation experiments reported below and in Fisher [3] (Chapter 8). Here the issue is that of why aggregate production functions should appear to exist at all, rather than that of what form they will take given that a constant distribution of capital over firms ensures their existence. See pp. 21–4. The books by Johansen [5] and Sato [9] give excellent discussions of aggregation from several points of view.

This program of research was begun in Chapter 8; individual firms (with a single homogeneous output and single homogeneous labor but different capital types) were given different Cobb–Douglas production functions, underlying capital and labor data were generated in various ways, and labor was assigned to firms to maximize output. An aggregate Cobb–Douglas production function was then estimated and its wage predictions examined.

A number of subsidiary results were found in these experiments, and we shall comment on some of them below. The principal conclusion, however, was the following. It is obvious, of course, that an aggregate Cobb–Douglas production function which fits input and output data well cannot give good wage predictions unless labor's share of total output happens to be roughly constant. What is not obvious is that such an aggregate production function will turn out to give good wage predictions even if rough constancy of labor's share happens to hold. Yet this is overwhelmingly the case in the experiments reported in Chapter 8.

This observation has occasionally been misinterpreted, so we dwell on it here. To say that an estimated Cobb–Douglas function fits input and output data well is to say that it will predict output accurately, given the inputs. Any Cobb–Douglas function will predict that the real wage is proportional to calculated output per worker (and therefore to actual output per worker if it fits well). Therefore, a Cobb–Douglas that fits input–output data well cannot hope to predict wages accurately unless the observed share of wages is roughly constant. If the observed wage share happens to be roughly constant, the fitted Cobb–Douglas can still go wrong if and only if the elasticity of output with respect to labor input, as estimated from input–output data, deviates from the actual wage share by a lot. The content of Fisher's observation about the earlier experiments is that, whenever the simulated economy exhibited roughly constant factor shares, the Cobb–Douglas elasticity estimated from input–output data was close to the observed wage share, and thus that predicted wages were close to actual wages.

If the same thing should happen in empirical work with real data, it requires interpretation. One cannot simply conclude that, under such-and-such a circumstance, the Cobb–Douglas gives a good representation of the "underlying aggregate technology" because it gives a good representation of wages. This is because the simulation examples were generated in just such a way that there is no "underlying aggregate technology" to be represented. No one seriously supposes the situation to be different in real economies. The next thought is likely to be that the estimated aggregate functions work as good approximations only so long as all variables move roughly together. The results of the Cobb–Douglas experiments in Chapter 8 suggest that aggregate production functions will work in wider circumstances than that. In particular, an aggregate Cobb–Douglas gives good results whenever labor's share is relatively constant, even though there is quite a lot of relative movement in the underlying variables.

In any case, it is obviously of interest to know the extent to which the results of Chapter 8 are limited to a highly simplified case in which not only is the aggregate production function estimated Cobb–Douglas but so are all the underlying micro production functions. Indeed, there is some reason to suppose that such a limitation might hold because the heuristic argument given on pp. 210–11 as a partial explanation of the principal result appears heavily dependent on the Cobb–Douglas form of the underlying production functions being aggregated.

This chapter generalizes the experiments of Chapter 8 in two obvious ways. First, the underlying production functions of firms are not restricted to being Cobb–Douglas but are taken to be Constant Elasticity of Substitution (CES) functions with the parameters chosen in various ways described below. Second, not only is an aggregate Cobb–Douglas production function estimated and its wage predictions examined, but an aggregate CES production function is also estimated and analyzed.

In general, it turns out that the principal result of Chapter 8 continues to hold in this more general context. The aggregate Cobb–Douglas production function predicts wages well whenever labor's share is roughly constant, and the relationship is quite close. We have not found any similar organizing principle with which to explain when the aggregate CES production function does or does not give good wage predictions, but this may possibly be due to the fact that the wage predictions of the aggregate CES are generally very good in these experiments, almost always being better than the predictions of the aggregate Cobb–Douglas, even in those cases in which distributive shares are "roughly constant." In particular, the conjecture of Chapter 8 that what matters is how closely wages are a log-linear function of output per man is neither verified nor disproved.

In addition to verifying the principal result of Chapter 8, however, the present set of experiments is sufficiently rich as to suggest a number of conclusions concerning the estimation of aggregate CES production functions, and a good deal of attention will be paid to these results below. It is hoped that they will be of use to researchers using real rather than simulated data.

9.2 The experiments

We worked with underlying units which we shall call "firms." Each firm is distinguished by having its own CES production function. There were N firms. In general we took $N = 3$, but a set of runs in which $N = 5$ did not present any very different features. It is important to recognize, however, that the term "firms" is somewhat misleading. Since each firm's production function exhibits constant returns to scale, two firms with the same production function are equivalent (with efficient allocation of labor) to one big firm. Hence, varying the number of true firms in the economy can take the form of varying initial capital stock rather than simply varying N. In effect, N is the number of different "industries" if we suppose that all firms in an industry have the same production function.

Note also that N cannot be varied with other things equal, because variations in N inevitably involve changes in the distribution of the parameters of the production function. Changes in the number of firms that do not involve changes in that distribution are equivalent to changes in firm size rather than in N.

Each of the N firms had a CES production function:

$$Y_f = \{\delta_f K_f^{-\rho_f} + (1 - \delta_f) L_f^{-\rho_f}\}^{-1/\rho_f}, \tag{9.1}$$

where $f = 1, \ldots, N$ is the firm subscript; δ_f and ρ_f are parameters; K_f is the fth firm's capital stock; L_f is the amount of labor assigned to the fth firm; and Y_f is the resulting output. The time subscript is omitted.

In each experiment, the elasticity of substitution $\sigma_f = 1/(1 + \rho_f)$ and the distribution parameter δ_f were chosen for each of the N firms, as described below. Then a twenty-year time series for each capital stock and for total labor was generated. The labor market is cleared in each period by finding the real wage (in terms of the common product of firms) that equates the sum of all firms' competitive demand for labor to the exogenously given inelastic supply, L. This process determines not only the real wage, w, but also each firm's employment, L_f, its output, Y_f, and the marginal product of its own type of capital, r_f. Since the competitive process equalizes the marginal product of labor across firms, clearly aggregate output $Y = \Sigma_f Y_f$ is maximized in each period subject to the constraint that $\Sigma_f L_f = L$. We denote the maximized output by Y^*.

More precisely, the maximization of aggregate output $(= \Sigma_f F_f(K_f, L_f)$, where $F_f(\cdot,\cdot)$ is the fth firm's production function) subject to $\Sigma_f L_f = L$ defines a function $Y^* = F^*(\{K_f\}, L)$. Here $\{K_f\}$ stands for the vector of individual firms' stocks of not necessarily comparable capital. The envelope property guarantees that $\partial F^*/\partial L = \partial F_f/\partial L_f = w$. There is no "aggregation problem" so far; everything is exact. The aggregation problem arises when we try to sum up the vector $\{K_f\}$ in a scalar J and write $Y^* = G(J, L)$.

At any moment of time $\{K_f\}$ is fixed and virtual changes in output occur only as a function of L. At the next moment $\{K_f\}$ has changed; a successful "aggregate stock of capital" J has to have the property that the change in Y^* is captured by the change in J. In our numerical examples we replace $\{K_f\}$ by $J = \Sigma_f \bar{r}_f K_f$; the constant weights $\bar{r}_f$ are defined in (9.2) below. Theory tells us that any aggregation could be exact only if the marginal rates of substitution between different capital types were independent of L; and this particular aggregation could be exact only if those marginal rates of substitution were constant. Neither condition holds in the simulations. The alternative possibility exists that for at least some paths of the $\{K_f\}$ some simple aggregation will give passable, though not exact, results. Our numerical exercises are an attempt to check out this possibility. The firms' capital stocks evolve in ways that are neither random nor strange; but neither are they the simplest possible.

In general, the marginal rates of substitution between different capital types vary in the efficient production of total output over time; otherwise there would be no aggregation problem. For each capital type, we compute the average marginal product as:

$$\bar{r}_f = \Sigma_t r_f(t) K_f(t) / \Sigma_t K_f(t) \quad (t = 1, \ldots, 20) \tag{9.2}$$

and an index of aggregate capital stock, $J(t)$, as:

$$J(t) = \Sigma_f \bar{r}_f K_f(t) \quad (f = 1, \ldots, N). \tag{9.3}$$

We then estimated both an aggregate Cobb–Douglas production function:

$$Y^* = AL^\alpha J^\beta \tag{9.4}$$

and an aggregate CES production function:

$$Y^* = \gamma(\delta J^{-\rho} + (1-\delta)L^{-\rho})^{-\lambda/\rho} \tag{9.5}$$

by least squares assuming a multiplicative error term e^u. Equation (9.4) was estimated by the usual logarithmic regression. The estimation procedure used with (9.5) is described more fully in the Appendix, where other computational details are also reported. Note that we have not imposed constant returns to scale in either case despite the fact that the underlying data are generated from a constant returns economy. It turns out to matter whether or not we impose such a constraint, as we shall see when considering the results.

In both cases, we examined the wage prediction obtained for each period as the marginal product of labor in the estimated aggregate production function at the observed $L(t)$ and $J(t)$, and compared those predictions with the actual wages, w.

In addition, an aggregate CES production function with constant returns to scale (but not one without) implies a log-linear relationship between wages and output per man. Moreover, that relationship implies an estimate of the elasticity of substitution, $\sigma = 1/(1+\rho)$ since:

$$\log(Y^*/L) = H + \sigma \log w, \tag{9.6}$$

where H is a combination of parameters. Hence, there is another way to estimate the elasticity of substitution for an aggregate CES in addition to estimating it directly from input and output data and we regularly estimated it by least squares applied to (9.6), which we shall call the "wage equation." Note that estimation of (9.6) does not require the *explicit* construction of an aggregate capital stock, although the theory which leads to it implicitly supposes that there is such an aggregate.

The log-linear relation (9.6) cannot be exact even for virtual movements of L and Y^* at a single moment of time, with $\{K_f\}$ fixed. That is because the well-defined function $F^*(\{K_f\}, L)$ is not a CES function when the $F_f(\cdot,\cdot)$ are CES with different elasticities of substitution. Nor is there any good theoretical reason to expect it to hold. Nevertheless, (9.6) might happen to hold approximately for such virtual movements, at least in the particular artificial industries we have constructed. (In retrospect, we wish we had checked this explicitly.) Even so, it takes even more luck or robustness for (9.6) to hold over time, with $\{K_f\}$ changing. Our simulations offer some evidence that this is often the case. That says little more than that an aggregate CES function often gives good wage predictions though it has no "right" to do so. (It does say a little more, because the elasticities of substitution estimated directly and from (9.6) could in principle differ widely.) It is tempting to infer goodness of approximation in the time-series sense from goodness of approximation in the virtual point-of-time sense. There is no rigorous warrant for that. We should perhaps have set ourselves the task of generating an example with good wage predictions in one sense but not in the other. No doubt such examples could be constructed. Our routine constructions do not generally fall into that category, however, and we think that fact has some interest.

We must now describe how the parameters were chosen and the data generated.

For each set of experiments, the elasticities of substitution, σ_f, were chosen as indicated in Table 9.1 which summarizes the various choices of parameters made. The distribution parameters, δ_f, were chosen in a more complicated way. Except in case H, where all distribution parameters were set at 0.25, the distribution parameters were first chosen to divide the range of 0.15 to 0.35 evenly. (The intent was to generate a share for labor approximately 0.75, this being roughly labor's share in US output.) For each choice of the elasticities of substitution, the distribution parameters were chosen in two sets, half the runs having distribution parameters and substitution elasticities positively correlated and half of them negatively correlated. All this is reported in detail in Table 9.2.

Since labor's share is a complicated function of the distribution parameters, we adjusted the initial choices for those parameters if the average wage share for the time series was not within the range 0.65–0.85. We did this by multiplying all the distribution parameters by the ratio of 0.75 to labor's average share, repeating the process until the average wage share for the time series was within the indicated range. However, such adjustments were only required in Cases D and G.

The series for total labor was generated in all experiments as:

$$L(t) = \exp\,(0.02t + 0.014\varepsilon_t), \tag{9.7}$$

where ε_t is a standard normal deviate.

The capital stock series were generated in a more complicated way. For each case (other than H) indicated in Table 9.1, there were twenty-two experiments. Half of these had distribution parameters positively associated with elasticities of substitution and the other half had a negative association. Within each half case, the capital stocks

Table 9.1 Actual and estimated elasticities of substitution.

Case	N	Firm elasticities of substitution σ_f	Run no.	$\hat{\sigma}$: CES[1]			$\hat{\sigma}$: CESW[1]		
				High	Low	Average	High	Low	Average
A	3	0.6, 1.13, 1.66	1–11	17.18 (10)	0.25 (1)	3.12	2.43 (11)	0.52 (1)	1.30
			12–22	2.18 (14)	0.60 (13)	1.12	1.21 (16)	1.00 (22)	1.09
B	3	0.6, 0.75, 0.9	1–11	2.92 (9)	0.22 (1)	1.08	1.28 (11)	0.47 (1)	0.86
			12–22	1.44 (21)	0.49 (15)	0.89	0.92 (19)	0.64 (12)	0.79
C	3	1.11, 1.385, 1.66	1–11	8.43 (10)	0.47 (1)	2.43	2.79 (11)	0.86 (1)	1.70
			12–22	4.43 (18)	0.73 (12)	1.98	2.07 (21)	1.18 (12)	1.62
D	3	0.3, 0.45, 0.6	1–11	1.59 (11)	0.33 (2)	0.80	0.80 (11)	0.23 (1)	0.50
			12–22	1.00 (16)	0.26 (21)	0.56	0.48 (12)	0.37 (22)	0.43
E	3	1.66, 2.495, 3.33	1–8	5.81 (8)	0.64 (2)	2.15	4.84 (8)	1.33 (1)	2.50
F	3	1.66, 1.66, 1.66,	1–11	3.75 (11)	0.62 (2)	1.63	3.35 (10)	1.23 (1)	2.17
G	3	0.6, 0.6, 0.6,	1–11	1.00 (9)	0.36 (1)	0.66	0.76 (11)	0.48 (2)	0.62
H	3	0.6, 1.13, 1.66,	1–11	3.65 (10)	0.45 (1)	1.52	1.54 (11)	0.69 (1)	1.08
I	3	0.95, 1.005, 1.06	1–11	1.93 (6)	0.59 (1)	0.99	1.49 (10)	0.78 (1)	1.13
J	3	0.25, 0.95, 1.65	1–11	4.37 (11)	0.29 (2)	1.50	2.19 (11)	0.30 (1)	1.02
			12–22	1.64 (13)	0.27 (22)	0.83	1.12 (12)	0.47 (22)	0.71
K	5	0.6, 0.865, 1.13, 1.395, 1.66	1–11	12.11 (6)	0.10 (1)	3.30	3.20 (9)	0.18 (1)	1.79
			12–22	4.79 (12)	0.44 (22)	1.44	1.51 (12)	0.67 (22)	1.05

[1]Corresponding run numbers are in parentheses.

Table 9.2 Actual and estimated distribution parameters.

Case	N	Firm distribution parameter δ_f	Run no.	$\hat{\delta}$: CES			$\hat{\delta}$: CESW			$\hat{\delta}$: CD		
				High	Low	Average	High	Low	Average	High	Low	Average
A	3	0.15, 0.25, 0.35	1–11	0.51	0.006	0.28	0.43	0.09	0.28	0.31	0.23	0.27
			12–22	0.39	0.13	0.25	0.29	0.25	0.28	0.26	0.24	0.25
B	3	0.15, 0.25, 0.35	1–11	0.41	0.0008	0.18	0.29	0.04	0.16	0.23	0.18	0.21
			12–22	0.29	0.07	0.16	0.19	0.09	0.14	0.21	0.19	0.20
C	3	0.15, 0.25, 0.35	1–11	0.51	0.09	0.33	0.46	0.23	0.36	0.33	0.27	0.29
			12–22	0.47	0.20	0.35	0.42	0.31	0.37	0.31	0.27	0.28
D	3	0.30, 0.38, 0.46	1–11	0.31	0.007	0.13	0.17	0.0006	0.08	0.22	0.15	0.19
		0.29, 0.37, 0.46	12–22	0.18	0.04	0.06	0.04	0.01	0.03	0.19	0.16	0.18
E	3	0.15, 0.25, 0.35	1–8	0.50	0.21	0.39	0.50	0.37	0.44	0.34	0.32	0.33
F	3	0.15, 0.25, 0.35	1–11	0.48	0.18	0.34	0.48	0.34	0.41	0.34	0.29	0.31
G	3	0.25, 0.35, 0.43	1–11	0.24	0.03	0.14	0.19	0.06	0.13	0.25	0.22	0.24
H	3	0.25, 0.25, 0.25	1–11	0.46	0.07	0.28	0.36	0.16	0.27	0.28	0.25	0.26
I	3	0.15, 0.25, 0.35	1–11	0.37	0.08	0.23	0.34	0.17	0.27	0.27	0.23	0.25
J	3	0.15, 0.25, 0.35	1–11	0.46	0.006	0.23	0.41	0.007	0.20	0.28	0.20	0.24
			12–22	0.33	0.003	0.15	0.25	0.04	0.15	0.22	0.19	0.21
K	5	0.15, 0.2, 0.25, 0.3, 0.35	1–11	0.46	0.0001	0.32	0.43	0.007	0.31	0.35	0.26	0.30
			12–22	0.43	0.08	0.25	0.34	0.18	0.26	0.28	0.24	0.26

were chosen in eleven different ways, being generated from the equation:

$$K_f(t) = \exp\{\theta_f^0 + \theta_f^1 t + 0.03\,\eta_{ft}\}, \tag{9.8}$$

Where η_{ft} is a standard normal deviate (chosen independently in each run), and the two sets of parameters, θ_f^1 were chosen as follows:

$$\text{(a) } N = 3,\ \theta_f^0 = -1, 0, -1 \qquad \text{(b) } N = 5,\ \theta_f^0 = -1, -\tfrac{1}{2}, 0, \tfrac{1}{2}, 1 \tag{9.9}$$

$$\text{(a) } N = 3,\ \theta_f^1 = 0.04 + (2-f)\,\mu \qquad \text{(b) } N = 5,\ \theta_f^1 = 0.04 + \tfrac{1}{2}(3-f)\,\mu \tag{9.10}$$

$$\mu = +0.05, +0.04, \ldots, 0, \ldots, -0.04, -0.05 \tag{9.11}$$

determining eleven different runs.

In other words, with the firms numbered in increasing order of elasticity of substitution, the middle firm starts off with the largest capital stock, the firms at either end having initial capital stocks of $1/e$ as much (except for the random disturbance). The center firm grows at a rate of 4 per cent (plus a random term) while the other firms grow (or shrink) relative to that with the rates depending on the value of μ. Thus, for example, with three firms, when $\mu = -0.05$, the trend terms are -0.01, $+0.04$, and $+0.09$ while when $\mu = +0.05$, they are $+0.09$, $+0.04$, and -0.01. For $N = 5$, the trend terms cover the same range as for $N = 3$, with the additional two firms interpolated, in effect. Of course, the random term is far from negligible, to avoid collinearity.

Notice that the stream of investment for each firm is chosen arbitrarily as a distributed trend. We have incorporated no tendency for profitable firms to add to their capital faster than relatively unprofitable firms. There is no strong theoretical reason to believe that endogenous investment of this sort would make aggregation easier, although it does not seem implausible to conjecture that approximate equalization of marginal products across types of capital might in practice tend to make aggregation conditions more nearly satisfied. That may be a subject for further work. In any case, in these experiments, when one of the estimated aggregate production functions works well that outcome is unlikely to be the result of some hidden long run efficiency consideration of the type just described.

9.3 Summary of results

9.3.1 *General remarks*

It will be remembered that each "case" in Tables 9.1 and 9.2 consists of twenty-two "runs." A case is characterized by the parameters of the individual firms' CES production functions. Within each case, the runs fall into two groups of eleven each. In one group of eleven, the firms with the larger elasticities of substitution have the larger distribution parameters; in the other, a large elasticity of substitution goes along with a small distribution parameter. Within each group of eleven, the runs differ according to the relative growth rates of the capital stocks of the different firms.

We then fit Cobb–Douglas and CES production functions to the aggregate time series of each run. We remind the reader that the elasticity of substitution in these production functions is an "estimate" of nothing; there is no "true" aggregate parameter to which it corresponds. Of course, comparison of the calculated aggregate elasticity of substitution with the range of firms' elasticities of substitution, or with their average, is irresistible. We comment on this kind of comparison in due course.

Now each estimated aggregate production function gives us a series of twenty wage predictions for each run. In each run, the predicted wage can be compared with the "true" market equilibrium wage series. As a measure of accuracy, we calculate the relative root-mean-square error, i.e., the root-mean-square deviation of predicted wage from "true" wage, expressed as a proportion of the average "true" wage over the twenty-year period.

In addition, we estimate the wage equation (9.6) from the data for each run. This gives us another estimate of the (non-existent) aggregate elasticity of substitution. The wage equation, introduced in Arrow *et al.* [1], is sometimes used in empirical work as a vehicle for estimation of the elasticity of substitution in the absence of complete data on inputs and outputs. We shall comment on the relation in our artificial data between the estimate obtained from the wage equation and that obtained from the direct estimation of the production function.

In our data, as apparently in much empirical work on production functions, the elasticity of substitution is poorly determined in the sense that the residual sum of squares has a very flat minimum around the best estimate. On the other hand, it is our experience that a small variation in the estimated elasticity of substitution can make a substantial difference to the predicted wage series, even while it makes only a trivial difference to the ability of the estimated production function to track aggregate output. This suggests a hybrid estimate of the aggregate production function: we impose the elasticity of substitution estimated from the wage equation on the production function, and use the input–output data only to estimate the distribution and efficiency parameters γ and δ in (9.5). Naturally, this hybrid production function gives us yet another series of wage predictions for each run. As will appear, these hybrid wage predictions are uniformly the best of the lot.

This outcome is, in a vague sense, expectable. The "true" wage series has played a part in the prediction process, because the elasticity of substitution has been lifted from the wage equation. When you think about it, however, the role of the true wage series is rather peripheral: it gives rise to an elasticity of substitution which is grafted onto a production function whose other parameters are estimated without benefit of the wage series, and which is then differentiated to give wage predictions. We confess to some surprise that this hybrid prediction is so consistently and so substantially superior to the others.

Before giving a systematic summary of our "empirical" results, we make two general statements that we shall not bother to document in detail because they lead nowhere in the present series of experiments.

First, in all of our runs, the fit of the aggregate production function, as measured by R^2, is very good. This goes for both Cobb–Douglas and CES functions, estimated from the same data. An attempt to make the fit deteriorate by introducing enough random variation into the exogenously generated investment and labor-supply series ran into difficulties with the labor-allocation algorithm used. We have not pursued this line because our main interest is not in goodness-of-fit *per se*, but rather more in wage predictions. Since all of the production functions track aggregate output extremely well, we have not tried to use third and fourth decimal place differences in R^2 as an explanation of differences in the ability to predict wages.

Second, as already mentioned, we did some experiments in which the degree of homogeneity of the fitted production function is determined freely in the estimation process. (Remember that the firms' underlying production functions all have constant returns to scale.) We found that, with very few exceptions, the estimated degree of homogeneity is close to unity, say within the range 0.95–1.05, and often closer than that. Nevertheless, free estimation of returns to scale is not innocuous. If constant returns to scale is imposed, the other parameters change only slightly, and the goodness-of-fit deteriorates only slightly, but the wage predictions usually become considerably better. Presumably such small parameter changes have negligible effect on the ability of the estimated function to track aggregate output, but a larger effect on the slopes of the function, and therefore on its wage predictions. It is, of course, interesting that giving the estimation process correct information about the underlying returns to scale actually improves the ability of the (nonexistent) production function to predict market wages. It could, in principle, have gone the other way.

9.3.2 Wage predictions

We have (see Table 9.1) 184 runs altogether. Each run gives us an estimated Cobb–Douglas function and two CES functions (one from input–output data only, the other using the elasticity of substitution from the wage equation). Figures 9.1 (a)–(c), show the frequency distributions of the relative root mean square errors (RRMSEs) of the wage predictions over all runs in the form of a histogram for each of the production functions. (The hybrid estimate is labelled CESW.)

Our first observation is that the errors are generally small. The relative root mean square error in predicting the period-by-period market wage is often less than 1 per cent, usually less than 2 per cent, and rarely gets as high as 5 per cent. This observation is of limited value, naturally, because it refers entirely to our model world inside the computer and tells us nothing about practical experience. It does, however, help to calibrate our findings.

A second observation is that when all runs are taken together, the CES function out-performs the CD function and is in turn quite substantially out-performed by the hybrid CESW function. This conclusion can be read from the medians plotted in Figure 9.1. The superiority of the CESW predictions is rather remarkable

In this respect, Case I is especially interesting: the three firms have elasticities of substitution of 0.95, 1.005, and 1.06 respectively, so they are all essentially Cobb–Douglas, but with different distribution parameters. There are only eleven runs in this case: the CES has better wage predictions than the CD in four of them, two or three of the runs are essentially ties, and the CD is better in the remaining runs. But the CESW wage predictions are the best of all in every one of the eleven runs (although essentially tied with CES in one of them). We remark here – in anticipation of more extensive discussion below – that the eleven estimated CES functions in this case have elasticities of substitution ranging from 0.49 to 1.93 and averaging 0.99. The eleven wage equations give estimates of the elasticity of substitution ranging from 0.78 to 1.49, and averaging 1.13. Thus, in this case, where the firms all have elasticities of substitution near unity, both methods of estimation of the (nonexistent) aggregate elasticity put it near unity on average, though with considerable range from run to run. It is characteristic, as we shall mention later, that estimation of σ from the wage equation provides a narrower range than does direct estimation of a production function.

A third observation, with respect to the CD estimates, is that Fisher's earlier finding is confirmed in these simulations. The estimated aggregate Cobb–Douglas gives good wage predictions when the

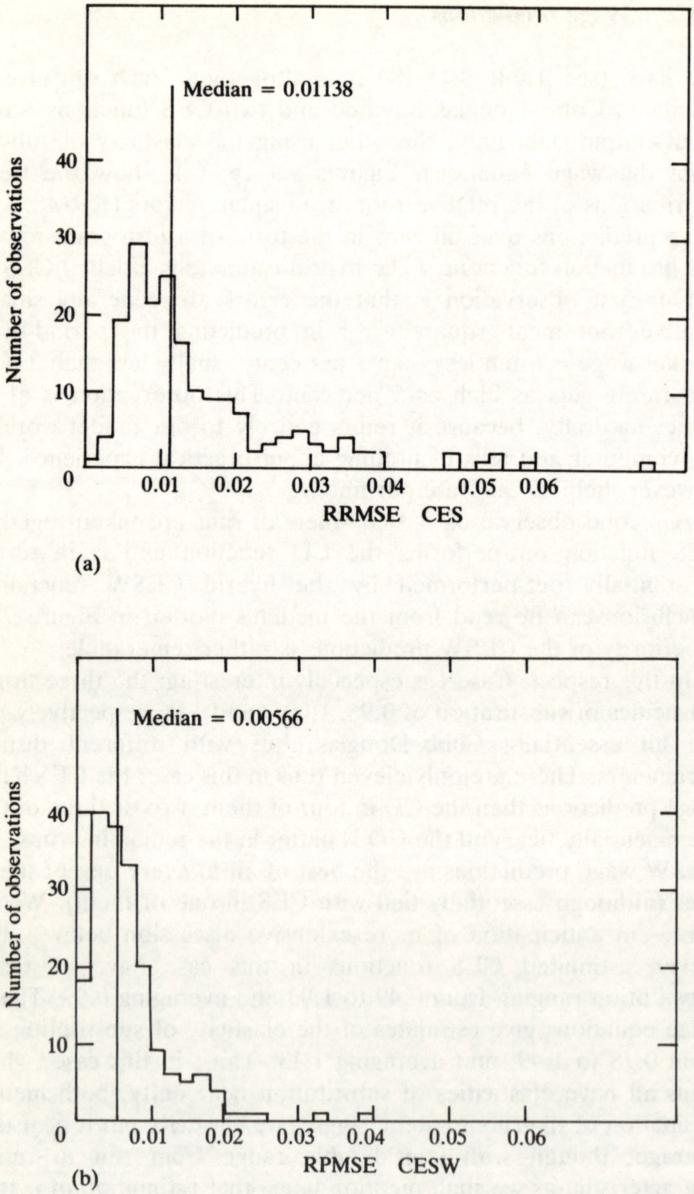
Median = 0.01138
Number of observations
40
30
20
10
0
0.01
0.02
0.03
0.04
0.05
0.06
RRMSE CES
(a)
Median = 0.00566
Number of observations
40
30
20
10
0
0.01
0.02
0.03
0.04
0.05
0.06
RPMSE CESW
(b)

Figure 9.1

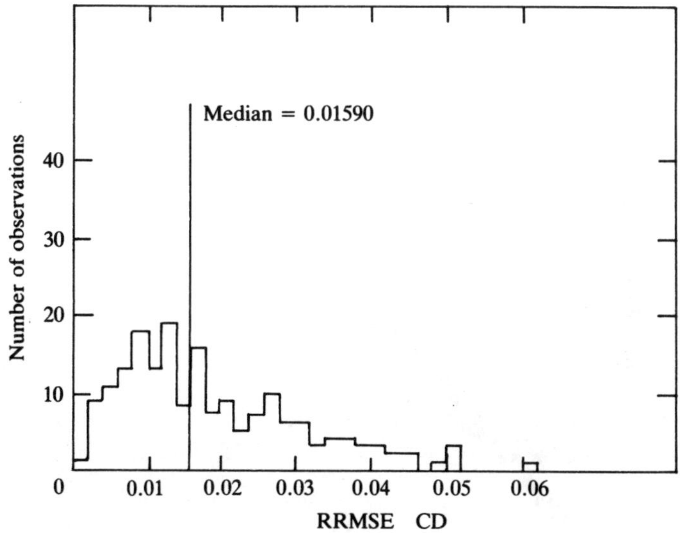

(c)

Figure 9.1 (continued)

"observed" wage share is fairly stable and poorer predictions (as it must) when it is not. As remarked earlier, this means that when the wage share is approximately constant, the CD estimation yields a labor-exponent near the observed wage share. In fact, the accuracy of the CD wage-predictions diminishes rather smoothly as the wage share becomes more variable. This is demonstrated in Figure 9.2, which is a scatter diagram of the relative root mean square error of the CD predictions against the standard deviation of the "observed" wage share, with each observation representing a twenty-period run.

Our fourth observation is a nonobservation. We have tried to find some quantity that would "naturally" be correlated with the accuracy of the CES wage predictions, but we have failed. Accuracy is not correlated with the variability of the wage share, but there is no intuitive reason to expect it to be. We wondered if the accuracy with which the fitted CES function predicts wage rates might be correlated with the goodness-of-fit of the wage equation in the same run (as conjectured in Chapter 8) because they are both indicators of the extent to which the data behave as if they came from an aggregate CES production function. But in fact there was no such correlation to speak of. We did not try to correlate the accuracy of wage prediction with the goodness-of-fit of the production function, because the variation in R^2 is so small. And we did not try to correlate the accuracy

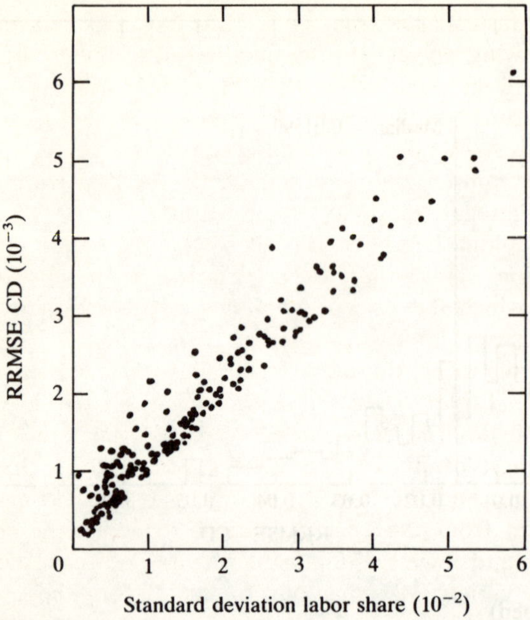

Figure 9.2

of the CESW wage predictions with anything, because the predictions are almost all very accurate. Indeed, it is quite possible that our failure to find an organizing principle to "explain" the relative accuracy of CES wage predictions in different runs occurs simply because almost all the predictions involved are pretty accurate to begin with.

9.3.3 *The aggregate elasticity of substitution*

Each of our cases is characterized by six numbers: three elasticities of substitution and three distribution parameters. Recall that the twenty-two runs within each case fall into two groups of eleven each: in runs 1–11, the elasticities of substitution and distribution parameters are assigned to firms so that the highest value of one goes with the lowest value of the other, while in runs 12–22 the high elasticity of substitution goes with the high distribution parameter, and low with low. Now fix attention on one of these subgroups of eleven runs. These runs differ among themselves in one respect, namely the pattern of investment (and output) across the three firms. In the low-numbered runs within any subgroup, the firm with the low elasticity of substitution is growing fastest and the one with the high elasticity of substitution is growing slowest. In the middle run (numbered 6 or 17) all three firms are growing at about the same rate. And in the higher-numbered runs, the firm with the highest elasticity of substitution grows the fastest. We emphasize this pattern here because it turns out to be a very important determinant of the behavior of the estimates of the aggregate elasticity of substitution.

Since the technology has been chosen so that no exact aggregate production function exists, there is no true aggregate elasticity of substitution with which the various estimates can be compared. One would like to know, however, whether the estimated aggregate elasticity at least falls within the range of the single-firm elasticities that generated the data. Table 9.1 shows, for each subgroup of eleven runs, the underlying single-firm elasticities of substitution, the lowest, average, and highest estimated aggregate elasticity from the direct production function, and the lowest, average, and highest aggregate elasticity estimated from the wage equation. (The run numbers at which the highest and lowest estimates occur are shown in parentheses.) We have a variety of inductions to make from these experiments.

First, if one looks only at subgroup averages, the estimated aggregate elasticity of substitution is clearly in the ballpark, whether it comes from the production function or from the wage equation. That is to say, the (subgroup average) aggregate elasticity of substitution is inside the range defined by the lowest and highest single-firm elasticities of substitution. Moreover, these (theoretically illegitimate) aggregative methods do succeed in distinguishing a situation like case B from one like case C, i.e., an industry whose firms have moderately weak possibilities of factor substitution from one whose firms can substitute rather more freely. *A fortiori*, cases D and E are even more sharply distinguishable.

Second, however, if one looks inside the subgroups, the range of estimated aggregate elasticities of substitution is very wide. Indeed, many of them do lie outside the range defined by the single-firm elasticities. To see more clearly what is happening in the various experiments, we must distinguish between the subgroup of runs 1–11 and the other subgroup comprising runs 12–22. In the course of run 1, the firm with the lowest elasticity of substitution and the highest distribution parameter is growing relative to the others; in run 11 it is the firm with the highest elasticity of substitution and the lowest distribution parameter. Within this subgroup it is an excellent generalization that the estimated elasticity of substitution is higher for higher-numbered runs. That is to say, when output is shifting to firms with high (low) elasticities of substitution, the estimated aggregate elasticity tends to be high (low). In the extreme runs (say, 1, 2, 10, 11), when the firm with high (low) elasticity of substitution is growing much faster than the others, the estimated aggregate elasticity is likely to fall above (below) the range of single-firm elasticities. If this process were to go on long enough, the most rapidly growing firm would come to dominate the model economy and presumably the aggregate production function, and the wage equation would come (properly) to estimate the characteristics of that firm. But it appears that during the long interval before that process is complete, the effect of shifting input and output from firms with high elasticity to firms with low elasticity is to make the aggregates look as if the elasticity of substitution were lower still. This is an insight of unfortunately little practical use: in any real case, if one knew enough to expect such shifts one would probably have access to information which would make it unnecessary to resort to highly aggregative methods. Still, it suggests that the aggregate estimates of the elasticity of substitution can be very badly thrown off by systematic compositional effects.

Third, these observations have to be modified when we look at runs 12–22. In some cases (B and C) one sees the phenomenon just described, but considerably attenuated. In other cases (A and D) it is reversed. We think this can be understood in the following way. In all of our runs, "capital" accumulates faster than the supply of labor, and so the real wage rises. An interpretation of events using an aggregate production function will certainly want to say that a small wage increase is evidence of a high elasticity of substitution, given the evolution of labor supply and "capital." Now in run 11, for instance, as time goes on the firm with the highest elasticity of substitution and lowest distribution parameter (measuring labor intensity) bulks larger and larger in the industry. On *both* counts the increasing demand for labor is tempered and the rise in real wages is gentle. So the data suggest a very large elasticity of substitution indeed. In run 22, on the other hand, the rapidly growing firm has a high elasticity of substitution but also a relatively high labor intensity. These two factors have opposite effects on the demand for labor and thus on the course of the equilibrium real wage. So it perhaps is not surprising that the results are variable from case to case.

In cases F and G (for which only runs 1–11 exist) all firms have the same elasticity of substitution, so the increase in estimated elasticity with run number must be due entirely to the effect of the distribution parameter. In case H, on the other hand, all firms have the same distribution parameter, so the outcome is entirely due to the different elasticities of substitution.

Fourth, the effect we have been describing is present in both methods of estimating the aggregate elasticity of substitution, but it is considerably attenuated in the estimates stemming from the wage equation and considerably more pronounced in those coming from the production function. In fact, generally speaking, the wage equation estimates seem more reliable than the production function estimates (though one must remember that the notion of "reliability" is not terribly well defined in these experiments).

Finally, we repeat here an observation made earlier: the elasticity of substitution – a curvature parameter – is not well determined by the data. The other parameters seem to be able to compensate easily for variations in the elasticity of substitution when it comes to tracking the input–output data. But the wage predictions are more seriously affected. The changes in the distribution and efficiency parameters required to compensate for vagaries in the elasticity of substitution seem to distort the calculated marginal products significantly.

9.3.4 *The distribution parameter*

Less general interest attaches to the estimates of "the" distribution parameter δ (which also does not exist as a true aggregate parameter). Nevertheless, we report some observations here because they may be useful in interpreting the results of econometric work on real data. Table 9.2 shows actual and estimated distribution parameters. In most of the cases, the three firms have distribution parameters equal to 0.15, 0.25, and 0.35. These were chosen so that aggregate quasi-rents would average about $\frac{1}{4}$ of total output and aggregate wages about $\frac{3}{4}$ of output over the twenty periods. (Of course, the functional distribution of income changes in the course of each run, depending on the inter-firm pattern of growth and its interaction with the firms' technological parameters.) Cases D and G have higher values of δ because they have low elasticities of substitution; for a fixed capital–labour ratio – as long as it exceeds one – a lower elasticity of substitution lowers the capital share, and a higher value of δ is needed to pull it back up to $\frac{1}{4}$. Case H was designed to give all firms the same distribution parameter.

It is evident from Table 9.2 that δ is poorly "estimated" in the sense that the estimated distribution parameter in the aggregate CES function may easily lie outside the range of the firm's distribution parameters. This occurs both with the directly estimated CES functions and with the CESW estimates using the wage equation. For cases B, C, D, E, F, and G, even the average over the various cases is far from the centre of gravity of the microeconomic δs.

In the columns devoted to Cobb–Douglas estimates, the distribution parameter is simply the estimated elasticity of aggregate output with respect to aggregate "capital." The various cases illustrate a generalization made earlier. In cases like B and D, in which the three firms have elasticities of substitution well below unity, the aggregate Cobb–Douglas underestimates the share of capital, overestimates the share of labor, and therefore gives poor wage predictions. In cases C, E, and F all firms have elasticities of substitution above unity, and the Cobb–Douglas overestimates the share of capital. The robustness of the Cobb–Douglas comes from cases like A, G, H, I, the first half of J, and the second half of K, in which the Cobb–Douglas manages to estimate a capital-elasticity near 0.25, although the estimating process does not use factor-price data.

More can be said about the estimates of δ, however. Figure 9.3(a) is a scatter plot of estimates of δ against estimates of σ for all 184 CES estimates described in Tables 9.1 and 9.2. Figure 9.3(b) does the same thing for the 184 CESW estimates. Obviously, there is a strong curvilinear relation between estimates of δ and estimates of σ. A run yielding a high estimate of the elasticity of substitution tends to yield a high estimate of the distribution parameter. (By the way, the scatters for individual cases look just like pieces of these combined scatters; there is no misleading composition effect.)

One can understand in a loose way why this should happen. Present a least-squares program with time series labeled output, labor, and capital, and instruct it to estimate a production function under constant returns to scale. When will it tend to generate a large elasticity of substitution? A natural answer is: when output per worker rises rapidly as capital per worker increases, i.e., when the effect of diminishing returns appears to be mild. One way of making this intuition more precise is to calculate from (9.1) that the elasticity of output per worker with respect to capital per worker (k) is

$$\delta k^{-\rho}/(\delta k^{-\rho} + (1-\delta)) = \phi,$$

say. Next, one can easily verify that $\partial\phi/\partial\delta > 0$ and that $\partial\phi/\partial\rho < 0$ provided that capital per unit of labor exceeds one, as is the case in our model economy with our artificially constructed "capital." Since $\sigma = 1/(1+\rho)$, $\partial\phi/\partial\sigma > 0$ under the same condition. Thus, if output per worker seems to increase freely with capital per worker, the least-squares program can register this fact by imputing either a high elasticity of substitution or a high distribution parameter. Not surprisingly, it does both of those things, in proportions which must depend on finer details of the artificial time series.

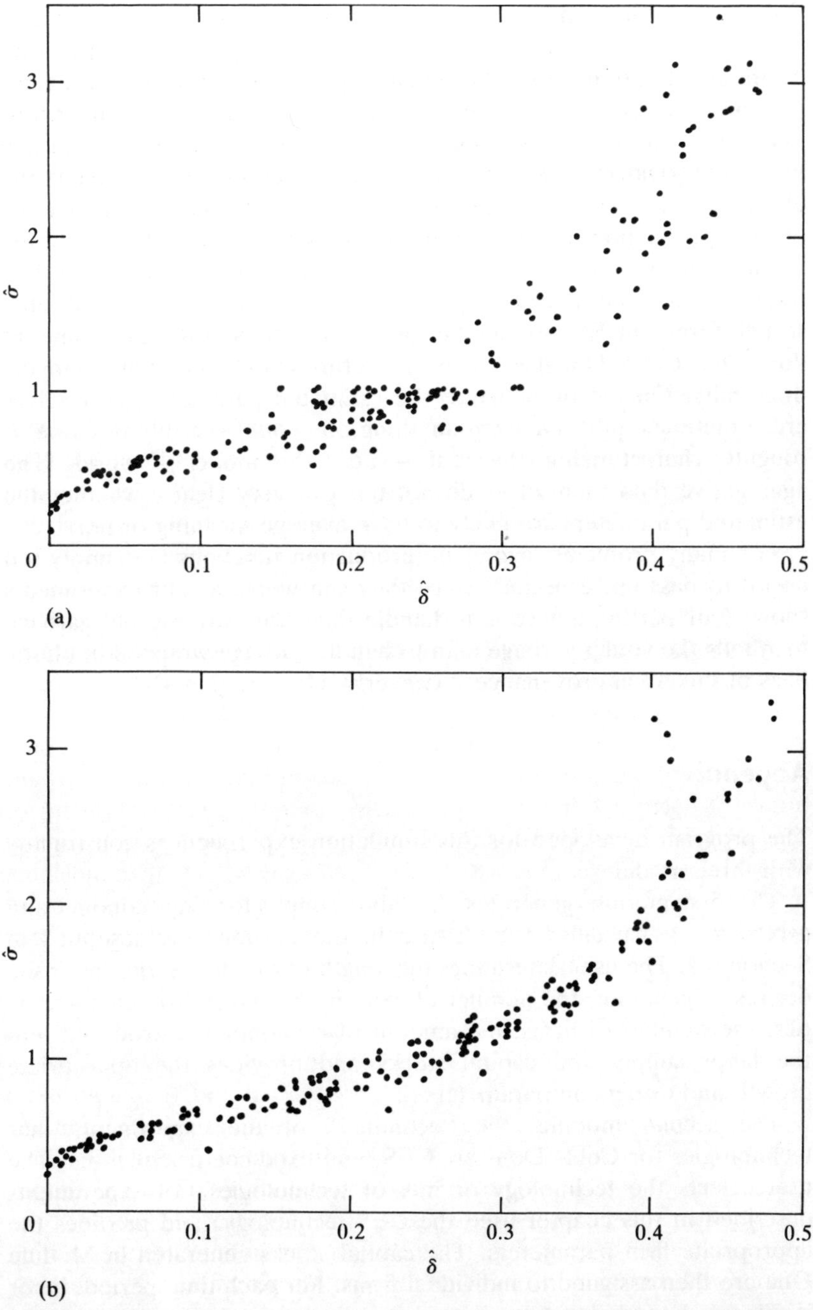

Figure 9.3

9.4 Conclusions

There are situations in which aggregate production functions will work (in the sense of the first paragraph of this chapter) without any assistance from formal theorems on aggregation. In particular, we had uniformly good results from the hybrid procedure that estimates the elasticity of substitution from the wage equation and other parameters of the production function from input–output data. The resulting production function tracks output very closely, and its partial derivatives capture the behavior of factor prices quite well. Even the straightforward CES estimate performs adequately most of the time, as does the Cobb–Douglas, if only factor shares are not changing drastically. On the other hand, the estimated parameters themselves are sometimes quite far from anything one could sensibly describe as roughly characterizing the real – i.e., the model – world. The aggregative data themselves do not tell you very clearly whether the estimated parameters are likely to have average meaning or not.

For many problems, aggregate production functions are simply too useful to pass up, especially since they can work, as our experiments show. Our parting advice is to handle them the way the old garbage man tells the young garbage man to handle garbage wrapped in plastic bags of unknown provenance: "Gingerly, Hector, gingerly."

Appendix

The program developed for this simulation experiment is constructed with three modules:

The first module generates the labor supply for the economy and capital stocks specific to each firm in the economy as described in Section 9.2. The user determines the length of the time series he or she desires to generate, the number of experiments given firm characteristics, the number of firms, the amount of randomness introduced into the labor supply and capital stocks and provides the appropriate growth and dispersion parameters.

The second module, the "economy" of the experiments, has technologies for Cobb–Douglas, CES, and fixed-coefficient firms. The user selects the technology or mix of technologies (all experiments described in this chapter used the CES technology) and provides the appropriate firm parameters. The capital stocks generated in Module One are then assigned to individual firms. For each time period, labor is allocated to each firm using an iterative procedure, moving labor from low to high marginal product firms until the marginal product of labor is virtually uniform across firms. This determines the wage rate for the economy of that time period, and all firm marginal products must be within 1 per cent (approximately) of this wage. Simultaneously, the total labor allocated to the firms must be within 0.5 per cent of the supply generated in Module One.

Given the allocation of labor to each firm and the capital stock one can generate a measure of aggregate capital. The firm's technology with the firm's capital and the firm's allocated labor yields output. Thus we get aggregate output and a measure of aggregate capital.

Using the labor supply from Module One, the aggregate measure of capital and the output generated by the economy, Module Three estimates Cobb–Douglas and CES production functions. For the CES estimation we use a nonlinear least-squares algorithm developed by Marquardt [7], modified to impose simultaneous convergence on the parameters and the sum of squared residuals, the percentage change in both being less than 10^{-5} for convergence. The aggregate production function is then used to predict labor's share which is compared with the actual share generated in Modules One and Two.

References

[1] Arrow, K. J., H. B. Chenery, B. S. Minhas and R. M. Solow, "Capital–labor substitution and economic efficiency," *Review of Economics and Statistics*, **43** (1961), 225–50.

[2] Fisher, F. M., "The existence of aggregate production functions," *Econometrica*, **37** (1969), 533–77 (reprinted as Chapter 1).

[3] Fisher, F. M., "Aggregate production functions and the explanation of wages: A simulation experiment," *Review of Economics and Statistics*, **53** (1971), 305–26 (reprinted as Chapter 8).

[4] Houthakker, H. S., "The Pareto distribution and the Cobb–Douglas production function in activity analysis," *Review of Economic Studies*, **23** (1955–56), 27–31.

[5] Johansen, L., *Production Functions*, Amsterdam: North-Holland, 1972.

[6] Levhari, D., "A note on Houthakker's aggregate production function in a multifirm industry," *Econometrica*, **36** (1968), 151–4.

[7] Marquardt, D. W., "An algorithm for least-squares estimation of nonlinear parameters," *Society for Industrial and Applied Mathematics Journal* (June 1963), 431–41.

[8] Sato, K., "Micro and macro constant-elasticity-of-substitution production functions in a multifirm industry," *Journal of Economic Theory*, **1** (1969), 438–53.

[9] Sato, K., *Production Functions and Aggregation*, Amsterdam: North-Holland, 1975.

10

On perfect aggregation in the national output deflator and generalized Rybczynski theorems (1982)

10.1 Introduction

Fisher and Shell [6] attempted to place the theory of output deflation on a production-theoretic foundation in the same way as the theory of the cost-of-living index is based on a consumer-theoretic foundation. It developed a production-theoretic output deflator to which actually computed indices, such as the GNP deflator, serve (sometimes) as bounding approximations.

This chapter continues that work. In it, I inquire as to the possibility of building up the production-theoretic deflator from subindices each of which is a deflator for a particular sector or industry. In what sense, if any, is it possible, for example, to talk of the steel industry's contribution to inflation? Clearly, such a statement would be well defined if the full output deflator could be expressed in terms of specific industry deflators; the question is whether this is possible.

Obviously, such questions are trivial when considering the Paasche approximation to national output deflation, the GNP deflator. Paasche or Laspeyres indices can be expressed in terms of subindices in a simple, arithmetic way. Yet to be content with this answer is, in effect, to ignore the question. The steel industry deflator in the Paasche approximation is a bound on the production-theoretic deflator for the

---

This research was carried out under contract to the Bureau of Labor Statistics, the United States Department of Labor. I am indebted to Karl Shell for helpful conversations. I take sole responsibility, however, for the views expressed and any errors.

steel industry. The full Paasche approximation is a similar bound on the production-theoretic deflator for the economy as a whole. Yet if the economy-wide, production-theoretic deflator is not simply a function of production-theoretic deflators for separate industries, it is not at all plain that much interest should attach to the percent of Paasche-approximated deflation accounted for arithmetically by the Paasche deflator for the steel industry.

More generally, someone attempting to construct deflators for a particular sector or industry will do so without regard for prices outside that sector. If this is done for every sector of the economy, can the results then be used directly to construct the national output deflator? If not, then what can one say concerning the errors that are likely to be committed in proceeding on a sector-by-sector basis? What approximation theorems can be proved?

This chapter is only the beginning of research into such questions. It asks only whether perfect aggregation is likely to be possible. Not surprisingly, in view of what is known of similar questions in cost-of-living theory,[1] the answer turns out to be that perfect aggregation requires certain separability properties in the structure of the overall technology. However, while "*de gustibus non est disputandum*," this is not true about production-possibility sets and it is therefore possible to inquire further. While the conditions for perfect aggregation remain quite stringent, it is moderately interesting to see what they come down to in terms of individual production functions.

A second purpose of this chapter appears in the course of the analysis. As we shall see below, the conditions for perfect aggregation in the national output deflator turn out to be intimately related to the well-known Rybczynski theorem of international trade theory.[2] It turns out that some of our results can be interpreted as at least mild generalizations of that theorem in ways which do not appear to be fully covered in the literature. I discuss this in detail in a separate section below.

Interestingly enough, the results of this chapter (and therefore also of the Rybczynski theorem) turn out also to be related mathematically to the theorem on capital aggregation which I proved some time ago.[3] Indeed, the method of proof below is often to establish an isomorphism. It is perhaps not surprising that theorems on aggregation of prices and of factors should have the same general structure; it seems less obvious that the Rybczynski theorem should also. The relation ceases to appear coincidental, however, when one realizes that the Rybczynski theorem gives conditions under which a change in factor supplies makes the same relative output prices correspond to different output ratios. The condition that this should *not* occur is a condition that the marginal rates of substitution among different outputs depend only on the output ratios. By Leontief's well-known theorem, this is seen to be a theorem about aggregation over outputs.[4]

10.2 Formal statement of the problem

We begin with a formal description of the production-theoretic deflator; for present purposes, we can use a slight simplification of the description in Fisher and Shell [6] (to which the reader is referred for extensive discussion).[5]

The economy produces outputs $x_1, \ldots, x_r$. The column vector of the x_j is denoted by x. The corresponding row vector of prices is denoted by p' and the money value of output by y. Hats are used to denote base-period magnitudes and are omitted on current-period ones.

The production possibility frontier (PPF) in the base period was:

$$\Phi(\hat{x}) = \hat{\mu}, \tag{10.1}$$

where $\hat{\mu}$ is a shift parameter which will simply be constant in the present analysis. To construct the deflator, we find that current output, x, which lies on the base-period PPF and which maximizes value at current prices, p. That is, we solve

$$\text{Maximize } p'x \text{ subject to } \Phi(x) = \Phi(\hat{x}). \tag{10.2}$$

Let y be the resulting value of $p'x$ and $\hat{y} \equiv \hat{p}'\hat{x}$. The deflator is then given by $y/\hat{y}$.

To study aggregation in this context, it will suffice to consider two sectors. The first of these will consist of the first r_1 outputs and associated prices and the second of the remainder. Sectoral vectors will be denoted by superscripts, so that, in particular, p^1 is the vector of the first r_1 prices, and so forth.

Now, consideration of the deflation problem as posed makes it plain that we can focus on the way in which y depends on p, since the dependence of $\hat{y}$ on $\hat{p}$ will be essentially the same (because a competitive economy locates the value-maximizing point on the PPF). Certainly, y is a function of p and hence of p^1 and p^2. We seek the circumstances under which the goods of the first sector can be considered together and the function in question written as:

$$y = R[r(p^1), p^2] \tag{10.3}$$

where $r(\cdot)$ is a scalar-valued function.

10.3 Independent output ratios and the Rybczynski theorem

By Leontief's well-known aggregation theorem [9] such aggregation will be possible if and only if the ratio of the partial derivatives of y with respect to any two prices in sector 1 is independent of every price in sector 2. Consideration of the maximum problem in (10.2) and application of the envelope theorem now yields immediately:

Lemma 10.1: A necessary and sufficient condition for prices in the first-sector to be aggregated in the deflator is that any ratio x_i^1/x_j^1 be independent of p^2, where x_i^1 and x_j^1 are any two outputs in the first sector.

Thus, aggregation over first-sector prices will be possible if and only if all first-sector output ratios are independent of prices not in that sector. We must now explore what such a requirement implies about the underlying technology. The first possibility is a simple one. Suppose that none of the factors of production used in the first sector is used anywhere else.[6] Then the prices of goods not in the first sector will have no effect on outputs in that sector which will be determined entirely by their own relative prices and the amounts of the first-sector-specific factors which are available. By Lemma 10.1, aggregation will then be possible. I shall refer to this as the completely decomposable case.

Consideration of the completely decomposable case points the way towards analysis of more general cases. The prices of goods not in the first sector can influence the relative outputs of goods in that sector only by changing the amounts of the common factors (i.e., not sector-specific factors) which it is optimal to devote to that sector. It is possible, however, that such changes leave relative outputs in the first sector unchanged.

This can happen in the following manner. Given the inputs (sector-specific and common) to be devoted to the first sector, the PPF of the first sector considered in isolation is determined. Now vary the amounts of the common factors. This will shift the PPF. Such shifts will leave relative outputs unaffected at any given set of first-sector prices if and only if the collection of PPFs so generated is homothetic.

Analytically, drop sector superscripts from now on and consider the technology of the first sector taken in isolation. Let x be the t-vector of first-sector outputs; v be the m-vector of common factors devoted to the first sector; and u be the n-vector of first-sector-specific factors.

The efficient frontier is given by:

$$F(x, u, v) = 0. \qquad (10.4)$$

Lemma 10.2: A necessary and sufficient condition for prices in the first sector to be aggregated in the deflator is that there exist functions $J(\cdot,\cdot)$ and $G(\cdot,\cdot,\cdot)$ such that

$$F(x, u, v) = G[J(x, u), u, v]. \qquad (10.5)$$

If v actually affects the value of F, then $J(x, u)$ must be homothetic in x.

***Proof*:** By Lemma 10.1 and the remarks following, aggregation is possible if and only if given output ratios correspond to the same marginal rates of substitution among outputs, varying v (but taking u as fixed). This means such marginal rates of substitution can depend on u but must be independent of v. A second application of Leontief's aggregation theorem yields (10.5). If v actually influences F, then the requirement that the same marginal rates of substitution correspond to the same output *ratios*, given u, implies that $J(x, u)$ must be homothetic in x.

To see that this result is the same as that of homotheticity in generated PPFs described above, observe that if (10.5) holds, (10.4) can be solved for J, obtaining:

$$J(x, u) = M(u, v). \qquad (10.6)$$

Parametric on u, this gives the PPF for each v. Changes in v which shift the PPF will generate a homothetic map if J is homothetic in x.

Obviously, if there are no common factors, (10.5) is automatically satisfied and the homotheticity requirement is vacuous, so that, as we already know:

Theorem 10.1: Aggregation is always possible in the completely decomposable case.

We shall explore the other ways in which the conditions of Lemma 10.2 can be satisfied. This means looking behind (10.4) to see what restrictions the conditions of Lemma 10.2 put on individual production functions. Obviously, one possibility is that all the outputs of the first sector are jointly produced with the conditions of Lemma 10.2 describing the technology of such joint production. If that is so, then there is no more to be said. We proceed, therefore, by examining the other extreme (and leading) case in which each element of x is produced from a separate production function with the PPF (10.4) derived by efficient allocation of resources in the usual way. We shall discuss the extension of our results to the intermediate case of coproduction of some but not all of the first sector outputs in a later section.

As promised, we are now dealing squarely with the Rybczynski theorem [12] which states that for a two-factor, two-output constant returns world in which production of the two outputs differs in factor intensities, a change in a factor supply *always* shifts the relative production of the two outputs. In terms of the underlying production functions, the absence of such Rybczynski effects would require the two production functions to differ only by a Hicks-neutral technical change so that factor intensities will *always* be the same. (Note that in this case the PPF will be a straight line and it is thus not surprising that it is easy to aggregate over the prices.)

It is not surprising that our attempt to aggregate over prices turns out to involve the Rybczynski theorem. It was shown in Fisher and Shell [6, p. 85] that an increase in the supply of the ith factor would increase (reduce) the importance of the kth output price in the deflator if and only if an increase in the kth output price would increase (reduce) the share of the ith factor in total factor payments. But this latter condition essentially involves the Stolper–Samuelson theorem [13] which is well known to be dual to the Rybczynski theorem.[7] Hence, if we ask for conditions under which a change in factor supplies to the first sector leaves the deflator for that sector unchanged, we should expect to encounter conditions under which the Rybczynski effect is absent.

The literature contains a number of generalizations of the Rybczynski theorem. The two articles which come closest to accomplishing the present purpose are Ethier [2] and Kemp and Wan [7].[8] While the results proved in the present chapter are, of course, consistent with those of Ethier and Kemp and Wan and occasionally overlap them, they are not identical to them.

In particular, the results below do not assume a nonsingular factor-intensity matrix as does Ethier. Indeed, as do Kemp and Wan, I allow different numbers of goods and factors. However, whereas Kemp and Wan explore the consequences of assuming constant factor prices, I take the "other path" of assuming full employment of factors with factor prices adjusting. (See [7, p. 56].)[9] In addition, I consider some cases of nonconstant returns providing some generalization of the Rybczynski theorem in that direction.

My concentration is on the properties of the underlying production functions required for there *never* to be any Rybczynski effects. The results thus turn out as already indicated to be in terms of the relations among the individual production functions rather than in terms (directly) of factor-intensity conditions (although the implications are usually obvious). In what follows, I do not explicitly restate the theorems in terms of Rybczynski effects but the foregoing discussion (and Lemma 10.2) makes it plain how to do so; except for the completely decomposable case, aggregation over first-sector prices is possible if and only if there are no Rybczynski effects. In general, Rybczynski effects are the rule, rather than the exception, as we should expect. Indeed, most nonhomothetic production functions have the property of leading to Rybczynski effects whether or not the different production functions are related to each other by Hicks-neutral technical changes or are even the same. It is an open question whether there are *any* nonhomothetic cases which do not generate Rybczynski effects.

It turns out to be useful (after a preliminary lemma) to organize the discussion by considering first the case in which there are no sector-specific factors, u, used in the first sector. Our results are easiest and most complete for this case. After that, we reintroduce such factors but divide the discussion between the very difficult case in which all such factors are used for all outputs and the easier contrary case which we shall term that of "output-specific" factors. The case in which there are only sector-specific and no common factors is the completely decomposable case already handled.

Translation of these different cases in Rybczynski-effect terms is straightforward. The case of price aggregation with no sector-specific factors is the case of no Rybczynski effects. The case of price aggregation with some sector-specific and some common factors is the case in which changes in *some* factor supplies (the common factors) generate no Rybczynski effects although changes in *other* factor supplies (the sector-specific factors) may generate such effects. The interpretation of output-specific factors is immediate.

The possibility of having sector-specific factors which are also output specific raises a question which it is convenient to dispose of now. Can there be common factors which are output specific? Is aggregation possible with some of the factors used both in and out of the first sector, the elements of v, not used everywhere in the first sector? The answer is in the negative as shown by the somewhat more general:

Lemma 10.3: If at some point on the first sector PPF (10.4) optimal allocation results in a corner solution with a particular common factor, v_j, not employed in the production of some output, x_i, then aggregation over the prices of the first sector is impossible.

***Proof*:** Add a little more v_j to the first sector. Because of the corner solution, at the same output prices as before it must be optimal to assign the extra input entirely to outputs other than x_i. Evidently the resulting shift in the PPF cannot leave output ratios unchanged, i.e., it is not a homothetic outward shift.

For the remainder of the chapter we shall assume that common factors are always employed in the production of all first-sector outputs. (Actually, tangency conditions at zero employment would make no difference, as the lemma suggests.)

10.4 Homotheticity and additivity

It will be useful to proceed by stating the following lemma.

Lemma 10.4: Suppose that, for some $n > 1$,

$$J(x) \equiv \sum_{i=1}^{t} H^i(x_i) \tag{10.7}$$

is homothetic and that, for all i, $H^i(0) = 0$, and for $x_i \geqslant 0$, $H^i(\cdot)$ is twice differentiable with $H^{i'}(x_i) > 0$. Then for all $x_i \geqslant 0$,

$$H^i(x_i) = C_i x_i^{\alpha} \tag{10.8}$$

with the same $\alpha > 0$ for all i.

***Proof*:** This follows from Lau [8, Lemma II, p. 383], the logarithmic case being ruled out by $H^i(0) = 0$.

10.5 No sector-specific factors

We now consider the case of no sector-specific factors. Here the production functions of the first sector can be written as:

$$x_i = g^i[v(i)] \qquad i = 1, \ldots, t, \tag{10.9}$$

where $v(i)$ is the vector of common factors devoted to the production of x_i and

$$\sum_{i=1}^{l} v(i) = v. \tag{10.10}$$

We assume $g^i(\cdot)$ monotonic in all arguments and $g^i(0) = 0$. In addition, save where separable cases are specifically considered, we assume that the factor demand functions generated by production functions here and below all have positive definite Hessians in their factor arguments (outputs held constant).

It is convenient to begin by considering the very special case of $m = 1$.

Theorem 10.2: If the only factor employed in the first sector is a single common factor, then a necessary and sufficient condition for aggregation over the prices of the first sector is that every production function (10.9) be in the form:

$$g^i[v(i)] = b_i v(i)^{\beta} \tag{10.11}$$

where β is the same for all i.

Proof:[10] Solve (10.9) for $v(i)$ to obtain the factor demand functions

$$f^i(x_i) = v(i) \tag{10.12}$$

where $f^i(\cdot)$ is the inverse function of $g^i(\cdot)$. Summing (10.12) over i, the first-sector PPF is given by

$$\sum_{i=1}^{l} f^i(x_i) = v, \tag{10.13}$$

recalling that some factor is employed in the production of every output. Lemma 10.2 now shows that a necessary and sufficient condition for the aggregation in question is that the left-hand side of (10.13) be homothetic in the x_i. This makes Lemma 10.4 applicable with $H^i(\cdot) = f^i(\cdot)$ and the theorem follows from (10.8) with $b_i = 1/C_i$ and $\beta = 1/\alpha$.

Thus aggregation will be possible in this case if and only if every production function is homogeneous of the same degree and differs from the others by at most a multiplicative parameter (Hicks-neutral) shift. In particular, under constant returns, this makes the PPF linear, and relative prices in the first sector will never change so long as the corresponding outputs are produced, making aggregation trivial. As the Rybczynski theorem suggests, these results will recur in more interesting and complicated cases.

We now go on to consider the case of more than one common factor, $m > 1$. As in the proof of Theorem 10.2, it will be convenient to solve (10.9) for a particular element of $v(i)$, say $v(i)_m$, and obtain the factor-demand functions:

$$f^i[x_i, \tilde{v}(i)] = v(i)_m, \tag{10.14}$$

where $\tilde{v}(i)$ is the subvector of $v(i)$ obtained by deleting $v(i)_m$.

Now, we can consider the derivation of the aggregate technological frontier (10.4) as follows. Let the x_i be fixed and minimize v_m given (10.14) and the first $m-1$ of the factor constraints in (10.10). We then wish to aggregate over the x_i (homotheticity comes later). This problem, however, is precisely isomorphic to the standard capital aggregation problem studied in Chapter 2[11] with the x_i playing the role of capital, the $\tilde{v}(i)$ the role of labor, and $v(i)_m$ the role of output. We can therefore proceed by adapting the capital-aggregation results to the present case.

There are two possibilities. The first of these, which we shall refer to as the "Nataf case,"[12] is that, *for every choice of m*, and *every i*, the factor demand functions (10.14) are all additively separable in x_i and $\tilde{v}(i)$, being written as

$$f^i[x_i, \tilde{v}(i)] = H^i(x_i) - M^i[\tilde{v}(i)], \tag{10.15}$$

where the form of $H^i(\cdot)$ and $M^i(\cdot)$ depend on the choice of m. The other possibility is that for some i, this cannot be done for at least one choice of m. We begin with the Nataf case and prove:

Theorem 10.3: In the Nataf case, aggregation is possible over first-sector prices if and only if every first-sector production function (10.9) is in the form:

$$g^i[v(i)] = b_i \left[\sum_{j=1}^{m} a_j v(i)_j \right]^{\beta} \tag{10.16}$$

where β and the a_j are independent of i.

***Proof*:** It is obvious[13] that since separability (10.15) of the factor demand functions must hold for every choice of m, (10.14) can be rewritten as

$$H^i(x_i) = \sum_{j=1}^{m} a^i_j v(i)_j. \tag{10.17}$$

Then, letting $G^i(\cdot)$ be the inverse function of $H^i(\cdot)$, the production functions (10.9) are all in the form

$$g^i[v(i)] = G^i\left[\sum_{j=1}^{m} a_j^i v(i)_j\right]. \tag{10.18}$$

Examining marginal rates of substitution between pairs of factors, it is evident that the absence of corner solutions (Lemma 10.3) implies that the ratios a_j^i/a_k^i $(j, k = 1, \ldots, m)$ must be independent of i. It is then a matter of notation to absorb any common multiplicative difference into the definition of $H^i(\cdot)$ and to take the a_j^i as themselves independent of i, dropping the superscript.

Now sum (10.17) over i, obtaining the first-sector PPF as:

$$\sum_{i=1}^{I} H^i(x_i) = \sum_{j=1}^{m} a_j v_j. \tag{10.19}$$

Lemma 10.2 now shows that a necessary and sufficient condition for the desired aggregation is that the left-hand side of (10.19) be homothetic in the x_i. This makes Lemma 10.4 applicable (the remaining properties of the $H^i(\cdot)$ present no difficulty) and the theorem follows from (10.17) and (10.8) with $b_i = 1/C_i$ and $\beta = 1/\alpha$.

Once again, aggregation requires all production functions homogeneous of the same degree and with only Hicks-neutral differences. Under constant returns this makes the PPF linear and relative prices unchanging so long as the corresponding outputs are produced. These results carry over to what is perhaps our most straightforward generalization of the Rybczynski theorem:

Theorem 10.4: Suppose that all first-sector production functions (10.9) are homothetic. Then aggregation over first-sector prices will be possible if and only if all such production functions are homogeneous of the same degree and differ by at most Hicks-neutral shifts.

Proof: For the single-factor case, this holds by Theorem 10.2 and for the Nataf case by Theorem 10.3. We must therefore take $m > 1$ and consider the non-Nataf case.

Consider the factor demand functions (10.14) for that choice of i and m for which separability does not hold. We know from pp. 36–7 and 64, Note 7 that aggregation over the x_i requires that for the same choice of m, separability not hold *for any i*. Since a homothetic function is a monotonic transformation of a function homogeneous of degree one, it is easy to see that the factor demand functions (10.14) can be written as:

$$f^i[x_i, \tilde{v}(i)] = F^i[H^i(x_i), \tilde{v}(i)] \tag{10.20}$$

where the $H^i(\cdot)$ are monotonic with $H^i(0) = 0$ and the $F^i(\cdot,\cdot)$ are all homogeneous of degree one.

This means, however, that all the factor demand functions are in a class isomorphic to the class of capital-generalized, constant-returns (CGCR) production functions introduced on pp. 41–3 and Theorem 2.4 therein applies to the present problem. That theorem, however, which is a generalization of the standard capital aggregation theorem for constant returns,[14] states that aggregation over the x_i will be possible if and only if the $F^i(\cdot,\cdot)$ can all be taken to be the same, differences being absorbed in the $H^i(\cdot)$. Moreover, it is not hard to see[15] that, in that case, the aggregate is the sum of the $H^i(x_i)$ so that Lemma 10.4 becomes applicable. Putting all this together and solving (10.20) for x_i, routine calculations show that aggregation over prices will be possible if and only if we can write:

$$g^i[v(i)] = b_i[N[v(i)]]^{\beta} \tag{10.21}$$

where $N(\cdot)$ and β are independent of i and $N(\cdot)$ is homogeneous of degree one. This proves the theorem.[16]

Theorem 10.4 covers the leading case of homothetic production functions. It includes, in effect, the earlier two theorems, since in both the scalar and Nataf cases it turns out that aggregation requires homotheticity (indeed, homogeneity). It seems quite possible that the homotheticity requirement of Lemma 10.2 can only be satisfied if all production functions (10.9) are themselves homothetic, but I have been unable to prove this.

This is about as far as it seems possible to go, largely because complete closed-form results for the isomorphic capital aggregation problem are not known. It is an open question whether there exist any nonhomothetic cases which fail to generate Rybczynski effects and thus permit aggregation. Most nonhomothetic production functions will create such effects regardless of how they are related to each other. This is the equivalent statement to that of capital aggregation theory that most production functions do not permit capital aggregation over any set which contains them (see Chapters 1 and 2).[17]

10.6 Sector-specific but no output-specific factors

These results can be used to study the case in which there are sector-specific factors present. In this section I do so, assuming that such factors are not also output specific; that is, I assume that such factors, u, are allocated across outputs so that marginal revenue products are equalized. The case of corner solutions where such factors are productive only in some but not all of the outputs of the first sector is taken up later. Note that since aggregation will require the ability to aggregate over subgroups of outputs and prices within the first sector there is no loss of generality in assuming each sector-specific factor used in all outputs and each output-specific factor used in only one.

Obviously, any condition which is sufficient for pure aggregation when there are no sector-specific factors remains so when such factors are present. To see this, observe that the preceding section found necessary and sufficient conditions for the absence of Rybczynski effects when *any* factor supply changes. Such conditions are certainly sufficient to ensure the absence of such effects when only certain factor supplies (the common factors) change. What is new about the present case is that such strong conditions may not be necessary if we are only interested in ruling out Rybczynski effects from changes in the supply of some but not all factors. Unfortunately, the problem considered in the present section turns out to be very difficult and, except for the case of a single sector-specific factor, I can only give partial answers. Lengthy proofs are omitted. Some readers may wish to skip to the next section.

Write the production functions of the first sector as:

$$x_i = g^i[v(i), u(i)] \tag{10.22}$$

where the $g^i(\cdot,\cdot)$ are monotonic in all arguments and $g^i(0,0) = 0$. Consider solving (10.22) for the demand for a particular sector-specific factor, $u(i)_n$, obtaining

$$k^i[x_i, v(i), \tilde{u}(i)] = u(i)_n \tag{10.23}$$

where $\tilde{u}(i)$ is $u(i)$ with its nth element deleted. Similarly, I shall write the factor demand functions for a particular common factor, $v(i)_m$, as

$$f^i[x_i, \tilde{v}(i), u(i)] = v(i)_m. \tag{10.24}$$

As before, I begin by considering special cases. The case of $m = 1$ turns out to be no longer special unless, in addition, it turns out that every one of the factor demand functions for the sector-specific factors (10.23) for every choice of n is separable into the sum of a function of

x_i and a function of $\tilde{u}(i)$ and $v(i)$. I shall refer to this as the "sector-specific Nataf case." It is not hard to show that the factor demands must be linear in $u(i)$ and then to generalize Theorem 10.2 as:

Theorem 10.5: If there is only a single common factor employed in the first sector and the sector-specific Nataf case is present, then a necessary and sufficient condition for aggregation over the prices of the first sector is that every production function (10.22) be in the form

$$g^i[v(i), u(i)] = b_i\left[v(i) + \sum_{h=1}^{n} d_h u(i)_h\right]^{\beta} \tag{10.25}$$

where β and the d_h are the same for all i.

The Nataf case considered in the previous section similarly generalizes. Now it becomes the case in which, for every i and every choice of m and n, each of the factor demand functions (10.23) and (10.24) are additively separable in a function of output and a function of the remaining factors. We shall call this the "general Nataf case." A proof substantially identical to that of Theorem 10.3 then shows:

Theorem 10.6: In the general Nataf case, aggregation is possible over first-sector prices if and only if every first-sector production function is in the form:

$$g^i[v(i), u(i)] = b_i\left[\sum_{j=1}^{m} a_j v(i)_j + \sum_{h=1}^{n} d_h u(i)_h\right]^{\beta} \tag{10.26}$$

where β, the a_j, and the d_h are independent of i.

Suppose then that neither of the special cases so far considered is applicable. Then for some i, there is some factor demand (10.23) or (10.24), with an element of $v(i)$ on the left-hand side, which cannot be written as the sum of a function of x_i and a function of the factors on the left-hand side. We shall refer to this as the "absence of Nataf separability" for the particular factor demand. In this case, it is not hard to show that aggregation will only be possible if the corresponding factor demand function is also not Nataf-separable for all i. We may therefore suppose that such Nataf-separability does not hold for any i for the factor demand in question. In what follows, it does not matter whether that factor demand is for a common or a sector-specific factor, and, we shall suppose that it is the latter,[18] in the form (10.23), leaving the other case to the reader.

This leads us to consider the generalization of Theorem 10.4 to the present case. As it turns out, this is not so straightforward, and there are a number of cases to consider.

In the first place, Theorem 10.4 implies:

Corollary 10.1: Suppose that all first-sector production functions, $g^i[v(i), u(i)]$ are homothetic in the $v(i)$ when $u(i) = 0$. Then a necessary condition for aggregation over first-sector prices is that the $g^i[v(i), 0]$ all be homogeneous of the same degree and differ by at most Hicks-neutral shifts.

Corollary 10.2: Suppose that all first-sector production functions $g^i[v(i), u(i)]$ are homothetic. Then a necessary condition for aggregation over first-sector prices is that the $g^i[v(i), 0]$ all be homogeneous of the same degree and differ by at most Hicks-neutral shifts.

Now consider the special case in which, for every i, the factor demand function for the particular choice of n under consideration can be written as

$$k^i[x_i, v(i), \bar{u}(i)] = K^i(J^i[x_i, \bar{u}(i)], v(i)). \tag{10.27}$$

We shall refer to this as the "weakly separable case." Note that it is automatically present if there is only one sector-specific factor.

Now, Lemma 10.2 can be regarded as stating two requirements for price aggregation. The first of these, the "existence requirement," is given by (10.5). The second, the "homotheticity requirement," involves homotheticity of the function $J(x, u)$. It is easiest to consider these requirements separately.

Lemma 10.5: In the weakly separable case, suppose that every production function (10.22) is homothetic. If the existence requirement of Lemma 10.2 is satisfied *and* if aggregate factor demand for u_n can be written as $K[J(x, \bar{u}), v]$ (the aggregate equivalent of (10.23)), then the $K^i(\cdot,\cdot)$ of (10.27) can be taken to be independent of i.

***Proof*:** The aggregation problem involved here is isomorphic to that of aggregation over fixed and movable capital goods considered in Chapter 4. See especially Corollary 4.2, p. 115.

It is important to realize that the condition of Lemma 10.5 is not sufficient for aggregation. Apart from homotheticity, the existence requirement involves marginal rates of substitution among the x_i independent of v for *every* factor demand optimum problem. This was not a problem with Theorem 10.4.

We now consider homotheticity in these cases. It is not hard to show.

Lemma 10.6: In the weakly separable case, suppose that all production functions are homothetic. Suppose that aggregation over first-sector prices is possible *and* that aggregate factor demand for u_n can be written as $K[J(x, \tilde{u}), v]$. Then all production functions (10.22) must be in the form

$$g^i[v(i), u(i)] = Q^i(N[v(i), u(i)_n], \tilde{u}(i)) \qquad (10.28)$$

where $N(\cdot,\cdot)$ is homogeneous of degree one and independent of i, and

$$Q^i(N[v(i), u(i)_n], 0) = b_i\{N[v(i), u(i)_n]\}^{\beta}. \qquad (10.29)$$

Unfortunately, Lemma 10.6 is not directly very interesting because it requires the aggregate equivalent of (10.27), that $\tilde{u}$ not enter the factor demand for u_n directly. This would be satisfied if $\tilde{u}$ (or even stronger, u) entered the function $G[J(x, u), u, v]$ of (10.5) only through $J(x, u)$ and not directly, but it seems likely that this is not required for aggregation.

We can state, however:

Theorem 10.7: Suppose that all production functions (10.22) are homothetic and that there is only one sector-specific factor. Suppose further that for some i the demand for that factor is not Nataf-separable. Then a necessary condition for aggregation over first-sector prices is that all production functions (10.22) be in the form

$$g^i[v(i), u(i)] = b_i\{N[v(i), u(i)]\}^{\beta} \qquad (10.30)$$

where $N(\cdot,\cdot)$ is homogeneous of degree one and, like β, does not vary over i. That is, all production functions must be homogeneous of the same degree and differ by at most Hicks-neutral shifts.

***Proof*:** In this case $\tilde{u}$ does not exist and Lemma 10.6 is immediately applicable. Further $Q^i[\cdot, \tilde{u}(i)] = Q^i(\cdot, 0)$.

It is easy to see from Theorem 10.4:

Corollary 10.3: A sufficient condition for aggregation over first-sector prices is that all production functions be in the form (10.30).

Corollary 10.4: Suppose that all production functions (10.22) are homothetic and that there is only one sector-specific factor. Suppose further that for some i the demand for that factor is not Nataf-separable. Then a necessary and sufficient condition for aggregation over first-sector prices is that all production functions (10.22) be homogeneous for the same degree and differ by at most Hicks-neutral shifts.

There are a number of problems in going beyond these results. First, the aggregate will be the sum of the $J^i[x_i, \tilde{u}(i)]$. The $\tilde{u}(i)$, however, are functions of the elements of u and of all the elements of x (but not of v in this case). This makes each of the $J^i(\cdot,\cdot)$ a function of all the x_i and of u. Even with u held constant, therefore, Lemma 10.4 does not apply so that further restrictions on the form of the functions $Q^i(\cdot,\cdot)$ are not readily available.

Moreover, one cannot be sure, in general, even if (10.28) and (10.29) hold, that the solution of (10.28) for one of the common factors or for one of the sector-specific factors other than $u(i)_n$ will result in a weakly separable factor demand function. This makes most of our results necessary but not sufficient conditions. Further, even necessary conditions in the weakly separable case, however, are not directly of great interest because of the requirement that separability hold not only for factor demands in the ith production process (10.27) but also for aggregate factor demand.

In the nonweakly separable case, closed-form conditions for aggregation are not known, even under homotheticity. Some idea of the problems involved may be obtained from the following discussion.

Consider the demand for a sector-specific factor (10.23). The Leontief conditions for aggregation require that the marginal rates of substitution between any pair of the x_i with optimized demand for u_n constant must be independent of v when the $v(i)$ *and* the $\tilde{u}(i)$ are adjusted optimally. This is certainly a weaker requirement than the requirement that such independence hold when the $v(i)$ are optimally adjusted and the $\tilde{u}(i)$ arbitrary *and* that such marginal rates of substitution be independent of the $\tilde{u}(i)$. Imposing that requirement, however, produces a problem isomorphic to that of capital aggregation with some capitals (the x_i) in the aggregate and some [the $\tilde{u}(i)$] left out. This problem was considered on pp. 47–57, and complete closed-form results are not known for it. *A fortiori*, we shall not be able to obtain complete closed-form results for our problem.

An example may help here. Suppose that there are only two sector-specific factors and a single common factor. Suppose further that every production function (10.22) is in the form:

$$g^i[v(i), u(i)] = D^i(S^i[u(i)] + c_i v(i)), \tag{10.31}$$

where the $D^i(\cdot)$, $S^i(\cdot)$, and c_i can all vary with i. Then the factor-demand functions for either sector-specific factor are in the form:

$$u(i)_n = L^i[H^i(x_i) - c_i v(i), \bar{u}(i)]. \tag{10.32}$$

It can be verified by direct computation that the conditions of Theorem 2.6, p. 49 are satisfied[19] so that at least the existence requirements of Lemma 10.2 are met. Whether or not the homotheticity requirement is also met depends on the nature of the aggregate, and this is not known. Note that (10.31) can be homothetic or even constant returns, although it would then be further restricted by Corollary 10.2. Note further that common factor indispensability would rule it out. I have not found it possible to go further along these lines.[20]

10.7 Output-specific factors and co-production

I now take up the two matters which have been postponed, the introduction of output-specific factors and the case in which a single production function produces more than one output.

Begin with the case of output-specific factors. The amounts of such factors can be arbitrary; there are no Leontief conditions involved in their factor demands; and aggregation must hold for all such amounts. Hence, such factors act as parameters of the production functions. For given amounts of such factors, all of our earlier results must apply.

Unfortunately, this is not so simple a matter as it appears. If a production function is homothetic in all the factors, it will generally (not always) fail to be so in the remaining factors when one or more are held constant. We have nice closed-form results only for homothetic cases, however. It follows that simply holding output-specific factors constant and applying earlier results only leads to definite answers in a rather restricted class of cases, even given homotheticity, although Corollaries 10.1 and 10.2 above obviously apply here also.

The nicest of the new results is a generalization of Theorem 10.4 when all sector-specific factors are also output-specific.

Corollary 10.5: Suppose that all sector-specific factors are also output specific. Suppose further that every production function (10.22) is homothetic in the elements of $v(i)$ for every value of $u(i)$. Then a necessary and sufficient condition for aggregation over the prices of the first sector is that all such production functions be in the form

$$g^i[v(i), u(i)] = b_i[u(i)]\{N[v(i)]\}^{\beta} \tag{10.33}$$

where $N(\cdot)$ and β are independent of i and $N(\cdot)$ is homogeneous of degree one.[21]

Note that for given amounts of the sector-specific factors this reduces to Theorem 10.4. In particular, for constant returns it will again be the case that relative first-sector prices do not vary.[22] Unfortunately, the conditions of Corollary 10.5 are much stronger than simple homotheticity, so it is of interest to look further.

There is another class of special cases which can be generated in a different way. Suppose that in (10.5) the output-specific components of u only entered through $J(x, u)$ and not directly as arguments of $G(\cdot,\cdot,\cdot)$. Then we could think of (10.5) as involving aggregation over outputs *and* output-specific factors. Exploring this possibility, however, is obviously equivalent to supposing that there are no output-specific factors but that certain production functions involve more than one output. I now turn to that problem and shall not give the interpretation of the results in terms of output-specific factors explicitly.[23]

Denote the vector of outputs produced by the ith production process by x^i, using the superscript instead of the subscript. For simplicity, we assume no sector-specific factors, although not all results depend on this. We begin by writing the production frontiers for this case as:

$$F^i[x^i, v(i)] = 0, \tag{10.34}$$

with $F^i(\cdot,\cdot)$ monotonic in $v(i)$ and $F^i(0,0) = 0$.

We prove:

Theorem 10.8: A necessary condition for aggregation over the prices of the first sector is that the production frontiers (10.34) can be rewritten as:

$$H^i(x^i) = g^i[v(i)], \tag{10.35}$$

where $H^i(\cdot)$ is homothetic.

Proof: If there is a single factor this is trivial. If there is more than one factor, solve (10.34) for the factor demand for $v(i)_m$. Aggregation in the resulting optimum problem in which v_m is to be minimized is isomorphic to the capital aggregation problem in which each production function has more than one capital and these are all to be included in the aggregate. The existence of (10.35) follows from p. 54.

Moreover, observe that aggregation must remain possible when some outputs are zero. Then (10.35) is the equivalent of (10.5) when only the *i*th production process is active. Homotheticity of the $H^i(\cdot)$ follows by similar reasoning.

This result makes it relatively easy to proceed since we can treat each production process (10.35) as having a single output, $H^i(x^i)$, and aggregate over such outputs. Further, since the $H^i(\cdot)$ will have to remain homothetic when all elements of x^i save one are set equal to zero, our results derived from Lemma 10.4 will stand as well.

I shall not spell out all those results in formal detail. In general, for the cases considered in Theorems 10.2–10.4, which include homotheticity of the $g^i(\cdot)$ and thus constant returns, it turns out to be necessary and sufficient that the $g^i(\cdot)$ all be homogeneous of the same degree with only Hicks-neutral differences. For constant returns this will make the relative prices of the $H^i(\cdot)$ constant, so to speak, but it will no longer invariably follow that relative prices of actual outputs in the first sector should be so.

In terms of the Rybczynski theorem this last result implies that, even when production functions involve more than one output, Rybczynski effects are to be expected under constant returns (unless *all* outputs are jointly produced).

Notes

1. See Pollak [11] and Blackorby and Russell [1].
2. Rybczynski [12]. I am indebted to M. Machina for first calling the relationship to the Rybczynski theorem to my attention, and to him, J. Bhagwati, E. Helpman, and A. Razin for helpful references.
3. Fisher [3] and [4] (Chapters 2 and 4). A nontechnical summary is given in Fisher [5] (Chapter 1).
4. Leontief [9]. It is also not surprising to find some relation here to the theorem on correcting for quality change by simple price adjustments proved in Fisher and Shell [6, pp. 105–7].
5. Appropriate differentiability and regularity conditions are assumed throughout.

6. As we are dealing with production possibility frontiers, intermediate outputs are netted out and we consider production from primary factors only.
7. Indeed, the duality results proved in Fisher and Shell [6, pp. 86–7] essentially re-prove this.
8. Other references are given in these papers.
9. As a matter of fact, the results below are more general than this. What matters are the assumptions on which the PPF is drawn. It can be drawn as usual with fixed factor supplies or with some (or all) factors purchased at fixed factor prices and the total expenditure on such "variable" factors fixed along with the individual amounts of the remaining factors. The results below would still apply considering expenditure on "variable" factors as a factor in an "indirect" production function. (One can show that the same conditions developed below would have to hold for the original production functions in order to hold for the desired "indirect" production functions.) Such an interpretation of the case of some or all factor prices fixed leads to a different case from that analyzed by Kemp and Wan, however.
10. I am indebted to A. Dixit for suggesting the first part of the proof.
11. See Chapter 1 for an expository discussion of this and related works.
12. See Nataf [10] and Chapter 1.
13. A similar proposition occurs in the course of the proof of Theorem 10.5.
14. Theorem 2.2, p. 38.
15. See p. 8.
16. Note that, concerning sufficiency, the form of (10.21) eliminates the asymmetry between $\tilde{v}(i)$ and $v(i)_m$ and thus presents no problem as far as aggregation in factor demands other than (10.20) is concerned.
17. The class of examples given on p. 44 appears to lead back to the Nataf case here if it is to apply for every choice of m in the factor demand functions (10.14). In the present notation that class would involve two factors, v_1 and v_2, with every factor demand function in the form
$$v(i)_2 = f^i[x_i, v(i)_1] = \psi^i[H^i(x_i) + d_i v(i)_1]$$
where $\psi^i(\cdot)$, $H^i(\cdot)$, and d_i can vary with i. It is known (R. Feenstra has shown me some results on this point) that this does not exhaust the set of cases permitting aggregation, although the conditions are very restrictive.
18. It *would* matter if no element of $v(i)$ appeared on the left-hand side. This possibility was taken care of in Theorem 10.5.
19. Note that (10.32) with $\tilde{u}(i)$ constant involves the same class of examples as that given in Note 17.
20. Nor have I found it profitable to drop weak separability at the aggregate level while retaining (10.27).
21. Note that for the $u(i)$ to be output-specific in (10.33), they must be nonzero in different components for each i.
22. For constant returns, the $b_i(\cdot)$ of (10.33) must be homogeneous of degree $1-\beta$. This means that if the ith production function has a single output-specific factor it cannot be in this class.
23. Much of this development is similar to that of the weakly separable case of Section 10.6, however.

References

[1] Blackorby, C. and R. R. Russell, "Indices and subindices of the cost of living and the standard of living," *International Economic Review*, **19** (1978), 229–40.

[2] Ethier, W., "Some of the theorems of international trade with many goods and factors," *Journal of International Economics*, **4** (1974), 199–206.

[3] Fisher, F. M., "Embodied technical change and the existence of an aggregate capital stock," *Review of Economic Studies*, **32** (1965), 263–88 (reprinted as Chapter 2).

[4] Fisher, F. M., "Embodied technology and the aggregation of fixed and movable capital goods," *Review of Economic Studies*, **35** (1968), 417–28 (reprinted as Chapter 4).

[5] Fisher, F. M., "The existence of aggregate production functions," *Econometrica*, **37** (1969), 553–77 (reprinted as Chapter 1).

[6] Fisher, F. M., and K. Shell, *The Economic Theory of Price Indices*, New York: Academic Press, 1972.

[7] Kemp, M. and H. Wan, "Relatively simple generalizations of the Stolper–Samuelson and Samuelson–Rybczynski theorems," in M. Kemp (ed.), *Three Topics in the Theory of International Trade*, New York: Elsevier, 1976, Chapter 4.

[8] Lau, L. J., "Duality and the structure of utility functions," *Journal of Economic Theory*, **1** (1969), 374–96.

[9] Leontief, W. W., "Introduction to a theory of the internal structure of functional relationships," *Econometrica*, **15** (1947), 361–73.

[10] Nataf, A., "Sur la possibilité de construction de certains macromodèles," *Econometrica*, **16** (1948), 232–44.

[11] Pollak, R. A., "Subindexes in the cost of living index," *International Economic Review*, **16** (1975), 135–50.

[12] Rybczynski, T. M., "Factor endowment and relative commodity prices," *Economica*, **N.S. 22** (1955), 336–41.

[13] Stolper, W. F. and P. A. Samuelson, "Protection and real wages," *Review of Economic Studies*, **9** (1941), 58–73.

11

The commodity pattern of trade and the Heckscher–Ohlin theorem in the presence of aggregate and commodity-specific factor-intensity reversals (1984)

Written jointly with Arye L. Hillman

11.1 Introduction

Theoretical analyses of the two-factor multicommodity model of trade usually make the assumption retained from the standard ($2 \times 2 \times 2$) Heckscher–Ohlin setting that individual goods can be uniquely ranked by relative factor intensity – see, for example, Bhagwati [1], Jones [16], Deardorff [4], Dornbusch *et al.* [8], and Brecher and Choudri [2]. On the other hand, while the theoretical literature tends to assume away factor-intensity reversals, the empirical literature with its beginnings in Minhas [20] (see the review by Stern [21]) adopts the two-factor multicommodity framework to investigate whether the technologies of particular traded goods do exhibit a relative factor-intensity reversal and seeks to relate the outcome of absence or presence of reversals in individual goods' technologies to whether an observed commodity–trade pattern conforms to Heckscher–Ohlin predictions.

In this chapter we consider the multicommodity trade model when factor-intensity reversals between individual goods' technologies are not in principle ruled out. Leaving the possibility of reversals open makes for compatibility with the setting of the empirical literature concerned with testing whether reversals take place. Our purpose is to investigate the influence of factor-intensity reversals on the Heckscher–Ohlin theorem when many individual traded goods are competitively produced via their own production technologies. In so doing, we are able to establish the extent to which, if at all, outcomes of the commodity-specific studies are relevant for the theorem.

If indeed only two goods are traded, then the traditional $(2 \times 2 \times 2)$ setting offers a precise portrayal of how the H–O prediction that a country's exports will be relatively intensive in its abundant factor may fail as a consequence of a factor-intensity reversal between the two goods' technologies.[1] However, when an economy's exports and imports comprise many goods, each produced via its own individual production technology, the requirement that 'a factor-intensity reversal not occur' becomes less precise. In principle, reversals may occur between some goods' technologies but not others. Such commodity-specific reversals taking place in a multicommodity setting then do not fall readily into the $(2 \times 2 \times 2)$ framework of analysis wherein the consequences for the H–O theorem of a factor-intensity reversal are precisely specified.[2]

Since the $(2 \times 2 \times 2)$ setting does offer a precise statement of how a factor-intensity reversal affects the H–O theorem, one can seek to reconcile a multicommodity world with an analytical framework defined for two goods via aggregation. This is the approach explored in this chapter.[3] The standard H–O assumptions facilitate aggregation over the technologies of individual goods to establish well-defined aggregate technologies for the exportables and importables observed in an economy's free trade equilibrium. These aggregate technologies can then be applied to a consideration of the factor-intensity reversal question in the usual $(2 \times 2 \times 2)$ model, in particular enabling one to consider relations between possible factor-intensity reversals exhibited by the aggregate technologies, possible factor-intensity reversals exhibited by individual goods' technologies, and the posited H–O link between relative factor intensities in production and the commodity pattern of trade.

In Section 11.2 we derive the aggregate technologies for an economy's exportables and importables in a free-trade equilibrium from the underlying commodity-specific technologies of the individual goods traded in that equilibrium. Section 11.3 considers the implications of factor-intensity reversals in the aggregate and commodity-specific technologies when the free-trade equilibrium exhibits factor–price equalization. Section 11.4 considers cases where factor prices are not equalized by free trade. Conclusions concerning the interpretation and significance of the no-reversal assumption in the context of the multicommodity model are then presented in Section 11.5, and we also comment on the relevance of the evidence provided by Minhas-type commodity-specific tests for reversals to the question as to whether a particular observed trade pattern is consistent with H–O predictions.

11.2 Industry-specific and aggregate technologies

Our setting is that of the basic two-factor multicommodity model of trade between two competitive economies, one of which we designate the home country and the other the rest of the world. All goods are produced via CRS strictly quasiconcave technologies using intersectorally mobile capital and labor, such that, for the jth of n goods, output q_j is

$$q_j = \phi_j(K_j, L_j), \qquad j = 1, \ldots, n, \tag{11.1}$$

where K_j and L_j are, respectively, capital and labor inputs. The industry-specific technologies described by (11.1) are internationally identical.

Given prevailing and observed free-trade goods' prices p_j ($j = 1, \ldots, n$) characterizing a given free-trade equilibrium, one can construct exportable and importable aggregates. Suppose that in the free-trade equilibrium the home economy is revealed to have s exportable and $(n - s)$ importable goods.[4] The respective exportable and importable aggregates are then

$$Q^X = \sum_{j=1}^{s} p_j q_j; \qquad Q^M = \sum_{j=s+1}^{n} p_j q_j, \tag{11.2}$$

which are, of course, Hicksian composite commodities.

The technologies for these aggregates are derivable from the problem of maximizing the values of exportable and importable outputs at the given free-trade prices. That is,

$$\max Q^X = \sum_{j=1}^{s} p_j q_j$$

subject to

$$q_j = \phi_j(K_j, L_j), \qquad j = 1, \ldots, s,$$

$$\sum_{j=1}^{s} K_j = K^X, \qquad \sum_{j=1}^{s} L_j = L^X; \tag{11.3}$$

$$\max Q^M = \sum_{j=s+1}^{n} p_j q_j$$

subject to

$$q_j = \phi_j(K_j, L_j), \qquad j = s+1, \ldots, n,$$

$$\sum_{j=s+1}^{n} K_j = K^M, \qquad \sum_{j=s+1}^{n} L_j = L^M.$$

The solution to (11.3) yields the aggregate technologies:

$$Q^X = \phi^X(K^X, L^X), \qquad Q^M = \phi^M(K^M, L^M). \tag{11.4}$$

A competitive economy will solve the maximization problems (11.3) in the course of finding its way to its production possibility frontier. Competitive firms will maximize the value of output, solving

$$\max\left(\sum_{j=1}^{s} p_j q_j + \sum_{j=s+1}^{n} p_j q_j\right) \tag{11.5}$$

subject to industry production technologies and aggregate factor supplies $\bar{K}$ and $\bar{L}$ of capital and labor, respectively.

$$q_j = \phi_j(K_j, L_j), \qquad j = 1, \ldots, n,$$

$$\sum_{j=1}^{s} K_j + \sum_{j=s+1}^{n} K_j = \bar{K},$$

$$\sum_{j=1}^{s} L_j + \sum_{j=s+1}^{n} L_j = \bar{L}.$$

The factor allocation solution to (11.5) is clearly the same as that derived from the problem,

$$\max(Q^X + Q^M)$$

subject to

$$Q^X = \phi^X(K^X, L^X), \qquad Q^M = \phi^M(K^M, L^M), \tag{11.6}$$

$$K^X + K^M = \bar{K}, \qquad L^X + L^M = \bar{L}.$$

That is to say, the sum of exportables and importables is maximized (both measured in common value units), subject to the aggregate production technologies (11.4) and the factor-endowment constraints. Competition thus results in equilibrium outputs of the specific exportable and importable goods, which yield maximized values of aggregate exportable and importable outputs, and hence competition suffices to ensure that the economy's aggregate production technologies for exportables and importables are as described in (11.4).

The industry-specific technologies can be expressed in intensive terms as

$$y_j = l_j \cdot f_j(k_j), \tag{11.1'}$$

where $y_j = q_j/\bar{L}$, $l_j = L_j/\bar{L}$, $k_j = K_j/\bar{L}$, and $\bar{L}$ is the economy's labor endowment. Denoting by α^X and α^M, respectively, the proportions of labor employed in exportable and importable production, for a given competitive factor allocation solution, the relative factor intensities of the exportable and importable aggregates are

$$k^X = \alpha^X \sum_{j=1}^{s} l_j \cdot k_j, \tag{11.7a}$$

$$k^M = \alpha^M \sum_{j=s+1}^{n} l_j \cdot k_j. \tag{11.7b}$$

Keeping the total labor allocations and hence α^X and α^M constant, these aggregate relative factor intensities may be preserved by changing the l_js to change equilibrium outputs of individual goods, while at the given equilibrium free-trade wage–rentals ratio competitive firms maintain the cost-minimizing relative factor intensities k_j, $j = 1, \ldots, n$. Hence, output combinations may change without any attendant change in the value of the marginal products, giving rise to flats in the unit value isoquants of the aggregate technologies.

Figure 11.1 depicts an aggregate unit-value isoquant *CDEF* as the envelope of individual goods' isoquants reflecting those combinations of capital and labor which *at given free-trade goods' prices* produce a unit value of output. The aggregate isoquant consists of a flat section bounded on either side by segments of the isoquants of the most

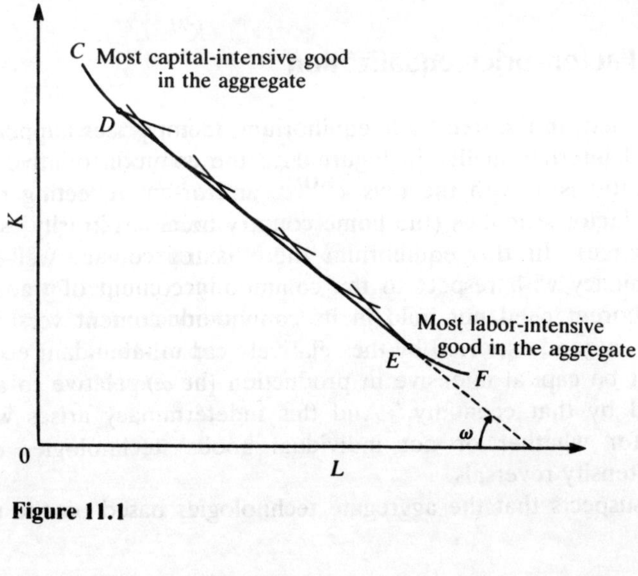

Figure 11.1

capital-intensive and most labor-intensive good (at the given free-trade relative factor price) contained in the aggregate.

The given free-trade goods' prices for which the aggregate technologies are specified may be viewed as parametrically given to the home economy as a small country unable to influence world prices.[5] Or, more generally, these prices may be viewed as determined in conjunction with relative factor prices in the international trade equilibrium.[6] In either case, the conditions for perfect aggregation over individual goods' technologies are satisfied,[7] but we are obliged to confine ourselves to a given free-trade equilibrium. This is, however, for our purposes, not a hindering restriction, our subject of investigation being precisely a given trade pattern with attendant specified free-trade prices. The aggregate technologies are well defined and are appropriate in principle for application to questions concerning the character of such a given pattern of trade.[8]

Furthermore, since the aggregate technologies are based on common output prices and common commodity-specific technologies, they are common to both economies, although each country will in general produce different equilibrium combinations of the goods comprising the respective aggregates. Hence, the aggregates conform to the standard H–O requirement of internationally identical technologies.

In our multicommodity setting, rather than viewing trade as taking place in many different goods each with its own individual production technology, we can now treat the aggregates as the basic data and regard a revealed trade pattern as if it entailed exchange of two goods produced according to the aggregate technologies.

11.3 Factor–price equalization

Suppose that, in the free-trade equilibrium, factor prices happen to be equalized internationally. In Figure 11.2 the common relative wage–rentals ratio is ω with the rays $\bar{k}^{\text{HOME}}$ and $\bar{k}^{\text{ROW}}$ reflecting relative physical factor scarcities (the home country being arbitrarily assumed labor scarce). In this equilibrium there is, of course, well-known indeterminacy with respect to the commodity content of trade. The H–O theorem need not hold in its commodity content version; for example, a good exported by the relatively capital-abundant economy need not be capital intensive in production (at ω) relative to a good imported by that economy.[9] And this indeterminacy arises without regard for whether or not individual goods' technologies exhibit factor-intensity reversals.

One suspects that the aggregate technologies based on the under-

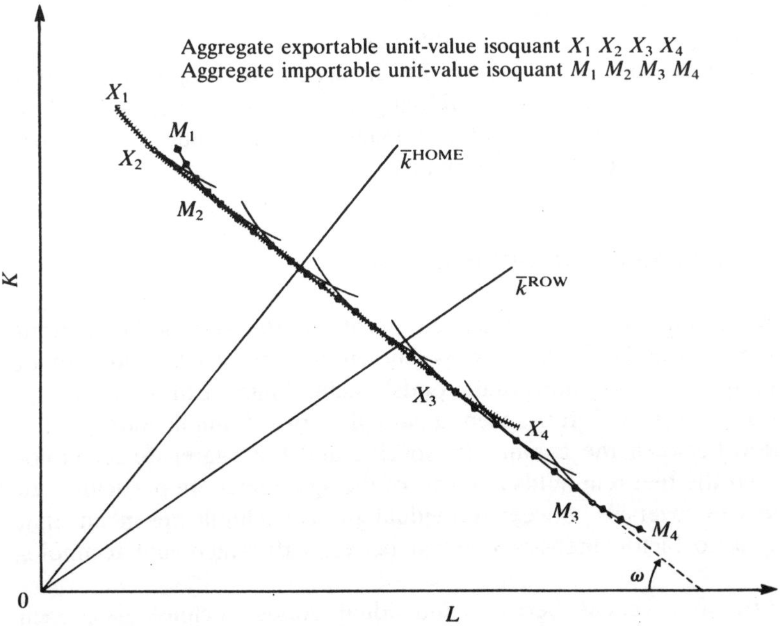

Figure 11.2

lying individual goods' technologies will fare no better than the individual goods themselves in necessarily adhering to the H–O commodity-content trade pattern, and this is readily borne out. Assume that, *on the basis of goods observed to be exported and imported in the realized free-trade equilibrium*,[10] the aggregate exportable and importable technologies are representable in Figure 11.2 as the unit-value isoquants $X_1X_2X_3X_4$ and $M_1M_2M_3M_4$, respectively. In this case the home country's exportable aggregate is relatively capital intensive, and, capital being the relatively abundant factor in the home economy, the trade pattern conforms to Heckscher–Ohlin predictions in terms of the aggregate technologies. But, of course, because of *ex ante* indeterminacy as to which individual goods might be exportables or importables, a comparison of the relative factor intensities of the two aggregate technologies could just as well have gone the other way. Moreover, the equilibrium could be such that the exportable aggregate includes both the most capital-intensive and the most labor-intensive good,[11] in which case reference to the relative factor intensities of the exportable and importable aggregate technologies would indicate a factor-intensity reversal. But just as reversals between individual goods' technologies are of no significance, neither are reversals exhibited by the aggregate technologies.

Indeed, no matter what outcomes investigations of possible factor-intensity reversals between individual goods or the aggregates based on those goods reveal, the indeterminacy of the commodity-content version of the H–O theorem remains.[12]

11.4 Unequalized factor prices

In the absence of factor–price equalization, the commodity-content version of the H–O theorem is known to hold (independently of preferences) if no individual goods' technologies exhibit a factor-intensity reversal.[13] It is then a straightforward implication of the relation between the commodity-specific and the aggregate technologies that the theorem holds in terms of the aggregates. In particular, an absence of reversals between individual goods' technologies means that there is no factor-intensity reversal between the aggregate technologies.

With no reversals between individual goods' technologies, each country specializes in production to its own exportables (with the possible exception of a single good).[14] If, on the other hand, we observe more than one good produced both at home and abroad, then the multicommodity model implies that factor-intensity reversals have occurred between individual goods' technologies.[15]

From the one extreme case of no commodity-specific reversals at all, now let us go to the other extreme where each and every pair of commodity-specific technologies exhibits a factor-intensity reversal. To contrast further with the (all but) complete specialization outcome of the no-reversal case, suppose that the free-trade production equilibrium is consistent with competitive production of each good in each economy. In Figure 11.3 the set of the home country's exportables is denoted by A and its importables by B; as a consequence of the individual goods' reversals in relative factor intensities, each good in the A set (unit-value isoquants are not drawn for all goods) is capital intensive in production at the home economy's relative factor–price ratio relative to each good in the B set, but this factor-intensity ordering is precisely reversed at the foreign relative factor–price ratio. The aggregate unit-value isoquant $X_1X_2X_3X_4X_5X_6$ for the exportable and $M_1M_2M_3M_4M_5M_6$ for the importable, reflect the reversal behavior of the individual goods and themselves exhibit a factor-intensity reversal. One can accordingly make an analog ($2 \times 2 \times 2$) statement of failure of the H–O theorem because of factor-intensity reversal. We

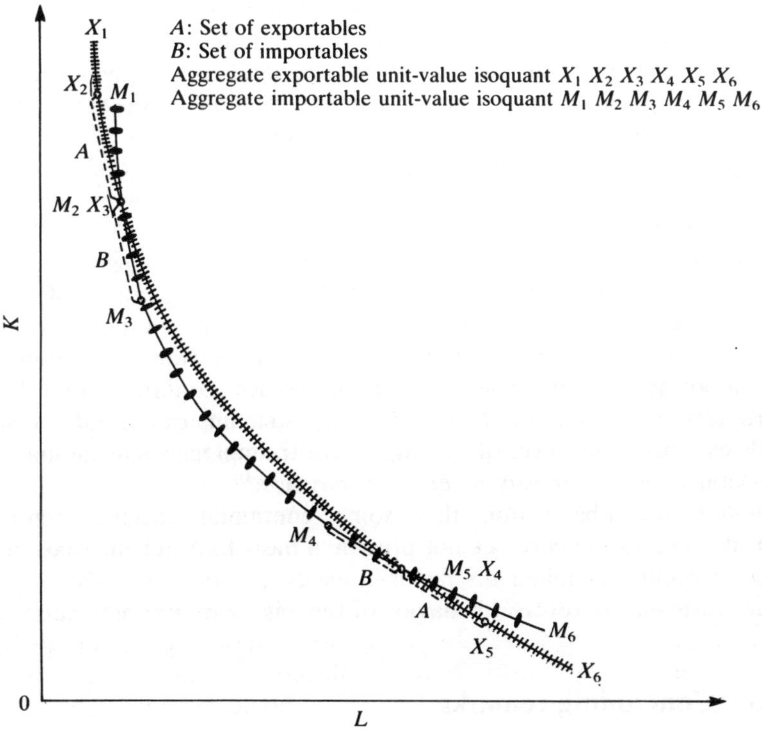

Figure 11.3

observe that in particular, in the foreign economy, production of the aggregate composed of B goods (its exportables) is capital-intensive relative to the aggregate composed of A goods (its importables), whereas capital is this economy's physically relatively scarce factor.

The two polar cases of (1) no reversals between any individual goods' technologies and (2) reversals between all individual goods' technologies are, of course, extremely special – although if it could be confirmed empirically that no technologies for the individual exportables and importables observed in a particular trading equilibrium exhibited a factor-intensity reversal, one could conclude that the H–O theorem held in its aggregate ($2 \times 2 \times 2$) form. Similarly, one could conclude that the theorem failed in this form because of factor-intensity reversal if all individual goods' technologies were revealed to exhibit reversals. More generally, however, some individual goods' technologies might be expected to exhibit reversals and others not.

Once we depart from the limiting cases of no reversals or universal reversals and allow this latter more general case, the exact correspondence between reversals in the aggregate and commodity-specific technologies is lost. For example, suppose that in Figure 11.3 one individual exportable technology and one individual importable technology, in each case for neither the most capital-intensive good nor the most labor-intensive good in its respective aggregate, were not to exhibit a factor-intensity reversal. At least one of the goods will then be produced in one country only. The aggregate technologies by the nature of their construction are unaffected by this change and continue to exhibit a factor-intensity reversal. Or, alternatively, let there be but one factor-intensity reversal revealed between individual exportable and importable technologies. It can be readily confirmed that by appropriate manipulation of the unit-value isoquants of the individual goods exhibiting the reversal, the aggregate technologies may be made to exhibit a factor-intensity reversal or may not.[16]

Hence, the observation that some commodity-specific factor-intensity reversals occur does not provide a basis for inferring that the H–O theorem has failed on factor-intensity reversal grounds. Such failure rests on the reversal behavior of the aggregate technologies.[17]

11.5 Concluding remarks

Adopting the procedure of aggregation over individual goods' technologies, we have in this chapter portrayed the basic two-factor multicommodity model of trade between two competitive economies as a $(2 \times 2 \times 2)$ analog to the traditional $(2 \times 2 \times 2)$ case. The aggregate exportable and importable technologies derived from underlying commodity-specific technologies and free-trade prices facilitate a $(2 \times 2 \times 2)$ commodity-content statement of the H–O theorem for the trade pattern exhibited in the particular free-trade equilibrium where the prices prevail. This enables the question to be framed whether the relative factor intensities revealed by the trade pattern for the aggregate exportable and importable technologies exhibit the relation to relative factor scarcities proposed by the H–O theorem. Our interest has in particular been in the factor-intensity reversal question when the $(2 \times 2 \times 2)$ framework has been achieved by aggregation over individual commodity-specific technologies which may or may not exhibit reversals with respect to one another.

We have observed that in the case where factor prices are equalized, the aggregate technologies do not lend themselves to a commodity-content formulation of the H–O theorem. Of course, since when there is factor price equalization the H–O theorem may fail in terms of the commodity-content factor-intensity ranking of the individual exportables and importables, it is not all that surprising that the theorem need not hold in terms of the aggregate technologies which are themselves based on the underlying individual exportable and importable goods' technologies. In this case of equalized factor prices, whether the aggregate technologies exhibit a factor-intensity reversal is of no consequence for the H–O theorem, nor is there any relevance for the theorem of assumptions ruling out reversals between individual goods' technologies, nor of discoveries that particular goods do or do not exhibit a reversal.

When factor prices are not equalized, the aggregate technologies do facilitate a $(2 \times 2 \times 2)$ analog statement of the H–O theorem if the usual assumption is retained that there are no factor-intensity reversals between individual goods' technologies. The aggregates then reflect the consistency of the relative factor-intensity rankings of the underlying technologies with the commodity content statement of the theorem. The aggregate exportable and importable technologies also facilitate an analog $(2 \times 2 \times 2)$ statement of failure of the H–O theorem due to factor-intensity reversal in the other extreme case where the relative factor-intensity rankings of all individual goods' technologies are precisely reversed at the unequalized free-trade factor–price ratios.

In a multicommodity world, however, the more reasonable supposition is that some goods' technologies will exhibit a factor-intensity reversal and others not. In this more general case, anything can in principle happen in terms of the reversal behavior of the aggregate technologies. However, the aggregates nevertheless remain well defined and allow a statement as to whether the relative factor intensity of an economy's aggregate exportable and importable technologies reflects relative factor scarcities in the predicted H–O manner.

Accordingly, when factor prices are not equalized, the analog $(2 \times 2 \times 2)$ structure achieved via aggregation accommodates various patterns of factor-intensity reversals in the technologies of the underlying individual goods of the multicommodity model. The pattern of reversals exhibited by the commodity-specific technologies may affect the nature of the aggregate technologies. But factor-intensity reversals revealed to be exhibited by particular commodity-specific technologies offer no necessary indication that the prediction of the H–O theorem has failed in the form appropriate for the aggregate version of the multicommodity model, i.e., in terms of the relation between relative factor intensities of the aggregate exportable and importable technologies and relative factor scarcities.

Since this is the case in the absence of factor–price equalization, and since in the case of factor–price equalization aggregate or commodity-specific factor-intensity reversals are in any event of no relevance for the H–O theorem, one can only conclude that results of investigations examining individual technologies for presence or absence of reversals have in themselves no direct bearing on the theorem. Yet taking an example from the pioneering Minhas study [20], we find emphasis on results such as 'the paper industry [is] more capital-intensive than the dairy products industry at all values of *w/r* greater than $2,136, while it is relatively labor-intensive for all smaller values of *w/r*' (where $w/r = \omega$).

Moreover, it still has remained common practice in recent expositions of some popular texts to associate this type of evidence with the question of whether particular trade patterns conform to H–O predictions. For example, in Grubel's text [11] one finds a $(2 \times 2 \times 2)$ exposition of the theoretical possibility of a factor-intensity reversal followed by the observations and appeal to evidence that:

> To find out whether such factor intensity reversals do take place in the real world, it is necessary to collect data on production techniques used in different countries. B. S. Minhas (1962) collected such statistics for 24 industries and 19 different countries and found factor reversals in 5 of the industries. Furthermore, he found a low correlation of +0.328 between the capital/labor ratios of 20 industries existing in both the United States and Japan. Leontief and Moroney have raised some questions about how great the probability is that factor intensity reversals do take place in the real world by analyzing Minhas's statistics somewhat more closely. (p. 68)

Similarly, in Caves and Jones' textbook exposition [3], the $(2 \times 2 \times 2)$ theory of reversals is followed by the observations with respect to the real-world importance of reversals that: 'One can only examine the evidence directly to see if intensity reversals seem to afflict *an important group* of internationally traded commodities. . .' (p. 150, emphasis added). They go on:

> Agriculture is an activity that seems particularly prone to factor-intensity reversals. Rice is raised in the United States using elaborate mechanical equipment, in the Far East with large quantities of hand labor. That fact does not explain the Leontief paradox for the United States, because capital-intensive agriculture is an export industry and thus supports our normal expectation that U.S. exports would be capital-intensive. However, Japan's heavy imports of foodstuffs that would be produced with labor-intensive technology by the Japanese may explain why the exports that pay for the country's food imports appear capital-intensive. (p. 151)

Here, too, there is a jump in the interpretation of evidence on factor-intensity reversals from the (2×2×2) theory appropriate if really only two goods are traded to the interpretation of empirical results drawn from a multicommodity framework where trade is observed to be taking place in many distinct goods, each with its own individual production technology.[18]

Notes

1. See Johnson [14] and Jones [15].
2. Melvin [18, pp. 1260–1] portrays factor-intensity reversals in a three-good, two-factor setting but is concerned with the prospects for factor–price equalization. The factor–price equalization theorem in the presence of factor-intensity reversals is likewise the subject of Finger [9] and Melvin [19].
3. Jones [16] also adopts an aggregation approach to the multicommodity model. Whereas we shall aggregate to secure two tradable goods, Jones views all traded goods as an aggregate, i.e., in the manner of the traded/nontraded goods dichotomy. Various aspects of aggregation in trade theory are discussed in Jones [17].
4. That is, information regarding classification of goods as exportable and importable is taken as given, revealed by the prevailing trade pattern. Prospective indeterminacy in production and trade (see, for example, Melvin [18]) is not an issue in this classification of goods.
5. This is the approach adopted by Jones [16].
6. See Dixit and Norman [6] for an insistence on this approach, but of course this neglects the traditional small country framework.
7. See Fisher [10] (Chapter 1). Note that we have assumed away all problems of factor aggregation by assuming that both capital and labor are homogeneous.
8. Of course, if prices change, so do the aggregate technologies, as does the equilibrium trade pattern. The new aggregate technologies then apply to the new observed trade pattern at the new equilibrium prices. A referee has made the observation that requiring foreknowledge of the equilibrium prices in order to examine the properties of an equilibrium appears to require having an answer before one can proceed with the question. However, this is not a valid objection to our procedure. We are not seeking to explain the determination of the equilibrium configuration of a particular trade pattern. On the physical definition of relative factor scarcity, the relative factor endowment relation between a given country and the rest of the world is constant over all equilibria, and it is this relative factor endowment together with goods' production technologies (and preferences) which the H–O theorem takes as given. It is perfectly sensible to ask what that theorem says about the relative factor intensities of the aggregate goods traded in the particular equilibrium we happen to observe, and if we are to test the predictions of the theory, it is the relative factor intensities revealed to be employed by firms producing goods in that equilibrium which we must examine. Similarly, if we wish to employ the aggregate technologies to ask what the theory predicts for

some other equilibrium, it is not a problem of principle that we must first inquire as to what the relative prices in that equilibrium will be – that is the cost of aggregation.

9. See Bhagwati [1].
10. That is, we take the *ex ante* indeterminacy as resolved by the revelation of an *ex post* trade pattern. As we have stressed, we are not in this chapter concerned with how particular equilibria come about, but rather with the character of revealed trade equilibria.
11. See Melvin [18, p. 1263] on this possibility in the three-good, two-factor model.
12. Of course, identical homothetic preferences suffice for the H–O theorem to predict unambiguously the *factor content* of trade. See Melvin [18, pp. 1263–4]. Also, revealed preference arguments can be used to establish correlations involving factor endowments, autarkic prices and trade which sustain the theorem in an average sense. See Deardorff [5], Dixit and Norman [6], Dixit and Woodland [7], and Helpman [12].
13. See Bhagwati [1]. Deardorff [4] shows, however, that the theorem can fail in this version in the simultaneous presence of intermediate goods and impediments to trade.
14. See Deardorff [4] and Brecher and Choudri [2].
15. See Melvin [18, p. 1260].
16. The critical consideration in each instance is whether the reversal behavior of the individual goods' technologies changes the identity of the most capital-intensive or most labor-intensive goods in one of the aggregates.
17. Failure refers here, of course, to the validity of a commodity-content-of-trade statement of the theorem as applied to the aggregate technologies which facilitate the $(2\times2\times2)$ analog of the multicommodity model. In the absence of factor–price equalization, the theorem holds (independently of preferences) in its factor-content form; see Brecher and Choudri [2] and Helpman [12].
18. This jump is avoided in Hillman and Hirsch [13] where factor-intensity reversals are considered in terms of baskets of traded good aggregates. However, aggregate technologies are not derived along the lines of this chapter.

References

[1] Bhagwati, J. N., "The Heckscher–Ohlin theorem in the multicommodity case," *Journal of Political Economy*, **80** (1972), 1052–5.

[2] Brecher, R. A., and E. U. Choudri, "The factor content of international trade without factor price equalization," *Journal of International Economics*, **12** (1982), 277–83.

[3] Caves, R. E., and R. W. Jones, *World Trade and Payments*, Boston Little, Brown, 1981.

[4] Deardorff, A. V., "Weak links in the chain of comparative advantage," *Journal of International Economics*, **9** (1979), 197–209; reprinted in J. N. Bhagwati (ed.), *International Trade: Selected Readings*, Cambridge, Mass.: MIT Press, 1981, 76–87.

[5] Deardorff, A. V., "The general validity of the Heckscher–Ohlin theorem," *American Economic Review*, **72** (1982), 683–94.
[6] Dixit, A. K., and V. Norman, *Theory of International Trade*, Welwyn: Nisbets, and Cambridge: Cambridge University Press, 1980.
[7] Dixit, A. K. and A. Woodland, "The relationship between factor endowments and commodity trade," *Journal of International Economics*, **13** (1982), 201–14.
[8] Dornbusch, R., S. Fischer, and P. A. Samuelson, "Heckscher–Ohlin trade theory with a continuum of goods," *Quarterly Journal of Economics*, **95** (1980), 203–24.
[9] Finger, J. M. "Factor price equalization and the factor proportions theorem when commodities outnumber factors: The case with intensity reversals," *Metroeconomica*, **25** (1973), 194–9.
[10] Fisher, F. M., "The existence of aggregate production functions," *Econometrica*, **37** (1969), 553–77 (reprinted as Chapter 1).
[11] Grubel, H. G., *International Economics*, Homewood, Ill.: R. D. Irwin, 1977.
[12] Helpman, E., "The factor content of foreign trade," *Economic Journal*, **94** (1984), 84–94.
[13] Hillman, A. L., and S. Hirsch, "Factor intensity reversals: Conceptual experiments with trade goods aggregates," *Weltwirtschaftliches Archiv*, **115** (1979), 272–83.
[14] Johnson, H. G., "Factor endowments, international trade and factor prices," *Manchester School of Economic and Social Studies*, **25** (1957), 270–83.
[15] Jones, R. W., "Factor proportions and the Heckscher–Ohlin theorem," *Review of Economic Studies*, **24** (1956–57), 1–10; reprinted in R. W. Jones (ed.), *International Trade: Essays in Theory*, Amsterdam: North-Holland, 1979, pp. 5–19.
[16] Jones, R. W., "The small country in a many-commodity world," *Australian Economic Papers*, **13** (1974), 225–36; reprinted in R. W. Jones (ed.), *International Trade: Essays in Theory*, Amsterdam: North-Holland, 1979, pp. 21–32.
[17] Jones, R. W., *Twoness in Trade Theory: Costs and Benefits* (Special Papers in International Economics, No. 12), International Finance Section, Princeton; reprinted in R. W. Jones (ed.), *International Trade: Essays in Theory*, Amsterdam: North-Holland, 1979, pp. 289–326.
[18] Melvin, J. R., "Production and trade with two factors and three goods," *American Economic Review*, **58** (1968), 1249–68.
[19] Melvin, J. R. "Factor-intensity reversal in a three-factor, three-commodity model," *Economic Record*, **55** (1979), 164–71.
[20] Minhas, B. S., "The homohypallagic production function, factor intensity reversals and the Heckscher–Ohlin theorem," *Journal of Political Economy*, **70** (1962), 138–56.
[21] Stern, R. M., "Testing trade theories," in P. B. Kenen (ed.), *International Trade and Finance*, Cambridge: Cambridge University Press, 1975.

Permissions

1. "The existence of aggregate production functions," *Econometrica*, 37 (4) (1969).
2. "Embodied technical change and the existence of an aggregate capital stock," *Review of Economic Studies*, XXXII (4) (1965).
3. "Embodied technology and the existence of labour and output aggregates," *Review of Economic Studies*, XXXV (4) (1968).
4. "Embodied technology and the aggregation of fixed and movable capital goods," *Review of Economic Studies*, XXXV (4) (1968).
5. "Aggregate production functions revisited: The mobility of capital and the rigidity of thought," *Review of Economic Studies*, XLIX (4) (1982).
6. "On the simultaneous existence of full and partial capital aggregates," *Review of Economic Studies*, L (1) (1983).
7. "Approximate aggregation and the Leontief conditions," *Econometrica*, 37 (3) (1969).
8. "Aggregate production functions and the explanation of wages: A simulation experiment," *Review of Economics and Statistics*, LIII (4) (1971). Reprinted with permission of the President and Fellows of Harvard College.
9. "Aggregate production functions: Some CES experiments" (written jointly with R. M. Solow and J. M. Kearl), *Review of Economic Studies*, XLIV (2) (1977).
10. "On perfect aggregation in the national output deflator and generalized Rybczynski theorems," *International Economic Review*, 23 (1) (1982).
11. "The commodity pattern of trade and the Heckscher–Ohlin theorem in the presence of aggregate and commodity-specific factor-intensity reversals" (written jointly with A. L. Hillman), *Journal of International Economics*, 17 (1/2) (1984). Reprinted with permission of Elsevier Science Publishers, Academic Publishing Division.

Index

Index